THE LAND, THE SEED AND THE BLESSING

A CHRONOLOGICAL BIBLICAL COMPENDIUM

T0163774

WILLIAM T. KUMP

New York

THE LAND, THE SEED AND THE BLESSING

A CHRONOLOGICAL BIBLICAL COMPENDIUM

WILLIAM T. KUMP

Copyright 2007, 2010

Book layout by Bonnie Bushman
bbushman@bresnan.net

Morgan James Publishing, LLC
1225 Franklin Ave. Ste 325
Garden City, NY 11530-1693
800-485-4943
www.MorganJamesPublishing.com

Kump, William T.
    The Land, The Seed and The Blessing
A Chronological Biblical Compendium/
William T. Kump
ISBN 978-1-933596-05-1 Paperback
ISBN 978-1-60037-008-3 Hardcover

Acknowledgments

To my family during the years of working on this chronology: to my wife Agnes for her support and encouragement, and to my son Cyrus and daughter Sterling, for whom primarily I wrote; and also to my insightful proofreaders Claire Hudgins, Matthew Murphy and Ann Finley, and, of course, to my publisher and staff.

TABLE OF CONTENTS: SUMMARIES

Chapter 5 Leviticus & Deuteronomy   39
The laws of Leviticus were given at the end of the book and time of Exodus at the end of the first year of the exodus. That Deuteronomy is the second stating of those laws by Moses. What some of those were, and are.

Chapter 6 Joshua   47
The story of Joshua leading the multitude westward from modern Jordan across the Jordan into the land promised and then taking them to victories over part of the land. Joshua telling the people that all of the promises of God to the land to that date are fulfilled.

Chapter 7 Judges & Ruth   55
Stories of "judges" Othniel, Ehud, Shamgar, Deborah, Barak, Gideon, Tola, Jair, Jephthah, Ibzan, Elon, Abdon and Samson. Continual syncretism and apostasy of the Hebrews. Failure to capture the pockets of land of pagans. Also, the story of Ruth, Boaz and Naomi and redemption.

Chapter 8 First Samuel   65
A brief mention of Samuel followed with the stories of Saul and David. The Philistines, the Sea Peoples, the iron age, the battle of Troy. The demands of the people for a king to rule over them. Goliath, Jonathan, and Michal. The enmity of Saul toward David.

Chapter 9 Second Samuel   71
David restores cosmos out of Saul's chaos. David succeeds Saul as king and enlarges the small kingdom, including the capture of "Jerusalem." Ishbosheth and also Mephibosheth. David's sin against Uriah and with Bathsheba. Taking the census. David not to build the temple, but to gather the supplies and the artisans.

Chapter 10 First Kings   77
Solomon spends his first four years building the temple then the rest of his life in apostasy with 700 pagan wives and places of worship leading to the division of the kingdom. God goes outside the line of Abraham and David to make his promises to Jeroboam, who does not accept. Elijah and Jezebel.

Chapter 11 Psalms   85
A Pentateuch of hymns and prayers attributed to David and Solomon. The word of man to God.

Chapter 12 Proverbs   91
Solomon's pithy wisdom teachings. What proverbs are. A good book for a teenager, to know wisdom and instruction. "In Psalms we find the Christian

on his knees. In Proverbs we find the Christian on his feet." A division of the Psalms. An interlude in the heaviness of Kings leading to the calamitous prophecies.

Chapter 13 Ecclesiastes & Song of Songs   97
With Ecclesiastes all life and wisdom end with God. It is a record, man's or God's, of one man's, and each person's, progression to true wisdom and to God. It is good reading for a person with some life experiences. Song is human love poetry, a love story with many ancient mid-eastern phrases for which a Bible dictionary would be helpful. Like many stories, it has one message for the younger person and another for the older.

Chapter 14 Second Kings   103
In agonizing detail this narrates the disastrous events of the divided kingdom until Israel's fall, and Judah's captivity. Early prophets Elijah and Elisha. The people and their kings continued to do evil in the eyes of the Lord. Isaiah causes the shadow to go backward as a sign to Hezekiah that he would live. All of the valuables of the temple treasury are paid out as tribute, but the captivity comes any way.

Chapter 15 Chronicles 1 & 2   111
These are of things omitted from previous books, mainly genealogies and histories. They re-tell a period of about 440 years, the stories of David, Solomon and the kingdom of Judah, with but little mention of Israel. The omission of the battle of Carchemish.

Chapter 16 Obadiah, Joel & Jonah   117
Begins by pointing out the problem with inserting the prophets in their proper chronological location in the Bible, and of which and as to which of the peoples any specific prophet speaks. Fifteen of the seventeen prophets must be rearranged and placed within the 275-year period of Second Kings. Obadiah speaks of the Edomites, who will be brought down. Joel speaks to Israel and its coming collapse. Jonah is vomited out by a large fish and goes to Nineveh, northern Iraq, to preach repentance.

Chapter 17 Amos, Hosea & Micah   125
Judgment will come from a loving God. Amos and Hosea are the last two prophets to the small nation of Israel as it collapses into captivity. Micah, with Isaiah, is the first to the nation of Judah, as its collapse sits on the horizon.

Chapter 18 Isaiah 1-39   133
Surrounding related secular history and geography. Contemporary of Hosea,

saints. The pregnant woman. The dragon. The beast of the sea. The beast of the earth. The scarlet harlot. Babylon. The kings of the evil world. The *parousia* and Armageddon. The new earth and new Jerusalem.

PREFACE

The purpose of this book is to introduce and to reintroduce readers to the Bible, the combined old Hebrew scriptures (Old Testament) and new Christian scriptures (New Testament). It is written to be read much as one might read a historical novel, without the necessity of any other books, though one or two would be helpful. It is probably true that most people in the world and many in the United States have absolutely no knowledge of the contents of the Bible. Many who do have some knowledge have but a scattered sprinkling of unconnected bits and pieces, such as the 23rd Psalm, the Good Samaritan, the Feeding of the Multitudes and John 3:16, and most of the remainder have a very restricted knowledge of most books of the Bible. An extremely small portion of people have a working knowledge of the order, flow and connectedness of all of the books of the entire Bible.

This is a compendium of the Bible. It is neither a Bible dictionary nor an encyclopedia; nor is it a commentary, as it is not intended to explain anything. It may be considered a handbook, as it may easily be carried about in one's hand. In Latin and Old English we have the word *pendeo* which means "hang". From this we get words like "pendant", "pending", "suspend" and "depend". The prefix "com-" means "with" or "together." A compendium is a "together hanging." The purpose of this book is to show how the books of the Bible "hang together" both between and among themselves and also in the general history, and geography, of human civilizations. *The Random House Dictionary of the English Language*, Random House, Inc. (1967), defines compendium as "a brief account of an extensive subject; a full inventory; a weighing." One might describe this book as a "complete compendium."

As the purpose is to introduce and reintroduce one to the Bible, there is the obvious sequential purpose to encourage one to read broader and deeper and to do so upon a broad and solid foundation. It is a purpose here to give a person a sweeping overview of the structure of the Bible. In a sense, when one constructs a house the house is already there; one now must put the wood, wiring, plumbing and bricks in the correct locations. The window frames usually do not go on the inside wall separating the bathroom from the kitchen, but on the outside wall. The materials for the second floor bathroom do not go into the first floor sitting room. That is not to say one should never memorize any verse or hear and love a wonderful story from the Bible without first having a comprehensive overview as to where and how that fine piece fits.

Those things will have occurred with a person before they ever even pick up this book.

It is the intention that everything in this book is in the Bible, or is accepted common knowledge found in several or many reference books. Matters which are not directly in the Bible are a relatively minor portion and are at times prefaced with "this refers to." These are facts which are on the periphery of the verses discussed. Comments which are in the nature of commentaries are at times prefaced with "some scholars say." There are no footnotes or endnotes to distract the reader. Biblical quotes are from *The New King James Version*, Thomas Nelson, Inc. (1982). There is a bibliography of suggested helpful writings, and one or two of these, such as maps and a dictionary, in addition to a Bible, may be of assistance while reading.

This book avoids any intentional criticism of the Bible, such as "higher criticism." There is no intended "historical-critical" analysis, unless so stated, nor any analysis of literary devices, such as allegory, poetry, metaphor or hyperbole, nor who may have written which book, in whole or in part. That means very rare comments as to parts of Genesis or Isaiah or whether 2nd Corinthians is one letter or a combination of three to six letters or where some scribe may have made a copy error, insertion, omission, amendment or emendment. There are ample commentaries and textbooks offering positions on all of those debates, none to very few of which have any impact on the message of the Bible.

This book is structured and ordered to rearrange the books of the Bible as events occurred chronologically in ancient history. The standard old Hebrew scriptures do not arrange the books according to their place in time but rather as law, then history, then poetry-wisdom, and then the prophets, which are arranged primarily by length. This book may be used, with the Bible and other texts, as a course on an overview of the Bible, each chapter being one 55-minute class. Also, each chapter may be used as a sermon, of about twenty to thirty-five minutes. For a sermon introduction, one may consider the first twenty or so lines, two-and-a-half paragraphs, of those anecdotes used at the beginning of each book in the *Holy Bible*, *New Living Translation*, Tyndale House Publishers, Inc. Wheaton, IL (1996).

The exact chronological arrangement and order of all of the books and many specific events of the Bible may be lost to history, but a fairly, or very, accurate workable order can be established from an analytical combination of those many timelines found in most modern study Bibles, textbooks and encyclopedias. *The Reese Chronological Bible*, Bethany House Publishers, Minneapolis (1980), contains the entire Bible text, verse by verse, arranged in a chronological order and may be the "granddaddy" of such projects. That book has been a most helpful "backstop" in this endeavor.

In compiling and writing this book, a persistent effort has been made to avoid any and all purely personal bias, philosophy, politics, interpretation and the like from the book and its words, phrasings and inclinations. However, one must recognize that a person's deep beliefs and convictions are part and parcel of the person and enter into the selection of virtually each word, phrase and inclination. There has been no intentional, and certainly no erroneous, manipulation by the author of the words and phrases. The author comes from a lineage and family of lawyers and teachers and practiced law for forty years. After decades of taking complicated matters and reducing them to brief and understandable wordings, the same is here applied to the Bible.

INTRODUCTION:
BIBLE GENERAL OVERVIEW

One might say we will fly over the land below, seeing only the most prominent peaks and valleys of the Bible. Some will think it is too much too fast; some will think it is too little with no depth. Both will be correct. I exhort, implore and encourage you to look through this greatest and most influential of all books this week.

What is the Bible? From where did it come? Who wrote it and how and why? What is its purpose? In one sentence, what is its story? Why should a person read it?

The Bible, the combined Old Testament and New Testament, is God the Father's call to and search for lost mankind, who runs from God, until hearing the call, stops and stumbles to return to a reconciliation. The purpose of the entire Bible is to present, to reveal, one unified Trinitarian Godhead, God the Father, God the Son and God the Holy Spirit, as the creator of the universe and the redeemer and sustainer of the humans of earth. The Bible is not the story of mankind searching for or forming God, though many trifle with that notion.

In ancient days, in Egypt, primarily in the Nile Delta around Cairo, (Northern) Lower Egypt, there grew many grass-like plants, as bulrushes and sedges. One of these sedges was the *cyperus papyrus*, which was used for many purposes, and from which we got our word "paper." Its root was burned as a fuel, and its pith eaten as a food. The fibers of its stem could be woven into many items, such as seats, boxes, mats and a cloth-like material, which could also be used for writing, as it was for centuries. In antiquity the papyrus was so plentiful that it was the symbol for Lower Egypt, but today it is nearly extinct. From the name of the inner bark of the papyrus came the name *biblios*, which became the Greek word for "book," and the plural *biblia*, that for "books." Shortly after the time of Jesus the Christ, the Chinese began to make a similar, but better, material for writing from other plant fibers. During the following eight centuries this product moved into Japan then westward to Egypt, where it replaced the papyrus material, and was called paper.

The Bible is simultaneously both one book and many separate books. It is technically a *bibliotheca*, a collection of books, a library, which is the title used by Jerome when he translated the Hebrew and Greek scriptures into the Latin Vulgate Bible around 450 A.D. However, the collection compiles such a unified and continuing story as to be one book, a *biblios*. To say the Bible is the "book of books" is to state a double meaning. It is both the greatest of all books and is composed of and contains sixty-six separate little books.

Things of God and the Bible have been denounced, renounced and attacked since the very beginning of mankind. We can turn that great gift of intelligence against God by that other great gift of free will. Throughout history many have believed they have studied the Bible and do not believe it, and that anyone who does believe the Bible simply has not studied it. In our days it seems even more so, but it is only a small change of percentages. But, such a slight change of percentage, say from forty-nine to fifty-one, easily chooses a President, a Governor, a Judge and the course of the people, for better or worse.

A theologian is simply one who sees and speaks words about God working in the lives and history of humans. The Bible is history. The Bible is the action of God in the history of mankind. Some groups breed confusion in this aspect as their free will allows them to pick and choose their own personal theology. Some teach that the first eleven chapters of the Bible, as to creation and the flood, are true history but, in an honest attempt to keep people from secularizing the Bible, erroneously teach that the rest is somehow not history. Others teach that the first eleven chapters are not history but the rest is history. Our word "theology" simply means "God words."

The first five books of the Bible, Genesis, Exodus, Leviticus, Numbers and Deuteronomy, contain a great deal of history and God's law. They cover the period from the beginnings, through the centuries in Egypt to the time of return under Moses. This group of five is referred to by three names. They are called *Torah*, the Hebrew word for "Law." They are called the *Pentateuch*, the Greek word for "five tools." They are called the "books of Moses." Humans have always, including today, stumbled over many parts of these first five books.

The actual dates of the very beginnings, of creation, the first eleven chapters of the Bible, of Genesis, are extremely difficult, maybe humanly impossible, to establish. Some set these dates of creation from about 10,000 B.C. to 4000 B.C. Archbishop Usher, of the Irish Church, around 1650 A.D., calculated many of these dates from the Bible, with those of the first eleven chapters being somewhat uncertain. His calculations put creation at 4004 B.C. Calculating from the annual *Rosh HaShana*, the Jewish New Year's Day, the Jewish date of beginnings would be September 6, 3761 B.C. Others, who opine that God needed more time to create, put the date of the first five verses of Genesis, the "first day," the "big bang" of the universe, at 15,000,000,000 B.C.; the date of verses six through nineteen, days two through four, the formation of earth, at 5,000,000,000 B.C.; the date of verses twenty through twenty-three, the fifth day, the formation of sea-life, at 500,000,000 B.C.; the date of verses twenty-four through thirty-one, the sixth day, the formation of animals at 50,000,000 B.C.; and of humans at 100,000 B.C.

However, from the end of chapter eleven, the approximate time of Abraham, true scholars are in fairly accurate agreement as to dates, with minor uncertainty as to some specific times and places. The early stories recorded in Genesis (and Job) were most certainly handed down by word of mouth long before they were written. Writing was in use centuries before 2000 B.C., the time of Abraham, the end of Genesis chapter eleven. However the stories of the book of Genesis may have been preserved, it is Moses, around 1460 B.C., who is credited with writing the book of Genesis and the four books concerning his life and work, being Exodus, Leviticus, Numbers and Deuteronomy. Although it is quite probable that Moses did write these first five books, and the Bible states that he did, there is some thought that he may not have written them but that there were four unknown writers (J,E,D and P) who wrote between 850 and 500 B.C.

Abraham is the earliest patriarch for Jews, Christians and Muslims. Both the date and place of Abraham's origin are most interesting. His history begins in Genesis 11:26, hard upon the story of the tower of Babel, and concludes at 25:11. He came from "Ur of the Chaldeans." There were two Urs on the Euphrates River in what is modern Iraq. In the early twentieth century it was suggested that this Ur was about 150 miles south of Babylon, just north of modern Kuwait. Mid-twentieth century research suggested it was a different Ur some 550 miles northerly up the Euphrates in the mountainous land of those people we today call the Kurds. Late twentieth century research again suggested it was that Ur near Babylon. The dates of Abraham's life range from 2500 to 1400 B.C. but most settle in the range of 2000 to 1700 B.C. At the time of Abraham the main pyramids in Egypt were already 1,000 years old, and Stonehenge was just being built in England. Peking (Beijing) was a beginning settlement in what was to become China. Many centuries after the pyramids, Abraham was born and raised in Iraq.

Babylon plays a big part throughout the Bible, from Genesis through the prophecies of Revelation. It was located sixty miles west of what is modern Baghdad, Iraq. Babylon is one of the oldest known cities in the world, along with Jericho and Damascus, having been a settlement from around 5000 B.C. Babylon was a very advanced and cultured civilization with books, libraries and settled laws. Abraham was an older contemporary of Hammarubi, who ruled Babylon from 1792 to 1750 B.C. He is credited with composing the "Code of Hammurabi," not so much a formal legal code or recitation of existing laws as a collection of edicts, which was the fairly common practice of most monarchs. This Code has much in common with the *Decalogue*, the Ten Commandments, of Exodus chapter 20, and with the Covenant Code of Exodus chapters 21-23, which includes at 21:23-25 the *lex talionis*, the "law of retaliation" of precise retribution, and no more, an eye for an eye, a tooth for a tooth. These similarities and relationships would indicate that the laws of God for his people and their societies are universal and eternal.

A confusion, more major than minor, for most people as they move into a slightly deeper study of the Bible, is that the sixty-six books that make up the Bible are not arranged in their correct chronological order. This can, and frequently does, cause an out-of-context misinterpretation of certain parts. This is especially true of the thirty-nine Hebrew books that make up the Old Testament which are grouped generally as Law/History (five), History (twelve), Wisdom/Poetry (five) and Prophets (seventeen, five major and twelve minor). The Prophets are further out of order as they are arranged according to length and not date. The twenty-seven books which form the Christian Scriptures of the New Testament are grouped as Gospels/Life of Christ (four), History (one), Epistles/Letters (twenty-one, thirteen by Paul and eight by others) and Prophecy (one). The Epistles, as are the Prophets, are arranged largely by length and not date, but this does not cause any great misinterpretations as they were written over such a relatively short time span. Though some of these could have been written first in Hebrew, they all have come to us in the Greek language of that fading empire at that time.

There is a movement and flow of several very powerful kingdoms during the 2,000-year period from Abraham to Jesus, which is easily missed, or at the least confused, by most readers. One really should understand the constancy of these kingdoms and the life-and-death power of these rulers to fully appreciate the supreme King and kingdom of God. Two embryonic kingdoms began 1,000 years before Abraham. They were 1,000 miles apart. One was as the mouth of the Nile growing 1,000 miles southward, upstream. It would always be called Egypt. The other was at the mouths of the Tigris and Euphrates growing 1,000 miles northward, upstreams. It would change names as it grew, from Babylon, to Assyria, to Nineveh, to Neo-Babylon, to Persia (essentially modern Iran). These two empires would grow for two millennia, and 1,000 years after Abraham would seriously rub against one another in the vicinity of a very small kingdom caught in the middle, generally called Canaan, Palestine and Israel. The new Iron Age would be in full growth as used in the chariots and weapons of the Assyrians.

The 250-year growth of this little Israel is told in the books of Joshua, Judges, 1st and 2nd Samuel, 1st and 2nd Chronicles, and 1st Kings. It grew westward from the River Jordan, and by 1000 B.C. Solomon, son of David, ruled a small area of 250 miles north to south by 100 miles east to west, lying between the two growing giants of Egypt to the south and Assyria to the northeast. The Greek Empire was then but an embryo, and the Roman not yet conceived. First Kings covers about 118 years, the years of Solomon and of the division of the kingdom. Second Kings covers about 282 years of huge mid-east "world wars," changes of empires and the fall of Israel and Judah. Nearly all of the prophets, major and minor, were during the last twelve chapters of Second Kings. Ezekiel and Daniel were probably followers of Jeremiah in Judah before it collapsed and they were taken to Babylon, into exile. During the exile these three prophesied as to the return to Israel, which prophecy was fulfilled under Cyrus. Haggai and Zechariah were prophets of the return from exile. Only Malachi prophesied after the return, and his was of yet another and final collapse.

At the very end of the old Hebrew scriptures there were thunderings over the horizon of the coming Greek Empire. Under Alexander the Great they would swiftly sweep over the territories of both Egypt and Assyria-Persia, taking the former Israel in stride. At the beginning of the new Christian scriptures, the Roman Empire would be taking the biblical territory over from the Greeks, and also moving westward into Europe.

There is also that group of a combination of thirteen writings which are either parts of various Old Testament books or separate little books of that era. These are called the Apocrypha, which means in Greek, "off writings," as they are not a part of the canonically recognized Protestant Bible nor of the modern Jewish scriptures, the Tanakh. These are 1st and 2nd Esdras, Tobit, Judith, Esther Additions, Book of Wisdom, Ecclesiasticus/Son of Sirach, Baruch, Epistle of Jeremiah, Daniel Additions (Prayer of Three Young Men, Susanna, Bel and the Dragon), 1st and 2nd Maccabees and Prayer of Manasseh (at 2 Chronicles 33:18).

At the time of Christ the Apocrypha was being used increasingly by both the Jews and the early Church, though none of these writings are quoted in the New Testament. However, at the time of the Reformation the Church of Rome officially accepted all of the Apocrypha except 1st and 2nd Esdras and the Prayer of Manasseh. The Church of England, in its sixth Article of Religion, followed Jerome's view of these "other books" as deutero-canonical in that "the Church doth read for example of life and instruction of manners; but yet doth it not apply them to establish any doctrine." In more recent times many other English-speaking churches increasingly have cast aside these books. Such disregard is a loss as some of these writings transport the readers from the Jewish to the Christian era, especially 1st and 2nd Maccabees which cover much of that 400-year interval between the Old and the New Testament, of the rise and fall of the Greek empire, and the rise of the Roman.

We communicate primarily with words, spoken and written, and the sender and receiver of such words must have the same understanding of their meaning. This can be a minor problem within the same language and a very serious problem in translations from one language to another. Although Hebrew most certainly was not the primordial first language nor that in which God necessarily spoke or speaks, it is the one in which the earliest scriptures come to us. The better one's understanding of Hebrew and Greek, the better will be one's understanding of the written word of the Bible. For the more serious student, a good dictionary for at least key words would be helpful.

The old Hebrew scriptures were handed down to us in the Hebrew language, with a smattering of Aramaic, and the new Christian scriptures in the Greek. No doubt there are now thousands of translations of the Bible, of which several hundred are in English. Of course, in selecting a Bible one must first choose the language, such as English, German or Spanish. In English there are then two more categories from which to select. One of these is the level of vocabulary or reading. These usually range from the fourth to the twelfth grade levels.

The other category is the format of translation, of which there are three. First is the "word for word" or transliteral translation in which the Hebrew or Greek is translated into English in as close a word order as reasonable to retain the text as closely as possible. Second is the "thought for thought" or equivalent (dynamic or functional) translation in which the original word order is not followed so closely as it gives way to selecting the English words which convey the original thought. Third is a paraphrase, which is a translation from the original freely into a modern standard word selection and order. As the translations migrate from "literal" to "equivalent" to "paraphrase" they become easier to read but lose some quality of accuracy.

Twelve popular Protestant Bibles and one Roman Catholic Bible are as follows with name, abbreviation, date of completion, format and generally accepted reading level.

King James (Authorized) Version (KJV)	1611	literal	12th grade
American Standard Bible (ASB)	1901	literal	12th grade
English Standard Version (ESV)	2001	literal	11th grade
New American Standard (NAS)	1971	literal	11th grade
New American Bible (NAB)(Catholic)	1970	equivalent	10th grade
Revised Standard Version (RSV)	1952	equivalent	10th grade
New Revised Standard Version (NRSV)	1990	equivalent	10th grade
New English Bible (NEB)	1970	literal	10th grade
Jerusalem Bible (JB)	1966	equivalent	10th grade
New King James Version (NKJV)	1982	literal/equiv.	8th grade
New Living Translation (NLT)	1996	equivalent	8th grade
New International Version (NIV)	1984	equivalent	7th grade
Amplified Bible	1987	paraphrase	7th grade
Today's English Version/Good News (TEV)	1976	equivalent	4th grade

Two other considerations, which have nothing to do with the basic choice of Bible, are the type or print size and the intended use. The smaller the print the smaller the book. The print in most standard size Bibles is 9-point. A 7-point is fairly small and is used in "pocket" Bibles; and a 14-point is considered "Large" or "Giant" print, and is good for both pulpit use and for those with weaker eyesight. The intended use is important as an equivalent or paraphrase coupled with a lower grade or reading level is good for easy first-time reading; and a literal coupled with a higher grade or reading level is better for the majesty required for pulpit reading and memorization.

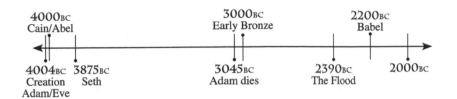

CHAPTER 1

GENESIS 1-11

BEGINNINGS, ADAM, EVE, NOAH, BABEL

In the beginning God created. Gen. 1:1

The Bible is history. The Bible is the action of God in the history of mankind. Some groups breed confusion in this aspect as they pick and choose their own personal theology. Some teach that the first eleven chapters of the Bible, as to creation and the flood, are true history but, in an honest attempt to keep people from secularizing the Bible, erroneously teach that the rest is not history. Others teach that the first eleven chapters are not history but the rest is history. Our word "theology" simply means "God words". A theologian is simply one who speaks words about God working in the lives and history of humans.

We build a culture and society with stories, of which some are true and some mostly untrue but for the purpose of sending a message. These stories have several names, including fable, legend and myth. A fable is an untrue tall tale. A legend is based upon factual history but with a lot of embellishment. A myth is an explanation of the beginnings of a culture or society, a people, and may or may not be true in fact. We communicate primarily with words, spoken and written, and both the sender and receiver of such words must have the same understanding of their meaning. We will describe about a dozen Hebrew words, and a couple of Greek words. For our purposes, the correct writing or pronouncing of these words is unimportant, as we are communicating in English.

The first eleven chapters of the Bible, of the old Hebrew Scriptures, of the Old Testament, of Genesis, tell of the earliest history of humanity in general. The first word in the Hebrew Bible is *b'resheeth* (בְּרֵאשִׁית), which translates into the English as "in the first." That Hebrew word is the Hebrew name of this first book. About 250 B.C., the Greeks translated the Bible, then only the old Hebrew scriptures, from Hebrew into Greek. They translated *b'resheeth* into the Greek as *en arche* (εν αρχη), "in first," and centuries later into the English as "in the beginning." The Greek word for "beginning" or "generation" is *geneseis* (γενέσεις). In that ancient Greek translation, this word *geneseis* was

1

not used in the very first verse but was used in subsequent verses many times, particularly at ten places where the beginnings or generations of heavens, earth, mankind and the families of Noah and Abraham were reported. With that Greek translation of 250 B.C. the name for this book became Genesis, "beginnings".

In the Hebrew scripture, the word *toldah* (תלדה) is used to separate the ten main sections of Genesis. About seven different English words are used to translate *toldah*, being origin, history, account, story, birth, descendant and generation. The first five sections are of primeval matters. At 2:4 is the generation of sky and land; 5:1 is of the children of Adam and Eve; 6:9 is of Noah; 10:1 is of Noah's sons; and 11:10 is of Shem's sons. The second five sections are of the patriarchs. At 11:27 is the account of Abraham; 25:12 is of Abraham's son Ishmael; 25:19 is of Abraham's son Isaac; 36:1,9 Isaac's son Esau; and 37:2 is of Isaac's son Jacob and his son Joseph.

The English word "generate" is derived from the Greek through Latin and means to beget, procreate, bring into existence (essentially from nothing). Genesis is the book of things being brought into existence, of origins, of generations. In chapter one we have the generation of the universe, the earth and its space, seas, plants, the sun and stars, fish, fowl, animals and *adam* (mankind, male and female). In chapter two we have a day of rest and the generation of the word of God and of marriage. In chapter three we have the generation of sin and of judgment, as Adam and Eve ate of the forbidden fruit and were punished. In chapter four we have the generation of family, with Cain and Abel and, also obviously, daughters, and the continued increasing effects of sin with the first horrendous conflict as Cain murdered Abel. In chapter five we have the generation of generations of descendants, the begats, of Adam and Eve. In chapter six we have the generation of worshipful obedience with the example of Noah. In chapters seven through ten we have continued disobedience and evil followed by judgment, as we are told of that great flood, which has been recorded by most of the ancient cultures of the world. In chapter eleven we have the generation of separate languages at Babel, and begin the generation of a chosen people, of Abraham and the Hebrews. The rest of the chapters, twelve through fifty are of the events of the beginnings of a people, a nation, a church, a Savior and God's plan for salvation.

The Hebrew word *bara* (ברא) means "to create" out of nothing, as distinguished from the words *asah* (עשה) and *b'na'* (בנא) which mean "to make or build" out of something. In Genesis *bara* is used eight times, but refers to only three events, those at which modern science fails in its attempts to explain. Out of nothing, God created: (1) at the first three verses the universe and light, day one; (2) at verse twenty, the living fish and fowl, day five; (3) and at verse twenty-seven mankind, male and female, late in day six. In the other three days, plus early day six, God made, formed or built from things already created: (1) at verse six the expanse of the earthly atmospheres, day two; (2) at verse nine the waters were gathered from the dry land, from which then came vegetation, day three; (3) at verse fourteen (from the light of the first day) the greater (sun) and lesser (moon and stars) luminaries, day four; (4) and at verse twenty-four, the land animals, early in day six. God set the example for human bio-rhythms as he rested on the seventh day. Three days of separation; three days of population; one day of relaxation.

The Hebrew word for God used in the first chapter, the creation chapter (and through much of the Hebrew scriptures), is in the plural, which causes some people some confusion. This use of the plural may be either the "royal plural" as used by kings and heads of state or, for Christians, the three-in-one unified trinitarian God of the Father, the Son and the Holy Spirit. This oneness is evidenced by the fact that the verb *bara* (create) is in the masculine singular. God is a person, one and incomprehensible. Within the limitations of the English language, the only pronouns applicable to God are the singular "who" or "whom" and a reverent and unsexualized "he", but not "she", in some vain attempt to sexualize God, nor "it" nor "which", though "which" is used for phonetic purpose in the most popular sung version of the Lord's Prayer.

Chapter two begins with what may be called the seventh day of creation, the day on which God rested and set aside as a hallowed day of rest. We are then focused back on the afternoon of day six, the creation of man and of woman. First, the scene is set with a reminder that God created heaven and earth. Some of the plants made from the earth on day three were set in a garden called Eden. Included were two trees in the middle of the garden, the tree of Life and the tree of Knowledge of Evil, and also of Good, of which the couple already knew.

At verse four, as we focus back on the afternoon, we see four different words used for "ground". They are used very specifically and rarely interchanged, one for the other. First is *eretz* (ארץ), which usually means "land" but here means the earthly globe, which God created on day one. Second is *adamah* (אדמה), the (reddish) fertile soil, the humus. Third is *ara'* (ארע), the lowly dirt. Fourth is *aphar* (עפר), loose dry dirt, the dust. In chapter one at verse twenty-seven, we are told God created *Adam* (male and female), indicating from the *adamah*, the humus, from which comes "human". In chapter two at verse seven, we are told more specifically that *Adam* was created from the *aphar*, the very top, loose layer of dust. Dirt to dirt. Dust to dust. Into *Adam* God breathed life, inspiration.

Immediately upon creating the male *Adam*, who knew only good, God commanded him not to eat of the tree of knowledge of evil. Then from the male *Adam*, God created a female *Adam*, a matching complement. Three times we are told that *Adam* meant both male and female, Mr. and Mrs. Ground, one flesh, she from him. The male had named all of the animals, and later he would give to the woman the wonderful name *Havah* (Eve), "life-giver". God had described her as a "help-meet", equally descriptive of both the male and the female, but Adam called her "life-giver".

Two different Hebrew words are used in chapter one with a sense of "dominion". Humans, *Adam*, are to subdue, *radah*, animals and fish and are to tread down, *kabash*, the earth. As to the earth, in chapter two, *Adam* is told that treading down the earth means to cultivate or farm it, to till the garden. Also, in verse twenty, the female *Adam* is described as *ezer b'negedo*, the best translation of which is in the King James Bible, as a "help-meet", which does not mean a person of lesser worth. Help simply means two working toward the same goal. Frequently a stronger one helps the weaker, but here the other is also a mate, a match, an equal, the other glove. Both are help-mates in the building of a unified family by one man, one woman, one flesh.

Marriage is of one man and one woman, and they are to have children which is the family. Many believe that some god did not make this rule but that it is simply the way societies throughout history have decided is the best way to do it. Today many would tell us that either way that system is no longer valid. Marriage and family have so many individual meanings as to have absolutely no meaning.

The true location of Eden is unknown. Four rivers flow out from Eden, two of which are unidentifiable today. The other two are the Tigris and the Euphrates, which through history have begun in southeastern Turkey, in the land of the Kurds, in the vicinity of what is thought to be Mount Ararat, and flow southeastward about 1,000 miles through modern Iraq to the Persian Gulf. This would place the Garden of Eden in the mountains of southeastern Turkey, the climate of which at the time is unknown. A more popular theory is that in *Adam*'s time the Tigris and Euphrates came together just north of the Gulf and then separated again, allowing Eden to have been in southern Iraq, in the vicinity of ancient Babylon.

In chapter three we are told of the fall of humans into sin as the result of temptation by Satan, who appears as a serpent. Some think that this satanic serpent possibly may have been either before "evolution" gave Satan legs and arms or that the serpent lost the ability to speak due to sin. Some think this is but an absurd fairy tale. God grew things in the garden that were "pleasing to the sight", "good for food" and " available for life". Sight, food and life. God planted two trees in the middle of the garden. God told Adam, of whom Eve was "one flesh", that they could eat of the tree of Life but not of the tree of Knowledge of Evil. Satan twisted both the words of God and the thoughts of Eve, as Adam stood by in silence allowing Satan to usurp his protective dominion over Eve. Satan tells Eve a series of half-truths to convince her to alter "sight, food and life" to "food, sight and death". Immediately they knew evil and that they were naked. Upon disobeying God, the very first and primordial evil was concupiscence, lust and a twisted sexuality.

Sin went from the serpent to the woman to the man, one flesh. Serpent, woman, man. However, as God had given Mr. Adam primary responsibility, he reverses that order as he speaks to them, beginning with four primordial questions, repeated by all good counselors to this day, three to Mr. Adam. "Where are you?" meaning we are all meant to be somewhere but may be lost and suffering from an identity crisis. "Who told you?" meaning we all are taught and led by some guide. "Have you been eating from the wrong trees?" meaning we are each fed on and by some culture. To Mrs. Adam, "What have you done?" is to make us examine our past actions, smoke out a confession, and, with his help, to make corrections so as not to repeat. God then gave his judgment in the order of the sin: serpent, woman, man. The serpent was cursed to creep on its belly and to be an enemy of the woman until her descendant shall crush his head. The woman was to have great pain in childbirth and would have increased desire for her husband who would rule over her, but within that fact of being one flesh. The man was to toil and sweat all of his days in thorns and thistles until he returned to dust. God covered the sins and shames of the man and woman with animal skins, a blood sacrifice. He then cast them out of the Garden, to a place east of Eden, and posted guards at the tree of Life.

Following the story of the expulsion from the Garden is the beginning of civilization at chapter four. We are told of the cancerous growth of sin and the effects of uncontrolled, selfish jealousy as we hear of the first conflict and murder. This is the first story of the pain of a child who does not get the blessing of the father. Eve gave birth to Cain and Abel, possibly twin sons. Cain was a tiller of the ground and Abel a keeper of sheep. God had set the example of an animal blood sacrifice to cover sins, and there must have been some firm understanding that an offering to God was to be the "first" of one's produce. Cain brings only "an" offering of fruit, but Abel brings the "first" of his flock. God indicates his lack of regard for Cain's offering. Rather than correct his error, Cain becomes angry and jealous toward Abel. God now asks the fifth great question, "Why are you angry?" God cautions Cain that sin crouches like a wild animal at the door to catch such a person. Cain then lures Abel into the field where he kills him.

God then asks his sixth great question, "Where is...your brother?" Insolently Cain replies, "Am I my brother's keeper?" The answer to that question is a resounding, "No!" We are not our brother's keeper; God is. We are to love and care for our brother, and we are not to murder, abuse, mistreat, steal from or falsely accuse our brother or sister, neither are we to keep him, her or them, not by slavery with wages earned or welfare given. God told Adam he was the keeper of all plants and animals. Humans "keep" animals and things, but only God is the keeper of humans. From a misreading of these verses can come volumes of erroneous sermons and a horribly distorted welfare system. God alone keeps humans, and he destroys any person or nation who does so. See herinafter page 277. God was not pleased with Cain's murder of Abel, and with this insolence God immediately cast Cain out of his presence to the land of Nod, east of Eden. Cain and his nine descendants are mentioned in chapter four but nevermore. Eve bears a third son, Seth, and in chapter five we are told she bore Adam other sons and daughters. In the beginning brothers could marry sisters.

In chapters six through ten we are told of Noah, his family, his ark and of the great flood. Noah was the grandson of Methuselah, who lives 969 years and probably dies in the year of the great flood. Probably due to the ultra clean and nurturing environment, from Adam to Noah many people lived to be 800 to 900 years. The fact of the great flood covering the earth has been recorded by many cultures, which is wide and disparate proof of the fact that such a flood occurred. This is a story of crime and punishment. God sees that wickedness and violence are great upon the earth and in the hearts of men. Noah is the one exception, the one man who is righteous, blameless and walks with God. God determines to make an end to all flesh by a great flood. He tells Noah to build an ark of gopher wood and that it is to be covered with pitch, being 450 feet long (300 cubits), 75 feet wide (50 cubits), 45 feet high (30 cubits), with three decks, about half the size, one-fifth the volume, of a modern aircraft carrier or large cruise ship, but obviously large enough to carry the young of the land animals and fowl described.

The people ridicule Noah as he builds, but the rains do begin. Some calculations put the flood at about 2300 B.C., about the time the Egyptian pyramids were being built, but it was most likely many centuries earlier. Then Noah and his three sons, Shem, Ham and Japheth with their wives, load the ark with provisions and male and female of each kind. As the waters rise, the people scream to get in, but God withdraws his protection and with his own hand closes the hatches, shutting them all out. It rains forty days, then those on the ark float for another 110 days. Noah sends out doves, but they return. Then one day a dove returns with an olive branch in its mouth, forever more the symbol of reconciliation. Dry land has appeared. The ark lands on Mount Ararat, in eastern Turkey, near the headwaters of the Tigris and Euphrates rivers, a possible site of that Garden of Eden.

God set a rainbow in the sky as a covenant never again to curse the ground nor destroy every living thing as he had done, forever more the symbol of peace. God also tells the people, "every moving thing that lives shall be food for you", meaning they are no longer restricted to vegetarianism, as all animals, fish and fowl now are allowed as food. God tells Noah and his sons, "Be fruitful and multiply, and fill the earth," and the three sons of Noah and their wives begin the repopulation of the earth. Their descendants are set out "according to their families, according to their languages, in their lands and in their nations."

Chapter eleven begins with another story of inordinate satanic human pride, striving to become God. It is the story of the tower of Babel and the confounding of human language. Many calling themselves scholars claim this is but a naïve child's tale, as language must "evolve" over eons and cannot happen fairly suddenly. However, the evidence as to languages seems to indicate that they do in fact peak to an excellence fairly rapidly then begin a period of deterioration. This story is that many descendants of Nimrod, great-grandson of Noah, settle at Babel, "gate of God", in the plain in the land of Shinar. Shinar (and Sumer) was the name of the area now known as southern Iraq, mainly ancient Babylon, modern Baghdad and also Kuwait. This was the area first known to use bronze. For building they make bricks of stone, using bitumen asphalt for mortar. In modern times that area is still rich in oil and bitumen. They decide to build for themselves "a city, and a tower whose top is in the heavens; to make a name for ourselves." This is so they not "be scattered abroad over the face of the whole earth," as God had decreed. But the Lord comes down to see the city and the tower and determines to "confuse their language, that they may not understand one another's speech." Now God is not a God of confusion and the languages do not divide families or tribes but do cause the people to scatter themselves abroad from there over the face of all the earth. Studies indicate there may be about seventeen separate and distinct languages around the world, one is Navajo, and all trace back to this land of Shinar. There is likely no "mother tongue".

The latter part of chapter eleven begins a major shift from the "pre-historic" to the historic as we are introduced to Abram/Abraham, a descendant of Noah's son Shem, and his descendants.

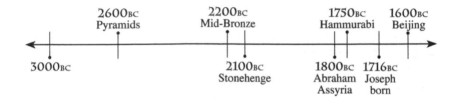

CHAPTER 2

GENESIS 12-50

ABRAHAM, ISAAC, JACOB AND JOSEPH

*I am the God of your fathers, the God of Abraham, the God of Isaac,
and the God of Jacob. Gen.28:13; Exo 3:5*

Again we are reminded always to keep in mind both the theme and
the purpose of the Bible. The theme of the Bible is reconciliation; God the
Father's call to and search for lost mankind, who runs from God, until hearing
the call, stops and stumbles to return. The purpose of the Bible is revelation;
primarily to reveal one unified Trinitarian Godhead, God the Father, God the
Son and God the Holy Spirit, as the creator of the universe and the redeemer
and sustainer of the humans of earth; and secondarily to reveal the true nature
of humans, of anthropology. The Bible is not the story of mankind searching
for or forming God, though many trifle with that notion. Whether or not one
believes that it was written by human hands as guided by the inspiration of
God, one should read it for guidance as to life. Also, always keep in mind the
LSB, the Land, the Seed and the Blessing, as they move from the nation of
Israel to the faithful believers, which is for Christians the followers of Christ.
Also, again we are reminded that the Bible is history. The Bible is the action
of God in the history of mankind.

There are three groups of people one must keep in mind throughout
the old Hebrew scriptures, as God strives to establish the nation of Israel,
which continually disobeys and falls away. The first group are the Egyptians,
those to the southwest, which were a world power all during the old Hebrew
scriptures. The second group are those living in the land the Hebrews were
invading. These were mostly Canaanites, descendants of Ham, a son of Noah,
as the Israelites were descendants of Shem, a son of Noah. The third group
are the Assyrians, those to the northeast, the land from which Abraham had
come, the land we today call Iraq, and the Babylonians of modern southern
Iraq. During the 400 years the Israelites were in Egypt this kingdom would
expand and continue for another 300 years until God allowed Assyria to
defeat the disobedient people of Israel and take them into captivity.

Genesis is the book of things being brought into existence, of origins, of generations. In chapter twelve we are told of the generation of a chosen people as the stories of Abraham and the Hebrews begin. The rest of the chapters, thirteen through fifty are of the events of the beginnings of a people, a nation, a church, a Savior and God's plan for salvation.

Genesis is an extremely important book of the Bible. Most people have a mere smattering of scattered little parts of tales. Nearly every verse of its fifty chapters is packed not only with history but some of the most profound character analyses in all of literature.

At the end of chapter eleven we met Abram/Abraham, son of Terah, a descendant of Shem, one of the three sons of Noah. As previously stated, we are told the family came from "Ur of the Chaldeans", of which there were probably two, both in modern Iraq. They may have come from both, the southern one south of ancient Babylon, the area of modern Baghdad, and the other 550 miles north up the streams between the Euphrates and Tigris rivers, near the land of the modern Kurds. The family moved from the southern area to the northern area both to work the caravan route and at God's early call. Secular archeology fairly well acknowledges the existence of Abraham and that he was born around 1950 B.C.

At that time of Abraham, the Bronze Age which began in his area of Ur, was about 1,100 years old. Egypt was in the period of its Middle Kingdom, and its pyramids were 700 to 1,000 years old. The cities of Jericho, Damascus and Babylon were easily of the same vintage, and Babylon had a population of 30,000 at the time. Ashkelon, a fortified Syrian city on the Mediterranean had 15,000 inhabitants. Stonehenge in modern England was maybe 200 years old. Beijing was just becoming a city. Hammurabi, the compositor of the early legal code of ancient Babylon was a young man. The Hindu religion would begin on the Indian subcontinent shortly after the death of Abraham. Job was a contemporary of Abraham, and some think may even have been Abraham.

The sons and daughters of Adam and Eve had been permitted to marry one another; however, over the centuries that closeness gradually widened. Terah had at least two wives and three sons, Abram, Nahor and Haran. Abram's wife Sarai was his half-sister. Nahor's wife was his niece, the daughter of Haran, who also had a son named Lot. Terah took most of this group northward between the Euphrates and Tigris Rives, the Meso-potamia. After Terah's death God called Abram, known later as Abraham, to go from there to a land he would show him later and that he would bless Abram.

At the age of seventy-five, Abram gathers his many possessions and livestock, and with Sarai, known later as Sarah, and his nephew Lot, begins the journey of some 550 miles southwesterly to the land of the Canaanites, named for Canaan who was the son of Ham cursed by God to serve the other descendants of Noah's sons. They settle in Shechem between what would later be Samaria and Jerusalem on what in modern times would be known as the West Bank. He builds two altars in that area. One of the places he calls Bethel, "house of God", and the other, six miles away, he calls Ai, "ruin". He is not yet fully committed and is between God and ruin.

God promised Abram that were he to go to this land, he would make him a great nation, bless him, make his name great and bless those who bless him and curse those who curse him. Abram went on faith. As Joshua will tell us some 500 years later, at the end of his chapter 21, God fulfilled his promises, "All came to pass." Abram/Abraham does give rise to a great nation from Joseph to Solomon; he indeed does become blessed; his name does become great to Jew, Christian and Muslim; other nations were blessed or cursed based upon their treatment of the Hebrews; and his people will be put on the land, time and again. God will so conditionally promise Abram four times, once including all of the land from south of Gaza north past modern Lebanon and east over both modern Jordan and Iraq. Some forty times, God will make this promise, each plainly conditional on obedience to God, but the Hebrews will constantly disobey and turn to other gods, especially during about 300 years that begin with Solomon. For such continual breach, about 1,400 years after Abram, God will remove the Hebrew nation from the land promised. Isaiah, Jeremiah and Ezekiel will prophesy of the coming of a new covenant and a new Spirit.

Abram moves about a hundred miles further south into the Negev desert where he faces a famine, which causes him to continue another 250 miles westward into Egypt. This begins an early pattern of Abram and his descendants running to Egypt for various reasons. To discourage the Egyptians from killing him to take Sarai, he says she is his sister, a half-truth. After about a year he returns, with his wife, livestock and possessions to Shechem. To avoid strife, Abram offers his nephew Lot the choice of land, neither of which they actually control except by the promise of God. Lot chooses the area of the plains in the valley of the Dead Sea, and moves to Sodom near Gomorrah. Abram moves to Hebron by the oaks of Mamre, and God again promises Abram the land of the West Bank.

At this time there are two empires on two separate river basins. Egypt lies on the Nile to the southwest of the land promised. Assyria lies on the Tigris and Euphrates, to the east of the land promised. The land promised lay between the two. For about 1,200 years, Assyria will continue to grow into a true rival of Egypt when God will allow Assyria to capture the northern Hebrew kingdom shortly before Assyria itself, even with the aid of Egypt, will be defeated by Persia.

In chapter fourteen we hear of Melchizedek, king of Salem. Salem was the city of the Jebusites. In Hebrew the letter "b" is similar to "r" and, no doubt, over time the name Jebu-Salem became Jeru-salem. There is no mention of the ancestry of Melchizedek nor of any descendants. He is described as a king-priest of God Most High and appears briefly to praise Abram who in return gives him a tenth of everything.

In chapter fifteen Abram tells God that he is promised land but has no heirs except his slave Eliezer. God tells him that the slave will not be the heir but that Abram will have a child of his own. Here we have that verse which will be quoted in the book of Habakkuk and Romans chapter four and upon which Martin Luther will base the Reformation. "Abram believed the Lord, and he reckoned it to him as righteousness." God simply counts us righteous based only upon our faith in him, which faith will produce good works. God then covenants that he will give Abram's descendants (seed) the land.

Abram believes they will have a child, but after ten years Sarai convinces him to try another route, as she is seventy-five and he eighty-five. She gives her Egyptian servant Hagar to Abram as his concubine, and she conceives and bears a child. Hagar looks with contempt upon Sarai who then causes her to flee, but God tells Hagar to return and that she will have many descendants, and that this son will be a wild ass of a man and against his kinsmen. She returns and delivers her son and names him Ishmael, which means "God hears". The son is born and through his twelve sons becomes the progenitor of the Arabs.

God again comes to Abram and Sarai, changing Abram's name from "exalted father" to Abraham, "father of a multitude" and Sarai's from "contentious" to Sarah, "princess". He says he will give Abraham a son by Sarah. He also covenants that as a sign every male child shall be circumcised on the eighth day, and so it will be with all, including Abraham and Ishmael. Abraham loves Ishmael, so God blesses the boy and agrees to make him a great nation. Sarah laughs that she is to have a son at her age of ninety, so God says her son will be named Isaac, meaning "he laughs", and so it will be.

During this time Lot, Abraham's nephew, is living down in the valley near the Dead Sea in Sodom. Sin is great in that city, and God says he will destroy both it and Gomorrah. Abraham pleads that surely God will not do so if fifty righteous live there and God agrees, then forty, then thirty, then twenty and finally ten. However, there are none righteous in Sodom so God proceeds. Two angels, as men, visit Lot in Sodom. The men of Sodom demand that Lot turn them over to them for illicit sexual relations, but Lot refuses, and he and his family flee as God begins the destruction with brimstone and fire. Lot's wife pauses to look back, perhaps longing for that life, and God turns her into a pillar of salt.

Many a man in the Bible had to overcome early sins and blunders, and could not look back in guilt. They looked forward and upward in faith. The culture and society, run by fallen men, of these great men of the Bible may have permitted, even encouraged, mistreatment of women, but these men rose above that.

There is no one left to carry on the line of Lot except his two daughters. They get their father drunk and lie with him and conceive. The son of one daughter is named Moab who settles the northeast of the Dead Sea, and the son of the other is named Ben-ammi, "son of my people", who settles the southeast of the Dead Sea as Ammon. A little over 500 years later, as Moses leads the multitudes back from Egypt, they will be forbidden to fight their kinsmen along the east of the Dead Sea and will negotiate their passage.

Sarah does conceive and deliver their son Isaac. One day she sees her son playing with the older Ishmael and in a sense of jealousy, insists that Abraham cast out Hagar and Ishmael, which he reluctantly does. God promises to make Ishmael a great nation, as he had with Abraham. Hagar and Ishmael run out of water, but God hears their cry and positions them near a well. At this time Abraham settles a dispute over another well, which he names Beer-sheba. Abraham lives on the southern West Bank in the area of Hebron and Beer-sheba. Water-wells are important in that area and in the book of Genesis. In Hebrew "beer" means "water-well". It is here that the designation "Philistine", centuries later "Palestine" is first used, meaning "rolling migrants". Ishmael lives in the wilderness and takes Egyptian wives as they settle in the area of the Arab and Sinai Peninsulas. Like Jacob, Ishmael will have twelve sons. The Arabs and the Hebrews are both descendants of Abraham and of Shem, and both Semites.

In chapter twenty-two is the story of the testing of Abraham. God tells him to take his son Isaac, then about fifteen, and go northward some twenty-five miles to the Mount of Moriah, the future Jerusalem, where he is to offer Isaac as a burnt offering. Upon arrival he has Isaac carry the wood for the fire up the final incline. (Much as will Jesus carry the wood centuries later.) Isaac asked where the lamb for the sacrifice is and is told that God will provide. Isaac is placed on the altar, and Abraham raises the knife. God directs him to stop, and they see a lamb caught in the brush. The test is also a message from God, early on, that there is to be no human sacrifice as is practiced by the Canaanites all around them.

Sarah dies, at the age of 137 years. Abraham negotiates and buys "the cave of the field of Mach-pe'lah east of Mamre," which will be repeated many times for the town of Hebron. There she is buried. Abraham grows old and concerned that Isaac not take a wife from the surrounding Canaanites. As he sits, he has his slave Eliezer put his hand "under his thigh" and covenant to return 550 miles northward to the ancestral home of Abraham to find a wife for Isaac, and so he did. The act of placing a hand "under the thigh" is the origin of the English word "testify".

Eliezer prays that he meet a woman at a well who will help him draw water and then also for his camels, as he wants a woman who is sufficiently wise and considerate for both man and animals. The prayer is answered as the beautiful Rebekah does so. At this time, marriage within fairly close blood lines is still permitted. She is the grand-daughter of Abraham's brother and niece and wife to be to Isaac, her first cousin-once-removed. She has a brother named Laban, a bit of a rascal and conniver. He sees the valuables Eliezer carries and obtains some for himself and his father as a dowry for Rebekah. She returns to the southern West Bank with Eliezer. In the distance she sees a man and is told it was Isaac, so she covers her face with her veil, as was the custom. At the age of forty, Isaac takes her for his wife and loves her immensely.

With Sarah gone and Abraham dying at the age of 175, the story shifts to Isaac and Rebekah. God becomes known as "The God of your father; the God of Abraham," and later known as--"I am the God of your fathers, the God of Abraham, the God of Isaac, and the God of Jacob."

Rebekah conceives twins who struggle within her womb. God tells her they are to be two nations and the younger will rule the elder. The first to come forth has a reddish hairy covering and is named Esau, meaning "red". The second comes forth holding the ankle of the first and is named Jacob, meaning "heel grabber". Esau becomes a hunter and is loved by his father Isaac. Jacob is a quiet tent-dweller and is loved by his mother, Rebekah. Such a division of love is usually disastrous for the children, and such it was between Ishmael and Isaac and now between Esau and Jacob.

Esau is a robust man of the fields who cares more for the fullness of life than for visionary or spiritual matters. Jacob, perhaps as an act of God or simply that his mother Rebekah had told him God had said he would rule and favored him, took a stronger interest in visionary and spiritual matters. One day, when the boys are about twenty, Esau comes in from the fields famished and asks Jacob for some of the red pottage. Jacob asks Esau to agree to give over his birthright as first son for the pottage, to which Esau agrees, not being concerned as to such matters. Esau receives his pottage and gives up his birthright. As he is of reddish complexion, sells out for some red pottage and eventually settles the reddish lands southeast to the Dead Sea, he is also known as Edom, very similar to Adam, meaning "red ground".

As with his father Abraham, a famine comes upon the land. God tells Isaac not to go to Egypt and that he will also give the land of Abraham to Isaac. So Isaac remains in the area of the West Bank, the area later known as Palestine. Unlike his wandering, adventurous father, Isaac conserves what he has and never leaves that small area.

As Isaac grows old he calls Esau, his eldest and favorite son, to him. He asks Esau to hunt some game, cook it and bring his favorite meal so that he may bless him. Rebekah overhears the conversation, and, due to impatience for God to work, she proceeds to violate her relationship with both her husband and eldest son and also her good name. Jacob, her favorite, has claim to the birthright of Esau, and she is determined that he have it. She cooks the meal, dresses Jacob in animal skins, and sends him to Isaac with the meal. Jacob tells his father three untruths: that he is Esau, that the hunt had been quick as God helped and again that he is really Esau. He draws near so Isaac can smell and feel the animal skins. Isaac then gives Jacob his blessing and claim to all he has. Jacob will later suffer for the deception, beginning with separation from parents and brother, followed by deception from his uncle Laban.

Then comes a very sad scene. Every child needs the blessing of the father, and parents should have no favoritism. Esau returns with the cooked meal. His aged father asks who he is, then tells him he has given all to another. Four times Esau cries out for the blessing of his father, each time more painful than the preceding, as he breaks down crying. Isaac can only answer that one day Esau will break the yoke of Jacob. Esau hates Jacob and determines to kill him. Mother Rebekah tells Jacob to flee those 550 miles northward back to her home, to brother Laban and her family. Isaac also tells him to go there, to find a wife. Jacob does so, going to the native area of his mother for a wife. Esau proceeds in the other direction, going to the land of his father's exiled brother Ishmael, to the Arabs.

Laban, Jacob's maternal uncle, has two daughters. The elder is Leah, a girl with pleasant eyes, but not as beautiful as the younger Rachel. Jacob first meets Rachel and falls in love. He asks for her hand, to which Laban agrees. Not having any possessions Jacob agrees to work for Laban seven years to pay a dowry for Rachel. Laban fails to tell Jacob that it is the custom that an elder daughter be married before the younger. At the end of seven years, Laban sends the veiled Leah to Jacob's tent. The next morning Jacob discovers the switch and demands Rachel. Uncle Laban tells him that he has to spend the seven-days of festivities with Leah and that he could then have Rachel but that he has to work off another seven years. It is agreed. Thus begins the birthing of the twelve sons of Jacob, whose name will be changed to Israel with the sons becoming the heads of twelve tribes. All but Benjamin are born in Paddan-haran in what is northern modern Syria and Iraq, the land of the Kurds. Seven of Jacob's children will be by Leah, including Dinah, the only daughter. Rachel will have only the last two. The maid-servants of Leah and of Rachel each will have two sons.

Jacob works twenty years for his uncle Laban, seven for each wife and six for livestock. He does well for both men. Finally, he heads south, some 550 miles, back to the area of the West Bank of the River Jordan. As his entourage passes on the east side of the Sea of Galilee, he sends messengers of peace to his brother Esau, who himself has done quite well with his small kingdom of Edom, at the southeast side of the Dead Sea. The messengers return to inform Jacob that Esau is headed north to meet Jacob with 400 men. In fear, Jacob encamps and divides his people and livestock to save at least half and sends about 500 head of livestock south to his brother Esau. Jacob is now a little over half-way from the Sea of Galilee toward the Dead Sea on the East Bank of the River Jordan. He takes his two wives, two maids and eleven children and crosses the deep canyon of the River Jabbok, then has the rest of his entourage cross over.

Jacob is alone when an unidentified man appears and wrestles with him until dawn. The man can not defeat Jacob so he touches the socket of Jacob's hip, and his hip is put out of joint as they wrestle. The man then asks to leave, but Jacob will not release him unless the man bless him. The man asks of Jacob his name, then tells him his name will henceforth be "Israel", meaning "he who struggles with God" and survives. The man will not tell "Israel" his name but does bless him and leaves. Jacob says, "I have seen God face to face, and my life is preserved." To this day the children of Israel are not to eat the thigh muscle. From here on the remainder of Genesis concerns Jacob/Israel and his twelve sons, including the giving of young Joseph to be taken to Egypt, and the resultant 400 years of bondage.

Jacob looks and sees Esau coming with his 400 men. Esau runs to embrace Jacob and declines the gift of livestock explaining that he has enough. Jacob tells Esau, "I have seen your face as though I had seen the face of God." Esau then accepts the gift of livestock and leads the way for Jacob back home. Jacob settles in Shechem, where he purchases land from Prince Shechem's father.

One day Dinah, the only daughter of Jacob, goes out visiting. Prince Shechem sees her and rapes her. He does fall in love with her and asks his father to obtain her as his wife. Jacob hears of the defilement and tells his sons. Shechem's father speaks with Jacob and even asks that their children be allowed to marry one another. Dinah's brothers insist that all of the males of Shechem's tribe first be circumcised, to which they agree. On the third day, when they are all sore, Simeon and Levi, two of Dinah's brothers, go in and kill all the males, including Shechem and his father, and take all of their livestock and claim their lands.

Beginning at chapter thirty-seven, the final fourteen chapters are concerned with Joseph, the second youngest son of Jacob, and his removal to Egypt leading to the resultant 400 years of bondage. Parental favoritism toward certain of their children will inevitably cause serious problems, as we have seen with Abraham and Sarah with their sons Ishmael and Isaac, with Isaac and Rebekah and their sons Esau and Jacob/Israel, and now with Jacob and his favoritism toward his son Joseph. He "loved Joseph more than all of his children...and made for him a tunic of many colors." When he was seventeen years-old, Joseph brings a bad report to his father about his brothers. On a subsequent trip to watch his brothers they conspire to kill him, but Reuben convinces them not to shed blood, so they strip him of his tunic and put him into a deep pit. When a caravan of Ishmaelites comes by on the way to Egypt they sell Joseph to them. The brothers then dip his tunic in goat's blood and tell their father a wild beast had devoured Joseph.

Upon arrival in Egypt, Joseph is purchased by the captain of the Pharaoh's guard and begins to become quite successful. The captain's wife takes a liking to Joseph and tells him to lie with her. When he refuses she cries out falsely and has him thrown into prison. While in the prison Joseph interprets several dreams of the Pharaoh's staff, and later is called to interpret a dream of the Pharaoh. The interpretation is that there will be seven years of plenty followed by seven years of famine. Pharaoh sets Joseph in charge of collecting extra stores during the first seven years, later rising to governor. During this time Joseph has two sons, Manasseh and Ephraim, who will eventually take the places of Joseph and Levi as heads of tribes.

As Joseph had interpreted, after seven years a famine strikes the entire area, including Egypt and that to the northeast where his brothers live with his father, Jacob/Israel. Jacob/Israel sends ten of the brothers, keeping back Benjamin, the youngest, to Egypt to buy grain. Not recognizing Joseph, they bow low to him. Speaking through an interpreter, he accuses them of being spies, takes their money and jails them. After three days he releases them to go bring Benjamin to prove themselves. He secretly puts grain and their money into their bags. The brothers return to home and convince Jacob/Israel to allow them to take Benjamin back with them.

Upon their return to Egypt they are all invited to a fine dinner with Joseph. He then allows them to head home, but hides a silver cup among Benjamin's items. When this is "found" he demands that Benjamin remain with him. After much wrenching discussion, Joseph reveals to his brothers who he is and begs them to go bring their father to Egypt. Jacob/Israel does travel to Egypt, where he eventually dies. The last chapter of Genesis is the prophecy and blessing of father Jacob/Israel as to the future of his twelve sons, the twelve tribes of Israel. There is no account in the Bible of those "400" years of bondage in Egypt, only a gap of silence from Joseph to Moses.

In this book of origins we find a brief explanation of the origin of many things, nineteen of which are: the Universe, Space, Earth, the Seas, Plant Life, Animal Life, Man, Woman, Marriage, Family, the Word of God, Sin, Conflict, Prayer and Worship, Judgment, Languages, Civilization, Chosen People and Redemption. A summary of this book of origins would be confined to the first twelve chapters. The rest of the chapters, thirteen through fifty, are of the event of the beginnings of a people, a nation, a church, a Savior and God's plan for salvation.

And here begins the story of Job.

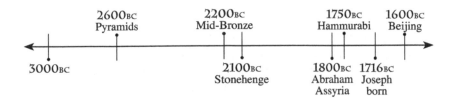

| 2600BC | 2200BC | 1750BC | 1600BC |
| Pyramids | Mid-Bronze | Hammurabi | Beijing |

3000BC   2100BC   1800BC   1716BC
Stonehenge   Abraham   Joseph
Assyria   born

CHAPTER 3

JOB
REMAINING FAITHFUL IN SUFFERING

Will a person worship God for nothing? Job 1:9

Job may be the oldest and earliest book in the Bible and Revelation the latest. Both are studied by students searching for deep and permanent answers. Job has probably been studied since the beginning of time, Revelation, in any depth, probably since our mid-nineteenth century. Studying these two books develops within a student's heart a deep sense of the awesomeness of the sovereignty and power of God and that he is in charge and does not account any human. They are true books of worship. Neither book really gives a person answers so much as they give faith and rise to even more questions. Excluding Psalms, the other Poetry- Wisdom books are timeless and personal, having nothing to do with the rise and fall of the ancient empires. Appropriate ages for comprehending four of these may be Proverbs fifteen, Song of Songs twenty and forty, Ecclesiastes forty and Job fifty. A person can travel half way, or all the way, around the world searching for specific answers, and Job will still be telling him or her to look to God.

We hear two clichés about Job which may be close but are just not correct. We hear that the book is about suffering or enduring suffering. That may be true but more accurately it is about worshipping God and demanding nothing in return. It is easier to talk about suffering than worshipping. We also hear about the "patience of Job", but that is inaccurate though it may touch the faith of Job. Impatience is mentioned about three times in the book but patience not at all. It is easier to talk about patience than about faith. Four key words in Job are worship, faith, integrity and almighty.

This book of Job is a wonderful vivid short story, a play. When any person writes a story or a book, that person sets the stage and the circumstances. In most books the first few chapters are important as for the introductions and staging. In the book about Mr. Job the very first chapter sets the stage and circumstances. We will take time to cover the early chapters and rapidly skim the others. The very first verse tells us "Job...was blameless and upright, and one who feared God and shunned evil." Nothing that happens to Job in this book is because he sinned or did anything wrong.

Beginning in verse six, the circumstances are further set forth. God called his sons to come to him. One of them was Satan, or more accurately "the Satan". In Hebrew "h-a" is the English definite article, "the". "Satan" means "adversary", or "prosecuting attorney", or "tester". HaSatan was a member of God's court, who turned bad.

"Now there was a day when the sons of God came to present themselves before the Lord, and haSatan also came among them. The Lord said to haSatan, 'From where do you come?' haSatan answered the Lord and said, 'From going to and fro on the earth, and from walking back and forth on it.' The Lord said to haSatan, 'Have you considered my servant Job, that there is none like him on the earth, a blameless and upright man, one who fears God and shuns evil?'" The writer again repeats, from the mouth of God, that Job is, in a sense, a perfect man. haSatan answered the Lord and said, "Does Job fear God for nothing?" Right there, in verse nine, is the theme of the book. Will a man, a woman, worship God for nothing, demanding nothing in return?

The book of Job, probably the oldest book in human history, is about why you did, or did not, go to church this week. We are to come to church simply to worship God. We are not to come demanding payment, such as a healing, a good feeling, to be seen, or for gold or silver in your account, nor because we are up nor down, but just as we breath or eat. This book also allows us to cry out to God. About 1,000 years after Job, David wrote Psalm twenty-two, which first verse was quoted by Jesus on the cross about 1,000 years after that. "My God, my God, why have you forsaken me?" Job, David and Jesus.

The very first question in the Westminster, the Presbyterian, Catechism is, "What is the chief end of man?" First we must decide the end, the ultimate goal, the purpose. "Man's chief end is to glorify God, and to enjoy him for ever."

HaSatan then challenges God to allow Job to lose all of his possessions, and God agrees. "The Lord said to haSatan, 'Behold, all that he has is in your power; only do not lay a hand on his person.'" Take all Job has, but do not touch him physically. Job promptly lost his oxen, his asses, his sheep, his camels, his sons and his daughters. To all of this, in verse twenty-one, Job states his life's purpose, from which he will not deviate and which is so often heard today at funerals, and so little followed. "Naked I came from my mother's womb, And naked shall I return there. The Lord gave, and the Lord has taken away; Blessed be the name of the Lord." And again we are told, "In all this Job did not sin nor charge God with wrong."

In chapter two haSatan returns to the court of God, and again God asks him, "'From where do you come?' HaSatan again answered the Lord and said, 'From going to and fro on the earth, and from walking back and forth on it.' The Lord said to haSatan, 'Have you considered my servant Job, that there is none like him on the earth, a blameless and upright man, one who fears God and shuns evil?'" To which God now adds, "He still holds fast to his integrity, although you incited me against him, to destroy him without cause."

This word "integrity" is both interesting in itself and the very heart and crux of this man and book called Job. When Job is described as "blameless" or "upright" that is a fairly good English translation of the Hebrew *tam* (תּם'), which means perfect, complete, whole, upright or blameless. Job was whole as to God. From that word comes another Hebrew word, *tummah* (תֻּמָּה), which means whole and which is best translated as "integrity". From the Latin we get our word "tangible" which means "touchable". Tangible properties are things like benches, tables, cars and computers. If we put "i-n" in front of it we get "intangible" which means "untouchable". Intangible properties are things like the stock market and maybe money, which represent things we cannot really touch. The "t-e-g" in "integrity" is the past participle form of tangible. "Integrity' is a form of "intangible" and "untouchable". A person of integrity is a person who is untouched, unchanged, unaffected by a change of environment or circumstances. That person remains true to his or her principle purpose at all times. Most people have integrity. The problem is identifying their principle purpose, which may be self. Job's principle purpose was faith in God.

In verse four haSatan again challenges God to let him now attack Job physically. "Skin for skin! Yes, all that a man has he will give for his life. But stretch out your hand now, and touch his bone and his flesh, and he will surely curse you to your face!" God consents, and tells haSatan, "Behold, he is in your hand, but spare his life." Do anything you please to Job, but do not kill him. So "haSatan struck Job with horrible burning ulcers from the sole of his foot to the crown of his head, so that he took for himself a broken pot with which to scrape himself while he sat in the midst of the filthy, loathsome ash dump." Powerful Job was in the pits.

When a person meets their king or queen, or in many churches before entering the pew, people bend their knee, they "genuflect." We get our word "knee" from the Greek *gonu*. To genuflect is to flex the knee in respect. The Hebrew does the same. The Hebrew word for "kneel" is *barak* (בֶּרֶךְ'). A person kneels to render respect and also to receive a blessing. This word *barak* can also euphemistically mean "curse". Today many people, when upset about something, say "bless it", when they really are thinking, "curse it". The Hebrews did the same thing.

As Job sat on the garbage heap, alone, his wife came to him. She too had lost all of her possessions and sons and daughters, but she did not divorce Job and go sleep with some other fellow. She stayed. She went to Job and "said to him, 'Do you still hold fast to your integrity? Curse God and die!'" That word "curse" is *barak*, and could be translated as "bless God and die". It seemed that every time Job blessed God he received some curse. Have you ever felt that way? "But Job said to her, 'You speak as one of the foolish women speaks. Shall we indeed accept good from God, and shall we not accept adversity?' In all this Job did not sin with his lips." Notice Job spoke of accepting from God. Later he will be somewhat corrected as to this thought.

In verse eleven we are told "Job had three friends who heard of all this adversity that had come upon him, each one came from his own place-- Eliphaz the Temanite, Bildad the Shuhite, and Zophar the Naamathite." All three of these places are east, a bit southeast, of the Jordan and the Dead Sea. Wise men were deemed to come from the East, as did the three to follow that star at the birth of Christ. "For they had made an appointment together to come and mourn with him, and to comfort him. But when they raised their eyes from afar, and did not recognize him, they lifted their voices and wept; and each one tore his robe and sprinkled dust on his head toward heaven. So they sat down with him on the ground...."

These four men sat there on the ground for "seven days and seven nights, and no one spoke a word to him, for they saw that his grief was very great." That is a fine example of a pastoral visit at a time of grief. Just be present and be quiet. There are no words more powerful than a simple presence, a friend sitting quietly in a chair near the bed, or the couch, hour after hour.

The stage and the circumstances are now set. The three friends will now take turns lecturing Job as to his problems. Three times the three will lecture and Job will respond. Then there will come a fourth person, a young man who will come closest to the truth. At the end of the book will come God to speak. The big chapters in this book are these first two and then the four of God at the end. About thirty-five chapters in between are worthless advice from the three "comforters". Our English word "comfort" does not mean to bring soft, mushy, warm fuzzies. The "f-o-r-t" means "strength," a "fort." The "c-o-m" means "with". To comfort means "with strength." However, these three were not comforters, but wind bags.

Before we hear what these three, or four, men have to say to Job, let's look at the men themselves. In this most ancient of stories we have the three, or four, types of so-called counselors found to this day. Try to remember these fellows. First comes Eliphaz. He is from a country famous for its wisdom. He presents the two main arguments we hear from many in our churches today. He states religious dogma, just rules of the religious; and he states his own personal subjective revelation. Second comes Bildad. He is less sympathetic and more narrow. He states the accumulated wisdom of the fathers, worn-out platitudes and proverbs. Third comes Zophar. He is even less sympathetic and very abrupt. He is an agnostic and argues from his personal reason and experience, very much a modern-day liberal churchman. When these three finish will come the fourth, Elihu, an impetuous young man who speaks but one long discourse and is partially onto the truth.

With chapter three Job himself begins the three cycles of discussions. "Job opened his mouth and cursed the day of his birth, and said: 'May the day perish on which I was born, and the night in which it was said, 'A male child is conceived.'" In verse eight he mentions Leviathan, of which we will hear later. In verse twelve he expresses a bitterness of soul as to his father's knees and his mother's breasts. This is not exactly a display of patience.

There are three cycles of speeches by these men. They cover virtually every thought as to why life can be so very difficult. Of course, today many would say it is not for them as there is no mention of the greatest calamity that many people have suffered, a computer crashing. Chapters four through fourteen are the First Cycle of speeches. These lectures are about the greatness and wisdom of God, but as viewed by three men who somewhat miss the matter.

Eliphaz, with his religious rules and personal visions, begins. "If one attempts a word with you, will you become impatient?" Eliphaz recognizes that Job is not patient. In verse five the Revised Standard translation reads, "Now it comes upon you, and you are impatient." There is no "patience of Job". In verse six we again have that word "integrity". "Is not...the integrity of your ways your hope?" Then in verse seven Eliphaz states an erroneous religious rule: "Remember now, who ever perished being innocent? Or where were the upright ever cut off?" He believes only the sinful suffer, but Job is blameless.

Beginning in verse twelve, Eliphaz tells Job he has had a personal vision from God. "Now a word was secretly brought to me, and my ear received a whisper of it. In disquieting thoughts from the visions of the night, when deep sleep falls on men, fear came upon me, and trembling, which made all my bones shake. Then a spirit passed before my face; The hair on my body stood up. It stood still, but I could not discern its appearance. A form was before my eyes; There was silence; Then I heard a voice."

In chapters six and seven Job will respond to the rules and visions of Eliphaz, but not directly. Job is not patient. In verse three he himself says, "My words have been rash, impetuous, wild." In verse eleven he says, "What is my strength that I should wait? And what is my end, that I should be patient?" At verse fifteen he speaks of losing his friends, not these three, with his fortune. "My brothers have dealt deceitfully like a brook, like the streams of the brooks that pass away....When it is warm, they cease to flow; When it is hot, they vanish from their place." In verse eleven the impatient Job says, "I will not restrain my mouth; I will speak in the anguish of my spirit; I will complain in the bitterness of my soul." Where do people get that "patience of Job" cliché?

In the play, or movie, *The Fiddler on the Roof*, Tevye regularly raises his fist and voice to yell at God. The Jews of the Old Testament knew theirs was an almighty God and could handle their little temper tantrums. They would cry out, "Why? Why me God? Answer me when I ask you!!" Christians have some idea that God is small and can't handle such plaintiff cries. It is far better to yell at God than to quit speaking to him altogether, as many do, some because they are too busy, some because they got upset about something some human did at church or had a bad break, so they punish God by not speaking to him. Teach God a lesson!

In chapter eight we have Bildad, with his worn-out platitudes and proverbs. How often do we get that from friends and church-goers? In verse eight Bildad tells us his source. "Inquire, please, of the former age, and consider the things discovered by their fathers." He then recites a series of sayings which sound good but mean absolutely nothing for Job, such as verse twenty: "Behold, God will not cast away the blameless, nor will he uphold the evildoers."   In chapters nine and ten Job replies, but not to Bildad, who has offered nothing to which to reply. Job continues to rage impatiently. In verse two Job fairly denies that he has sinned: "Truly I know it is so, but how can a man be righteous before God?"

It is interesting what Job says in verse nine, in this most ancient of books. The constellations and Zodiac were household names at the earliest of beginnings. "God made the Bear, Orion, and the Pleiades, and the chambers of the south." The Greater Bear of Ursa Major of the Big Dipper. Orion the constellation that pursues the constellation Pleiades across the night sky. Long before the Greeks named it Pleiades, the Hebrews called it *kiymah*. Its rising in springtime marked the beginning of the seafaring and farming seasons.

In verse nineteen, Job returns to law court. "If it is a matter of...justice, who will appoint my day in court and summon God to court?" In verse thirty-three he continues with, "Nor is there any umpire, referee, mediator, arbiter between us, who can lay his hand on us both" to bring us in to court to argue this thing out. This is Job's first of three thoughts as to a mediator, an impossible longing for a mediator, whom Christians interpret as Jesus the Christ.

In chapter eleven we have the third friend, Zophar, the unknowing agnostic, with his personal reason and experience. He is the ancient man of modern times. An agnostic says, "I don't know; you don't know, and nobody else knows. But let's talk about it anyway." His speech is short, as human reason cannot comprehend the nature of the world. He says only that we cannot comprehend God, as in verse seven, "Can you search out the deep things of God? Can you find out the limits of the Almighty?...What can you know?"

In chapter twelve verse two, Job gets a bit sarcastic with Zophar, and the other two. "No doubt you are the only wise people in the world, and wisdom will die with you!" Job then goes on to speak of the majesty of the universe and the rule of God. In chapter thirteen verse twelve Job turns away from the three toward God. "Your platitudes are proverbs of ashes; your defenses are defenses of clay. Hold your peace with me, and let me speak, then let come on me what may!" At the beginning of chapter fourteen, he again gives us one of our great funeral service readings. "Man who is born of woman is of few days and full of trouble. He comes forth like a flower and fades away; He flees like a shadow and does not continue."

The three again take turns speaking a second time, as they only say that the wicked are punished. This cycle covers chapters fifteen through twenty-one. Eliphaz is running out of his religious rules and personal visions, so he just accuses Job of being an unrepentant sinner, though we know Job is blameless. At chapter sixteen Job caustically asks him to be quiet. "I have heard many such things. Miserable comforters are you all! Shall words of wind have an end?" Then, in verse nineteen, he goes to a more definite hope for a mediator. "Surely even now my witness is in heaven, and my advocate is on high."

In chapter eighteen Bildad, quotes some more of his worn-out platitudes and proverbs, which serve only to accuse Job erroneously of having sinned. Job responds in chapter nineteen with a display of great impatience, with the three and with God. He cries out for help, and in verse twenty-five he goes to a certainty that there is an umpire, a mediator, with another saying much quoted at funeral services. "I know that my Redeemer lives, and he shall stand at last on the earth."

Zophar, the unknowing agnostic, pops in again with his fading personal reason and experience. In verse two chapter twenty he describes his theology and that of so many in the churches today. "Therefore my anxious thoughts give me an answer, because of the turmoil within me." Like so many today, he does not want to be guided by the scriptures or the Holy Spirit of some faithful authority. No, his own personal thoughts, reason and experience will dictate to him. In verse five he simply falls in line with the others. It is all Job's fault. "The triumphing of the wicked is short, and the joy of the hypocrite is but for a moment?...He will perish for ever like his own dung."

Job does not even reply to him. He goes on in chapter twenty-one to ponder why the wicked so often seem to win, as in verse seven. "Why do the wicked live and become old, Yes, become mighty in power? Their houses are safe from fear, and no rod of God is upon them." At the end of chapter twenty-one he tells the three to get lost. "How then can you comfort me with empty words, since falsehood remains in your answers?"

That statement sort of upsets his three "comforters". They have exhausted their cases and simply drop to calling Job a tyrant. Zophar the know-it-all know-nothing of personal reason and experience will not even rise to the third bell. In chapter twenty-two, Eliphaz, with his religious rules and personal visions, will presage Jesus (Matthew 25), about giving drink to the thirsty and food to the hungry. In verse seven he accuses Job of "having not given the weary water to drink, and of having withheld bread from the hungry."

In chapter twenty-three Job cries out for a chance to debate with God. In verse three he cries out, "Oh, that I knew where I might find Him, that I might come to His seat!" However, in verse fifteen he says, "Therefore I am terrified at His presence; When I consider this, I am afraid of Him." In chapter twenty-four Job rants on about his, and our, perplexities as to God and religion, but he does not doubt or lose faith. The first verse of chapter twenty-four is one for all of us. "Why are times not stored up by the Almighty, And why do those who know Him not see His days?"

Bildad then pops in at chapter twenty-five with six worthless platitudes. He is finished, and Job totally ignores him. Job then talks on for six chapters, about the greatness of God and man's inability to comprehend God. He again reaffirms his innocence, and concludes with words as to the wisdom of God. His three friends now sit mute. It is chapter thirty-two. From out of nowhere comes one Elihu, an impetuous young man with his honest and open partial truth. He will talk through chapter thirty-seven.

In chapter thirty-two, verse eight, he corrects the others as to what brings an understanding. "There is a spirit in man, and the breath of the Almighty gives him understanding." In chapter thirty-five, verse seven, Elihu corrects Job as to what he had said in chapter two as to "receiving both good and evil from God," and gets back on course as to simply worshipping God. "If you are righteous, what do you give Him? Or what does He receive from your hand?" Job does not respond to Elihu. All is quiet, before the storm.

Beginning at chapter thirty-eight Job meets God. In 1 Kings 19:12 we hear of Elijah sitting on a mountain to hear from God. There came a strong wind, but God was not in it; There came an earthquake, but God was not in it; There came a fire, but God was not in it; There came a light breeze, a still small voice, and God was in it. Now for Job, God spoke out of a whirlwind, a raging storm. What a wonderful scene. Job wanted to debate God in court. "Who is this who darkens counsel by words without knowledge? Now gird up your loins like a man; I will question you, and you shall answer me."

Then for four chapters God throws out one unanswerable question after another, beginning with, "Where were you when I laid the foundations of the earth? Tell Me, if you have understanding." He speaks of the constellation Pleiades. In verse eleven he tells them it is okay to pour out the overflowing of your anger, the fury of your wrath. In chapter forty, at verse fifteen, God speaks of Behemoth, which many deem to be a hippopotamus. Read it again. It eats grass; his strength is in his loins; he makes his tail like a cedar tree of Lebanon. That is a dinosaur. In chapter forty-one God speaks of Leviathan, of which Job spoke, and which many deem to be a crocodile. At verse eighteen he says his sneezings flash forth light; out of his mouth go burning torches;

sparks of fire leap forth; and out of his nostrils smoke goes forth, as from a boiling pot and burning rushes. That is a dragon. At Isaiah 27:1, Leviathan is certainly defined as a dragon.

In chapter forty-two verse six, Job simply says he will "repent in dust and ashes," an ancient phrase and a reminder of the much neglected Ash Wednesday of Lent. The property and children of Job, and his wife, are restored at double the amount of what they had lost. Of course, not the very same beloved children.

And here begins, the story of Moses and the Exodus of the Hebrew nation out of Egyptian bondage.

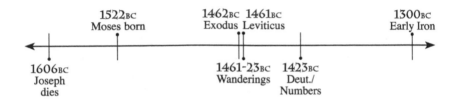

CHAPTER 4

EXODUS AND NUMBERS
MOSES; FROM EGYPT TO CANAAN

The pillar of cloud led them by day and the pillar of fire by night. He wrote on the tablets the words of the covenant. Exo. 14:19,21; 34:28

As with fixing the dates of Abraham and Joseph in Genesis, fixing the dates of Moses and the Exodus are also very difficult as the people of those days did not keep time by one calendar of consecutive years, and those involved were slaves. The Book of Genesis ended with the death of Joseph, and as previously stated, with the 300-year time spread down to about 250, being from about 1725 to about 1425 B.C. This writer chooses 1606 B.C. as the date of Joseph's death, at the age of about 110 years. As to the time of the Exodus, most scholars think the year it began was about 1462 B.C., but some think about 1294 B.C., a 168 year spread. This writer chooses 1462 B.C., which gives 237 years of bondage, from Joseph to Moses. As previously stated, this gap continues to lessen until the time of David in 1010 B.C., and these dates and times have absolutely zero effect or impact on the biblical message.

These problems with these dates also give a problem with the date of the Exodus. We are told in Genesis 15:13 that the bondage in Egypt will last 400 years and in Exodus 12:41 that it "was" 430 years. If counting from 1699 when Joseph came to Egypt, the Exodus then would begin around 1269 B.C. But for decades of that the Hebrews could not have been in bondage, as Joseph was governor. The primary central conflict on definitely setting the beginning and ending dates of the Egyptian bondage comes later in 1 Kings 6:1. There we are told the Exodus began 480 years prior to the dedication of Solomon's temple, which was in 966 B.C. making the Exodus begin in 1446 B.C. Our present, possibly yet imperfect, knowledge of these irreconcilable numbers simply crunches out about 177 years as to the date of beginning bondage and the start of the Exodus. Various scholars attempt to reconcile these dates by moving the period of the four patriarchs, Abraham, Isaac, Jacob and Joseph, about 100 years earlier and then crunching another 100 years out of the period of the Judges. Both of which are reasonable adjustments, but the date-time discrepancies still exist, without any way affecting the story.

The Bible does say the Hebrews, the children of Jacob, renamed Israel, were in bondage for about 400 years, during which time they grew to over two million. With that there is a gap of silence between Genesis and Exodus of those 400 years. There is no direct report of the bondage, except that Moses led them out. Moses was born about eighty years before the Exodus, meaning his birth as recorded in the book of Exodus was 320 years after the Hebrews either arrived or were reduced to bondage in Egypt. There is a similar gap of about 400 years between the last book of the old Hebrew scriptures and Matthew's report of the birth of Jesus the Christ.

Joseph had come from Canaan (Palestine) as a young man after being sold by his brothers. In Egypt he had risen to be governor. Due to another famine in Canaan, Joseph's brothers and father Jacob, renamed Israel, moved to Egypt. Egypt was in its Middle Kingdom. The pyramids were about 1,000 years old, and Stonehenge in what would be England were about 400 years old. We are told the Israelites grew in great number while in Egypt and eventually became bondage slaves to the Pharaoh. As with most slaves, there are minimal to no records of these people. The bondage is reputed to have been about 400 years, but again the exact dates and period are debatable. Genesis ends with the death of Joseph, and Exodus begins with the birth of Moses, maybe 237, or only sixty-three, years later.

The Greek word for "way" or "road" is *odos*, and the prefix "*e-x*", means "out of". Exodus means "way out of ". For Christians Jesus will say, "I am the Way." This book is about the way out of, the successful escape of, these millions of Hebrews from slavery in Egypt to the land promised. It is about redemption and salvation. It may be divided into two sections of twenty chapters each, a 20-20 vision. The first twenty chapters are a continuation of the history of the people into the formation of the nation of Israel. The second twenty are a summary of the law, the law of God and the law of worship, and also the blueprint for the building of the Tabernacle. The book also may be divided into three sections of forty years each, about the life of Moses. The first forty are of Moses as a somebody who became a nobody, the second forty are of Moses becoming a somebody again, and the third forty are of what God can do with somebody who realizes he is a nobody. 20-20 chapters and 40-40-40 years.

The first twelve chapters are about the early life of Moses. At chapter one, verse fourteen, we are told of the Hebrews that the Egyptians "made their lives bitter with hard bondage -- in mortar, in brick, and in all manner of service in the field. All their service in which they made them serve was with rigor." There are no dates given as to when after Joseph and before Moses this bondage began, but it may have lasted in the range of only about 150 years.

However, the Hebrews continued to increase, so an order was issued to kill their newborn sons.

At chapter two, verse one, "a man of the house of Levi went and took as wife a daughter of Levi, and the woman conceived and bore a son. And when she saw that he was a beautiful child, she hid him three months." This child was of Levite parents and fully Hebrew. There came a time when she no longer could hide the boy, so she put him into a water-tight basket and floated him down the river to the area of Pharaoh himself, as his sister Miriam watched.

The maidens of the daughter (possibly Hatshepsut) of Pharaoh himself discover the boy in a basket, and Pharaoh's daughter takes pity. Out of hiding comes Moses's sister to volunteer to find a woman to care for the boy. Pharaoh's daughter agrees, and the sister takes the boy back to his mother as guardian and nurse. He is named *Mosheh*, which means "to draw out", as he was drawn out of the water, but he also will draw his people out of bondage. As he grows up his mother takes him to Pharaoh's daughter who brings him into her home as her son. This Hebrew nobody is now a somebody.

"It came to pass in those days, when Moses was grown, that he went out to his brethren and looked at their burdens. He saw an Egyptian beat to death a Hebrew, one of his brethren. He looked this way and that way, and when he saw no one, he killed the Egyptian and hid him in the sand. When he went out the next day, he saw two Hebrew men were fighting, and he said to the one who did the wrong, 'Why are you striking your companion?' Then he said, 'Who made you a prince and a judge over us? Do you intend to kill me as you killed the Egyptian?' So Moses feared and said, 'Surely this thing is known!' When Pharaoh heard of this matter, he sought to kill Moses. But Moses fled from the face of Pharaoh." He goes some 300 miles to the southeast, across the Sinai Peninsula, into what we today call Saudi Arabia, and dwells in the land of Midian. This somebody had become a nobody, a murderer and fugitive in the desert, a forty year-old man with no future, no reason to live. But his life, and this story, have only begun.

In this desert Moses becomes a shepherd and meets and marries Zipporah, the daughter of Jethro, a pagan priest used by God. One day Moses leads his flock to a mountain in the desert. It is called Mount Horeb, of which one summit is named Mount Sinai. At chapter three, verse two, "An Angel appeared to him in a flame of fire from the midst of a bush. Moses looked, and behold, the bush was burning with fire, but the bush was not consumed. Then Moses said, 'I will now turn aside and see this great sight, why the bush does not burn.' So when the Lord saw that he turned aside to look, God called to him from the midst of the bush and said, 'Moses, Moses!' And he said, 'Here I am.' Then He said, 'Do not draw near this place. Take your sandals off your feet, for the place where you stand is holy ground.' Moreover He said, 'I am the God of your father -- the God of Abraham, the God of Isaac, and the God of Jacob."

Several places in the Hebrew Scriptures God tells us this is his name. In an age of "political correctness" you will hear many, even clergy, commit the heresy of modifying this name to include the wives of Abraham, Isaac and Jacob. Moses hid his face, for he was afraid to look upon God, and those who would change the name of God should do likewise.

God then gives Moses his marching orders. We come and go. One must first come to God and then be sent. God sends Moses as his agent to deliver his people from Egypt back to the land promised. But Moses flinches, and asks for authority. God speaks, "*eyeh asher eyeh* (אֶהְיֶה אֲשֶׁר אֶהְיֶה)." That word *eyeh* (אֶהְיֶה), can be translated "I am" or "I will be". God said, "I will be who I will be" and/or "I am who I will be" and/or "I will be who I am", and/or the phrase most English bibles choose, "I Am Who I Am." This is the great "I AM" which Jesus will repeat several times as recorded by John. God again repeats his name as to Abraham, Isaac and Jacob.

Like most of us who flinch at telling people of God and inviting them to your church worship, Moses continued to debate God. In chapter four God shows him his power. Moses continues, that he is not a man of words and to send someone else. In verse fourteen God becomes angry and says he will also send along Moses' brother Aaron to speak. Finally Moses returns to Egypt to tell Pharaoh, now possibly his step-brother or a brother of the woman who raised him, "Let my people go!" After forty years in the desert this nobody came to realize God could use him as a somebody. He is now about eighty years old.

Pharaoh refuses the request of this murdering Hebrew vagabond. Moses throws down his rod, which turns into a serpent. But the magicians of Pharaoh match this display. Beginning at chapter seven verse twenty, God then sends ten plagues upon the Egyptians. The first is turning the Nile to blood, but the magicians of Pharaoh also match this. The second plague is to send frogs to cover the land, but the magicians match this. The third is to send gnats from all of the dust of Egypt. The magicians no longer can match the displays. The fourth is a swarm of flies. In chapter nine, verse six, is the fifth, all of the cattle of the Egyptians die, but none of the Israelites'. The sixth is boils and open sores on the Egyptians. The seventh is thunder and hail. The eighth is an east wind filled with locusts. The ninth is a thick darkness of three days.

Satan is not on the level of God, but on the level of the archangels; however, he always challenges God. Egypt is a symbol of worldliness. Pharaoh may be a type of Satan. Christians see Moses as a type of Christ. We see here the stages of deliverance, and that we are never to compromise with Satan. After the fourth plague Pharaoh agrees to give the people some freedom, but--they are to offer sacrifice and worship in Egypt, in a worldly manner. Then he agrees to allow them to go into the desert, but--not very far.

After the seventh plague he agrees to let the adults go, but--not the children. He does not understand that when a person is saved, although it is personal, it also is for the entire household, the entire "seed".

The tenth plague is the one that hit the Pharaoh at home, and is a prototype of the crucifixion of Jesus Christ. This is setout at chapter eleven verse four and chapter twelve verse twenty-nine. The Lord said, "At midnight I will go out into the midst of Egypt; and all the firstborn in the land of Egypt shall die, from the firstborn of Pharaoh who sits on his throne, even to the firstborn of the female servant who is behind the handmill, and all the firstborn of the animals." On the fourteenth day of the first month, each family is to sacrifice a year-old male lamb, and put its blood on the lintel and two doorposts of their front door. They are to roast the meat and eat it along with unleavened bread and bitter herbs, eating all and burning any excess. They are to collect all of the valuables they can and be dressed and packed, ready to leave.

The plague of death will pass over all homes marked with the blood of the lamb. This event was to be remembered in the springtime of every year as the Passover, the Feast of Unleavened Bread. In 2 Kings 23:22, we are told that the Hebrews did not celebrate the Passover from about 1120 B.C. to about 620 B.C., 500 years. For Christians, 1,480 years after the Exodus, this time of Passover will be the time of the Crucifixion of the Lamb of God. In Hebrew, Passover is *pesach* (פֶּסַח), which became *pascha* (πάσχα) in Greek. That name is still used today by the Orthodox churches. For some reason the King James Version of 1611 A.D. changed this to "Easter" in Acts 12:4. The plague of death comes, and Pharaoh loses his own son. He consents to let the people go. Moses, at the age of eighty-one years, is becoming the greatest prophet and man of God ever to live, except for Jesus.

For scholars only, at chapter twelve verse two, God changes the Hebrew religious calendar making *Nisan* (April) rather than *Tishri* (September) the first of the year, which remains the first of the year of the civil calendar, *Rosh Hashannah*.

At verse thirty-seven Pharaoh consents to let the people go. There are 600,000 men, plus women and children, totaling probably 2,000,000 people, walking into the desert, to a land 250 miles to the northeast, a land they had never long occupied and had abandoned approximately 400 years before, a massive migration of humanity! This is a powerful story. To people who remember a time of oppression and slavery, it is on a level nearly with those of Jesus himself. This is THE book of deliverance for the enslaved and oppressed. In the latter twentieth century, as it was taken out of its place in time, it became a book of sadness for Christian Palestinians, especially on the West Bank.

At chapter thirteen verse nineteen, we are told Moses takes the bones of Joseph, and that God leads them as a pillar of cloud in the day and a pillar of fire at night. Pharaoh decides to undo his consent, gathers his army and gives pursuit. At chapter fourteen the Hebrews are at the Red Sea. From here on things are done by the right hand of God. In Hebrew *yam* (יָם) means "hand" and *men* (מִין) means "right"; *yamen* (יָמִין) means "right hand". God did everything by his right hand. From that we get "amen". We also get the English word "right" to which the opposite is "wrong", all deeply embedded in the language. Moses stretches out his right hand over the sea and the Lord drives the sea back by a strong east wind. The people of Israel cross over on dry land to the eastern side of the Red Sea. The Egyptians pursue them, God has Moses again stretch out his hand, and the water returns to its flow and covers the Egyptians.

The Israelites are three days on the Sinai peninsula without water. All they find is bitter water at Marah. The people begin the first of many occasions of murmuring against God and Moses. God shows Moses a tree and directs it be thrown into the bitter water which then becomes sweet. The people are then led to a camp with twelve springs. Later, when they are hungry, God provides quails, and bread and manna from heaven. Again the people are thirsty; God directs Moses to strike a rock, and he does so and water comes out. The Amalekites fight with the Israelites, and the Israelites prevail as long as Moses holds his hands high, but otherwise they lose. As Moses grows tired, Aaron and Hur hold high the hands of Moses.

After about three months (some say fifty days) the people come to the wilderness of Sin and encamp at the base of Mount Sinai. God calls Moses alone up the mountain and there gives him the laws of rituals, of society and of worship, including the Ten Commandments, all as set out in chapters twenty through thirty-one and in the following book of Leviticus and largely repeated in the book of Deuteronomy.

Moses makes several trips up the mountain over about two months. His final trip is long, and the people grow impatient and ask Moses' brother Aaron to make a god for them. They collect much of their gold and form a golden calf to worship, which they do with much pagan revelry of feasting and drinking. For this, God threatens to consume all of them in fire, but Moses intercedes successfully on behalf of the people. Moses then goes down from Mount Sinai, carrying the two large stone tablets on which the finger of God had written the Ten Commandments. Upon actually seeing the golden calf, Moses smashes down the two tablets, burns the calf, grinds its residue into power, casts it upon water and makes the people drink the mixture. He then directs the sons of Levite to slay 3,000 of them.

God then instructs Moses in the specifications for building a Tabernacle, a large tent, in which God will be present and meet with Moses. The Tabernacle is also called the Tent of Meeting and the Tent of Testimony. The people are to build and place in the tent an ark, a large trunk-case, the Ark of the Covenant, which is to contain the two replacement tablets prepared and written by God. When God is present the pillar of cloud will fill the Tabernacle in the day and the pillar of fire will be present at night. If neither is present the people are to pack up and journey on toward the land promised. About 500 years later, in the land promised, the Hebrews will replace the movable Tabernacle with the immovable Temple of Solomon.

****

NUMBERS

The book of Exodus is the story of the "way out" of Egypt. It concludes, probably about April 1461 B.C., one year after the exodus itself began at the Red Sea. The book of Numbers begins the following month, which would then be May 1461 B.C. The book is titled "Numbers" because God directed twice that a census be taken of all males twenty years of age and older, once in April 1461 B.C. and again about April 1423 B.C. as the multitude begins to cross the River Jordan into Canaan. Both times the number comes to a little over 600,000 men. There also are numberings of other groups. With no gap between them, Numbers is a continuation of Exodus. The journey from modern Cairo to Jerusalem is about 250 miles, which should have taken about one month; however, due to their lack of faith, the total for the Hebrew multitude was forty years.

At the conclusion of the book of Exodus and the beginning of Numbers, the multitude is at Mount Sinai. The Tabernacle (Tent of Meeting), containing the Ark of the Covenant (Testimony), is erected. The people celebrate the second Passover. After a year of camping, the people resume their journey northeastward to the land promised. The presence of God leads the people by a pillar of cloud by day and a pillar of fire by night. The people grumble, mumble and murmur regularly, and such is the primary story of the new Hebrew nation in Numbers, constant murmuring.

Shortly the multitude arrives at Kadesh-barnea, a little over 100 miles south of Jerusalem. God tells Moses to send out twelve spies, including Caleb and Joshua, into the land of Canaan, around Jerusalem, in preparation of the invasion. The spies scout all across the west bank of the Dead Sea and River Jordan well into modern Lebanon and return in forty days. They bring back grapes and pomegranates and describe the land as flowing with milk and honey. Ten of the men describe the occupants of the land as fearsome and that the Hebrew people would be but as grasshoppers to them. Only Caleb and Joshua remain steadfast in reminding the people that they will be victorious as God is with them.

Unreported in the Bible is that the very ancient Greeks of the day, known as "sea peoples" or "people of the isles", were gradually occupying the eastern perimeter of the Mediterranean Sea, probably including the area of Gaza and ancient Phoenicia. The battle of Troy, in western Turkey, was fought around 1200 B.C., and from that the Greeks spread around the Mediterranean. This is another facet of the argument that the exodus itself was probably closer to 1290 B.C. than 1463 B.C., the date preferred by this writer. At the time Moses' spies went across the area of Canaan, the occupants of the coastland line areas were indeed a warring people and to be feared. But God, who had provided food and water for nearly 2,000,000 people in the desert and garments and sandals which did not wear out, would continue to provide.

For their lack of faith and murmuring and grumbling, God directs that the people wander aimlessly in the wilderness around Kadesh-barnea until all over twenty years shall perish, all except for Moses, Caleb and Joshua. Some students of the Bible think it is silent as to the wandering itself, except to state that it occurred; that there is a thirty-seven year gap of silence between chapters nineteen and twenty, silence from late 1461 B.C. to early 1423 B.C. Others think chapters fifteen through twenty-one describe some of the wandering.

In short order, when they finish the aimless wandering and begin the fairly direct 100-mile trek to the land promised, three events occur. Miriam, the older sister of Moses, who had watched over him as he floated down the Nile in that basket, probably for her frequent criticisms of Moses, dies in the wilderness. God then tells Moses to tell a certain rock to yield water. Instead of simply telling the rock, to show God's power, Moses strikes the rock, as he had done with a previous rock. For that relatively minor disobedience God directs that Moses will not enter the land promised but would die before completing the journey. Aaron, the older brother of Moses, for his frequent lack of faith, also dies in the wilderness. Of the adults who exited Egypt, only Moses, Caleb and Joshua remain alive.

Moses moves the multitude northward up the eastern side of the Dead Sea into Moab (modern southern Jordan). Balak, king of Moab, fearing the multitude coming his way, calls on Balaam, a seer known for the giving of curses and blessings. He sends emissaries with fees who ask Balaam for a divination of cursing on the Hebrews, and are told that God blesses them. Balaam travels on his jackass with the emissaries, which angers God. The angel of God, with sword in hand, stands in the pathway of the jackass and rider. The jackass can see the angel, but Balaam can not. The jackass goes into the field. Upon returning to the road the angel again blocks the path, and the jackass presses Balaam's foot against a wall. A third time the angel blocks the path, and the jackass lies down under Balaam in the road. Balaam strikes the jackass, and God opens the ass' mouth and has him ask why he was struck. Regardless of payments from Balak, Balaam continues to bless the Hebrews, who then defeat Balak.

The Hebrews continue their march across the lands of the various kingdoms up to the edge of the River Jordan. They arrive at the end of the exodus and at the very edge of the land promised. Moses sees the land promised but he will die before crossing over the Jordan into the land.

And here begins, as follows on the next pages, the story of the laws and rituals as in Leviticus and Deuteronomy.

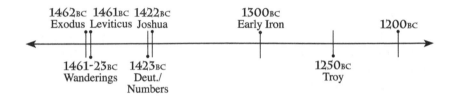

CHAPTER 5

LEVITICUS AND DEUTERONOMY

MOSES' THREE DISCOURSES; HOLINESS AND PRESENCE

Hear, O Israel: The Lord our God, the Lord is one. Deu. 6:4-5, You shall love the Lord your God with all your heart, with all your soul, and with all your strength. You shall love your neighbor as yourself. Lev. 19:18

The first five books of the Bible, Genesis, Exodus, Leviticus, Numbers and Deuteronomy, contain a great deal of history and God's law. This group of five is referred to by three names. They are called *Torah*, the Hebrew word for "Law". They are called the *Pentateuch*, the Greek word for "five tools". They are called the "books of Moses". Leviticus and Deuteronomy are the two books filled with the laws. Humans have always, including today, stumbled over many parts of these first five books. Except for the insertion of Job, the first eleven books of the Bible are in fine chronological order. There is a 400-year gap of silence between Genesis and Exodus, as to the captivity. Let's take a look at the chronology of four of these books.

In Exodus, the first twelve chapters, we were told of the call of Moses and his problems with the pharaoh. The next thirty-seven chapters told us of the first fifteen months as the multitudes moved eastward to Mount Sinai. There Moses went up to meet with God to receive the Ten Commandments and many other laws for the new Hebrew religion and society. These laws are set out in Leviticus. The book of Numbers then picked up where Exodus left off as the multitudes resumed their journey eastward. The first nineteen chapters told of the grumbling, mumbling, murmuring and weak faith of the people. God ordered that they wander aimlessly until that generation died away. There is a gap of over thirty-seven years between chapters nineteen and twenty, and very little about the wandering. The remaining seventeen chapters told of the movement around the Dead Sea to the east side of the River Jordan, positioned to move into the land promised. This book leaves no question of the power and sovereignty of God. He will give a people free will to destroy themselves.

Numbers covers some of the second year of the exodus and then jumps to the fortieth year of that the desert experience. Toward the end of Numbers, Moses gives a series of three speeches to remind the survivors, the children of the generation that had died during the wanderings, of the law and of what lay behind and what lay ahead. Leviticus is the words of God to Moses during the second year as the two met in the Tent of Meeting, over which that cloud covered when God was present. Deuteronomy is the words of Moses during the fortieth year to summarize.

Exodus tells of deliverance and redemption (of Jesus as the Passover Lamb?). Leviticus tells of worship, separation and communion (of Jesus as Sacrifice for our sins?). Numbers tells of failure and wanderings (of Jesus as the One Lifted-up to follow?). Deuteronomy tells of the great teaching sermons of Moses (of Jesus as True Prophet?).

****

LEVITICUS

Leviticus is so named as it is the handbook to the sons of Levi, who was the third son of Jacob, and a brother of Joseph. The descendants of the other sons of Jacob were all assigned tribal lands, not so those of Levi. They were the priesthood of the Hebrews. They were to be protected and provisioned by the other (twelve) tribes. The book begins with God speaking directly to Moses in the tent, as he had on Mount Sinai. Most of the book is in quotation marks as God himself speaks. For Christians, many of these rules as to sacrifices and offerings are greatly modified by Jesus Christ and the new covenant. Jesus being the fulfillment of the law, most to all of these now apply through Jesus the Christ.

It may have been about 430 years since God had called Abraham, and most of those years were spent in Egypt. During that time his descendants had not been a nation, and they had no specific laws and religion. Abraham and his sons had left the land promised to him. God was now going to give these people another opportunity to meet their part of the covenant, and he was going to be very specific about their part. Upon arriving at Mount Sinai, God called Moses up the mountain to have a word with him. The main part of these words is set out in Exodus chapters nineteen through thirty-one. God began with the primary ten words, the Decalogue, the Ten Commandments, as recorded in Exodus chapter twenty. These are followed by specific laws as to religion, crimes, the place of worship and the dress and duties of the ministers. Moses brought these laws down to the people only to find that his older brother Aaron, who served as Moses' spokesman, had helped them build a golden calf to worship. A poor start.

God knows that humans have a strong tendency to disobey and to fall into sin. Humanity had fallen from grace in the garden of Eden. In the first ten chapters of Leviticus God sets out his provision for sin. He had shown them the road out of Egyptian bondage and now he shows them the road back to him. The first seven chapters set out the five major sacrifices of which we frequently hear, and which were modified during the subsequent centuries, and totally changed for Christians.

First God explains the Burnt Offering, which was for trespasses in general. The sacrifice was to be the very best and first of the herd. We give to God first, not a little tip at the end. The very first substantial part of each paycheck is to go to the worship and work of God. God set this first because he knew people would resist this law in the year 2000, both 2000 before Christ and 2000 after Christ and every year and day in between. Another name for this is "holocaust", a whole burning of the entire sacrifice. This was not done because of any specific sin but as an act of dedication to God, and first. This is a blood offering, which gives people another excuse for ignoring it.

Second comes the Grain Offering, which was to honor God, simply worship. This was of some produce of the field, such as flour or corn and was a daily offering, daily morning prayer. We are promptly told to come to God daily. That is one of the lessons of that manna from heaven provided daily by God in the desert, which could not be stored away for another day. It is daily. The answer to the question, "Are you saved?" may be, "Yes, but only one day at a time." "Give us this day our daily bread."

Third comes the Peace Offering, which was essentially for thanksgiving. The animal that is sacrificed is not totally burned, but rather is eaten in part, a shared meal. For Christians, this is now fully replaced through Jesus and the communion service, as these offerings are to be read and understood with a view to the new covenant of God.

Fourth comes the Sin Offering, which was more a matter of purification for unintentional sins. This is not worship and peace but is an acknowledgment by a person of his or her sin. It is a blood sacrifice. The animal was not burned at the altar but was taken "outside the camp" and burned in a clean place. For Christians, the sacrifice of Jesus was a blood covering done outside the walls of the city.

Fifth comes the Trespass or Guilt Offering, which was for more intentional trespasses against God and others. "Forgive us our trespasses." This requires a recompense or repayment for a trespass. A person was required to compensate for the wrong done in full plus twenty percent. That law is probably still in effect in our court system today.

In chapters eight through ten, God sets out the rules for the Priesthood. Here we hear of the attire of the priests, of the breastplate and of the mysterious Urim and Thummim. The first verses of chapter ten tell of Nadab and Abihu, two sons of Aaron, the chief priest and brother of Moses. It simply says they offered a fire to God which was not as directed, and God allowed the fire to consume them on the spot. Coming to church, and especially to communion, with an evil or misguided heart, is not taken lightly. Judge yourself before God judges you.

God's people are a separate, a sanctified, people. The clean is to be separated and set aside from the unclean. This too has been very difficult for the people of the world to sign on to. Chapters eleven through twenty-four explain how his people shall separate themselves from others of the world, as we have God's Precepts for Separation. The Hebrew word used here is *tame*, which means to be unfit for religious and ritualistic reasons. Some of those reasons are based on good science and some on simple revulsion. We translate that as "unclean" which is not exactly what is meant. In chapters eleven through twenty God speaks of this people whom he is forming into his holy nation.

He begins in chapter eleven with the dietary laws, which were very necessary for the health of the people in that part of the world at that time. As one reads through them one sees that nearly every one of those rules applies today. Only very careful selection, curing and cooking can allow some items to be put on our tables today. Of creatures of the land, we are told we may eat only those which "part the hoof and is cloven-footed and chews the cud". Of birds, we are not to eat the scavengers. Of the sea creatures, we are to eat only those having both fins and scales, but no others. Of winged insects, we are not to eat those that walk on all fours.

In chapters twelve through chapter fifteen we are given various rules for hygiene and diseases. Here we again have a misunderstanding as to that Hebrew word *tame*, and its translation into English as "unclean" and our concept as evil. After childbirth a woman is not evil but should be allowed to rest in seclusion for one week, or even one month. Her first trip outside is to be to worship and give thanks to God. Rather than understand this concept, in the latter twentieth century many people turn their noses up in disgust at the scripture, but then ask that both the woman and her husband get two weeks off with pay to recuperate.

In chapters thirteen and fourteen we find the disease of leprosy, which no doubt included a variety of similar diseases. As we read this we see how like sin this disease is. It appears on the surface but the primary problem is that it is a disease of the nervous system and runs deep under the skin. It spreads throughout the body. It causes a person to be cast out from the community. Everything it touches is destined for destruction in the fire. We are given a very detailed procedure of examination before being allowed to return. Chapter fifteen speaks of various discharges of the human body being unclean and the method of cleansing.

In chapter sixteen is set out the Day of Atonement, *Yom Kippur*, *yom* meaning "day" and *kippur* meaning "atonement", one of the five Mosaic Festivals for the Hebrews. All five festivals are set out in chapter twenty-three.This is a time of national fasting and repentance which occurs sometime in September or October of each year.

Most of the remaining eleven chapters of Leviticus set out the Holiness Code to be obeyed by those who are to be set aside for God. Chapter eighteen sets out very clear rules for a man, and for the woman, as to marriage and sexual relations. A reading of these gives one a clear understanding of the wisdom of the rules. Verse twenty-two is one of which many people of this modern world are quick to say, "That is just an antiquated saying of the Old Testament which no longer applies." It states simply and clearly, "A man shall not lie with a male as with a woman; it is an abomination." Not much confusion there. Chapter nineteen is about worship. In verse eighteen is what Jesus will refer to as the second commandment. "You shall love your neighbor as yourself." A man is not to have sexual intercourse (or marry) with his sister, as had been permissible at the time of Abraham, upon pain of public execution.

Chapter twenty-three itemizes the five Mosaic feasts. The Feast of Passover commemorates the passing over of death of the homes of the Hebrews as they prepared to exit Egypt. Pentecost (indicating fifty days) commemorates the giving of the law to Moses on Sinai two or three months (or fifty days) into the exodus. The Feast of Trumpets commemorated the New Year, *Rosh Hashanah*, head of the year. Again we have the Day of Atonement, and then the Feast of Tabernacles, commemorating the living in tents during the exodus.

Chapter twenty-five itemizes a series of sevenths, of sabbaths. The seventh day of the week, the Sabbath. The seventh year, a Sabbatical. The seventh seventh year, being the year after the forty-ninth year, the Jubilee. The offering of lambs in groups of seven. Seven, the perfect number in all of scripture; the number for God. The book of laws concludes with the giving to God of the very first tenth of ones produce and income, a tithe. There is no record of the Israelites, the Hebrew nation, ever adhering to the seventh year Sabbatical, nor the fifty year Jubilee. They also failed as to celebrating the Passover for about 500 years, from Joshua through Second Kings.

****

DEUTERONOMY

Deuteronomy means "second law". The book of Deuteronomy is the second naming of the laws given by God to Moses. The first naming of the laws was the book of Leviticus which was given to the people during the first year of the exodus. Deuteronomy begins with a recitation of the history of the Hebrews, then moves on to the collection and recollection of the laws, statutes and customs. Due to their rebellion and murmuring God caused the multitude to wander aimlessly for over thirty-seven years, just eleven days' trek away from the land promised. This was to allow time for the entire generation of all over twenty years to perish. There was now a new generation. They were preparing to leave the nomadic life in the desert and move into the land promised. Moses felt it necessary to review with them the history and the laws. This greatest and most humble of all men of God here gives a series of three major discourses.

In the first verse of Deuteronomy we are told the multitude is on the east bank of the River Jordan preparing to cross into the land promised. In verse two we are told the people wandered for so long so near to the homeland. In verse three we are told it is about February 1422 B.C., forty years after leaving Egypt at the start of the exodus about 1462 B.C. Even today, when a person speaks of some period of aimless wandering, they describe it as a desert or wilderness experience. Moses looks back. He speaks to them of the tragedy of unbelief and pleads with them to obey God.

The first of his three discourses is in the first four chapters. Here Moses tells the new generation of the acts of God in their history during the exodus journey. He tells them the generation ahead of them lost faith and rebelled against God and thus were destined to wander aimlessly in the desert for thirty-eight years until that generation perished.

At the end of chapter four Moses begins his second discourse as he reminds the people of the laws of God. For the next twenty-four chapters Moses tells them of God's words as to rules for the Hebrews, as he looks within this new Hebrew nation itself. In chapter five he repeats the Ten Commandments, that of chapter twenty of Exodus. In chapter six is found the great Sh'ma' (hear) of the old Hebrew scriptures. "Hear, O Israel. The Lord our God, the Lord is one. You shall love the Lord your God, with all your heart, with all your soul and with all your strength." The Christian scriptures refer to this as the Great, or First, Commandment. In chapter seven he tells them of dangers from without, as he names seven small nation-tribes then living in the area of the land promised. The Israelites are told they shall not only not intermarry these people but shall utterly destroy them. The Israelites would later greatly disobey this directive of God, time and again. Foreseeing this failure, Moses also warns them of dangers from within, as the golden calf. He also cautions them of falling away in times of prosperity, as fitting for times when the securities market is flourishing. He cautions that forgetting God and chasing false gods will result in their being banished from the land promised and perishing.

In chapter ten, God speaks through Moses to answer a question most frequently asked. "What does the Lord your God require of you, but to fear the Lord your God, to walk in all his ways and to love Him, to serve the Lord your God with all your heart and with all your soul, and to keep the commandments of the Lord and His statutes which I command you today for your good?" Again the people are reminded that the promise of the land is conditional, though some may think it unconditional. They are told that they shall keep and do all that is commanded, and if they do not they shall quickly perish off the land.

Chapters twelve through twenty-six are what is called the Deuteronomic Code. This is the reiteration, rephrasing and recapitulation of the laws, many as found in Leviticus, some not. As God is using the Hebrew multitude to cleanse the land of Canaan of its many small kingdoms of evil and false gods, he commands the Israelites to destroy utterly both those people and their places of worship of other gods. This they failed to do as they intermarried with those people.

He tells them they may eat the flesh of slaughtered animals but not drink the blood, the life, of the animal. They may eat ox, sheep, goat, deer, gazelle, roebuck and ibex and antelope. Any animal that both has split hooves and chews the cud may be eaten; therefore, they may not eat camel, hare or rock badger, nor pig. They may eat any marine animal that has both fins and scales. They may eat any clean bird, which excludes eagle, vulture, osprey, buzzard, kites, ravens, ostrich, hawk, seagull and owl. They may not eat winged insects. They may not eat anything which has died a natural death.

They shall tithe all the yield of their seed of the field. Every seven years they shall forgive all indebtednesses. They shall not shut their hand against the poor, and the poor will never cease out of the land. If one holds another Hebrew, man or woman, as a slave, they shall be released after six years with sufficient goods to sustain them for a new start. Annually, they shall observe the Feasts of the Passover (Unleavened Bread), of Pentecost (First Fruits, Weeks) and of Booths (Tabernacles, Tents). (This would also include *Rosh Hashanah* and *Yom Kippur*.)

In chapter twenty-six is the first profession of faith as it relates the travels of Jacob and his sons into Egypt. "My father was an Aramean (Syrian), about to perish, and he went down to Egypt and dwelt there, few in number (70); and there he became a nation, great, mighty, and populous. But the Egyptians mistreated us, afflicted us, and laid hard bondage on us. Then we cried out to the Lord God of our fathers, and the Lord heard our voice and looked on our affliction and our labor and our oppression. So the Lord brought us out of Egypt with a mighty hand and with an outstretched arm, with great terror and with signs and wonders. He has brought us to this place and has given us this land, "a land flowing with milk and honey". In fulfillment of the promise of Gen. 12:2, Abraham had become a great nation, he was blessed, and his name had become great, and they were being put on the land as promised.

This second discourse concludes with curses and blessings. Chapter twenty-seven contains twelve curses, seven of which are used in the twelve curses of the historical Commination (Denunciation) service of the Anglican churches, particularly at Ash Wednesday. These seven are, "Cursed be he who -- makes a carved image -- dishonors his parents -- removes his neighbor's landmark -- misleads a blind man -- perverts justice -- attacks his neighbor secretly -- takes a bribe to slay an innocent person." Chapter twenty-eight contains a series of conditional blessings, all of which are conditioned upon obedience to the commandments as voiced by the Lord. If the condition of obedience is not meant, all will turn into additional curses; "So the Lord will rejoice over you to destroy you and bring you to nothing; and you shall be plucked from off the land which you go to possess." Chapters twenty-nine and thirty compose the third discourse and conclude with another promise to remove them from the land promised should they fail to obey. "If your heart turns away so that you do not hear...you shall surely perish; you shall not prolong your days in the land."

Deuteronomy concludes with two poetic songs given by God through Moses. Then God directs Moses to go to the top of Mount Nebo, on the east bank of the River Jordan at the north end of the Dead Sea, where he looks to the west and sees the land promised. Moses is forbidden to cross over as he had momentarily lost faith and struck the rock instead of simply speaking while in the desert. Moses dies, at the age of 120 years, is buried in an unknown location in Moab, east of the Dead Sea, and his leadership role is assumed by Joshua.

And here begins, as follows on the next pages, the story of Joshua.

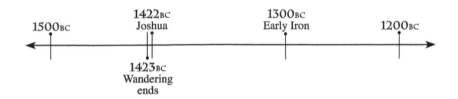

1500BC

1422BC
Joshua

1300BC
Early Iron

1200BC

1423BC
Wandering
ends

CHAPTER 6

JOSHUA
JOSHUA LEADS HEBREWS IN CONQUEST OF LAND

*Choose for yourselves this day whom you will serve; but as for me and
my house, we will serve the Lord.* Jos. 24:15

The first five books of the Bible, Genesis, Exodus, Leviticus, Numbers
and Deuteronomy are called the Torah, or the Pentateuch, "five tools".
Genesis covers the beginnings, Adam, Abraham, Isaac, Jacob and Joseph, and
the move into Egypt. The other four books cover the exodus and the forty-
year wanderings in the wilderness, as God provided the laws and sustenance
for his rebellious people. In the history of time and years, they cover the time
from the eternal beginning until about 1420 B.C., being the estimated time
of the end of the Exodus. With Joshua the stage is set for the rest of the old
Hebrew scriptures.

The term "patriarch" generally includes only Abraham, Isaac and Jacob,
father, son and grandson, the three by which God named himself, "The
God of your fathers, the God of Abraham, the God of Isaac and the God of
Jacob." Some wrongly try to modify that name by inserting Sarah, Rebekah
and Rachel. To the list of patriarchs many understandably add Joshua, and
Job. To *Pentateuch*, the "five tools", the first five books of the Bible, many
understandably add the book of Joshua, to make a *Hexateuch*, and complete
the return to the land. The only Bible Joshua had was the *Pentateuch*.

This book tells of the invasion, the migration, of about two million people
up and down the east side of the River Jordan then across the river into the
hill country of the land of the Canaanites, the land of Palestine. It is the story
of those who had found God while in the desert, the children of those he had
led out of Egypt, those who had come of age during forty years of wandering.
It is also about the "good news" of God leading his people, the revelation of
the power of God as he works in human history. This book has inspired many
hymns and spirituals. In modern time some erroneously use these stories out
of time context to support the invasion of the land by a displaced European
people in 1947 and 1967 and the subsequent occupation of a people who
currently had occupied the land for about 1,900 years.

We are reminded that in Numbers, a little over a year after exiting Egypt, Moses sent twelve men 300 miles north into Palestine to reconnoiter the land for the invasion. Two of those men were Caleb and Joshua. Ten of the men reported that they could not capture the land as the inhabitants were like mighty giants and the Israelites were like grasshoppers to them. Only Caleb, and then Joshua, disagreed, saying that they could indeed capture the land. The people resisted, and God directed that they would wander until that generation died away, and that only Caleb and Joshua would live to enter the land of promise. At that time Moses changed the name of his successor from "Hoshea", which means "salvation", to "Jehoshua", which means "the Lord's salvation". This is the name given to the child of Mary and Joseph, which name was called in the Greek, "Jesus".

At the beginning of this book, Moses was 120 years old, Caleb, eighty and Joshua sixty. At the direction of God, Moses appointed Joshua to be his successor. Forbidden by God to cross the Jordan, Moses died on Mount Nebo, directly east across the Jordan from Jericho and Jerusalem, and was buried by God at some unknown location. Moses took the people out of bondage. Joshua was to take the people into the land.

There are four groups of people one must keep in mind throughout the old Hebrew scriptures, as God works to establish the nation of Israel, which continually disobeys and falls. The first group are the Egyptians, which were a world power all during the old Hebrew scriptures. The second group are those living in this land the Israelites were invading. These were mostly Canaanites, descendants of Ham, a son of Noah. The Israelites were descendants of Shem, a son of Noah. In this area, along the coast of the Mediterranean Sea, was found a shell fish from which came an expensive purple dye. The name "Canaan" may have come either from the Aramaic word for "lowland", or from *kinahhu*, the word for purple. The invasion by the Israelites under Joshua pushed most of these people westward, out of the mountains into the coastlands. The Hebrews would not obey God and eliminate these people, but would struggle with their remnant and gods for about 400 years until the time of David and Solomon, as told in the books of Judges, Samuel and First Kings.

The third group of people are those called "Sea Peoples" or "people of the isles of Kittim", which was generally the area of the Aegean Sea. These people occupied most of the eastern Mediterranean coast line. Also on the coast was the heavily fortified Syrian city of Ashkelon. The exact dates of Joshua and Judges are difficult to establish. Many of these people are thought to have been early Greeks who came following some climatic change in Greece and for those who think the battle of Troy preceded Joshua possibly from wars, such as the Battle of Troy, of which Homer wrote. At the time of Joshua, the name of this land changes from Canaan to Palestine.

The Greek word for the *murex* shellfish was *porphura*, meaning purple. Their word for red-purple was *phoinix*, from which later came the name Phoenicia, the Greek name for this area today known as Lebanon and south near to Tel-Aviv. Along the southern coast these Sea People were called Philistines, from the Aramaic word for the rolling hills of the area. The people along the coast, especially the north coast at Phoenicia, were fairly prosperous, and the trade route between Egypt and Assyria was through the coastlands. Also, around Hebron on the West Bank, lived the Anakim who grew to around eight feet tall, and from whom Goliath may have descended. These were some of the people Caleb and Joshua had seen as they scouted for Moses. The Hebrews have never conquered the ancient coastlands of either Phoenicia or Gaza, from which would come the nine-foot tall Goliath to be felled by a stone from the sling of young David.

The fourth group of people are the Assyrians. Abraham had come from the land we today call Iraq. In his day there were two small kingdoms in that area, one in the north at Nineveh and one in the south around Babylon. During the 400 years the Israelites were in Egypt, the northern kingdom had expanded and absorbed that in the south. At the time of the Exodus and Joshua, Egypt was the ruling world power. As the Hebrews moved into Palestine, they began to settle in between the two giants of Egypt to the southwest and the ever-expanding empire of Assyria and Babylon to the northeast. The books of Kings are the story of God allowing Assyria to defeat the continuously disobedient people of Israel and take them into captivity.

Another part of the scene one begins to see with Joshua is cycles of about 400 years. As with many nations, the Israelites repeatedly spend 200 years rising, 50 sitting on top and 150 decaying, followed by a relatively rapid collapse. This scene is observed with a high with Abraham at 1800 B.C. followed by a low in 1600 B.C. in Egyptian bondage, followed by a high in 1400 B.C., as Joshua leads the invasion of Palestine. Judges will be a low as the separate tribes regularly need a deliverer to salvage them. In 1000 B.C. there is the high of David and Solomon, followed by the many warnings of the prophets and the captivity and exile of Israel around 700 B.C. In 500 B.C. Cyrus allowed the Israelites to return, but they again refused to obey, and at 400 B.C. we have the end of the old Hebrew scriptures with the book of Malachi, as God would change his approach. There also seems to be a seventy-year cycle as seen with Babylon of old and the Soviet Union of modern times.

In about five places in scripture the boundaries are given of that land promised over forty times on condition of obedience. It is fairly difficult to determine these boundaries exactly. All definitions agree that the Mediterranean coast forms the western boundary, and that the land runs at least to the River Jordan on the east. All agree the southern boundary is at least fifty miles south of Gaza and the Dead Sea, and the northern at least fifty miles north of the Sea of Galilee. Most agree the eastern boundary may be at least about sixty-five miles into Syria and parts of Jordan, being fifty miles beyond Damascus, Syria. Some think the eastern boundary goes to the Euphrates River of Syria and of Iraq. One can but ponder that prospect for WWIII or WWIV and some Armageddon, if the boundaries of modern Israel steadily move northward and eastward.

The book of Joshua may be divided into four sections. First are chapters one through five which tell of the preparation and then the crossing of the River Jordan. Second are chapters six through twelve which tell of the military campaigns, the "biblical conquests", of which there were actually only four. Third are chapters thirteen through twenty-one which tell of the division of the land among the tribes, the claiming of the inheritance, the possession of the possession, even though it is not all conquered. Fourth are the final two chapters which relate the final discourse and the death of Joshua.

The book begins with the commissioning of Joshua to lead the people into the land. God again promises a new people that they will possess the land, and again cautions and conditions such on their obedience. In verse seven he says, "Only be strong and very courageous, that you may observe to do according to all the law which Moses my servant commanded you; do not turn from it to the right...or to the left, that you may prosper...."

In chapter two we are told of Joshua first sending two spies, as Moses had sent Caleb and Joshua, about twenty miles across the Jordan to report back on the town of Jericho, which covered about six acres. Damascus, Syria and Jericho both are said to be the two oldest towns still in existence. The river was in flood stage and the men had to swim across then entered Jericho. They came to the house of the woman Rahab, a harlot, whose house was on the top of the double wall surrounding the town. The men of Jericho suspected the men and went to Rahab in search of them. She hid the two and told the searchers they had left town. Later she lowered the two out a window, and they hid in the hills for three days until crossing back over to Joshua. Rahab would be converted to Judaism and marry a Hebrew. We hear of her son Boaz in the book of Ruth, whom he marries. Ruth will have a son who will be the grandfather of King David. This we are told in the first chapter of Matthew. Rahab is also listed in Jas. 2:25 and in Heb. 11:31, as one of great faith.

In chapters three and four we are told of the crossing of the Jordan. We also hear of the Ark of the Covenant, of which we heard during the exodus. This English word "ark" comes from the Latin and simply means a container or enclosure, usually to transport something and regardless of size. An ark, a *tebah*, was used to float Noah in the bulrushes and for Noah to enclose and contain the people and animals. An ark, an *aron*, was used to enclose and contain the two tablets of Moses, the Covenant, and probably also the Urim and Thummim, for casting lots. This Ark was about the size of a large personal shipping trunk as loaded on the rear of early automobiles. It was carried only by the Levitical priests, and we hear of it until the capture of Jerusalem by the Babylonians.

As was a frequent use, the Ark was carried across the Jordan to lead the tribes of Joshua. When the feet of the priests touched the water the flow of the flooded river ceased, and they crossed on dry land. Chapter four tells of two memorials built on the spot. One man from each tribe placed a stone in the middle of the dry river bed and also carried a stone to Gilgal, the first place of encampment in the land. This new generation had not been circumcised in the wilderness, and such was done at Gilgal upon crossing the Jordan. They began to live off the land, and the manna from heaven ceased.

Chapter six tells of the battle of Jericho. Pursuant to directions from God, Joshua has his army march around the city once a day for six days led by seven priests, each blowing a trumpet of a ram's horn before the Ark. On the seventh day, all of the people (2,000,000 plus) circled the city seven times and then let out a great shout at the long blast of the trumpet. The wall of Jericho collapses, and the Hebrews capture the city and all therein. Rahab the harlot and her house are saved. Joshua does as directed by God, as he utterly destroys all of the people of Jericho and all of the livestock. The silver, gold, bronze and iron are devoted to the treasury of the Lord. None of the Israelites are to take anything at all as booty; however, Achan keeps a cloak and some silver and gold.

Chapter seven tells of a minor defeat at Ai. Joshua sends a reconnaissance party to spy on the city of Ai. The party returns and tells Joshua there are but a few there and to send about 2,500 soldiers to capture the city. Joshua so orders. The soldiers are repelled by the soldiers of the city and thirty-six men are killed in the retreat. Joshua and his men are dismayed and tear at their clothes. They wonder why God had so deserted them and allowed this defeat. God informs Joshua that the Israelites have sinned and disobeyed by keeping items captured from Jericho and that they are to determine the person who has done this and destroy all of the items.

Joshua calls each of the twelve tribes forward separately until God selects one tribe, which then comes forward by families until God selects one family, which then come forward by households until God selects one household, which then come forward by man until God selects Achan as the villain. Achan confesses his misdeed. The cloak, silver and gold are destroyed, as was Achan's livestock. Achan, and his sons and daughters (not his wife?), are stoned to death. God then tells Joshua to attack Ai again with a small force as he conceals his larger force for an ambush. The small force feigns a retreat, the soldiers of Ai are defeated in the ambush, the city is captured, and all is destroyed except the cattle which God permits to be kept as war booty.

Upon hearing of the defeat of Ai, six regional kingdoms encompassing most of the West Bank of the Jordan form a confederation to fight the multitude of Israel. However, the people of the city of Gibeon and surrounding terrain decide upon a stratagem of trickery and deception as to the advancing Israelites. They plan to enter into a treaty of peace. They send to Joshua a delegation which has worn-out sacks on their donkeys, and with worn-out and patched wineskins. Their clothing and sandals are also worn-out and mended. They carry dry and moldy bread. They tell Joshua they are travelers from a far country and that they want peace and to be the servants of Israel because they have heard of the might of Israel and its God. So, without asking God for direction the people of Israel make an alliance with the Gibeonites and make them woodcutters and water bearers.

Joshua continues the military campaign in the central area of the land promised. Hearing what has happened to the city of Ai and that the city and environs of Gibeon have surrendered to Israel, five small city-kingdoms form a coalition to attack Gibeon. The Gibeonites plead with Joshua to help them, which reveals the previous deception of their being from a far country. Upon learning of the deception Joshua still honors the treaty and comes to their defense. This association, the first of many disobedient comminglings, will last about 300 years, until the reign of Saul. Allied with God, the Israelites defeat the five city-kings. In the process of routing the opposing armies, more are killed by a hailstorm than by the sword. To conclude the defeat Joshua prays to God that the sun "stand still" to allow more daylight time. "So the sun 'stood still,' and the moon stopped...for about a whole day." The five kings hide in a cave but are captured and killed and their cities taken. The Israelites also capture the Anakim, the giant people, and all of the Negeb south to the area of the wilderness in which they had wandered those thirty-eight years.

Joshua then turns his armies northward to capture or control most of the land from the Dead Sea area to north of the Sea of Galilee, into modern western Syria and Lebanon. God directs that after capturing opposing armies they are to hamstring their horses and burn their chariots. It is the time of the late bronze-age and the very early iron-age, which had moved slowly southward from the area of modern Turkey, but the Israelites were still a slave and agrarian people and not yet knowledgeable of iron. Usually a victorious army takes and uses the buildings, tools and weapons of the vanquished, but as God is using the multitude to eliminate the pagan regions, they usually destroy everything within a captured area.

After waging war for over six years, there still remained much land to be possessed, most of which would not be taken, and there were a lot of pockets within lands possessed which contained pagan people yet to be cleared away. God tells Joshua that he is growing old. (Some biblical students think Joshua was seventy and others ninety and that he would live to be 110). He is directed to complete the allotment of all of the land promised to the eleven tribes of Israel, with Joseph's two sons' tribes getting his share and the tribe of Levi getting no share of the land as they were to care for the religious aspects of the Israelites and live off the tithes of the others. They cast lots for the land, and the distribution comes out exactly as their ancestor Jacob (Israel) had said some 450 years earlier.

At the end of chapter twenty-one we read: "So the Lord gave to Israel all the land of which He had sworn to give to their fathers....Not a word failed of any good thing which the Lord had spoken to the house of Israel. All came to pass." At the end of chapter twenty-three we read a similar verse. All of the good promises that the Lord had given Israel had come to pass. This refers to such passages as Gen.12:2-3; 15:18; and 17:8. They now possessed the land promised as promised to their forefathers. It was theirs to keep through obedience to his commandments or to lose by disobedience. Some think the time was about 1372 B.C.

There is about a forty-three year gap between chapters twenty-two and twenty-three. The years pass as God gives rest to Israel, and Joshua indeed grows very old. Joshua calls all of the people and their leaders before him and reminds the people of the new nation of Israel of the condition of their keeping the land promised. "Therefore take careful heed to yourselves, that you love the Lord your God. Or else, if indeed you do go back, and cling to the remnant of these nations--these that remain among you--and make marriages with them, and go in to them and they to you, you know for certain that the Lord will no longer drive out these nations from before you. But they shall be snares and traps to you and scourges on your sides and thorns in your eyes, until you perish from this good land which the Lord your God has given you." The people of Israel would promptly and boldly be disobedient and violate this admonition.

The worst among them in violation of this specific admonition would be Solomon. In 427 years, at the death of Solomon, the kingdom would divide and splinter due to continuing disobedience, primarily due to the actions of Solomon himself, the wisest and probably wealthiest man ever to live. Wisdom and wealth will be destroyed by disobedience. About 358 years after Solomon, the then divided and splintered kingdom of Joshua, David and Solomon would disappear.

In chapter twenty-three, verse fourteen, Joshua again states, as to promises of the land, "You know in all your hearts and in all your souls that not one thing has failed of all the good things which the Lord your God spoke concerning you. All have come to pass for you; not one word of them has failed." They possessed the land. At verse sixteen Joshua continues "When you have transgressed the covenant of the Lord your God...and served other gods...then...you shall perish quickly from the good land which He has given you." They promptly transgressed and served other gods, apostasy and syncretism.

The people had carried the bones of Joseph from Egypt and buried them in the city of Shechem in a portion of the land his father Jacob had purchased. Just before Joshua died, at the age of 110, he told the people, "Choose for yourselves this day whom you will serve; but as for me and my house, we will serve the Lord."

And here begin, as follows on the next pages, the stories of the Judges and of Ruth.

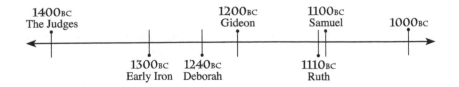

CHAPTER 7

JUDGES and RUTH
HEROES AND ZEROES IN DARK AGE
OF APOSTASY; REDEMPTION

The people of Israel did what was evil in the sight of the Lord, and served the Baals and the Ashtoreths, as every man did what was right in his own eyes. Jdg 2:11; 21:25

As has been stated, scholars debate the most likely dates for various events from Abraham, about 2000 B.C., until the time of David, about 1000 B.C., with most favoring the older dates. The dispute of time difference is about 200 years at the time of Abraham's birth, then narrows to about 155 years for the time of Exodus through the end of Joshua, then during the time of Judges narrows to about eight years at the time of Samson, and comes to agreement at the time of David. That means that there is also a disagreement as to whether the time of these judges covers 325 or 165 years. From the chariots and weapons, the area of Canaan was in a very late bronze age and a very early iron age. The exact dates will probably be determined in the future and are not important to the biblical message

As previously stated, there are four groups of people one must keep in mind throughout the old Hebrew scriptures, as God strives to establish the nation of Israel, which continually disobeys and falls away. The first group is the Egyptians, those to the southwest, which were a world power all during the old Hebrew scriptures. The second group is those living in the land the Israelites were invading, the locale of these books of Judges and Ruth. These were mostly Canaanites, descendants of Ham, a son of Noah, as the Israelites were descendants of Shem, a son of Noah. The third group is those called "Sea Peoples" or "people of the isles of Kittim", which was generally the area of the Aegean Sea, and occupied most of the eastern Mediterranean coast line. They are thought to have been early Greeks who came following some climatic change in Greece and possibly from wars, such as the Battle of Troy, of which Homer wrote. They occupied the areas of Phoenicia and Gaza, which areas were not and never have been captured by the Israelites.

The fourth group is the Assyrians, those to the northeast, the land from which Abraham had come, the land we today call Iraq. During the 400 years the Israelites were in Egypt this kingdom had expanded and would continue for another 300 years until God allowed Assyria to defeat the disobedient people of Israel and take them into captivity.

The Hebrew word used early in this book is *sho'tim*, which is translated as "judges", but it also may be translated as "governor", which conveys a better meaning for us in English than does "judges". Later in the book the word *yasha'*, is used, which means "deliverer" or "savior". They did not merely decide legal disputes, but they were leaders of the people who delivered them from their oppressors. The word *yasha'* is the same for the name Joshua and for its Greek counterpart, Jesus. Even more so than governors, these twelve heroes, and one heroine, were actually deliverers, as they delivered the failing Israelites from intermarriage with the surrounding pagans and worship of their gods back to the God of their fathers, and they did it time and time again for about 200 years. Their names are Othniel, Ehud, Shamgar, Deborah, Barak, Gideon, Tola, Jair, Jephthah, Ibzan, Elon, Abdon and Samson.

God raises up these heroes (and a heroine) to deliver a given local tribe of Israel from apostasy and then govern them. The people of Israel have become a very disorganized, loose confederacy after their conquest of the land of Canaan under Joshua. Therefore, without leadership, they repeatedly fall into idolatry, foreign political domination, intermarriage with pagans, and other major sins. They are in a general state of confusion and apostasy.

We began to see with Joshua the cycles of about 400 years of most nations, as the Israelites repeatedly spend 200 years rising, 50 sitting on top and 150 decaying, during which decay a relatively rapid total collapse can occur at any time. We observed a high with Abraham at 1800 B.C. followed by a low in 1600 in Egyptian bondage, followed by a high in 1400 as they invade Palestine. In the book of Judges we look at separate tribes and seem to find cycles more like forty (or seventy) years. Judges will be a bit of a low as the separate tribes regularly need a deliverer to salvage them. Later in 1000 B.C., there will be the high of David and Solomon, followed by the many warnings of the prophets and the captivity, all ending in captivity and exile in 721 B.C. In 539 B.C. Cyrus, King of Persia, will allow them to return, but they will again refuse to obey, and at 435 B.C. we have the end of the old Hebrew scriptures, the book of Malachi, God would change his approach. If one follows the later date for the exodus of 1280 B.C., then Israel peaks with Solomon in 970 B.C. and is taken captive in 721 B.C. a total of 459 years from valley to peak to valley. Sir Alex Fraser Tyler, Scottish jurist and historian (1801 A.D.), suggested that declines begin after 200 years due to loose fiscal policy which leads both to the populace discovering it can tap the treasury and by the rise of a despotic dictator.

With the Israelites we also see a repeating cycle like a clock with twelve, or ten, hours. The ten-hour clock begins at the top with bondage, then spiritual faith, then great courage, then liberty, then abundance at the bottom, then selfishness, then complacency, then apathy, then dependence, then back to bondage at the top. The twelve-hour clock begins at the top with God, then comes apostasy, then moral corruption, at three comes political corruption, then an enemy is raised up, then the enemy defeats the people, and at six the people are at the bottom, in slavery to the enemy and at death's door. Since "there is nothing else to do but pray," they do so, and then is repentance, and at nine is regicidal, then a deliverer is raised up, then comes deliverance, so that at twelve God is again primary.

As with most things in life, exactitude is debatable and schematic flow charts are general examples. A 400-year cycle may be a century more or less, and a 70-year cycle may be a decade more or less. The Greek and Roman empires of biblical times were on 400-year cycles. Babylon of biblical times and the Soviet Union of modern times were on 70-year cycles. It is interesting to ponder which, if any, cycle the United States is on and where, if any, it may be on the ten-hour or twelve-hour clock. It is also interesting as to where the United States may be in relation to biblical Israel from the exodus 1463 B.C. to the heights of David and Solomon around 1000 B.C. to the division of the kingdom in 930 B.C. and the beginning of captivity in 721 B.C.

There are two words for the problem we find continuously with the biblical Israelites, "apostasy" and "syncretism". Each word is a combination of two Greek words. Apostasy means "away stand", as the people stand away from God, and is usually fairly obvious. Syncretism means "together Crete", and is a futile attempt to combine two opposing cultures. For centuries the island of Crete has been occupied by Greeks and Turks, and they just cannot be blended and merged. A cretan, in days of politically incorrect speech, is a person who seems to have been put together by some disorganized committee. Syncretism is trying to blend cultures or religions, as you end up with one or the other or a third. It is an ancient form of multi-culturalism or new tolerance. God commands the Israelites not to assimilate with other religions, though they probably may assimilate politically.

Apostasy and syncretism were the creeping and crushing problem with the biblical Israelites. We read a lot of the primary god and the primary goddess of the world. They are with us today in abundance. One is the primary male god, the god of power, storms and war, the national god. There are many gods and names, but he is usually called by the Canaanites Baal, by the Babylonians Marduk, by the Egyptians Re, by the Greeks Zeus and by the Romans Jupiter. The other is the primary female goddess, the goddess of fertility, fecundity and sex, a national goddess. There are many goddesses and names, but she is usually called by the Canaanites Ashtoreth or Astare, by the Babylonians Ishtar, by the Egyptians Hathor, by the Greeks Artemis or Athena or Gaea and by the Romans Diana or Minerva or Cybele. God commanded the Israelites not to mix with these, the first of the ten commandments. From Ashtoreth and Ishtar most certainly comes Eostre, the name for the Anglo-Saxon goddess of Spring, and the words "estrogen" and "Easter." Five hundred years after these judges and their book, the prophet Jeremiah will point out that the Israelites are worshipping Ashtoreth, "Queen of Heaven", which fact will cause God to allow the fully grown Assyrian empire to take the Israelites into captivity.

It is interesting to ponder which, if any, of these specific primary gods and goddesses the United States may be worshipping. As we turn on our televisions, read our newspapers and magazines, watch our movies and follow their subject matter and advertisements and as we follow the public debates as to abortion, homoeroticism, evolution and similar subjects, how many of us even care about some primary god? Do not the subjects pervade even our church councils? Do we not hear time and time and time again that, "This may not be right for you, but it is right for me?" that, "Every man can do that which is right in his own eyes."

At the beginning of the book of Joshua, the Israelites crossed the River Jordan into the land as one body united under the one God. The land was promised to them as an inheritance on condition of obedience and of driving out the heathen. Joshua assigned each tribe its own territory to be purged of the heathen, but they failed and left pockets of pagans all around. The tribes became isolated from the others and were easy prey for enemy invasion. They began to lose their sense of national purpose.

Throughout the old Hebrew scriptures, one must continuously keep in mind four groups of people, as God encourages the establishment of the nation of Israel, which continually disobeys and falls. The first group, whom we met in Genesis and Exodus, is the Egyptians, a world power all during the old Hebrew scriptures. The second group, whom we meet in Joshua and Judges, is those living in the land the Israelites were invading. These were mostly Canaanites, descendants of Ham, a son of Noah, and cousins of the Israelites. The third group, whom we will meet later, is those called "Sea Peoples" or "people of the isles of Kittim", who are thought to have been early Greeks who came following some climatic change around the Aegean Sea, and possibly from wars, and occupied the areas of Gaza and Phoenicia, modern Lebanon. These also may have been people from the break up of the Mycenean confederacy. The fourth group, whom we will meet in later books, is the Assyrians, the area from which Abraham had come and which we today mostly call Iraq. As the Hebrews moved into Palestine, they began to settle in between the two giants of Egypt to the southwest and the ever-expanding empire of Assyria and Babylon to the northeast. The books of First and Second Kings are the story of God allowing the fully grown Assyrian empire to defeat the disobedient people of Israel and take them into captivity.

****

JUDGES

Some specifics of this book called Judges include that the author is unknown. The book begins with compromise and ends with anarchy. It sets out seven apostasies, seven bondages, seven deliverances and has thirteen deliverers. Five of the deliverances involved only one of these heroes, but one of the deliverances involved three deliverers and another involved four. The shortest story is about Shamgar, being but one verse long, and is frequently combined with Ehud to give six rather than seven periods of deliverance. The two longest stories are about Gideon and Samson. These stories of heroes are separate stories of a separated people going their separate ways, and are not directly connected nor in any fixed chronology. Each of these stories of deliverance begins with essentially the same statement as to the apostasy.

A quick look at the first chapter picks up at the end of the preceding book with the death of Joshua. In verse thirteen we again meet Othniel, the brother, or possibly, nephew, of Caleb, who with Joshua were the only adults who left Egypt and entered this land. Chapter one fairly repeats the final chapters of Joshua. In these first two chapters we find widespread apathy toward God, just as in many modern nations. The early victories become repeated defeats. In verse nineteen we are told these wandering Israelites could not move westward out of the hills and across the coastal plains because those people had chariots of iron. The iron age had arrived from the fallen Hittites (modern Turkey) to the Assyrians and "sea people".

In chapter two we find the moral lesson of this book, the beginnings of the problems of the people. In verse two the angel of the Lord reminds them that they were told, "You shall make no covenant with the inhabitants of the land; you shall break down their altars. But you have not obeyed.... Therefore...I will not drive them out before you; but they will become as thorns in your sides, and their gods shall be a snare for you." Since the people did not drive out the sin, but compromised with it and the local heathens, God will turn them loose. In modern days we are told to tolerate sin and compromise. When the people heard these words of divine rebuke they wept and called on the name of God. However, verse seven tells us, "The people served the Lord throughout the lifetime of Joshua and of the elders." They called on God only until the death of Joshua and his generation. Then comes verse eleven, and the first of many times we will hear, "The Israelites did evil in the sight of the Lord, and forgot the Lord their God, and served the Baals (masculine) and the Ashtaroth (feminine)."

Chapter two is essentially a summary of the entire book, as it sets the stage for the repeated cycle of falling away, corruption, defeat, repentance, revival and deliverance, and again falling away. In chapter three we find the first cycle. The people exchange daughters in marriage. The hand that rocks the cradle rules the nation. The daughters of the pagan heathens raise the children of the sons of Israel. In verse seven we hear for the second time, "The Israelites did evil in the sight of the Lord, and forgot the Lord their God." This sin of idolatry leads to the people being overrun and oppressed by Assyria for a period of eight years. Then God raises up the first deliverer and judge, Othniel, and the people enjoy forty years of peace.

In verse ten of three we meet the Holy Spirit, who had hovered over the face of the deep waters in Genesis. In the old Hebrew scriptures, there are seventeen instances that "the Spirit of the Lord came upon" someone. Unlike these days following the resurrection and ascension of Jesus the Christ, as the Spirit remains, in those days the Spirit came only for a brief time and for a specific purpose. For the purpose of leadership, it came upon Moses, Joshua, and four of these delivering judges, being Othniel, Gideon, Jephthah and Samson. It will so come upon David.

Othniel is called against the oppressor Mesopotamia. The final verses of chapter three cover the first of seven apostasies, of the sin of immorality and more idolatry. God's punishment is eighteen years of oppression by the Moabites under King Eglon, the second apostasy. The people cry out to God, and he raises up Ehud, a left-handed man who hid a small sword under his garment and killed King Eglon. Ehud was called against the oppressor Moabites. Beginning at verse twenty-one of chapter three is a very vivid description of this stabbing then calmly walking past the guards, who did not go in as they thought the king may be relieving himself. Verse thirty-one gives but brief mention of Shamgar, who is called against the oppresor Philistines, for the third apostasy.

Chapters four and five are the story of Deborah and her assistant Barak and years of peace. For doing evil, the fourth apostasy, for twenty years God had put the people under the hand the king of all Canaan, who had 900 chariots of iron. The people cry to God for help. Having been told by God that he would deliver the Canaanite army to them, Deborah summons Barak to take the field against the Canaanites. Barak agrees on condition that Deborah join him, which she does. The two armies meet on Mount Tabor where God renders their chariots and weapons ineffective and routs the Canaanites so that there is not one soldier remaining. Ruth, of the book of Ruth, was probably a contemporary of Deborah.

Chapters six through eight cover the story of Gideon fighting the oppressor Midianites, to whom God gave them up for seven years for doing evil, the fifth apostasy. The Midianites come and destroy all of the crops of the Israelites as they hide in caves with their livestock and crops. The people cry to God for help. God sends an angel to tell Gideon, who is beating wheat in a winepress to hide it, that Gideon is a man of great valor and is to deliver his people. Gideon, sort of wondering whether he was the right man, asks for a sign. The angel tells Gideon to put a goatskin and some cake on a rock, which he does. The angel then taps the skin and cake with his staff and a fire comes from the rock and consumes them.

Believing, Gideon makes a night attack on one of the pagan altars of Baal. Upon discovering that, the next morning the people come to kill Gideon, whose father meets with them and makes an agreement to let Baal himself contend against Gideon. The Midianites form an army to come against the Israelites, and Gideon begins to form an army. Finding his faith lagging, Gideon asks God for another sign. He rolls out a woolen fleece that night and asks that the sign be that in the morning the fleece be wet with dew but the ground be dry. The next morning, so it is, and Gideon wrung out a bowl of water.

Gideon begins to form his army from 32,000 men. God tells him that was too many and to tell them any who are fearful could leave for home, and 22,000 leave. God then says the remaining 10,000 are too many and that they are to be led to a stream to drink. Those who lap water like a dog, with there heads down, are to be sent home. Those who scoop the water up in the hands, still looking out, are to be kept. Three hundred are kept. Gideon is concerned as the opposing army is so large its camels are as sand on the beach. That night God tells Gideon to sneak into the enemy camp to hear what they say of him. He hears of a dream which they interpret as God giving the victory to Gideon. Gideon returns, awakens his men, divides them into three groups of 100 each and gives each a trumpet and a clay jar. The groups separate, circle the enemy camp, then each man blows his trumpet and smashes his jar. The Midianite enemy begin to fight among themselves, and then flee. Gideon's men pursue and capture the land and the leaders. Gideon refuses an offer to rule over the people as God would rule, but he does ask and receive all of the gold earrings taken as war booty.

At Gideon's death the Israelite people return to the worship of Baal. He leaves seventy sons by his many wives and one by his concubine. Abimelech, the son of the concubine, campaigns to be the ruler of the Israelites. To help his campaign he kills all but one of his brothers. That one warns the people and encourages an overthrow of Abimelech. A civil war ensues in which Abimelech is successful in quashing revolts, until a woman throws a millstone down on his head. Thereafter, two judges, Tola and Jair, govern for fifty-five years of peace. Then the Israelites again return to the worship of the various gods of the surrounding people doing evil in the sight of God who turn them over to the Philistines and the Ammonites. The sixth apostasy.

After eighteen years the Israelites cry out to God, who says he would no more deliver them. They then go to Jephthah, an illegitimate son of Gilead, who has been cast out and runs with some worthless raiders. On condition of being restored to his respected position as a son of Gilead he agrees to lead them. The Spirit of the Lord comes upon Jephthah, who promises God that if he gives him military success against the Ammonites he will give as a burnt offering the first person to come out of his door upon returning home. He has his military victory. The first person to come out of his door is his only child, a loving daughter. The two agree she should be so offered, and it is done.

After several more victories, the Ephraimites, another Israelite group, come to Jephthah complaining that they have not been allowed to participate in the booty of victory, although they had been invited and refused. There is a civil war between the two and 42,000 Ephraimites are killed. As many retreat across the fords of the River Jordan, they are asked to speak the word for stream, being "shibboleth". They would pronounce only the "s" of the "sh" and be killed. Jephthah judges Israel six years and is succeeded by Ibzan, then Elon and then Abdon for a total of forty-two years of peace.

The Israelites then again do evil in the sight of God who turns them over to the Philistines for forty years. Chapters thirteen through sixteen are of Samson, the last of these twelve "judges", partially delivering the Israelites from oppression by the Philistines. The story of Samson is essentially one of wasted potential frittered away by a man, except when temporarily empowered by the Spirit of God, largely controlled by sensuality and revenge. When the woman to be Samson's mother was barren and childless, an angel told her she would have a son who would be a Nazirite, separated for life unto God. She bore Samson. As a young man he sees a Philistine woman and demands that his parents get her for him. In spite of their objections the three travel to her hometown. En route a lion roars at him, and the Spirit of God allows him to tear it apart with his bare hands. On a second journey he sees the lion's carcass with a swarm of bees and honey in it. He eats some of the honey. As they are preparing for the wedding, he tells a riddle involving the lion and the honey to some Philistines and bets them sixty fine robes they can not solve it. Samson's new wife entices him to explain the riddle to her, which he does and she tells the men. Realizing he has been tricked he goes to another town, kills thirty men and gives their robes in payment of the debt. He then gives his wife to his best man.

After a while Samson comes back to take his wife, but she belongs to another. So Samson catches 300 foxes, ties their tales together, sets them on fire and sends them running through the standing grain of the Philistines. He then hides in the cleft of a rock. The Philistines come to Samson's town and tell the people they want him, so they go to Samson who agrees to be bound up and delivered over. As they approach the town the Philistines come to get him. He breaks his bonds, picks up the jawbone of a donkey and, with the Spirit of God, slays 1,000 of them. A while later he goes to Gaza and sleeps with a prostitute. The townspeople surround the house to wait on him until morning. At midnight he comes out and pulls up the two posts of the main city gate and carries them into the hills.

After this he falls in love with Delilah, another Philistine woman, one motivated by greed. The Philistines enlisted her to inform them of the source of Samson's strength for the payment of 1,100 pieces of silver. First Samson tells her he will lose his strength if tied with seven fresh undried bowstrings. She so binds him, but he easily breaks free. Second he tells her he will lose his strength if bound with new and unused ropes. She so binds him, but he easily breaks free. Third he tells her he will lose his strength if his hair were bound into seven locks and held with a pin. She so weaves his hair as he sleeps, but he easily loosens his hair. Day after day she nags him as to their love relationship until he finally tells her. If his hair is shaved he will lose his strength. She encourages him to sleep with his head on her knees and has a man shave his head as he sleeps. He is captured.

The Philistines gouge out Samson's eyes, bind him with bronze chains and make him grind grain at the mill wheel. But his hair begins to grow back. They give credit to their god Dagon and call Samson out to make sport of him. They make him stand between two pillars of the temple, which is full of people and has about 3,000 on its roof. He asks a servant to place his hands on the two pillars. He pushes against the pillars, prays to God for strength and asks to die with the Philistines. He kills more Philistines at his death than during the previous part of his life. He had been a "judge" of Israel twenty years.

The last five chapters, seventeen through twenty-one, tell of events which many fine scholars think occurred at the time of chapter three. They may be correct. These five chapters are about the idolatry, immorality, anarchy and civil war, particularly of the tribes of Dan and Benjamin. They begin and the book ends with, "Every man did that which was right in his own eyes." Doing right in your own eyes! Is not that the very cause of idolatry, immorality, anarchy and civil war?

****

RUTH

Most students of the Bible place the story and book of Ruth contemporaneously with Deborah of Judges. Let's look at some background. In chapters two and six of Joshua we heard of Rahab, a harlot who lived on the walls of Jericho. Rahab took in the two spies sent by Joshua and covered the escape. For that she was spared during the destruction of Jericho and went to live with the Israelites.

The very last verses of the book of Ruth and the first chapter of Matthew and the third chapter of Luke, in the genealogies of Jesus, tell us that this harlot Rahab married an Israelite named Salmon and that they had a son. That son was Boaz, the very same man who married Ruth, a woman of Moab. Rahab gets special mention in Heb. 11:31, among those of great faith. This is the direct beginning of the house of king David. Rahab is David's great-great-grandmother. Ruth is David's great-grandmother. David's close lineage includes a harlot from Jericho and a Moabitess.

The story of Ruth is of an Israelite couple, Elimelech and his wife Naomi, with their two sons, moving eastward across the River Jordan into Moab due to a famine. One of the sons marries Ruth, another marries Orpah. The father and two sons die, and Naomi decides to return home, back across the Jordan. She frees her two daughters-in-law. Orpah chooses to remain in Moab. Ruth chooses to go with her mother-in-law, and says to her, as in verse sixteen, "Wherever you go, I will go; and wherever you lodge, I will lodge; your people shall be my people, and your God my God. Where you die, will I die, and there will I be buried." What Ruth says to her mother-in-law we now hear at so many weddings, usually by the bride.

Naomi and Ruth return home to Bethlehem. Naomi has a relative, a kinsman, named Boaz, who has some land and wealth. In chapter two verse four we are told that Boaz greets his field workers by saying, "The Lord be with you," to which they respond, "The Lord bless you." In many of our churches we retain and repeat this saying regularly. Boaz is a good man, and Naomi places Ruth under his care. The two fall in love. The law was that Ruth's brother-in-law was to care for her and redeem her. Boaz negotiates her redemption unto himself. The two marry and parent Obed, the father of Jesse and grandfather of David.

And here begins, on the following pages, the story of Samuel and Saul, the first king of Israel, and of young David.

CHAPTER 8

FIRST SAMUEL
SAMUEL, SAUL AND YOUNG DAVID

Fear the Lord, and serve him in truth with all your heart; but if you still do wickedly you shall be swept away. 1 Sam. 12:24-25

In Exodus and Numbers we heard of God's redemption of the people as Moses led them out of bondage in Egypt and of their arrival on the East Bank of the River Jordan. Because the generation that left Egypt lost their faith, God directed that they wander aimlessly for about thirty-eight years as that generation died off. Leviticus is tacked on to Exodus to set out the laws. Deuteronomy is tacked on to Numbers to remind the new generation of the exodus and laws. Joshua records the invasion of the land occupied primarily by Canaanites. That invasion was incomplete and left many pockets of pagans. Judges records the problems of the separate tribes as they slip into idolatry and syncretism, and God in his mercy sends a deliverer to salvage them. Now we are at another major demarcation for the Israelites.

These next four books, First Samuel, Second Samuel, First Kings, and Second Kings record the rise and fall of the kingdom of Israel, a period of about 460 years. Originally these four were one book. They were first separated to fit the ancient scrolls, and later separated according to their length. As First Samuel opens it is about 1125 B.C. Depending on which system of counting one uses, it has been between 175 and 340 years since Moses led the masses out of Egypt. The Israelites have not yet completely possessed the land, not even most of it. In about forty years David will pass the kingdom to Solomon as it sits at its peak for about seventy years then splits and spends 200 years falling into exile.

First Samuel tells us of Samuel in its first quarter, then of Samuel and Saul in its second quarter, then of Saul and the young David in its second half. Second Samuel tells of the rise of King David as he consolidates the kingdom. First Kings tells of Solomon overtaxing and dissipating the kingdom. Second Kings tells of the division and collapse of the kingdom followed by its capture by Assyria.

The old Hebrew scriptures tell of the people as they continuously fall away from God as he calls them to build a nation. This work is in the midst of four other peoples. First was Egypt, of whom we hear little after the exodus. Now, for about 500 years they deal with those people in and around the land. These are primarily the Canaanites and those called Sea People of early Greece, the Philistines and Phoenicians. We do not hear much of the fourth group, Assyria until Second Kings. Shortly after Abraham left the area of what we call northwestern Iraq and his grandson Jacob moved into Egypt, the little kingdom of Nineveh captured the area of Abraham's homeland. At the time of Joshua, Assyria expanded to the northeast. The second great empire, behind Egypt, was building. We will hear of them a little in First Kings with Solomon, as the two expanding kingdoms rubbed up against one another. During the time of Second Kings, as the Israelites begin to collapse upon themselves, we will see this Assyrian empire as it literally explodes westward into what we call Turkey and southwest across the land of the Israelites and on into Egypt. For about 700 years Assyria, the area we call Iraq and Syria, grows into the world empire replacing Egypt. Modern Iraq may no doubt very much like to repeat that history.

First Samuel begins with the scene of Elkanah and his two wives. One wife has two sons, but the other wife, Hannah, is barren. The family travels to the town of Shiloh, which is the primary holy city on the West Bank before David took Jerusalem. All except Hannah enjoy themselves, but she weeps and will not eat. She makes a vow to God saying, "If you will indeed look on the affliction of your maidservant, and remember me, and forget not your maidservant, but will give your maidservant a male child, then I will give him to the Lord all the days of his life, and no razor shall come upon his head."

In the presence of Eli, the priest and a judge, Hannah pledges that her son will be a Nazirite, as was Samson and as would be John the Baptist. A Nazirite was a person consecrated to God. The consecration was usually done by the parent before birth, and the mark of such separation was that the hair was never cut, nor could they come near a dead person. In verse twenty we are told God remembered her and she gives birth to a son, whom she names Samuel, which means "heard of God". She turns the newly weaned baby over to Eli. In chapter two verse twenty-six is written the same that will be said of the youth of Jesus. "The boy Samuel continued to grow both in stature and in favor with the Lord and with men."

As God had called Abraham and Moses and will call Isaiah, each of whom eventually responded, in chapter three God calls the boy Samuel. The prophet and judge Eli is growing old and his eyesight is failing. He lies down to rest. Samuel rests in the temple where the Ark of the Covenant is, a teenage boy alone with a large trunk that he is told not to touch. The Lord calls, "Samuel, Samuel," and he says, "Here I am," and runs to Eli, who says he had not called him. Samuel returns to his resting spot. Again God calls, "Samuel," and again he goes to Eli and says, "Here I am." Again Eli tells him he had not called. Yet a third time God calls and Samuel goes to Eli, who now perceives it may be God calling, and tells the boy to respond, "Speak, Lord, for thy servant hears."

A fourth time God calls, and Samuel responds, "Speak, for thy servant hears." God tells Samuel he is going to punish Eli because his two sons have blasphemed God and Eli has not restrained them. God wants us to worship him, but not to neglect the care for our family. The next morning Eli presses Samuel to tell him what God had said, and he tells him. In verse twenty we have a phrase that appeared one time in Judges, and will appear a total of nine times, four in second Samuel. "From Dan to Beer-sheba" means all of the land of Israel. Dan was thirty miles north of the Sea of Galilee and Beersheba in the vicinity of the southern end of the Dead Sea.

Chapter four is the first of a long line of battles between the Israelites and the Philistines. These people were called "Sea Peoples". Beginning at the time of Judges the people of Mycea and Greece, were beginning the bump and grind of building an empire. This building will continue through the rest of the old Hebrew scriptures. The period of Moses was the late bronze age, and the early iron age, as Assyria captured the Hittites of modern Turkey and their uses of iron. Weapons and utensils were changing. The people of Macedonia, Sparta and Athens began to flex muscles, as did the people of ancient Turkey. They fought over the Aegean Sea, the passageway at the Black Sea and the island of Crete. Just as they do today. Scholars place the Battle of Troy at 1183 B.C. during the period of the Judges. People from around the Aegean and Crete migrated onto Cairo and onto the Mediterranean coast, the western land of Canaan. Along the southern coast they were called Philistines, and along the northern coast Phoenicians, a sea people, of the iron age, with chariots, too powerful for the Israelite farmers.

The Ark of the Covenant contained the Ten Commandments and was kept in the tabernacle, the large tent, as it was the resting place of God. The Israelis took the ark from Shiloh, on top of the west bank, down the mountains near the coast. They did not inquire of God as to this and did so placing their faith in the utensils, vestments and trappings and not in God. The two wicked sons of Eli participated in this. In verse eleven we are told the Philistines captured the Ark of the Covenant. As God had told young Samuel, these sons were killed in the battle, and Eli, at ninety-eight, fell backward and broke his neck when told of these events.

In chapter five, the Philistines place the ark in the house of Dagon, one of their gods, half man and half fish, as a mermaid. The next day they find Dagon face downward on the ground. They set him back up. The next morning they find Dagon broken. They move the Ark to another town, then to another, as they are afflicted with tumors. After seven months they decide to return the Ark to the Israelites and to send offerings.

Samuel becomes a judge of the people. As had Eli, he appoints his two sons priests. As had the sons of Eli, the sons of Samuel do not walk in his ways and take bribes. Eli and Samuel fail as nurturing fathers and suffer for it. In chapter eight verse five is a point of change, from judges to kings. The people demand that Samuel "appoint a king to govern us like all the nations." God assures Samuel that they were not rejecting Samuel but were rejecting God. God had regularly directed that they not be like the other nations but have God work through the rulers. In verses ten through eighteen Samuel warns the people about kings, but they refuse to listen. God consents to give the people what they want. God may not so much punish us for our sins as step back and allow our sins to punish us.

In chapter eight at verse ten Samuel passes on to the people the warning of God as to having a king. The ways of a king are that he will take your sons for his military, appoint his own commanders, take your daughters for cooks, take your best fields, and take a tenth of your produce and livestock. But the people refuse to listen to words of Samuel as they demand a king. God consents to their disobedience in demanding a king.

In chapter nine we are introduced to a handsome, tall young son of a wealthy man, one Saul by name. In verse fifteen God reveals to Samuel that he will send to him a man whom Samuel is to anoint as prince, later king. At that time Saul's father sends him to search for lost jackasses, and Saul goes to Samuel for advice as to finding these animals. In chapter ten Samuel anoints Saul with oil and tells him to go to Gilgal, which had been Joshua's starting point at Jericho. He tells him to wait seven days and then he will also come. Trouble arises and Saul is called out of the field, and the spirit of God comes mightily upon him. He musters 330,000 men. In chapter eleven verse fifteen the people make Saul king. God does not.

In chapter twelve verse twenty-three, Samuel speaks the great words on intercessory prayer. "Far be it from me that I should sin against the Lord by ceasing to pray for you." It is a sin not to pray regularly and consistently for other people.

In chapter thirteen we are told of the chariots and horsemen of the Philistines, and troops as sand. Saul waits at Gilgal as directed by Samuel. He waits seven days. Being impatient and anxious, Saul himself offers the burnt offering and the peace offering, then Samuel arrives. Only a priest makes these offerings, and Saul had not waited the full seventh day. For that disobedience Samuel tells him, in verse fourteen, that God will seek out "a man after his own heart." It was the beginning of the end of Saul and of the beginning of David. Saul will disintegrate from a gifted prince to a paranoid suicide.

At verse nineteen we read of the problem at the start of the iron age. Israel has no blacksmith and has to go to the Philistines for their tools and the sharpening of them, paying exorbitant costs. They also destroy the chariots of the Philistines when they capture them. Solomon will bring the people into the iron age.

Saul has children. One is a son Jonathan and one a daughter Michal. They are both godly people who love and obey their father. Later they will both also love and obey David. Saul declares a rash edict that nobody is to eat until success at battle. Jonathan is away and has not heard and eats some honey. Saul orders that Jonathan be executed, but the people ransom him.

In chapter fifteen we again find Saul disobeying God as he speaks through Samuel. The Amalekites, who live in the Negeb, south of Gaza, had interfered with the people under Moses and are still doing so. Through Samuel God directs Saul utterly to destroy them, man, woman, sucklings and livestock. Things dedicated to a false god are dedicated to destruction. Saul attacks with 210,000 men, but brings back the king and the livestock. He tells Samuel he has obeyed, to which Samuel says, "What then is this bleating of the sheep in my ears, and the lowing of the oxen, which I hear?" In verse twenty-eight he tells Saul that God has torn the kingdom from him and given it to a neighbor. Samuel orders that the Amalekite king be brought before him, then proceeds to hew him into pieces. When God directs that something which opposes him is to be destroyed, he means utterly and without compromise or our modern tolerance. In verse twenty-two we have the earliest biblical criticism of the sacrifice of animals.

In chapter sixteen we meet young David. The rest of First Samuel is of the disintegration of Saul as he turns paranoid, and the rise of young David. We meet Jesse, the root, the grandson of Boaz and Ruth. He lived and farmed in Bethlehem, the "House of Bread" in which would be born the Bread of Life. Samuel visits and views the sons of Jesse, as God will tell him which to choose. In verse seven God says, "The Lord sees not as man sees; man looks on the outward appearance, but the Lord looks on the heart." The sons come forward in order of age. Until there is but one, the youngest, out in the field tending the sheep. He did not spend hours at the TV or the Internet. Samuel asks for him. He was ruddy and handsome with beautiful eyes. God instructs Samuel to anoint him, which he does, and the Spirit of the Lord departed from Saul and an evil spirit tormented him. This was about the time of Samson at the end of Judges.

Most people know the next chapters, of the Philistine soldier Goliath, a man about nine foot six. The armor of Saul is too cumbersome for David, the player of the lyre. Saul does not much notice David. Goliath has four brothers. David selects five stones. With his sling he had killed animals that attacked the sheep. The first stone from the sling lodges in the forehead of Goliath, and he falls. David takes Goliath's sword and severs his head. Saul and the people now take great notice of David. Abner, the commander of Saul's army, takes notice.

At the beginning of chapter eighteen we are told the soul of Saul's son Jonathan becomes knit to the soul of David, and they make a covenant. Jonathan was about twenty-five years older than David. In verse sixteen we are told that all of Israel loved David, and in verse twenty that Saul's daughter Michal loves him and is to be his wife. Saul becomes ever more afraid of David. He seeks to kill David, as Jonathan continues to assist David and even aid in his escape from Saul into the hills. This fleeing and hiding continues through these chapters. In chapter twenty-four David sneaks into Saul's cave as he sleeps and cuts of the skirt of his robe, and the next morning, from a safe distance, shows the robe to Saul. About this time Samuel dies. In chapter twenty-six David sneaks up on Saul and takes his spear and water bottle, then flees across a deep ravine to call back to Saul as to what he has done.

Having no place else to go, David then joins forces with the Philistines, the enemy of Israel and of God. He will attack other enemies of Israel and tell the king of the Philistines he has been attacking Israel, which he never does. Saul has ordered all wizards, mediums and witches out of the land. In chapter twenty-eight, without God, without Samuel, without Jonathan and at the depths of his paranoia, Saul tries to inquire of God, but there is no answer, not by dreams, nor by the lot of Urim, nor by the prophets. He seeks out a woman, a medium, the witch of Endor, to advise him. He asks her to divine up Samuel. She panicks as Samuel does in fact appear, to tell Saul that on the next day he and his sons will die. Their deaths are reported in the final chapter. Saul commits suicide. During this time David most likely wrote many of the psalms.

And here begins, as on the following pages, Second Samuel, the story of King David.

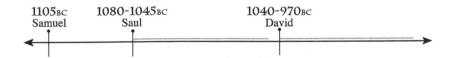
CHAPTER 9

SECOND SAMUEL
DAVID RESTORES COSMOS OUT OF SAUL'S CHAOS

The Lord is my rock, my fortress and my deliverer. The God of my strength, in Him I will trust. 2 Sam. 22:2-3

The four books of First and Second Samuel and First and Second Kings were no doubt originally one book. The second half of First Samuel tells of Saul as the first king of the twelve tribes of Israel and the efforts to bring them together as one nation under God. In the middle of that book God tells Samuel, the last of the judges and powerful priests and the first of a long line of prophets, that he is to anoint another to replace Saul as king. We are introduced to the young David, whose success in slaying Goliath endears him to the people and gives rise to a destructive paranoia in Saul. For nearly a decade Saul searched out David, who hid in the hills as a fugitive.

At the end of First Samuel we are told that Saul, wounded in battle, committed suicide near the battlefield following defeats by resurgent Philistines by falling on his spear. His son Jonathan, David's dearest friend, was also killed. Second Samuel opens with David returning from battle against the Amalekites, whom Saul had not completely destroyed as directed by God, when an Amalekite comes up to him telling him of the deaths of Saul and Jonathan and claiming to have killed Saul himself. David orders his troops to kill the man.

Though David was called of God, his reputation for taking blood and his many fallings away from God's commandments would prevent him from building the temple and perfecting the nation. His love of God and his remaining steadfast and prompt repentance sets the great example for us. Such an example is that upon learning of the death of King Saul, David immediately asks of God what he is to do, and is told to go to Hebron, an ancient town up on what is the West Bank of the Jordan, about twenty miles south of the town later known as Jerusalem.

The area Saul consolidated was mostly what may be called the West Bank plus some land east and north of the Sea of Galilee and some east of the Jordan. It was about seventy miles north to south and fifty east to west, being some 10,000 square miles, about the size of the U.S. state of Maryland. David would enlarge this to 400 miles north to south and 100 miles east to west, being some 40,000 square miles, about the size of the state of Virginia. Solomon would further enlarge this to 500 miles north to south and 100 miles east to west, being some 50,000 square miles, about the size of the states of Virginia and Maryland combined. They would never conquer the area of either Gaza or Phoenicia. The area of modern Israel and the West Bank, about 100 miles north to south and 50 east to west, being some 5,000 square miles, is about the size of the Florida panhandle or the Shenandoah Valley of western Virginia, smaller than Saul's kingdom. During the 250 years Joshua and these three kings were enlarging and consolidating this small empire, the Assyrians, off to the northeast in the area of modern Iraq, were enlarging and consolidating their empire. The Assyrians were moving westward across our modern countries of Syria and Turkey.

About 200 years after David's time, the Assyrian empire would grind southward across the divided and crumbling empire of David and his son Solomon and into Egypt, to become the world empire. For the disobedience of Solomon in bringing pagan wives and allowing pagan worship to remain, for the disobedience of many successor kings, who ignore the warnings of the many prophets, God will allow the Assyrians to eliminate the nation of the people he first called and reduce them to but a remnant of exiles.

As directed by God, David goes up to Hebron, where he is crowned king of Judah, that southern part of Israel west of the Dead Sea. He is thirty years old. Saul's son Ishbosheth claims the crown for all of Israel to the north. The scene is set for the coming civil war which will last throughout the remaining years of David. Solomon will suppress the internal wars, but the names and lines of division are sketched for the division of the empire which will come in eighty years upon the death of Solomon. With that division, the internal strife and assassinations will resurface and increase until God eventually allows Assyria and Babylon, to remove them all.

Abner, Saul's nephew and chief executive officer, supports Saul's eldest son Ishbosheth in his claim for the throne of Israel. Joab, David's nephew and chief executive officer, another man of great personal ambition, supports David's claim. Abner and Joab agree that each send twelve men to fight. The twenty-four all kill each other quickly. Joab's younger brother pursues the elderly Abner who kills him, and Joab determines to kill Abner. The civil war between Saul's house and David's house, between northern Israel and southern Judah is underway and will remain for over 1,000 years through the days of Christ.

The early stages of this civil war keep the Israelites from molesting the Philistines, who remain down along the coast of the Mediterranean as David consolidates his little kingdom. Abner is elderly and approaches David in peace. David directs him to bring to him Michal, the youngest daughter of

Saul, who had promised her to David for circumcising 100 Philistines, without their consent. She is now married to Paltiel. Ishbosheth removes Michal from Paltiel and takes her to David, as Paltiel follows weeping. In rapid succession, Joab hears of this agreement, Abner falls out with Ishbosheth and is killed by Joab, and Ishbosheth is assassinated. In chapter five, after serving seven-and-a-half years as king of only Judah, David is annointed king of all Israel.

In chapter five David captures a last stronghold, the city of the Jebusites at Salem, to be renamed Jerusalem, and moved the center of his operations from Hebron. The hill at the southeastern corner of Jerusalem was known as Zion, the City of David. As they are moving the Ark of the Covenant into Jerusalem, the oxen stumble and Uzzah puts out his hand to steady the ark. Only the priests, at certain times, are to touch the ark. God smites Uzzah dead. David becomes angry at God and will not allow the ark to proceed for some time. When the ark proceeds, David dances in front of it, and strips himself virtually nude, to the great displeasure of his seventh and new wife, Michal, daughter of Saul, who thereupon despises him and will have no child by him.

In chapter seven David discusses with the prophet Nathan his desire to build a great house for God and to move him out of the tent. Nathan tells him such a temple will be built by another, but that "your house and your kingdom shall be made sure for ever before God; your throne shall be established for ever." For Christians this is a reference to the kingdom of Jesus the Christ. We are told in First Chronicles chapter twenty-two that David gathered and stored all of the workmen and materials for the temple Solomon would build.

Beginning in chapter nine and spread across several chapters is the story of Mephibosheth, and David's care for him. Mephibosheth was the son of Jonathan, now dead, and the grandson of Saul. He was five years old when Jonathan was killed and Saul committed suicide. As his nurse fled with the boy, he fell and crippled both of his feet. David promises to care for the young man, and does so, even though the lad is not completely loyal.

In chapter eleven is the great sin of David. In the spring of the year a king is to go forth to battle, but David is idle in his successes and stays in his new castle. From the roof he looks down and sees a beautiful woman bathing. There is a high probability she knows David watches. There is no sin in seeing something. The sin begins with the second look, and is completed in the third stage of acting on it. David looks, sends, inquires and takes. Bathsheba is the wife of Uriah, one of his soldiers. She becomes pregnant by David. He tries to cover the deed over by giving Uriah time off to stay home with her, but he does not. Then he gets Uriah drunk, but he still will not go to her. Then he has Joab, commander of the army, put him at the front of battle where he is killed.

God sends Nathan to David. He tells him of a wealthy man with many sheep taking the one little lamb of a poor man. David rages that such a man should be punished. Nathan tells him, "You are the man," and that the child so conceived will die. That child dies on the seventh day, and on that day David ceases to grieve publicly for the child. Shortly David goes to comfort Bathsheba. They sleep together, and she bears a son and names him Solomon, but the prophet Nathan names him Jedidiah. This was at the time David's seventh son, along with one daughter.

Absalom, one of David's older sons, has a full sister named Tamar, who is beautiful. Amnon, their half-brother by David, falls in love with Tamar, so much so that he makes himself somewhat ill. He explains the situation to his cousin who convinces him to feign serious illness and request that Tamar bring food and prepare it in his chambers. King David honors his request and sends Tamar to Amnon. There, Amnon entices her into his bed chamber, and over her strong protestations he forces her and lies with her. Then he hates her with a hatred greater than the love he had held for her. He orders her to leave. She will not so he calls his servant who puts her out. Whereupon she tears her long robe of a virgin and puts ashes on her head. Absalom asks Tamar, and she tells him of the rape, and from then on he hates Amnon.

Two years later Absalom has a sheep shearing party and invites all of the family. King David declines but clears the way for Amnon to attend. Absalom instructs his servants to wait until Amnon gets drunk and then to murder him, which they do. Word of the deed gets back to David. Absalom flees to his grandfather's and remains there three years. David has grieved for his dead son but now longs for Absalom. Joab, David's nephew and Absalom's cousin, talks with David, then has a wise woman talk with David, who consents to allow Absalom to return. Absalom does return to Jerusalem but on condition that he remain in his own house and not approach David.

Absalom is a handsome young man, without a blemish. He has three sons and one daughter, whom he names Tamar, after his sister. He lives two years without seeing his father. Then he has Joab again go to David, who then consents to have Absalom come to him. Whereupon David kisses Absalom, who promptly acquires a chariot and horses and fifty servants. He begins politicking at the town gates and sets himself up as judge and steals the hearts of the people. After four years he asks for and receives the king's permission to go twenty-five miles south of Jerusalem to the town of Hebron. There he has himself proclaimed king of Hebron. The people in favor of Absalom increase and over time David gets word that all of Israel favors Absalom, causing David to flee, with a great entourage of followers. As he was from Saul, David is again a fugitive.

Chapters sixteen through eighteen tell of Absalom's continued rebellion against his father David as the vicissitudes, scheming and treachery in David's family and court peaked during his early sixties. The subordinates of David choose sides and change sides as the family splits. David takes his thousands of troops and crosses to the east bank of the River Jordan. King David gives explicit orders to all of his troops not to harm Absalom. The opposing armies meet. Absalom is riding his mule and his head gets tangled in the branches of an oak; he is left hanging from the tree. The fact is reported to Joab, David's chief officer, and a pragmatic and ambitious man. In spite of David's order, Joab takes three daggers and ten men, goes to Absalom and stabs him having the men complete the job. Two messengers take word of the death to David, and he and his army grieve his son's death.

The concluding chapters tell of more national unrest. The nation of Israel was in need of chastisement so God allowed Satan to incite David to do a numbering, a census, on the men of military age only. A census was an impious act of looking to the people and army rather than to God for increase and safety. The total number of such men in Israel and Judah was 1,300,000. In David's concluding days he completed the preparation for his son Solomon to build the temple denied to himself. He purchased the threshing floor of Araunah (Ornan), a large fairly flat and smooth rock upon which Solomon would build and upon which the Muslims would eventually erect the golden Dome of the Rock. We are reminded that in First Chronicles chapter twenty-two we are told that David assembled the material and workmen for Solomon's task.

And here begins, as on the following pages, the story of the rule of Solomon and of the division of the kingdom, as in the book of First Kings.

991-930BC
Solomon

930BC
Kingdom Divided
(Rehoboam/Jeroboam)

931BC
Civil Wars

CHAPTER 10

FIRST KINGS
SOLOMON AND DIVISION OF KINGDOM

*Be strong and prove yourself a man, and keep the charge of the Lord
your God, to walk in his ways, to keep his commandments, his judgments
and his testimonies.* 1 Kgs. 2:2

Remember, there are three groups of people one must keep in mind
throughout the old Hebrew scriptures. The first group is the Egyptians, those to
the southwest, which were a world power all during the old Hebrew scriptures.
The second group is those living in the land the Israelis had invaded, mostly
Canaanites. This is the group dealt with in First Kings. The third group is the
Assyrians, those to the northeast, the land from which Abraham had come,
the land we today call Iraq.

Depending upon one's system of counting, about 300 years earlier Moses
had admonished, as written in Deuteronomy 12:2, that they were to "destroy
all the places where the nations whom you shall dispossess served their gods
upon the high mountains," (12:2) that they were not to do "whatever is right
in one's own eyes"(12:8), nor was a king to "multiply horses, wives or silver
and gold for himself"(15:17). Solomon, even more so than David, would
violate all of these commandments, and reap the consequences. The wisest
man in all the world would but prove a fool.

The Israelites never removed the Canaanites and Sea Peoples from the
land. They left pockets of pagans across the land. God's choice of the Israelites
required their exclusive worship and wholehearted allegiance. In First Kings
we read of the pollution of apostasy and syncretism as the creep became a
sweep. God sends Elijah, the first of many prophets to warn the Israelites,
but they refuse to listen and feel the first press of the coming world power of
Assyria which God will allow to sweep the Israelites from the land in Second
Kings. The people will not listen, not then and not today. Neither religious
tolerance nor multi-culturalism means believers are to turn their back on God
and adopt the ways and customs of others, becoming like them.

In Judges there were clock-like cycles of falling and rising. In the
Samuels these cycles became a slope of steady rising. In the Kings this slope

77

turns to one of steady falling. As we read so often in the book of Judges, we read repeatedly in the books of Kings, "The Israelites did evil in the sight of the Lord, and forgot the Lord their God, and served the Baals (masculine) and the Ashtaroth (feminine)." Baal is the general masculine name for the gods of the Canaanites. Ashtaroth, also known as Asherah and Astarte, is the feminine name of the Canaanite goddess of fertility, the Mother-goddess. It is the "Queen of Heaven" of which Jeremiah will warn as the kingdom is swept away 300 years after Solomon. The two books of Kings are the depressing tale of collapse, as God sends many prophets to warn the Israelites. The people refused to listen then and people do not want to hear the warnings today.

First Kings opens as David, that young shepherd boy who slew Goliath and became king of Israel, lies on his bed an old and weak man. He is covered with clothes, but he remains cold. His aides search the country for a beautiful young maiden to minister to him and keep him warm. They find and bring to him Abishag, most beautiful in the kingdom, a Shunammite. David still had many concubines and at least eight wives, one of which was that seductive bathing beauty Bathsheba whom he had seen bathing on her roof top and took from her husband.

David's two eldest sons were killed in family feuds, and now his next eldest son, Adonijah, was preparing to become king. In chapter one verse eleven, Bathsheba talks with Nathan, that prophet who had told David of his great sins of first taking Uriah's wife and then having him killed. She then goes to David to remind him that God had said that her son Solomon was to be king. David agrees and pronounces Solomon to be king, and that he is to ride on David's mule. In chapter two David gives his partial charge to Solomon.

The charge includes that Solomon is to kill Joab, who had been David's right hand in battle, but who had killed too many, including his son Absalom as he hung by his hair in a tree. He is also to kill Shimei who had turned against David and cursed him. This causes Adonijah, and later Joab, who had led David's armies and now joined Adonijah, to run into the tabernacle and take hold of the horns of the altar. By this they gained a measure of forgiveness and protection from God and David. David then slept with his fathers.

Adonijah promptly came to Bathsheba to have her ask Solomon to give to him the beautiful young Abishag who had warmed and ministered to father David. One of the first acts of Solomon as king was to select Benaiah, a soldier who had become a priest, to be his enforcer. Benaiah promptly killed Adonijah, and Joab and Shimei. These were the first official acts of Solomon and set the stage and pattern for the uncivil civil wars of First and Second Kings.

In chapter three, after first killing his challengers, Solomon made "a marriage alliance with Pharaoh king of Egypt; he took Pharaoh's daughter, and brought her into the city of David." At this time "Solomon loved the Lord, walking in the statutes of David his father; only, he sacrificed and burnt incense at the high places," the holy places of the pagans. Solomon may have loved the Lord, but he not only failed to remove those altars, he sponsored his own services with his own ministers. Moses had said services were to be held only in certain places and conducted only by priests of the Levites. This is still the practice today, with most of our churches following it, with chosen ministers leading the services. However, Solomon did not follow the commandments of God, as he selected his own priests and pagan altars as places of worship and increasingly chose the gods of his wives.

In verse five we are told God "appeared to Solomon in a dream" (or in reality), and told him to, "Ask! What shall I give you?" At verse nine Solomon responds, "Give to your servant an understanding heart to judge your people, that I may discern between good and evil" (right and wrong). This was of the fruit of that tree in the garden of which Adam and Eve were not to eat, but did eat. We have to turn to Second Chronicles chapter one verses seven and ten for a commentary on this. Samuel and Kings are books written from the view of humans. Chronicles are written from the view of God and his priests. There we find two changes from Kings. God may not have appeared in a dream but in actuality. Solomon may not have asked exactly to discern good and evil, but rather for "wisdom and knowledge".

God gave him a wise and discerning mind. He also said, "none like you has been before you and none like you shall arise after you. I give you also... both riches and honor." God then placed a condition on Solomon's rule and life. It is the same condition he had placed on Abraham and David. "If you will walk in my ways, keeping my statutes and my commandments, as your father David walked, then I will lengthen your days." God had made to his people many promises, all with that one basic condition.

In verse sixteen begins that event of Solomon having two women, actually two harlots, come before him for a decision as to which of them was to have custody of a baby. Solomon first suggests that the baby be cut in twain. One of the women consents to that, and the other consents to have the baby go to that other. Solomon gives the baby to the one who would give it over rather than have it cut in two.

In chapter four Solomon sets up his government. In chapter five he begins his extravagant spending and debt as he enlarges his armies and his kingdom. He purposes to build a house for the name of the Lord God, using the materials and workers set aside by David. He cut a very expensive deal with Hiram, king of Tyre, for the cutting and shipping of great cedars, of modern Lebanon. We cannot say that Solomon strengthened his kingdom, because for all of the construction he began to overtax the people and enslave non-Israelites. He raised a levy of 30,000 men in forced labor and sent them in shifts to Lebanon to cut, load and ship timber. He enslaved 70,000 burden-bearers and 80,000 hewers of stone, and put 3,300 officers in charge of them. It had been about 300 years since Moses led the people out of Egypt, during which time the Israelites had been ruled by Joshua, then by Judges and now by kings. We continue to see that 400-year cycle of the Israelites, made up of 200 years climbing from the depths to the top followed by 200 years of collapsing to the pits.

In chapter six Solomon begins twenty years of construction. The temple was part of a larger scheme enclosed within a great court surrounded by three courses of hewn stones and one course of cedar beams. The temple took seven-and-a half years to build. His own palace took thirteen years to build. There was also the palace with the house of Pharaoh's daughter, and a Throne Hall, a Hall of Pillars and the House of the Forest of Lebanon. From Tyre in Lebanon, Solomon paid King Hiram for lumber and hired another Hiram who was a craftsman in metals, for his bronze and gold. There is serious scholarly thought that during this time, about 940 B.C., not having coal or oil, Solomon stripped his lands for timber for his metal furnaces, leaving a much larger desert.

In verse eleven, God again warns Solomon of that condition on his powers. "Concerning this house which you are building, if you will walk in my statutes and obey my ordinances and keep all my commandments and walk in them, then I will establish my word with you." If-then, if-then. Walk. Obey. Keep. All commandments. Commandments as clearly given, not as some person may freely interpret them. Not just some as one picks and chooses. Solomon rebelled against those absolutes, just as people rebel today.

Chapter seven gives some details of the buildings. One impressive detail is the extensive use of gold in the temple, for plating and for plates. A heavy tax was placed on his people. Chapter eight tells of moving the Ark of the Covenant, containing the two tablets of stone which Moses received at Mount Sinai, into the new temple. Beginning at verse twenty-five, God again gives Solomon the conditions. "There shall never fail you a man before me to sit upon the throne of Israel, if only your sons take heed to their way, to walk before me as you have walked before me." God continues to warn Solomon, as to false oaths, sins, draughts and famines. In chapter nine, verse four, God yet again gives Solomon the conditions to the land and the blessing. "If you walk before me...then I will establish the throne...as I promised David,,,(but if not)...then I will cut off Israel from the land which I have given them...and this house will become a heap of ruins."

Not taking heed of these conditions, promptly upon completing the construction, Solomon, as wise as he was, the writer of many Psalms and Proverbs, the builder of an empire, changed from seeds of construction to seeds of destruction. He gave twenty cities in the land of Galilee to King Hiram, no doubt mortgaged for timber. Hiram considered the cities worthless. A friendly relationship was destroyed. Solomon built a navy, a fleet of ships to operate from the Red Sea to the Orient. The Queen of Sheba came bringing great gifts from the area of modern Yemen at the southwest tip of the Arabian Peninsula. No one seems certain where the land of Sheba was, and many think it was in Arabia. Annually Solomon collected gold, the weight of which was 666 talents, an interesting number later to be used by John in Revelation.

Chapter eleven tells us of the collapse of Solomon. He "loved many foreign women: the daughter of Pharaoh, and Moabite, Ammonite, Edomite, Sidonian and Hittite women, from the nations concerning which the Lord had said to the people of Israel, 'You shall not enter into marriage with them, neither shall they with you, for surely they will turn away your heart after their gods.' He had 700 wives, princesses, and 300 concubines; and his wives turned away his heart....Solomon went after Ashtoreth the goddess of the Sidonians, and after Milcom the abomination of the Ammonites." These are the same gods being honored today in many false groups designated as "ultra liberal churches". This heart of hearts which God had filled with wisdom and understanding, was now corrupted and lost. The people of Solomon would suffer through 200 years of collapse and then captivity.

The story of Solomon is but nine chapters long. God himself raised up foreign adversaries to Solomon. He also raised up one within Israel, Jeroboam an Ephraimite. The second half of chapter eleven is a sad picture of God searching for a faithful servant. Rehoboam was the son of Solomon and the natural successor to kingship. However, God spoke through the prophet Ahijah to Jeroboam. Because Solomon had chosen pagan gods, goddesses and wives, God was going to take the kingdom of Israel away, at least ten of the twelve tribes, and give them and it to Jeroboam. Two tribes would remain with Rehoboam. Jeroboam was to rule over all his soul desired and to be king over Israel. God placed the same condition on him as to being king of Israel as had been placed on all of the line since Abraham. "If you heed all that I command you, walk in my ways, and do what is right in my sight...I will be with you and build for you an enduring house, as I built for David, and will give Israel to you." God went outside the line of Abraham and David and promised Israel and its house to Jeroboam. Solomon slept with his fathers. Jeroboam and Rehoboam began the division of the lands and the peoples. Solomon was the wisest man and had been handed the greatest of a wealthy kingdom, but he turned his back on God and the kingdom and wealth was divided.

In chapter twelve we are told that Rehoboam, his son, went north a few miles to Shechem to become king. His advisers told him to become as a servant to the people. Not liking this advice, he called some younger men, who told him to increase the burdens on the people. He made this announcement to the people, and they sent Jeroboam to object. Rehoboam rejected the objection, and Jeroboam and the people sent him packing back south to Jerusalem. The kingdom was divided. Ten tribes of the northern area retained the name Israel, and the tribe of Judah, with that of Benjamin, took the name of Judah, with its capital in Jerusalem under Rehoboam.

The north kept the name of Israel but not the heritage intended for Israel proper, not of the house of David. Solomon had broken all of the conditions. Jeroboam did not want his people going south to Jerusalem to the temple so he built two temples, one in Bethel and one north of the Sea of Galilee in Dan. He appointed his own priests for them. His people were to continue the apostasy of Solomon, of worshipping other gods in other buildings. Over the next 200 years, Israel, the small northern kingdom, would have nineteen kings, every single one of them worse then his predecessor. Many of them would come to power by assassination of the other.

Rehoboam would continue the line and house of David, as ruler of the small southern kingdom Judah. The land, the seed and the blessing would flow through the line of Judah as it began to move away from the Israelite nation. This very small southern kingdom would have twenty kings, only eight of which would be good.

Chapters thirteen through twenty-two are filled with the stories of the first six of the thirty-nine kings of these two little kingdoms. The words on the pages are written in blood polluted with greed. In chapter seventeen God sends Elijah, the first of a series of prophets. He rose in the horrible northern kingdom, Israel. He will be followed by Elisha and both will be written of in Second Kings. During the time of Second Kings will come every prophet of the books of prophets in the Bible except Haggai, Ezekiel and Malachi. From the middle of First Kings to the end of Second Kings is a time of horrors. This is that portion of the Bible, along with most of Judges, from which those known as "ultra liberal churches" are liberated, as they recognize no apostasy or sin.

The last six chapters of First Kings tells of Elijah and his contests with Ahab, king of Israel in the north. Ahab's lifestyle was compounded by his choice of wife, one Jezebel by name and reputation. An evil woman who controlled a fairly evil king for her own purposes. God even sent a "lying spirit" to confound Ahab. Elijah had the 450 prophets of Baal and the 400 prophets of Asherah, who ate at Jezebel's table, meet him at Mount Carmel, near the Mediterranean coast. There they cut and prepared two bulls upon an altar to see whose god/God would cause a fire to come. The pagan prophets called on their god and cut themselves all morning. Nothing. Elijah then told them to douse his sacrifice with water, then more water, then still more water. Elijah called on the true God, and fire came and consumed the sacrifice and the altar. Elijah then had all of those false prophets killed.

For doing this Jezebel took on Elijah directly. He ran. He ran to Mount Sinai, which is believed to be 400 miles to the south, all of the way to the tip of the Sinai peninsula. He hid forty days in a cave on the mountain waiting for a word from God. The Lord passed by and a great and strong wind came, but no word. Then there was an earthquake, but no word. Then there was a fire, but no word. Then there was a light breeze carrying the word of God. Elijah arose to return to destroy Ahab and Jezebel.

And here begins, on the following pages, the book of Psalms, the words of man to God.

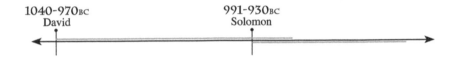
Chapter 11

PSALMS

Pentateuch of Hymns and Prayers; David, Solomon

Truly my soul waits upon God: from him comes my salvation. Psa. 62:1

The Hebrew word for praise, a verbal noun, is *halal*. The plural, praises, is *t'hillim*, which means songs of "praises". If we tack the suffix letter "u" onto *halal*, we get *halalu*, which is the second person plural imperative and means "you will intensively praise." If we then also tack on *jah*, one of the words for God, we get *halal-u-jah*, which commands, "you will intensively praise God." (Is it possible that God at times spoke in a southern accent with "hallal-you ah?") About 250 BC, when the Greeks translated the Hebrew, they used their word for "songs", *psalmoi*. Centuries later the translators into English kept that Greek word, *psalms*, with a silent "p". Another word used frequently in psalms is *selah*, which means "pause and think on that."

The books of Job, Psalms, Proverbs, Ecclesiastes and Song of Songs are termed poetry, or more accurately wisdom literature. A fancy term is "sapiential literature". From the Latin *sapientia*, we get our English word "sapient," which means "wisdom." From the Latin *humus*, for "ground or soil", which was modified to *homo*, "human", we get the Latin phrase *homo sapien*, English for humankind. God took soil and gave it life and wisdom. "God formed man from the dust of the ground." He created "sapiential humus", a wise dirt-ball, the *homo sapien*. What people think is a scientific phrase, is actually a theological phrase. In Greek *homo* means "same".

A quick look at the last psalm shows there are 150 separate psalms in this book. Half are attributed to David, twelve to Asaph and two to Solomon; many are anonymous. Each one speaks of God, but each one is separate and independent from the others. It is true that the Bible is the word of God to man, all of it except for this book of 150 psalms. The psalms are the word of man to God. Psalms give voice to man's sense of dependence upon and need of God. These voices to God have been reduced to the bare essentials of the highest quality. The great preaching in the history of the church has been on the psalms.

In Ecclesiastes, we are told, "To every thing there is a season, and a time to every purpose under the heaven." The Hebrew language will never again reach the level it had in the season of the scriptures. The English language will never again reach the level it had at the season of Shakespeare, King James and Milton. Music will never again reach the level it had at the season of Bach, Mozart and Chopin.

The psalms have a vocabulary of their own, a spiritual language that can no longer be composed or written. The more one reads and studies the more one builds a sense of language, and the language transforms the person. Psalms uses a lot of non-literal language, not all of which is a true metaphor. The floods clap their hands, the hills sing for joy, the mountains shake in the heart of the sea, and the gates lift up their heads. The traditional vocabulary of the psalms cannot be traded off for some lower level and more easily understood vocabulary of the vernacular, the vulgar. We are to rise to the level of the vocabulary of the psalms, of the entire Bible, and not lower the vocabulary to our lowest common denominator. That is not to say that many of our modern translations are not fine and accurate. This includes the New International, a seventh grade vocabulary, and the Good News, a fourth grade vocabulary.

There are about forty key words in the psalms. Listen to some of them. Perish, needy, Lord, man, enemy, swear, curse, God, angels, firmness, faithfulness, disturb, come, go, trust, marry, son, shape, create, covenant, road, flesh and blessing. The Hebrew word for blessing is *b'rakah* which comes from the word for knee, *berek*. We knee flex, genuflect, as we knee-el for a blessing. We see churches named Berachah.

We hear many people say they do not like prayers that are already written by somebody else, that they like spontaneous impromptu prayers from the heart straight to God. What they are saying is that they have torn the book of Psalms out of their Bible. The psalms are not spontaneous prayers out of a stream of consciousness, but rather a controlled thought line. They are the quintessential pre-written prayers. They are not written for a quick one-time read over. No indeed. One must stay with a psalm to get the subtle flow and interrelationship, and allow it to carry you to a higher level. Pray through a psalm. Take each verse and lift it to the Lord in prayer. The Gideons hand out little pocket New Testaments, most of which have added the books of Psalms and of Proverbs, very personal prayers and thoughts.

We hear people proudly say, "There was nothing else we could do, so we prayed." First things last! They say this as though prayer is not doing anything, doing nothing. Prayer is action. Prayer is moving a thought into spoken words, to put the problem, suffering or thanksgiving right out there where one can see it. It is shared, suffering is diminished, and thanksgiving is shared. Any wall of lonely alienation is breached. Regardless of some modern concept of spirituality, prayer must be spoken; otherwise it is only a thought. Speaking out loud crosses the threshold of thought. Martin Luther said, "You have not prayed unless you have asked. You have not asked unless you have spoken. Before God we all are beggars."

The only true way to read or study these psalms is in such wise hear them, read, mark, learn, and inwardly digest them, ruminate on them, chew them, swallow them so they become flesh. These psalms very obviously speak of God, but they also speak of Jesus, the Word made flesh. They are to be internalized, to be memorized. "To every thing there is a season." In our culture, the season of memorization has long passed, and we have moved into the season of having it in a book, on file or on the Internet. One of the early fatalities of this season was this book of Psalms. The first group of psalms to fall by the wayside was those great laments. They fell from the sermons, then from the studies, and others followed in the fall from our culture.

These books are poetry. That confuses you and me, as these do not flow like, "Roses are red; violets are blue. Sugar is sweet, and so are you." There are two reasons for this. First, the Hebrews did not write with meter and rhyme, as would Europeans. They did use stressed words for some sense of rhythm. Second, rather than rhyming, they used parallelism, in three ways, repetition (synonymous), contrast (antithetic) or building (synthetic); repetition as, "I acknowledged my sin to thee, and I did not hide my iniquity;" contrast as, "The Lord knows the way of the righteous, but the way of the wicked will perish;" building as, "I cry aloud to the Lord, and he answers me from his holy hill." Of course, scholars can expand these three into ten or more. It is very difficult to translate this Hebrew meter and thought into English.

Unlike the other books of the Bible this book of Psalms cannot be outlined; however, there are three methods of grouping these separate psalms.

One method of grouping the psalms is by their form or subject and object. Different people use different groupings, from maybe six to maybe sixteen groups. The Anglican/English prayer books have grouped them in this manner since the mid-sixteenth century to the present. It's good to try to keep the groups to five, being Lament, Praise, Thanksgiving, Sovereignty and Penitence. All of these groups are simply prayer, speaking to God.

A second method of grouping is simply to set them out for daily reading to read through all 150 in the course of one thirty-day month, or to set them out according to the seasons of the year. The Anglican/English prayer books have grouped them in this manner since the mid-sixteenth century to the present. We are to pray daily, for six days then come together for Communion.

A third method, that used in the Bible, and in the Anglican prayer books, is a straight numerical sequence from beginning to end. The psalms follow very much the theological concepts of the first five books of the Bible, Genesis, Exodus, Leviticus, Numbers and Deuteronomy. Those are called the *pentateuch*, Latin for "five tools". The book of Psalms is also a *pentateuch*, "five tools". The first tool, or book, Book I, is psalms 1-41; Book II is psalms 42-72; Book III is psalms 73-89; Book IV is psalms 90-106; and Book V is psalms 107-150. Let's look at parts of some of the psalms in these books.

Book I follows the theme of Genesis, the creation, the fall into sin and redemption.

Psalm one speaks of two ways, two roads, for a person to walk. "Blessed is the man who walks not in the counsel of the ungodly, nor stands in the path of sinners." This tells us not even to stand near sinners, but to flee. Verse five says, "The ungodly shall not stand in the judgment." That means those people have already been judged during their lifetime and will not even be allowed to stand and plead in the final courtroom.

Psalm 8 continues to speak of this created man. Verse four says, "What is man that you are mindful of him?" yet "You have made him to have dominion over the works of your hands."

Psalm 15 sets out the character of a person who will abide in the house of God. Using the form of repeated parallel we read, "Lord, who may abide in your tabernacle? Who may dwell in your holy hill?" It then sets out a dozen ways of such a person. Then in Psalm 17:8 "Keep me as the apple of your eye." In Psalm 22: "My God, my God, why have you forsaken me?" In Psalm 23 "The Lord is my shepherd, I shall not want." In Psalm 40:6 "Sacrifice and offering you do not desire."

Book II follows the theme of Exodus, as to the establishment of the nation of Israel, its ruin and redemption of believers by God. In Psalm 51:10 "Create in me a clean heart, O God, and renew a steadfast spirit within me."

Book III follows the theme of Leviticus, and the Tabernacle, Temple and God's holiness. In Psalm 84:10 "I would rather be a doorkeeper in the house of my God than dwell in the tents of wickedness."

Book IV follows the theme of Numbers, the nation Israel and its relationship to its neighbors and God's kingdom. In Psalm 95 "O come, let us sing unto the Lord; let us heartily rejoice in the strength of your salvation." In Psalm 100 "O be joyful in the Lord, all ye lands, and come before his presence with a song." These two are set into the Anglican Morning Prayer service.

Book V follows the theme of Deuteronomy, the law and the word of God. The shortest and the longest psalms come nearly together. Psalm 117 is the shortest chapter, two verses, yet covers all of the basics. Psalm 118 is the center chapter in the Bible, with 594 preceding and 594 following, which total 1,118; with verse 8 of 118 being the center verse and the central message of the Bible. Psalm 119 is the longest chapter in the Bible, with twenty-two sections arranged alphabetically by the Hebrew alphabet. The first eight verses begin with the first letter of the Hebrew alphabet, the next eight begin with the second letter, and this sequence continues to the end of that psalm.

Every verse except three speaks of the statutes, commandments or word of God, including precepts, testimonies, promises and judgments.

Psalm 136 is the Great Hallal, the Great Praise, which is read at the Jewish Passover meal. Every verse ends with the Hebrew phrase *ki lolam chesedo*, meaning "for eternal is his loving-kindness". *Chesed* is translated into English as a different word more than any other. It really has no accurate English equivalent, so we get goodness, favor, loyalty, beauty, mercy, kindness, love and loving-kindness.

Psalm 139 tells us we cannot hide from God. "O Lord, you have searched me and known me....Where can I go from your Spirit?....If I make my bed in hell, behold, you are there....You have formed my inward parts and covered me in my mother's womb."

The final four psalms are simply praise songs.

The enemy lurks in our lives and in the psalms, the enemy of man and of God. The enemy tells us we are alone. We can not ignore the enemy. We must wrestle with him. We never get rid of our doubt completely, nor do we give up our trust in time of trouble. The laments focus on the enemy. They get him out there so we can deal with him. The primary troubles in life and psalms are sickness, conflict and social alienation. The enemy wants us to feel alone in all of these. We need these laments to remind us we are not alone.

The psalms are to be repeatedly prayed through, as they become a part of you. It is not how much you have been through the Bible, but how much the Bible has been through you. In many books set up to read through the Bible in one year, the psalms are repeated on a monthly basis.

And here begins, as follows on the next pages, the book of Proverbs, as attributed to Solomon.

991-930ʙᴄ
Solomon

930ʙᴄ
Kingdom Divided
(Rehoboam/Jeroboam)

931ʙᴄ
Civil Wars

CHAPTER 12

PROVERBS

SOLOMON'S PITHY WISDOM TEACHINGS

The fear of the Lord is the beginning of knowledge, But fools despise wisdom and instruction. 1:7

The Hebrew title of this book is *mashal*, meaning "likeness" or "comparison", but just exactly what is a proverb? What is a verb? We go to Latin where *verbum* means "a word". That prefix *pro-* means "before," "in favor of" or "for". It means something "for a word". It is saying something in "other words". A proverb is a very short parable. A parable is an extended proverb. Both are comparisons to the fact of life at hand. Both are "analogies". Proverbs are not riddles, nor allegories. They are maxims and precepts. They are short, pithy sayings of a truth based on common sense. They are passed down in a culture, or the culture is lost. Do these proverbs pass through you, from your parents to your children?

Knowledge is the accumulation of facts. Wisdom is the proper application of those facts to life. In the Bible, wisdom includes more than the mind. It includes the heart and the spiritual, moral and religious intelligence. Wisdom is more than the speculative or philosophical. It is practical and pragmatic.

When a person wants to begin to study the Bible, many tell them to begin with the Book of Mark, which is short and concise in telling of Jesus. That may be a good start, as would the Book of Genesis. It is my thought that the book with which to begin may be this Book of Proverbs. For most of these proverbs a person does not need a Bible teacher, or to know Hebrew or Greek, or geography. It helps to be at least fifteen years old and have experienced a bit of life. As a person gains a few more years they can continue reading on into the next Book, Ecclesiastes.

Proverbs was written, "To know wisdom and instruction; To perceive the words of understanding; To receive the instruction of wisdom, Justice, judgment, and equity; To give prudence to the simple, To the young man knowledge and discretion. A wise man will hear and increase learning, And a man of understanding will attain wise counsel, To understand a proverb and an enigma, The words of the wise and their riddles." This then concludes by identifying the source of all wisdom. "The fear of the Lord is the beginning of knowledge, But fools despise wisdom and instruction." In Psalm fourteen verse one, David, the father of Solomon, wrote, "The fool has said in his heart, 'There is no God.'"

At the pinnacle of all fools is the atheist, the person who says there is no God. For a person to say there is no God, is to say that he, or she, himself is god, and all-knowing. The person who claims to be an atheist, is claiming to be above and beyond all and everything and to have knowledge of every nook and cranny and to verify that there is no God.

In her book, *What the Bible Is All About*, Henrietta Mears, writes, "In Psalms we find the Christian on his knees. In Proverbs we find the Christian on his feet. The Psalms are for the Christian's devotions. The Proverbs are for the Christian's walk. The Psalms are for the closet of prayer. The Proverbs are for the business place, home, and playground." She also writes that "Wisdom in Proverbs is piety. Wisdom in Ecclesiastes is prudence and sagacity."

Some of these proverbs are but one sentence long. Many are two sentences long. As with the psalms, these two sentences are used in parallels in three ways, repetition (synonymous), contrast (antithetic) or building (synthetic); in repetition as, "Pride goes before destruction, And a haughty spirit before a fall;" in contrast as, "He who walks with wise men will be wise, But the companion of fools will be destroyed;" in building as, "Go from the presence of a foolish man, When you do not perceive in him the lips of knowledge." A few are much longer, as most of the final chapter is one long proverb.

These proverbs may be divided into sections, and different scholars divide them differently. Most agree that chapters one through nine are one group, and speak generally of the value of wisdom. These are directed to young people. Without the rest of the old Hebrew scriptures, especially Job and Ecclesiates, and Jesus of the new Christian scriptures, these early chapters could lead to purely human wisdomism and to nature worship Chapters ten through about twenty-one are the core of the book, the proverbs of Solomon. These are directed to all people of all ages. Chapters twenty-two through thirty are sayings of Solomon and wise sages. The final chapter is of the perfect wife, and does not at all describe a mistreated, abused woman nor one treated as a piece of property, which many like to think the Bible teaches. Scoffers would say most of these proverbs can be found in many cultures of the world. That is true. Men and women are and have been the same in all cultures and societies. Abraham came from the area of Babylon in modern Iraq and took his sons to Egypt. They later lived amidst the Syrians, Arabians, and Canannites. The call here is to the one true God.

Proverbs, and the other wisdom books of the Bible, were spoken long before they were written. They were reduced to writing probably around 950 B.C., some 450 years before Confucius of China and Buddha of India wrote being about 500 B.C. The seven wise men of Greece, including Socrates, Plato and Aristotle wrote about 450 B.C. The very definition of a wise person is that they seek instruction and follow it. The wise sages through the ages have learned from other wise sages, and passed it on. Only the "fool" and the "scorner" would think it wise to try to belittle the Proverbs, or other stories of the Bible, by saying the stories are also told by other peoples. The call in the Bible is to the one true God.

Dick Woodward, in his book *Old Testament Handbook*, sets out a schematic flow of these proverbs. "The Book of Proverbs is written for and addressed to young men. As these young men are given advice in the Book of Proverbs, some see a pattern that forms an outline for the book. As they see it, the young men are given counsel as they live with their parents, as they relate to their play or peer group, and then as they go out into the world. Young men are warned about seductive women and all the world's temptations. As young men settle down and marry, they are given marriage and family counseling. Since they are becoming breadwinners and businessmen by this time, there is a lot of counsel pertaining to the marketplace."

The Anglican Books of Common Prayer have the Psalms assigned to be read through each month. The Book of Proverbs has thirty-one chapters, each about one page long, so that one chapter may be read every day of the month. The *One Year Bible*, published by Tyndale House, has a small portion of the Psalms and of Proverbs to be read each day of the year.

As with the Psalms, Proverbs also has several key words. "Hear", "soul", and "spirit" are found about seventy times. There are four classes of people, the "fool", the "simple", the "scorner", and the "wise". The "fool" is dense, sluggish, careless and self-satisfied. The "simple" lacks understanding, will believe anything and everything and is easily led astray. The "scorner" mocks God's wisdom because it is too high for him or her. The "wise" seeks instruction, obeys, flees from sin and brings others to the Lord. There is also a running contrast between Wisdom and Folly, as the two are personified into women calling out for the attention and loyalty of three young men, the fool, the simple and the wise. There is no middle ground in the response to two calls. To reject wisdom is to accept folly. To reject folly is to accept wisdom.

The book begins by telling us that it was written by Solomon, son of David. We are told in the fourth chapter of First Kings that "God gave Solomon wisdom and understanding beyond measure" and that he uttered three thousand proverbs and a thousand and five songs. There are far fewer than 3,000 proverbs here. It then tells us the purpose of this book.

In verse eight the author speaks as a father to a son, as he will several times in this book. That is the reason a young person should begin a serious reading of the Bible at Proverbs. It is wisdom. The old Hebrew scriptures (Old Testament) contain their books of law, of history, of prophecy and of poetry, or more accurately of wisdom. The wisdom and poetry books are Job,

Psalms, Proverbs, Ecclesiates and Song of Songs. From Latin, we get our English word "sapient", which means "wisdom". These books are "sapiential literature". Human beings are *homo sapiens*, or "wise dirt balls".

In many languages nouns have the declensions of masculine, feminine and neuter. English does not have those declensions. The fact that a noun, and its matching verb, must be masculine, feminine or neuter has nothing to do with sex, with male and female, though many fools today try to have it that way with some words in the Bible. In both Hebrew and Greek, the two languages of the Bible, "wisdom" is a feminine word. So also in Greek are the words folly and fool. A great and ancient way to tell a story, a fable, is to give life and personality to animals and things. Both Aesop and Walt Disney are well remembered for that. In Proverbs, neither Wisdom nor Folly is actually a woman.

In chapter one at the twentieth verse we have just such a picturesque story. We are told, "Wisdom calls aloud in the street; She raises her voice in the open squares. She cries out in the chief concourses, At the openings of the gates in the city She speaks her words." In chapter two at verse sixteen we have the first introduction of the competitor of Wisdom. Folly is a seductive, adulteress, a loose woman who also calls out in the streets. Is there not a person beyond the age of fifteen years who has not experienced the competing calls of Wisdom and Folly?

In chapter five we have a comparison of these two. The word adultery is used frequently in the Bible. Rather than learn the meaning of the word, many people and translations avoid it entirely. It is from two Latin words. The "u-l-t" is the same as in our English words alternate, alternative and ulterior. It means "other" or "another". The prefix "a-d" means "toward" or "added". When a person adolesces into an adult, they mature into another person, and become more accountable. The words adult and adultery both refer to adding something other than was originally present. God is a zealous God and does not tolerate the adding of another god. A marriage is one flesh and does not tolerate the adding of a third person, except God.

At the end of the twentieth century, it may be that seventy percent of Americans do not understand nor agree with the writer of chapter five. They would think the writer either never experienced adultery's effects or is a total hypocrite to warn anybody else. Solomon lived in adultery, as did his father David. God did not approve of such actions of either man, nor of their having so many wives or concubines, to the contrary. It violates chapter two of Genesis.

In chapter six at verse six is the advice to look to the ant for an example of how to work. At verse twenty begins warnings against adultery, which continue throughout chapter seven, as the harlot of Folly is contrasted to true Wisdom. This is the contrast and the problem of which President Jimmy Carter said he has lusted in his heart, for which most news media belittled him.

In chapter seven, verse two is that phrase we hear so often, "the apple of the eye". At verse twenty-two we have a description of what happens to one following the call of Folly the seductress. "Immediately he went after her, as an ox goes to the slaughter, as a fool to the correction of the stocks, Till an arrow struck his liver. As a bird hastens to the snare, He did not know it would cost his life."

In chapter eight wisdom is personified, given the form and attributes of a human. This is what is called poetic license, a freedom to make things not as they truly are for the purpose of a story, as mountains that clap hands, gates that lift up their heads and waters that speak. Wisdom says, "The Lord created me in the beginning of his work....before the beginning of the earth."

In chapter nine we are told, "The fear of the Lord is the beginning of wisdom; and the knowledge of the Holy One is understanding." Readers of this book are such people and most likely not as the women described at verse thirteen. "A foolish woman is clamorous; She is simple, and knows nothing."

In chapter ten. "He who has a slack hand becomes poor, But the hand of the diligent makes rich." In chapter eleven, verse twenty-nine, we hear the verse from which was taken the title of book and movie of the Scopes trial as to teaching evolution in the public school, *Inherit the Wind.* "He who troubles his own house will inherit the wind, And the fool will be servant to the wise of heart."

From here to the end of Proverbs is scattered these teachings of the Teacher. "Whoever loves instruction loves knowledge, But he who hates correction is stupid....An excellent wife is the crown of her husband....He who guards his mouth preserves his life, But he who opens wide his lips shall have destruction....He who walks with wise men will be wise, But the companion of fools will be destroyed....He who spares his rod hates his son, But he who loves him disciplines him promptly....Go from the presence of a foolish man, When you do not perceive in him the lips of knowledge....He who is slow to wrath has great understanding, But he who is impulsive exalts folly....He who oppresses the poor reproaches his Maker, But he who honors Him has mercy on the needy....A soft answer turns away wrath, But a harsh word stirs up anger....Pride goes before destruction, And a haughty spirit before a fall....Wealth makes many friends, But the poor is separated from his friend....Most men will proclaim each his own goodness, But who can find a faithful man?....A good name is to be chosen rather than riches, Loving favor rather than silver and gold....Train up a child in the way he should go, And when he is old he will not depart from it."

And here begin, as on the following pages, the stories of Ecclesiastes and also of Song of Songs.

991-930ʙᴄ
Solomon

930ʙᴄ
Kingdom Divided
(Rehoboam/Jeroboam)

931ʙᴄ
Civil Wars

Chapter 13

ECCLESIASTES AND SONG OF SONGS
All life and wisdom end with God;
Human love poetry

That which has been is what will be, That which is done is what will be done, And there is nothing new under the sun. Ecc. 1:9

When a person begins to study the Bible, many people will tell them to begin with the Book of Mark, or Genesis, and that is good advice. It may be that the Book of Proverbs could be the place to begin, as it is short sayings about the marketplace of life, one after another. It is good reading for a person from age fifteen onward. The Book of Ecclesiastes generally requires a few more years of life-experiences, maybe for one from age thirty onward. To fully appreciate Ecclesiastes one needs to have experienced some failures and successes, some benediction and some malediction. Ecclesiastes of the old Hebrew scriptures is easily confused with Ecclesiasticus of the Apocrypha, but they are two separate books in two separate books.

Psalms is man's words to God, many prayers. Proverbs is man's record of wisdom in various aspects and respects of life. Ecclesiastes is man's record, or maybe God's record, of a man's progression to wisdom. In Proverbs an older man speaks to his son, saying, "Listen, my son." In Ecclesiastes an older man speaks to some young man, saying, "O, young man." Every young person needs a teacher, a mentor, a boy a man, a girl a woman. The older should be there teaching, guiding, even as the younger does not yet know they need it. Ecclesiastes is the book of human philosophy. Right here in the Bible we have all of the basic and essential philosophies taught in college.

The book begins by telling us these are the words of the son of David, king of Jerusalem, which son was also a king of Jerusalem. That narrows it down to only Solomon, a man who had everything, including great wisdom. He is called a *koheleth*, which some translations call "teacher" and some "preacher". Either is fine, but this book is more sapiential than sermonic, more teaching than preaching. Most people prefer a teacher.

There are some key words in this book. Wise or wisdom is used 52 times; man is used 47 times; vanity is used 37 times; labor is used 36 times; "under the sun" is used 20 times; and evil is used 22. The phrase "under the sun" means the secular world of man. The opposite of under is over; the opposite of below is above. Man is confined to under and below the sun; God rises over and above the sun. Man's wisdom, even at its highest and best, cannot fathom the plan of God.

Ecclesiastes is the progression of one man's philosophy, his world view. In chapter one he sets the stage. The Hebrew, or Aramaic, word *hebel* means vapor or breath. In 1611 the King James translators chose the English word "vanity". In verse two is that great and brief sentence. "Vanity of vanities! All is vanity." That is a great choice of English. Vanity and vain do not mean something, but rather nothing. Vanity and vain mean emptiness, meaninglessness. Many modern translations use just those words. "Emptiness of emptiness! All is meaninglessness." The third commandment is, "Thou shalt not take the name of the Lord your God in vain." When many people, most people, say, "Our Father who art in heaven, hallowed be thy name," they do so with empty meaninglessness and thereby sin at the very beginning of the Lord's Prayer. These words are also only a vapor a breath across their teeth.

Feel the utter frustration and sense of futility in this older man. "What profit has a man from all his labor?" "One generation passes away, and another generation comes." "The eye is not satisfied with seeing, nor the ear filled with hearing." "That which has been is what will be, that which is done is what will be done, and there is nothing new under the sun."

Nothing new under the sun. How often do we hear a person entirely miss the depth of that phrase. The breath across his teeth will say how there are indeed new things under the sun. We have fire, the wheel, the longbow, iron, locomotives, automobiles, airplanes, calculators and the internet. One's first thought upon hearing that is, "Is this guy putting me on," but if he repeats those things then one recalls Proverb 14:7, "Leave the presence of a fool, for there you do not meet words of knowledge."

Verse eighteen is one not fully grasped until one has felt the company of wisdom. "In much wisdom is much vexation, and he who increases knowledge increases sorrow." There is the heart of Mother Teresa, Abraham Lincoln, Robert E. Lee, the exhausted physician, lawyer or educator suffering with those under his or her care, of Jesus the Christ. Only the cynical fool would say, "Then do not gain wisdom."

In chapter two the teacher begins his progression through philosophies of life. His autobiography is very likely also yours. He begins where most young people begin, in the search for pleasure. He was probably about twenty years old. This is the philosophy of Hedonism, that good is pleasure in some form, seeking pleasure and avoiding pain. In this category we find Epicureanism and much of what may be called Secular Humanism and some of Relativism; Locke, Hobbes, and Dewey. The teacher got off on the wrong foot. We should all read this. The teacher filled his life with mirth, pleasure and laughter; he gratified the flesh with wine and folly. But that was emptiness.

Quickly, in verse four, he changed to begin to build his own little empire. Most of us make that change. He was probably about thirty. This is the philosophy of Naturalism, the Ethics of Power, good is power. In this category we find Psychological Egoism, Social Darwinism, Humanistic Ethics, Fascism and Communism; Machiavelli, Hobbes, Nietzsche, Marx and Dewey. The teacher filled his life with great works, building houses and vineyards, accumulating slaves and herds. Then he discovered all of that was emptiness.

In verse twelve, he changed to consider the relation of wisdom to folly, just as in Proverbs. He was probably about forty. This is the philosophy of Theories of Knowledge, of Materialism, Behaviorism, Skepticism and Group-Mind Theories; Hume, Descartes, Kant, Hegel, Freud and Dewey. The teacher saw that wisdom excels folly, and that the same end comes to both the wise and the fool. "As it happens to the fool, it also happens to me....This is also a vanity." He realized that there is a plan for this world and cosmos that human wisdom cannot fathom.

In verse twenty-four is a verse most unusual to many who think the Christian life is to be one of gloom and flogging and that it is not this life that really counts. Some even think the Jews are not good people because they seem to focus only on this life. "Nothing is better for a man than that he should eat and drink, and that his soul should enjoy good in his labor. This also, I saw, was from the hand of God." A man should eat and drink, not getting drunk, and his soul should enjoy his work. The teacher begins to elevate his thoughts from philosophy to religion.

Until the 1960's we were told in our public schools that we were to begin thinking about our life's vocation. That word "vocation" is derived from the word "vocal", as it was a calling. If it was a calling then who called. God called. So the word had to be changed to "career", which is the same as "carriage" or "car", as our work was but a vehicle to get us someplace. Since it was no longer a calling people began to change careers frequently and the word became "job." Our public schools have changed our lives from vocations to careers to jobs and wonder why greed has replaced devotion. One's soul should enjoy good in his labor.

In chapter three come those verses read at so many funerals. Life, and the Bible, is full of paradox and the balance of opposites. "To everything there is a season, a time for every purpose under heaven: a time to be born, and a time to die." Here the teacher begins his turn. He is now probably fifty years old. He has come to peace with himself. To understand the embryonic peace of the man who wrote these verses is to appreciate more fully the depth of them when heard at a funeral.

At verse ten comes what may be considered the climax, the turning point of this book. "I have seen the God-given task with which the sons of men are to be occupied. He has made everything beautiful in its time. Also he has put eternity in their hearts, except that no one can find out the work that God does from beginning to end. I know that nothing is better for them than to rejoice, and to do good in their lives." The teacher then comes to a full realization of what he spoke earlier so repeats it. "Every man should eat and drink and enjoy the good of all his labor--it is a gift of God." He repeats the thought in verse twenty-two.

At the beginning of chapter four, the teacher is probably fifty-five. He looks around at his world. He "returned and considered all the oppression that is done under the sun: And look! the tears of the oppressed, but they have no comforter." He becomes a true intercessory prayer warrior. Today he would volunteer at the hospital, the jail, the church or meals-on-wheels. He knows every person needs a friend. This is the injustice of the first station of the cross, the way of sorrows of Jesus, his unfair trial. In verse nine he says, "Two are better than one, because they have a good reward for their labor. For if they fall, one will lift up his companion, but woe to him who is alone when he falls."

Through the next four chapters the teacher speaks of many things of this world that seem unfair to us, of wealth lost in a bad venture, of wealth or honor gained when it seems undeserved, of the righteous dying early and the wicked living long. We humans live "under the sun," but we know our God is "above the sun". In chapter six verse three, he states, "If a man...lives many years..., but his soul is not satisfied with goodness..., I say that a stillborn child is better than he." The word used is *nephel*, which means not to be born, a miscarriage, stillbirth, untimely birth or abortion. In the Greek version, the Septuagint, it is *ektroma*, as it is in 1 Cor. 15:8, which means to wound at the time of origin. But the choice for the existing child not to be born is God's, not woman's nor man's.

In chapter eleven at verse nine, he begins to wrap up things for the young man, as he tells him to work while the sun shines, to seize the day, as Robin Williams told his students, *carpe diem*, seize the day. "Rejoice, O young man, in your youth.., but know that for all these God will bring you into judgment." In chapter twelve he cautions him that his youth will one day be gone. There will come time when he will take no great pleasure in his days. Strong men will be bent over and their teeth will cease to grind. Their eyes will grow dim and even shut. They will awake at the sound of a bird. Their hearing will fade as will sexual desire. Remember your Creator in your youth before the silver cord of life snaps.

Ecclesiastes is full of the realities of life. It is a companion to the Book of Job. If read in sequence it is a tremendously uplifting book, as it turns one's eyes to Jesus. Proverbs tells us Jesus is the source of all wisdom. Ecclesiastes tells us Jesus is the end and goal of all wisdom. It is for a person of some maturity as to life. As one finishes this book one longs to hand this teacher the Chrisitan scriptures, the sequel, so he can truly know his end.

****

SONG OF SONGS

If one should be fifteen before grasping Proverbs and thirty before grasping Ecclesiastes, then one should be forty before grasping Song of Songs. But it should be part of marriage counseling. The writer, Solomon, is probably sixty years of age. This book is barely seven pages long. It is said the ancient Jews did not allow a person to read this book until they were eighteen, although it is read in the synagogues during Passover. It is also said that one should not give a sermon on this book until the hair of his head has turned white.

This book is Hebrew poetry. It is a love poem involving a dialogue between a young man and a young woman. It is a sequel to Adam and Eve at creation. The language is Oriental, of the Ancient Near East, and a student needs a Bible dictionary on hand to broaden their vocabulary. You also need a Bible or handbook that tells you whether the words are of the man or the woman. It was canonized and included in the Bible by the Hebrews about 125 B.C., for a reason. That reason is that love between a man and a woman is to be holy and a blessing of God. God is love.

It is sad that our English language has deteriorated steadily from the heights of the days of Shakespeare and Milton and King James. It is sad that, unlike the Greeks, we have only one word for love, and that then means either lust or mush. In the Greek *eros* means sexual love; *philos* means brotherly love; *storge* means familial love; and *agape* means an elevated spiritual love. Of these true love is to desire the ever increasing spiritual growth of another toward God, be that your lover or your enemy. This is a poem of the mixture of erotic love and agape love between a man and a woman.

This poem, this short story, should be read for just what it is, the days of the wedding of this man and this woman. Once you get that story down, then you can allow yourself to draw an analogy from it to the relationship of God to the Hebrews of the old Hebrew scriptures and to Jesus and the Church in the new Christian scriptures. First, as you would any book, understand everything in the Bible as the author wrote it. Many do not see this as an allegory as such, but it is analogous to Jesus and his Church.

The first chapter is set on the wedding day. Most of it is the words of the bride. In verse five she apologizes somewhat for being so darkly tanned from having to work in the fields. In verse thirteen comes one of many times the reader needs a handbook. She speaks of her lover being a bag of myrrh that lies between her breasts. Myrrh is an aromatic, a perfume, that women would place in a bag and hang from their neck. In verse fifteen the man tells her that her eyes are as beautiful as doves. Again one needs that handbook to be informed that doves were the symbol of fertility, as he says her eyes are somewhat seductive.

In chapter two she apologizes that she is a "rose of Sharon" and a "lily of the valleys". That is to say that she is but one of the common flowers of the fields. He quickly tells her she is as a flower among thorns. In verse seven she asks her friends, "Do not stir up nor awaken love until it pleases," meaning that love has its season and must not be rushed. Quite the opposite of what television encourages people to do.

Most of chapter two is the bride reminiscing of their courtship days. In verse fifteen she, or her friends, say, "Catch us the foxes, the little foxes that spoil the vines," meaning to get things under control before they blow out of proportion and cause real trouble. The reminiscing continues through most of chapter three. The latter part of chapter three is either the arrival of the groom or the wedding procession. Chapter four is either the time of the proposal and acceptance or the actual wedding ceremony. The words are mostly of the groom. In verse one he tells her that her "hair is like a flock of goats, going down from Mount Gilead." Again your handbook will explain that Gilead was the greatest pasturage and refers to fertility. Time and again he compares the bride to a pomegranate, which has many seeds. The end of chapter four is the consummation of the marriage.

In chapter five the bride relates a troublesome dream, or nightmare, she had about the groom coming to her but she refuses to meet him, and he leaves. She then describes him and what he means to her. Some of the symbolism of the time and place used in the poem is: trees symbolize life and vegetation; winter is the rainy season, which precedes spring with its growth; raisins are of fertility; the soul is the very essence of self. At one time they are together "until the day breathes and the shadows flee," meaning the time of the evening breezes and the sunset.

The poem concludes with words as to the power of love. "Love is strong as death." "Jealousy is cruel as the grave." God is love, agape love.

And here begins, as on the following pages, the book of Second Kings, the story of the beginning of the end of the two small kingdoms, and the leading into captivity.

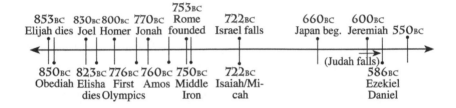

753BC
853BC 830BC 800BC 770BC Rome 722BC 660BC 600BC
Elijah dies Joel Homer Jonah founded Israel falls Japan beg. Jeremiah 550BC

(Judah falls)

850BC 823BC 776BC 760BC 750BC 722BC 586BC
Obediah Elisha First Amos Middle Isaiah/Mi- Ezekiel
        dies Olympics   Iron   cah   Daniel

CHAPTER 14

SECOND KINGS
ELISHA; KINGS-12 ISRAEL, 16 JUDAH; COLLAPSE

Turn from your evil ways, and keep my commandments and my statutes,...
(but) they would not hear...(and) did not believe in the Lord their God.
2 Kgs. 17:13-14

The area of King David's Israel, and of the two divided kingdoms, and of modern times, is about 200 miles long and 50 miles wide. It is about the size of the state of New Jersey and slightly smaller than the western panhandle of Florida. It is about the size of the Shenandoah Valley of Virginia from Winchester to Roanoke, from the West Virginia boundary to the top of the Blue Ridge mountain, where Samaria would be in the vicinity of Harrisonburg and Jerusalem in the vicinity of Staunton, but with both up on the Blue Ridge. With the kingdom divided there was a Northern Kingdom from Winchester to just below Harrisonburg, and a Southern Kingdom from just above Staunton to Roanoke. They were not very large kingdoms. The capitol of the Northern kingdom would be Harrisionburg, Samaria. The capitol of the Southern kingdom would be Staunton, Jerusalem. Thirty miles apart and all true cousins, engaged in a terrible civil war. The North contained ten tribes and kept the name Israel. The South had only two tribes and took the name of the larger, Judah. Each goes at times by any one of three names. The North is also called Israel or Samaria. The South is also called Judah or Jerusalem. Tiny kingdoms.

Throughout scripture, God's promises of the Land and of the Blessing always have one and the same condition attached. It is like a rental, a lease. As long as the rent is paid it is yours. Occasionally the rent can be late and on very rare occasion can even be forgiven. Through Moses God told his people, "You shall have no other gods before me. You shall not make for yourself any graven image. You shall not take the name of the Lord your God in vain. You shall remember the sabbath day, to keep it holy." This subjection to God is the one condition, the rent, on the promises of the Land and the Blessing. God clearly conditioned his covenant to Adam, Noah, Abraham, David and Solomon, If...then. If...then. If...then. He now repeats it again and again to these kings. Since about 1900 A.D., this condition to the ancient Israelites has been increasingly ignored in all too many of our pulpits.

Second Kings begins where First Kings left off, the end of Ahaziah's reign. In agonizing detail it narrates the disastrous events of the divided kingdom until Israel's fall, and Judah's captivity. The story began with Solomon in First Kings full of hope and promise; it ended with Second Kings as the skeletal remains of a nation. The God who had led them out of Egypt with awesome power was totally forsaken by the people. The two books combined, which were originally one book, cover a period of about 350 years, as long as the captivity in Egypt. The initial elements of the collapse began in First Kings with the apostasy of Solomon resulting in the division of the kingdom. We are taught in Second Kings that once a nation abandons its heritage it loses the ability to discern the difference between right and wrong. The final result of forsaking God and continued sins is always total collapse.

During the years of the divided kingdoms there were thirty-nine kings, nineteen in Israel and twenty in Judah. All of the twenty kings of the north, of Israel, were bad men. The phrase used for every one is, "He did what was evil in the eyes of the Lord." The same phrase was used for twelve of the twenty kings of the south, of Judah. Only eight kings, all of the south were good; they "did right in the eyes of the Lord." The north lasted 208 years, and the south 344 years.

First Kings ended with the gruesome death of evil Ahab, king of the north, of Israel. His evil wife, Jezebel, survived him and continues into nine chapters of Second Kings, as her son Ahaziah, and then her other descendants, reign. The prophet Elijah, who hid from Jezebel in a cave on Mount Sinai, and there heard the still small voice of God in a whisper of wind, also continues here. With Nathan, Elijah is the first of the prophets. He is the one who was to come at the time of Jesus, the one who John the Baptist was thought to be and the one who appeared with Moses on the mountain (Tabor) at the Transfiguration of Jesus the Christ.

King Ahaziah falls and lies sick to death. He sends out fifty men to bring in Elijah. God sends a fire to consume them. Ahaziah sends fifty more, and God sends another fire. Ahaziah sends fifty more. The leader of these fifty is respectful of Elijah, so Elijah goes back with them. He confirms that Ahaziah will die because he and his people worshipped other gods.

At this time Elijah had prophesied against the kings and people of the north for about seventy-five years. He had picked his successor, Elisha. In chapter two we are told that God was about to take Elijah up to heaven in a whirlwind. Three times he tells Elisha to tarry behind, and each time Elisha refuses to be put off. Elijah, who had miraculously caused a widow's food to multiply and had raised her son from the dead, now takes off his garment, his mantle, rolls it up and strikes the water of the River Jordan. The water parts and the two cross on dry ground.

Elisha asks for a double portion of the spirit of Elijah, to which Elijah agrees. Then comes "a chariot of fire, and horses of fire separated the two of them. And Elijah went up by a whirlwind into heaven." In church talk this is called the "translation" of Elijah, as he was carried over. Elisha rent his own garments and picks up the mantle of Elijah that had fallen, and strikes the river water, and it parts. The mantle, the torch, is passed. Elisha promptly performs one of his ten miracles. The city of Jericho is at an area of spring water, and oasis. Their water has gone bad and the land unfruitful. Elisha calls for a new bowl with salt in it. He throws this into the spring and the water becomes wholesome again.

About 100 years before this time, Jeroboam, the first king of the north, Israel, to keep his people from going south to Jerusalem to worship, had built two calves of gold and placed one in a temple in Dan, north of the Sea of Galilee and one in a temple in Bethel, about fifteen miles north of Jerusalem. He had appointed his own priests for these and other houses of worship. These two houses and others remained active throughout all of the days of the north, of Israel, and were known as "the sin of Jeroboam the son of Nebat, which he made Israel to sin, the golden calves that were in Bethel and in Dan." Bethel, meaning "house of God," was an evil place.

Elisha hikes from Jericho up the mountain to this Bethel, where some small boys come out and jeer him. Elisha curses them in the name of the Lord. Immediately two she-bears come out of the woods and tear forty-two of the boys. Scripture does not say Elisha directly causes this. The point is that God does not delight in people of any age, especially ones living in evil, being disrespectful of his messenger.

There are so many names in Kings, especially Second Kings, that one needs a chart to keep track of them. Many, usually the worst, have names beginning with "J-e-h-o," which means "Jehovah", and some change their names or take nicknames. Also, at the beginning of chapter three, Jehoram, the new king of the South, of Judah, marries Athaliah, a daughter of Jezebel of the North. Needless to say, this king and his son, Ahaziah, who succeeded him and who was named after his uncle, a bad king of the North, were both among the evil kings of the South. Then Athaliah, that daughter of Jezebel, became queen of the South. Jezebel and her gods severely infected and effected Judah in the South.

In chapter four Elisha performs two miracles for two women. A widow does not have enough provisions for herself and son. Elisha causes oil, not the black kind but olive, to flow unceasingly until she has ample funds from selling it. He also goes to the town of Shunem, where a wealthy Shunamite woman lives. She and her husband build and furnish a room for him as he visits. He tells her she will have a son, which she does. When the boy is big enough, he was working in the field with his father when his head begins to hurt. His mother sends for Elisha who comes to find the boy dead. Just as Elijah had done years before, Elisha now spreads out on this boy and his life returns.

Elisha then purifies a poisonous stew and multiplies the food of the prophets. The reputation of Elisha spreads all of the way north into Syria where Naaman, the chief commander of the army, suffers from leprosy. Naaman sends a messenger bearing silver and gold and festal garments to Elisha. Elisha accepts the messenger but not the gifts. Naaman then comes to Elisha who tells him to go wash in the River Jordan seven times. Naaman is furious at such impudent triviality. One of his servants convinces him to try it. He does and is cured. As Naaman leaves with the gifts, one of Elisha's prophets follows after him and tells him Elisha does want some of the silver and garments. He keeps these for himself, and when Elisha learns of it he curses the man with the leprosy from Naaman.

In chapter six another curious event occurs. Elisha told many of his prophets to go to the Jordan and cut a tree to bring it back to build a larger dwelling. As a man was cutting, the iron head of his borrowed axe flew off and into the river, where it naturally sank. Elisha was told where the iron axe head had sunk. He cut a stick and threw it on the spot. The iron axe head floats to the surface and is retrieved. God and his prophets are concerned with great events of kings and with small events of the people.

The king of Syria, also known as Aram, warred against Israel. First he surrounds the town where Elisha is. Elisha's servant advises him of the chariots surrounding them. Elisha prays that the servant have better eyesight. Then the servant reports that the mountain is filled with friendly chariots of fire. Elisha prays again, and the Syrian army is stricken with blindness. The blinded army is herded into Samaria and taken captive. These two tiny kingdoms regularly war between themselves and with those nations on their perimeters.

In chapter eight we are told that while Jezebel still lived in the North, her daughter Athaliah, who had married the king of Judah to the south, eventually becomes ruling queen of Judah. Her son the king had been shot by the king of the North. All relatives. To protect her throne she kills all of her grandchildren, except one who was hidden away. Most of these remaining rulers also suffer brutal deaths.

Jehu, the evil king of the North decides it is time to be rid of the evil Jezebel. As he approaches she fixes herself up to intimidate him. She paints her eyes and adorns her head and sits at the window. She calls him a murderer. He calls for her aides to rise up against her. They do and throw her down from the window, where her blood splatters and the horses stomp her. Jehu takes a short break. When he goes to check on her body there is nothing left except her skull, feet and hands. Her end is as Elijah had predicted about twenty years previously. This happened on that small farmland of Naboth, whom she had had assassinated to steal.

Jehu, king of Israel, continues his bloody rule. He then kills all seventy sons of Ahab the former king and husband of Jezebel. He invades Judah to the south, capturing his relative queen Athaliah, who had killed her grandchildren, and killing her and forty-two other relatives. He then returns north to Samaria and kills anybody who had anything to do with Ahab. He tricks all of the prophets, priests and worshippers of Baal to enter a pagan house of worship, where he has them all killed.

Some may think Jehu was doing the work of God in eliminating all of these people; but God had not directed him to do any of this killing. The fact was that there was nothing in the kingdom of Israel that was not evil, so whoever he killed was evil. That phrase regularly used of the kings of Israel is used of Jehu. He did not turn from "the sin of Jeroboam the son of Nebat, which he made Israel to sin, the golden calves that were in Bethel and in Dan."

Around the time of chapters thirteen and fourteen several events occurred. About 800 B.C. the prophet Elisha died at the time most think Homer was writing his Greek epics *The Iliad* and *The Odyssey*. In 776 B.C. the first Olympic Games were held in Olympia on the Peloponnesian island at the southern end of Greece. Around 770 B.C. the prophets Amos, Hosea and Jonah were prophesying and Isaiah was born. The traditional date of the founding of Rome by Romulus is 753 B.C.

The northern kingdom of ten tribes with its capitol at Samaria and its name of Israel was evil and apostate from its very beginning. Solomon had actually set the process of foreign gods in place. In this small kingdom arose the prophets of the Bible. First came Elijah then Elisha. The people did not listen. Then came Micaiah and Jehu. All of these are known to us only in the books of Kings. However, also at this time, the second half of the book of Second Kings comes all of the prophets of those books in our Bible except the last two, Zechariah and Malachi. Here come Obadiah, Joel, Jonah, Amos, Hosea, Micah, Isaiah, Nahum, Qephaniah, Jeremiah, Habakkuk, Daniel and Ezekiel. About twenty-eight percent of our Bible took place during a 150-year period around 675 B.C., that period of the final collapse of the two kingdoms, during which most of these prophets lived in the southern kingdom and warned of falling away.

The thirty-nine books of the old Hebrew scriptures are not in true chronological order. The first seventeen books, from Genesis through Esther are the history books grouped together. Then come the five books of wisdom and poetry grouped together, Job, Psalms, Proverbs, Ecclesiates and Song of Songs. Job belongs between Genesis and Exodus as Job lived at the time of Abraham. The other four belong between First and Second Kings as they are of David and mostly Solomon. Then come the seventeen books of the prophets. These are terribly out of chronological and historical order, which can cause a lot of confusion. They are grouped largely by the number of pages in them. Unless the reader constantly keeps a timeline on the table, confusion usually sets in.

The books and stories of the prophets were absolutely critical to the rulers and people of their day. They were ignored by all but a very few. Those books and stories of those prophets are absolutely critical to the rulers and people of this and every day. They are ignored by all but a very few. It seems the pulpits and people of those churches called "liberal" are liberated from these books, and rarely preach, teach and learn of them, except for some nice phrases here and there, and only the churches deemed ignorant, backward and fundamental study these fundamentals.

Israel, the northern ten tribes, hastens to its destruction and captivity. Egypt and then Assyria make Israel a vassal state, subject to pay tribute to them. Tiglath-pileser, king of Assyria, carries people of the northern part of the northern kingdom away in captivity. Prophets warn, Amos and Hosea in Israel and Micah and Isaiah in Judah. Ahaz, king of Judah, even takes silver and gold from the temple built by Solomon to buy off the king of Assyria, and then returns to restructure the temple altar to worship the gods of Assyria. He calls in Assyria to protect him from Israel. The rot comes from within. Samaria of Israel is fully invaded by Shalmaneser, king of Assyria, and besieged. In 722 B.C. Israel collapses and the ruling classes are transported to Assyria and Assyrians sent into Samaria. For the next 136 years, tiny Judah remains alone.

Hezekiah becomes king of Judah, and does his very best to follow the commandments of God, but the people drift. His prophet is Isaiah, who tells Hezekiah that his kingdom will be reduced to a remnant. The new king of Assyria, Sennacherib, threatens Jerusalem but returns to continue building his beloved Nineveh, the same city to which God had sent Jonah about seventy-five years earlier.

Hezekiah becomes sick to death, and calls in Isaiah, who tells him he will in fact die, causing him to weep. Isaiah walks out. God tells him to return and tell Hezekiah he will live yet longer. Hezekiah asks Isaiah for a sign, that the shadow of the sun turn backward ten degrees. It happens. That delay, combined with the time the sun stood still for Joshua makes the complete lost day discovered during modern calculations for space travel and millenniums.

Following the death of Hezekiah, who did his best, comes to the throne Manasseh. He rules Judah fifty-five years during which he rebuilds the pagan shrines and even sacrifices his own son. The sacrifice of children may very well be where our society is today with rampant abortion by choice. His actions were about the final apostasy for God. The rent on the land promised was not being paid and was beyond collection. Eviction was eminent.

In chapter twenty-two we are told Josiah becomes king of Judah. He is the best of all of the kings and "did right in the eyes of the Lord." He marries the daughter of Jeremiah the prophet. His faithful priest discovers the books of Moses, lost for centuries in the temple. Josiah finds the people had not observed the Passover since the days of the Judges, over 500 years before. All the good that Josiah does will not turn God from his wrath solidified by Manasseh. Josiah is killed in battle with the Pharaoh of Egypt, as he leads his army northward to world war with expanding Assyria, where Egypt will be defeated at Carchemish in 605 B.C. by Nebuchadnezzar. See page 115, Ninth Omission. The fall of Judah, the small southern kingdom, is but twenty-three years away.

Four more kings of Judah will come, sons of Josiah, grandsons of Jeremiah the prophet. However, with them come Nebuchadnezzar, king of Babylon, who had taken young Daniel captive. First he takes captives and all of the remaining treasures of the house of the Lord and of the king. Then he comes again and besieges Jerusalem for eighteen months. It collapses. He cleans out the temple and all valuables, burns the temple of Solomon and tears down all of the walls. The eviction, destruction, captivity and exile is complete, just as Solomon had warned in 1 Kgs. 9:8.

And here begin, as follows on the next pages, First and Second Chronicles, or as the Greek Bible of Jesus' day called them, "Things Omitted," a view of this history of the judges and kings from God's eyes.

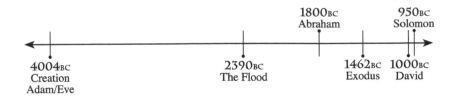

1800BC
Abraham

950BC
Solomon

4004BC
Creation
Adam/Eve

2390BC
The Flood

1462BC
Exodus

1000BC
David

CHAPTER 15

FIRST AND SECOND CHRONICLES

THINGS OMITTED; GENEALOGIES AND HISTORIES

If you keep all my commandments and walk in them, then I will establish my word with you; but if you turn away...and go and serve other gods...then I will uproot you from my land which I have given you and cast you out of my sight. 2 Chr. 7:17-20

The first nine chapters of First Chronicles is a recitation and listing of the genealogy of the line of David beginning with Adam. Names of parents and children are itemized to include Noah, Abraham, Isaac, Jacob, the twelve sons of Israel, David, Solomon, and his warring sons up to the collapse and captivity. A series of "begats", very boring except for roots. The next fifty-six chapters, twenty of First Chronicles and thirty-six of Second, is essentially a repetition of four books, being the two Samuels and the two Kings. They re-tell a period of about 440 years (1025-586 B.C.), the stories of David, Solomon and the tiny southern kingdom of Judah, with very little mention of the northern kingdom of Israel.

Why this repetition of one period of Hebrew history? The person who chronicled these stories wrote to bring the crushed people of Israel back to God by reminding them of their past. In the communion service of most churches we hear repeated, "Do this in remembrance of me." Remind and remember. News reporters, teachers and most good speakers, work on the adage, "Tell them what you are going to tell them. Then tell them. Then tell them what you told them." In the book of Genesis, a central part of the creation story of chapter one is retold in chapter two. The law of Leviticus is repeated in Deuteronomy. The biographies of Jesus are repeated by Matthew, Mark and Luke. Most repetitions are told from a different perspective, using different words. As with the four gospels, a handbook which blends and harmonizes the six books of Samuels, Kings and Chronicles is very helpful to the reader.

In his second letter to Timothy, Saint Paul tells of his being a pastor and preaching the word. His words to Timothy are used in some ordinations as a charge given at the time the ordinand is handed a Bible. "Be diligent to present yourself approved to God, a worker who does not need to be ashamed, rightly dividing the word of truth." (2:15) To rightly divide the word has several applications, mostly related to time. Various verses of the Bible must be kept in their proper context, as to time and recipients, otherwise a great distortion of the word will occur.

The word must be kept in its proper and orthodox place in human history and time. It is crucial and critical to know, teach and preach that essentially all of the prophets came during the time of Second Kings and Second Chronicles. Elijah arose sixty years after Solomon at the very end of First Kings. However, Elisha and all of the others, except Malachi, spoke and wrote at the time of the apostasy and collapse and exile of the Jews. Placing the word in its proper time will also place it before its proper audience, the people for whom it was meant. It is true that the word is eternal and unchanging, but also that creation had its time, the exodus had its time, the building of the temple had its time and the exile and return had their time. In modern times, "Rightly divide the word of truth," is a phrase and plumbline pressed only in but a few churches, because it does not permit false teachings.

Embedded in the genealogies, in chapter four verse ten, is the Prayer of Jabez. In that one verse he prays for four things: that God would bless him, enlarge his territory, keep his hand with him and keep him from harm. That one verse prayer gave rise to several short books about 1999 A.D.

As to time, these biblical books were written after the Kings, after the exile and probably during the time of the return from exile. They were most likely written by Ezra. The Jewish Bible titles these books "The Words of the Days," and places them at the very end of the scriptures, as they were a recapitulation of events from Adam to the return from captivity. When that Bible was translated into Greek, about 450 B.C., these books were moved forward to Kings and titled, *Paraleipomenon*, "Things Omitted." When Jerome translated the Bible into Latin (Vulgate), about 400 A.D., he gave them the name "Chronicles". All three titles fit. They are Chronicles of The Words of the Days which covered Things Omitted from Kings. Chronicles is also a commentary on the books of Samuels and Kings. Here we will look at things omitted from Kings. Remember, as God cautioned Solomon-- "If you keep all my commandments and walk in them, then I will establish my word with you; but if you turn away...and go and serve other gods...then I will uproot you from my land which I have given you and cast you out of my sight."

The books of Kings were written to record the secular, national and political history as seen from the eyes of the kings as events happened; the palace is central. The books of Chronicles were written to record the spiritual history as seen from the eyes of God's priests while returning from exile; the temple and altar are central. The Chronicles cover a period beyond Kings to the return from exile, about 500 B.C. They continue that regular 400-year cycle, of 200 years building and 200 years collapsing. The 200-year building period of the United States of America may have been 1750 to 1950.

Chronicles are a commentary, a defining of the other four books. For example, as to the death of Saul, at the end of First Samuel, it says that Saul committed suicide by falling upon his own sword, but Second Samuel begins with a messenger telling David that he had slain Saul pursuant to his request. In 1 Chr. 10:4, it is confirmed that Saul indeed did commit suicide upon his sword.

The events of Chronicles, and Kings, may seem extremely ancient and isolated history, but there were things in the world around them. About the time of the middle chapters of Second Kings and Second Chronicles, of the prophets Amos, Hosea, Isaiah and Micah, of the fall of the northern kingdom of Israel, Homer was writing his epics *The Iliad* and *The Odyssey*. About the time of the closing chapters of Second Kings and Second Chronicles, of the prophets Jeremiah, Zephaniah and Habakkuk, of the fall of the southern kingdom of Judah, Zoroaster was teaching his religious philosophies in Persia, and Pythagoras, Buddha and Confucius were but decades over the horizon. The Mayan civilization of the Yucatan Peninsula and Guatemala was in the midst of its pre-classic period.

Chronicles are the books of things omitted, both omitted from Samuels and Kings and also things notably omitted from Chronicles. Students of the Bible give us two sets of things omitted, both with nine items. One set is nine passages, eight found in the latter chapters of Second Chronicles but not in the other four books. We mention only the one from 1 Chr. 22:1-23:5, where we are told that David, forbidden to build the temple, made available all of the materials and workmen. We now look at the other set of nine omissions and corrections, but with the ninth being an omission from both Kings and Chronicles.

First Omission: Chronicles itself omits any mention of the conflicts between David and Ishbosheth or of the rebellions of Amon, Absalom and Adonijah.

Second Omission: The sin of David toward his servant Uriah and his wife Bathsheba is omitted entirely. In 1 Chr. 20, the phrase of 2 Sam. 11:1 is used, as to kings going to war in the spring but that David remained home. However, there is no mention of David's looking upon, sending for and taking Bathsheba. Some think this is omitted because God forgave David and no longer saw the sin. Chronicles also omits mention of the apostasies of Solomon as to altars to many gods. The good news is God's merciful pardon of his people who stumble and fall.

Third Omission: In 1 Chr. 22, we are told that although David was not to build the temple, the house of God, he stored up most of the material and personnel for Solomon to construct the temple.

Fourth Omission: At 2 Sam. 24:1, at the end of David's times, we are told "the anger of the Lord was kindled against David, and he incited David" to do a census of his people. However, in 2 Chr. 21, we are told that Satan, not God, actually incited David to number his people, which caused David to turn his eyes away from the power of God and toward his own power in his servants and armies.

Fifth Omission: An omission from Chronicles is that they speak mostly of the southern kingdom, of Judah, and barely mention the northern kingdom, of Israel. Chronicles essentially ignores the northern kingdom of Israel and speaks primarily of the southern kingdom of Judah, but uses the name Israel for the southern kingdom. We remember from Genesis, that Jacob's name was changed to Israel and the independent tribes of his twelve sons were collectively called Israel. After Solomon the ten tribes of the north kept the name Israel and the two tribes of the south took the name Judah. This distinction is made and kept in Kings, but somewhat lost in Chronicles. During the years of exile and upon return, the Jews collectively again were called Israel. It is important to know that Chronicles was written during the time of the return. The return was to Jerusalem, which was in the former southern kingdom of Judah, but for the Chronicler it was the place and people of Israel. In reading Second Chronicles one must pay heed that Israel can mean the southern kingdom of Judah, as God may consider them as one. Of the nineteen kings of Judah, Chronicles makes no mention of the eight evil kings and focuses on only the five best kings.

Sixth Omission: In 1 Kgs. 3, we are told that "God appeared to Solomon in a dream," but in 2 Chr. 1:7 the three words "in a dream" are omitted. From the view of the priest's of God, the vision was not a dream but a true theophany, an appearance of God.

Seventh Omission: When God appeared to Solomon, he said, "Ask what I shall give you." In 1 Kgs. 3:5 humans say Solomon asked for "an understanding mind to govern thy people, that I may discern between good and evil." These are the same words, *tov* and *rah,* of the fruit forbidden to Adam and Eve. In 2 Chr. 1:10, is a correction, as God heard Solomon ask for "wisdom and knowledge," and not discernment of good and evil.

Eighth Omission: As to God's blessing for David as to the people and the land, we first read this in 2 Sam.7, where there is no condition. However, in David's charge to Solomon in 2 Kgs. 2:3-4, and now in 1 Chr. 22:12-13, David himself adds God's condition, an "if-then." "Only, may the Lord grant you discretion and understanding, that when he gives you charge over Israel you may keep the law of the Lord your God. Then you will prosper if you are careful to observe the statutes and the ordinances which the Lord commanded Moses."

Ninth Omission: Any mention of Carchemish is omitted. At 2 Kgs. 23:28-30 and 2 Chr. 35:20-24, we are told of Josiah, the last actual king (and a good one), of the collapsing kingdom of Judah, riding off with his tiny army to stop the mighty Egyptians from marching northward across the lowlands at the Mediterranean. The Egyptians were headed to Carchemish, a place in northwestern Syria. The rising empire of Babylon had pushed the fading empire of Assyria, which had captured Israel, from Babylon up the Euphrates, out of Nineveh and to this place of Carchemish. King Neco of Egypt was marching to stop Babylon, under the father of Nebuchadnezzar, from replacing Assyria as the world power in the area. Egypt marched right over Josiah and killed him. A world war raged at Carchemish from 609 to 605 B.C. Babylon annihilated Assyria, and Egypt retreated. Babylon was set to move south and take Jerusalem in tiny Judah. Three mighty empires, with conquered northern Israel and southern Judah right in between, defeated Egypt and victorious Babylon, now ruling all of fallen Assyria. The southern kingdom of Judah would be no more.

In 2 Chr. 3, we have a retelling of the building of the temple. We are told that Solomon built the temple upon that threshing floor of Araunah, known here as Ornan, which David had purchased and that it was the same Mount Moriah upon which Abraham had taken Isaac to offer him as a sacrifice. We are told the temple's dimensions and artifacts.

One of the primary artifacts was the "Ark of the Covenant". In English the word "ark" means a vessel for carrying something, and can be of any size. The ark of Noah was a very large vessel, but the Ark of the Covenant was about the size of a large travel trunk. In Hebrew these two arks had separate names. From the days Moses received the stone tablets of covenant on Mount Sinai they were carried in an ark. This ark had three different names: "Ark of the Lord", "Ark of the Covenant" and "Ark of the Testimony". During camp, this ark was protected in the Tabernacle, which simply means a tent, a very large army type. The Tabernacle was also called "Tent of Testimony" and "Tent of Meeting", as Moses met with God there. Solomon's temple replaced the Tabernacle.

The very large threshing floor rock upon which the temple is thought to have been built is the same rock upon which, in 632 A.D., the horse of Mohammed would leave his hoof print as he sprung upward to carry Mohammed to the heavens. In 638 A.D. the armies of Islam captured Jerusalem, and over this rock sacred to Jews, Christians and Muslims, the Muslims built a large dome covered with gold which still stands today, guarded by Muslims as many non-Muslims talk of tearing it down to rebuild a temple, and thereby to precipitate World War III (IV?) thinking it will cause God to send Christ for the Armageddon of the book of Revelation.

In the first verses of First Kings, we are told that upon completion of the temple, Solomon, with all of his wisdom, immediately moved his new wife, Pharaoh's daughter, into her palace next door. He then continued to collect some 700 wives from the surrounding pagans and built altars to their gods. This was the beginning of the collapse, at the height of a burgeoning economy with extremely high taxes, the end began. God had very explicitly cautioned Solomon---"If you keep all my commandments and walk in them, then I will establish my word with you; but if you turn away...and go and serve other gods...then I will uproot you from my land which I have given you and cast you out of my sight."

And here, as we vault over about 500 pages in the Bible, begin the stories of the prophets, beginning with Obadiah, Joel and Jonah.

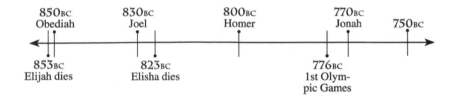

850BC
Obediah

830BC
Joel

800BC
Homer

770BC
Jonah

750BC

853BC
Elijah dies

823BC
Elisha dies

776BC
1st Olym-
pic Games

CHAPTER 16

PROPHETS AND OBADIAH, JOEL, JONAH

DIVINE JUDGMENT AND DIVINE GRACE

Rend your hearts and not your garments; for the day of the Lord is near in the valley of decision. Jol. 2:13; 3:14

****

PROPHETS GENERALLY

As one begins a closer look at the prophets, it is imperative to keep in mind six concepts.

One: Always keep in mind both the theme and the purpose of the Bible. The theme of the Bible is reconciliation, and the purpose of the Bible is revelation, primarily to reveal one unified Godhead and secondarily of the true nature of humans. With the prophets and prophetical statements, always keep in mind the L-S-B, the Land, the Seed and the Blessing, as they move from the nation of Israel, and as the Seed and the Blessing continue to move to the faithful believers, which is for Christians the followers of Christ.

Two: The Bible is history, and specifically the action of God in the history of mankind. We have heard much of that from Genesis through Kings and Chronicles, the historical books.

Three: There are three groups of people opposite the Israelites throughout the old Hebrew scriptures, as God encourages them to establish the nation of Israel, which continually disobeys and falls away. The first group is the Egyptians, with which the prophets are not concerned. They appear mainly in Genesis, Exodus and Second Kings 23-24. The second group is generally the Canaanites, those living in the land the Israelites invaded. The third group is the Assyrians, those off to the northeast, the land from which Abraham had come, the land we today generally call Iraq those God allowed to capture the disobedient people of small Israel and take into captivity, and also the

Babylonians from southern "Iraq", those God later allowed to capture small Judah. The prophets admonished mainly as to syncretism with and toleration of the gods of the Canaanites, which led to destruction by the Assyrians and then the Babylonians. Jonah was a prophet from Israel sent off to speak to the Assyrians.

Four: The books that make up the Bible are not arranged in their chronological order. The thirty-nine Hebrew books that make up the old Hebrew scriptures are grouped together primarily upon their content, being Law, History, Poetry and Prophecy. The seventeen books of the prophets should be re-arranged both according to chronology and then sprinkled across the book of Second Kings, or much confusion as to context and time will result. There are seventeen books of sixteen prophets (two by Jeremiah) in the old Hebrew scriptures. Five books are termed major and twelve minor. The shortest is Obadiah at two pages and the longest is Isaiah at about eighty-two. Following in this chapter are discussed three short books having a combined total of ten pages. Later we will divide Isaiah, Jeremiah and Ezekiel each into two sections, each section covering about forty pages. Don't be concerned if you feel it is too much. For all but the most familiar with these books the prophets indeed are a lot. That they are a lot very well may be the central point here, that there is a powerful lot in these old books, both for then and now.

As stated, the books of the old Hebrew scriptures (Old Testament) are not in chronological sequence, which can, and does, cause some confusion. It is organized, as are our modern libraries, according to subject matter, being four categories of books. The first five books are law (and history); the next twelve are history; then come five poetry or wisdom books; then come the prophets with five major books, by four prophets, and twelve minor books; five, twelve, five, twelve and five. The first seventeen books of the Bible, law and history, are in fairly good sequence, with Chronicles being essentially a re-telling of the books of Samuels and Kings. These end just about in the middle of the Bible, just before the five poetry-wisdom books of Job, Psalms, Proverb, Ecclesiastes and Song of Songs. The ending date of the old Hebrew scriptures is about 430 B.C., about ninety years after the return from exile in Babylon and the attempt at rebuilding a very small temple. The Prophets are very much out of sequence. As with the letters of Paul in the new Christian scriptures, the prophets are organized essentially according to page-length. Isaiah with its eighty-two pages is first, followed by Jeremiah with its seventy-eight pages, with Obadiah near the end.

Five: Very importantly, essentially all of the prophets, except the last two, Zechariah and Malachi, come during that period of roughly 275 years of the book of Second Kings. That includes Isaiah and Jeremiah, and also those prophets in exile in Babylon, being Daniel and Ezekiel and possibly Isaiah's second part. Of course, all of the prophets walk in the footsteps of the first and greatest prophet, Moses, and his five books. Likewise with the other prophets, such as Samuel who anointed Saul and David; and some for whom no book is named such as Nathan who chastised David as to his sin involving Bathsheba, and Elijah who admonished Ahab and his wife Jezebel at the end of First Kings; and Elisha at the beginning of Second Kings.

Some students of the Bible place Obadiah and Joel at the end and not the beginning of Second Kings. This then would have the first three prophets of the northern kingdom, Israel; then eight to the southern kingdom, Judah; then four during the exile. Beginning with Elijah and Elisha the prophets to the northern kingdom began to prophesy about 155 years before its collapse into captivity. Then the prophets to the southern kingdom began to prophesy about 155 years before its collapse into captivity.

There seems to be a general historical cycle for nations of 200 years rising then 200 years collapsing, some shorter and some longer. When the collapse phase begins, the final, total collapse can come very suddenly. These United States may have begun its rise about 1750. It may be that during the 1990's, serious U.S. of A. prophets began to raise their voices against the rise of ancient New Age philosophies and the syncretic mixing and toleration of other gods, as had been the on-going failing of the ancient Israelites.

Six: What and why is a prophet? The word prophet means both one who "tells forth" and one who "fore-tells". One who "tells forth" was of the "seer" category, who was clairvoyant as to existing facts. He either interpreted events or spoke truthfully of things he could not have known personally. One who "foretells" is of the "ecstatic" category, who would move himself into the distant future and speak of events yet to occur. Most people usually think of a prophet as one who "foretells" events yet to occur in the distant future. People who do this speak with a power that is highly distrusted and doubted. At times both types spoke of facts of which they could have no worldly knowledge, during which they were usually in a heightened and altered state of consciousness and awareness, an "altered state."

The biblical prophets were each called by God. There was a pattern to that call. It is a pattern that also exists to some degree in the call of God to all faithful believers, especially to those who go into the clerical ministry. First comes the call. Second comes the identification or awareness that it is of God. Third comes the purpose of the call. Fourth comes the person putting forth a strong resistance, even a denial. Fifth comes the overcoming proofs, the assurances, the signs. Finally the person succumbs and goes about the business of the Father, never fully understanding how it all happened.

There has always been a tension, a stretched out "holding together", between the priest and the prophet. The priest frequently inherits his position, and operates within and as part of the institution, leading the worship services. The prophet does not inherit his office, operates on the margins, and strongly exhorts the people to follow God, avoid sin and protect social justice. The tension between priest and prophet continues today, as we see the priest operating within and protecting the rituals and the prophet exhorting the people to a more pragmatic and practicable worship. An evangelistic sermon is one which calls the people to God, and lightly insinuates it is better to follow the God of the Bible than not to. A prophetic sermon moves the emphasis from the call to the punishment of God, a hell-fire and damnation sermon.

Some of these prophets are difficult to place in an exact time slot. The more conservative students struggle to place them as early as possible, so as to make their prophecies the more remarkable. The more liberal students struggle to place them as late as possible, so as to make their prophesies seem only reflections on historical facts.

****

OBADIAH (855-840 B.C.)

Obadiah means "servant of Yahweh". Some students of the Bible place Obadiah at the beginning of Second Kings and some 200 years later at the end. It makes no real matter as Obadiah speaks mostly of internal conflict. The conflict began back in chapter twenty-seven of Genesis, when Esau, the older of twins, gave over his inheritance to Jacob, the younger twin and continues to the present.

Jacob was renamed Israel, and his people settled on the west side of the River Jordan in the land of the Canaanites, the area later known as Palestine. The people of Esau settled on the east side of the Jordan and became known as the Edomites. Edom means "red", Esau was a "red and hairy" man, and the soil of that land is reddish in color. The fighting between these two brothers has continued through their descendants to modern times. The terrain is also a high plateau with deep ravines gutting down to the Dead Sea. At the time of Moses, the Edomites had not granted the migrating multitudes of Israel's children permission to cross their lands. Obadiah is words from the cousins on the West Bank, the spiritual, to the cousins on the east bank, the worldly and rebellious. Obadiah, of the tiny kingdom of Judah, begins by saying, "Thus says the Lord God concerning Edom."

In verse three he speaks of the Edomites living in the clefts of the rock, dwelling up high, and thinking that nobody can bring them down as their nests are among the stars. This is a reference to people living high up on the cliffs of those deep ravines. The main city was Sela, 800 years later renamed Petra by the Romans. The interesting remains of Petra were rediscovered in 1812 and are now the stop of many tourist buses. Many readers have seen pictures of the city carved in stone, some have been there.

Obadiah says the Edomites will be brought down by God, using those thought to be their friends. In verse ten he explains that this fall will be due to the violence which was both invading them and their standing to cheer as others invaded Jerusalem. Time and again they had looked on, gloating with delight, as Jerusalem was destroyed, time and time again. There will come a time of judgment, "the day of the Lord". That is an expression used by nine of these prophets, and then by Jesus. In verse fifteen he gives us an early version of the Golden Rule. "The day of the Lord upon all nations is near; As you have done, it shall be done to you. Your reprisal shall return upon your own head."

A few decades before the time of Jesus, the Romans pushed aside the collapsing Greek empire, captured Palestine and put an Edomite in charge. His name was Herod, and his descendants ruled during the time of Christ. Shortly afterward the Edomites as a nation, and the people of Petra, the Nabeteans, disappeared, just as Obadiah had prophesied.

****

JOEL (835-796 B.C.)

Joel means "Yahweh is God". He tells us that God will pour out his Spirit upon his sons and daughters in a time of renewal and salvation. Repentance precedes revival, and without repentance there will be no revival. Joel tells of spiritual deliverance. Obadiah, Joel and Jonah may have been the first three of these prophets for whom books are written, relatively early in the collapse phase of the small northern kingdom of Israel.

Joel speaks of national calamity and begins with descriptions of a plague of swarming locusts, and in verse fifteen is his first reference to the "day of the Lord", which phrase is used by nine of the prophets, but most strongly by Joel, then by Amos and Isaiah. The "day of the Lord" is not a day of great merriment but is rather the day of final judgments. Locust will cut, swarm, hop and destroy. Some think this "day of the Lord" will be the 1,000 years of Rev. 20:4, others think it is the Rapture, and others think the Tribulation. Each may be right or wrong.

In chapter two at verse thirteen we have the admonition to return to God as heard in many churches during the period of Lent. "Rend your hearts and not your garments; Return to the Lord, your God, for he is gracious and merciful, slow to anger, and of great kindness and relents from during harm." At verse twenty-eight we have the first prophetic mention of the coming of the Holy Spirit, which for Christians would be the Pentecost of the book of Acts. "I will pour out my Spirit on all flesh...Your old men shall dream dreams, and your young men shall see visions....I will pour out my Spirit in those days." The promises, as to Land, Seed and Blessings are in the early stages of moving.

The names of many kings of Israel and Judah began with the word "Jeho", which means "Jehovah, God". One of these was Jehoshaphat, which means "God judges". In chapter three Joel speaks of a very serious time of judgment and decision of God. In verse one he cautions of "those days", which refers to the time of the end, the judgment of God on the "day of the Lord". In verse two he uses the phrase "valley of Jehoshaphat", which he defines in verse fourteen as "valley of decision". There will come a day of decision and judgment by God as to all things and all humans. That day will be followed by an eternity of blessings.

****

JONAH (785-775 B.C.)

Jonah means "dove", the symbol of peace. The book of Jonah is a small book, only two pages long. Jonah begins by telling us he is the son of Amittai, a famous statesman who is mentioned in 2 Kgs. 14:25. Jewish tradition is that he was the son of Sarepta, the widow whose son Elijah had raised from the dead and that he was a disciple of Elisha. Jonah was born near Nazareth, in the hill-country just west of the Sea of Galilee, which was then in the divided northern kingdom of Israel. However, Jonah was a prophet living in the southern kingdom of Judah. The time was about 776 B.C., the time of the first Olympic Games in ancient Greece.

God called Jonah to, "Arise, go to Nineveh, that great city, and cry out against it; for their wickedness has come up before me." When a call comes from God, it is at first usually strongly resisted. Jonah was no exception. "Jonah arose to flee to Tarshish from the presence of the Lord. He went down to Joppa, and found a ship going to Tarshish." Jonah was a Jew living in the small kingdom of Judah. Nineveh was a great city of the Assyrian empire lying about 300 miles up the Tigris River from Babylon in southern modern Iraq and about 650 miles northeast of Judah. Nineveh was being developed to be the capital of the Assyrian empire. It had a population of over 120,000, was thirty miles by ten miles in size, with five great walls, each wide enough to drive four chariots side-by-side on top, all surrounded by three moats. The Assyrians were beginning seriously to threaten the small Jewish kingdoms of Israel and Judah, and about fifty-five years later would in fact take Israel into captivity. Jonah did not want to save Nineveh or Assyria.

God called little Jonah to travel to Nineveh to lecture the evil empire of Assyria, lecture and save these people "who cannot discern between their right hand and their left--and much livestock." Understandably, Jonah ran down the hills to Joppa on the Mediterranean coast, the very opposite direction, and caught a ship going to Tarshish, a town in Spain still trading in tin since the days of Solomon.

God hurled a storm at that ship. Being in fear the crew began to throw cargo overboard. They drew lots and decided Jonah must go over also. He was tossed into the Mediterranean Sea and sank downward. God "prepared a great fish (not necessarily a whale) to swallow Jonah. And Jonah was in the belly of the fish three days and three nights." All of this in chapter one. In chapter two, while in the belly of the great fish, Jonah reluctantly began to accept his assignment. He remembered the Lord, prayed to him, promised to make sacrifice and to keep his vows, as salvation is from the Lord. "So the Lord spoke to the fish, and it vomited Jonah onto dry land."

A second time God spoke his charge to Jonah to go to Nineveh and preach. We are not told what Jonah was to preach nor what he did in fact preach. Whatever it was, the people of Nineveh believed, and a fast was proclaimed with all putting on sackcloth and sitting in ashes, even the livestock. God saw what they did, and he relented of the evil he said he would do the Ninevites.

With that Jonah fumed and pouted, telling God that he knew and had said God would be gracious and not punish the people if they repented. Jonah went off to the east of the city, erected a small tent and sat watching. God made a large plant grow to shade Jonah, who was pleased. The next morning God had a worm destroy the plant so the sun and hot winds beat upon Jonah, who wanted to die. God chastised Jonah for not having pity on the Ninevites, reminding him of the freedom of God to forgive any who repent. This book is about evangelism to your enemy. It is not about some great fish, mentioned four times. It is not about Jonah, mentioned seventeen times. It is about a forgiving God, mentioned thirty-five times. Unlike Nineveh, neither Israel nor Judah would repent and return to God.

And here begin, as follows on the next pages, the prophecies of Amos, Hosea and Micah.

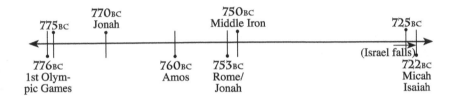

770BC
Jonah
775BC
750BC
Middle Iron
725BC

(Israel falls)

776BC
1st Olym-
pic Games
760BC
Amos
753BC
Rome/
Jonah
722BC
Micah
Isaiah

CHAPTER 17

AMOS, HOSEA AND MICAH
JUDGMENT WILL COME FROM A LOVING GOD

What does the Lord require of you but to do justly, to love mercy, and to walk humbly with your God? Mic. 6:8

The books of Amos, Hosea and Micah, are a combined total of twenty-six pages. Amos and Hosea are the last two prophets to the small nation of Israel as it collapses into captivity. Micah, with Isaiah, is the first to the nation of Judah, as its collapse sits on the distant horizon.

Always keep in mind both the theme and the purpose of the Bible. The theme of the Bible is reconciliation; God the Father's call to and search for lost mankind. The purpose of the Bible is revelation; primarily to reveal one unified Trinitarian Godhead, and secondarily the true nature of humans. Also, always keep in mind the L-S-B, the Land, the Seed and the Blessing, as they change from the nation of Israel to the faithful believers, which for Christians is of and in Christ. The Bible is history. The Bible is the action of God in the history of mankind.

Let's recall four points. One: The thirty-nine Hebrew books that make up the old Hebrew scriptures are not arranged in their exact chronological order. Two: The prophets are arranged in order of page length and are very much out of order. Three: Most importantly, fourteen of the seventeen books of prophets deal with the 275-year period of the book of Second Kings, and the remaining three deal with the period shortly afterward. Four: Prophets both "fore-tell" and "tell-forth" and operate from the margins in a tension with the priests. Moses was certainly the first and greatest prophet.

There are three groups of people one must keep in mind throughout the old Hebrew scriptures. The first group is the Egyptians, those to the southwest, with which the prophets are not concerned. The second group is those living in the land the Hebrews were invading, mostly Canaanites. The third group is the Assyrians, those to the northeast, the land from which Abraham had come, the land we today call Iraq, and the Babylonians of southern "Iraq." The prophets speak of God allowing the Assyrians to defeat the disobedient people of Israel and take them into captivity, and of the Babylonians later doing likewise with Judah.

****

AMOS (760-750 B.C.)

Amos is the first of the prophets of the coming judgment, so let's take a bit more time with him. The name "Amos" means "burden". The first verse of this book of Amos sets the stage, "The words of Amos, who was among the sheepherders of Tekoa." He was a shepherd from a small town about twelve miles south of Jerusalem, on what today we call the West Bank. This was well within the southern kingdom, Judah. About forty years previously, God had directed Jonah, who also lived in Judah, to pack up and go to Nineveh, the new capital of Assyria, to preach. Now God directs Amos to leave Judah and go about forty miles north to the small kingdom of Israel to preach, and he goes.

This first verse continues to set the stage as it names the kings of both kingdoms. This was "in the days of Uzziah king of Judah, and in the days of Jeroboam the son of Joash, king of Israel." With the help of the notes in many Bibles we take a quick look back to Second Kings, chapter fourteen beginning at verse twenty-three, and see a few historical facts. First, we see that both of these two kings were fairly successful in military ventures but neither had removed the false gods of the Canaanites. Second, we see Jonah and his father Amittai mentioned. Jonah was not much older than Amos, maybe thirty years. Just a few years apart, God directed these two prophets not only to prophesy but to leave home and go into the enemy lands to do it. The mighty call of God!

Amos, Hosea, Micah and Isaiah were contemporaries. Amos and Hosea were prophesying in Israel when Micah and Isaiah were much younger men living in Judah. Amos was most certainly an acquaintance of Hosea. Micah and Isaiah most certainly knew the older two. In their opening verses each of the four mention some of the same kings.

Amos begins with the words of the Lord against six neighboring nations and then includes Judah and Israel. As to each of them he says, "For three transgressions, and for four, I will not turn away." The phrase "three, and for four", is an idiomatic expression meaning "too many to be counted". Then the primary sin is named for each nation.

First named is Damascus of Syria, with its primary sin of extreme cruelty in war, that of running threshing machines over their captives. Second named is Gaza of Philistia, with its primary sin of carrying its captives off to Edom to be put into slavery. Third named is Tyre of Phoenicia, with its primary sin of also carrying its captives off to Edom to be put into slavery. Fourth named is Edom, with its primary sin of constantly pursuing its cousins of Israel and Judah with the sword. Fifth named are the Ammonites of the place we today call Jordan, with its primary sin of attacking Gilead just to add land and then ripping open the pregnant women. Does that sound like some of the things of which we read in the 1990's about the Balkans and places in Africa? Sixth named is Moab of modern south Jordan, with its primary sin of desecrating the tomb of the king of Edom.

Seventh named is southern Judah. Amos was born in northern Israel, lived in southern Judah, and was sent back to preach in northern Israel. Naturally, his words against Judah and its capital of Jerusalem were fine in Israel. Judah's primary sin was rejecting the law and the statutes of God, which included syncretism, the mixing of gods. However, then Amos named the eighth nation, Israel, with its capital of Samaria. Its primary sin was total corruption and the selling of honest people for silver and the poor people for a pair of sandals. But Amos does not stop, he adds that the Israelites stand on the heads of the poor, that a father and son go together to the temple of prostitution and all worship at false altars. Both Judah and Israel were momentarily prosperous, the military was strong, each person made his own personal individual bible and everybody marveled. No doubt their stock market was soaring, the singles bars expanded, entertainment once rated triple-X was rated GP, and they celebrated homoeroticism and the devaluation of life as with late-term abortion by choice, which could be deemed by some as child sacrifice for personal gain.

However, in chapter three, through Amos, God told them that none of their strengths would withstand the coming days. Their powerful bow and arrow will not help them, neither will their swift feet or swift horses, and not those of stout heart. The reason is that though they had been chosen and blessed of God they had turned their backs on him, but he will not turn his back on them. Though God is free to turn his back, he will stare right at and through them. He will discipline them. With privileges comes responsibility. With freedom comes accountability.

Amos explains the reasons for the coming judgment, giving seven rhetorical questions as to logical connective relationships. "Can two walk together, unless they are agreed? Will a lion roar in the forest, when he has no prey? Will a young lion cry out of his den, if he has caught nothing? Will a bird fall into a snare on the earth, where there is no trap for it? Will a snare spring up from the earth, if it has caught nothing at all? If a trumpet is blown in a city, will not the people be afraid? If there is calamity in a city, will not the Lord have done it?"

The people were enjoying a time of security and prosperity. Amos says their winter houses and their summer houses and their ivory houses will be destroyed. In the first verse of chapter four he calls them "cows of Bashan". Today we call the area of Bashan the Golan Heights. This was and is a fertile plateau on the east side of the Sea of Galilee in Syria, rich for farming and grazing livestock. The "cows of Bashan" are spoken of frequently in our old Hebrew Scriptures. Amos says they are well-fed people living in the lap of luxury. Of course, in times of prosperity, not everybody participates, some have to scrape along. The wealthy go to the temple but do not worship with their heart. They love to bring their sacrifices every morning and their tithes every three days. It is as in chapter eighteen of Luke where Jesus will tell the rich young ruler, "It is easier for a camel to go through the eye of a needle than for the rich to come into the kingdom of God," because they love their wealth on earth.

Solomon, the wisest person who ever was and ever will be and given a wealthy kingdom, turned his back to God, setting the stage for division and decimation. Now, cautioned by the prophets of God, continuing to worship false gods and, still having some luxurious power, Israel will be decimated, literally reduced by ninety percent and dispersed across the earth. The Land, the Seed and the Blessing are beginning their move, from the nation of Israel to the faithful believers and followers of the Messiah.

An amazing glory is a youth of eighteen with insights to know the Lord, and a deep sadness is a person near eighty who does not. An amazing glory is a person blessed with health and wealth with insights to acknowledge the Lord, and a deep sadness is such a blessed person who does not acknowledge God, and thinks it is all his or her own doing.

In chapter five verse fourteen we are told quite simply, "Seek good and not evil" and "Hate evil, love good." As it is said, "Do good and avoid evil." A society must have the word of God, the Bible, enculturated into the hearts and minds of their youth even to begin to know what good and evil are.

In verse eighteen Amos first uses the phrase "the day of the Lord", which phrase is used by nine of the prophets. It is "the day of judgment" which Joel couples with "the valley of decision". On that day it will be time for the decision of God, not of humans. Amos describes that day. "For what good is the day of the Lord to you? It will be darkness, and not light. It will be as though a man fled from a lion, and a bear met him! Or as though he went into the house, leaned his hand on the wall, and a serpent bit him!" There will be no escape from the valley of decision.

The people are told that God hates and despises their feasts and takes no delight in their solemn assemblies, and asks them to take away the noise of their songs as he will not listen to the melody of their harps. He simply wants them to "let justice run down like water, and righteousness like a mighty stream." They have turned things upside down and inside out, as they think horses run upon rocks and one plows the sea with a team of oxen. They had changed "life, liberty and the pursuit of happiness" to "the pursuit of happiness, liberty and life."

In chapter seven are given three visions. First, it will be as a plague of locusts devouring the land. A swarm of locusts can strip a large fig tree in fifteen minutes. Second, it will be as a devouring fire. Third, God will set his plumb line to measure any deviation and never again overlook their sins. That is to say he will measure them against those ten commandments and his other statutes and hold them strictly accountable to a standard. When God says he will "not pass by them anymore," he means there will be no passing over their sins.

The leaders of the people did exactly what most would do, they told Amos to get away from them, to return to his home in the southern Judah. That is what most do today, even in most of the pulpits. The people do not hear these cautions and admonitions, because they are not spoken from podiums and pulpits today. The people think this is "that God of the Old Testament" and not the loving God of the New Testament. It is the same God with the same ways and commandments. Jesus will quote from Amos.

In chapter eight Amos has a fourth vision, of a basket of summer fruit. The fruit is fully ripe for the picking. It's end has arrived. It will be destroyed either by eating or by rotting. So has the end arrived for Israel. One may say the "apple of his eye" is ripe for the end. This is concluded with a fifth vision, a vision of hope and return. God will again raise up the booth of David and repair its breaches, but not, not until after the decimation, deportation and disappearance of the ten northern tribes, which never had a descendant of David as king. In 135 years this would be followed by the decimation and deportation of the two southern tribes. There will be the "day of the Lord" in the "Valley of Decision". God will not turn his back on the people. He will stare right into the eyes of each and issue his decision. After 200 years, God will give his chosen yet another testing and chance. The land will be so plentiful that it will seem the abundance flows in faster than it can be handled. Yet they will fail again to walk in his ways.

And here begins, about thirty pages forward in most Bibles, the story of Hosea.

****

HOSEA (755-720 B.C.)

Hosea means "to save " or "salvation". It was the name of Joshua before Moses renamed him. It is the name of Jesus, before the Greeks modified it. In the first verse Hosea sets the stage as he names the kings of his time. This was "in the days of Uzziah, Jotham, Ahaz and Hezekiah," and he adds Jeroboam, one king of Israel. With the help of the notes in many Bibles we take a quick look back to Second Kings, chapter fifteen beginning at verse twenty-three, and see a few historical facts. There we read that the collapse of Israel, the north, prophesied by Amos is already now well under way, and its final capture is but thirty years away. Their wealth had been given away to protect them, and the military had been squandered.

Recall that Amos, Hosea, Micah and Isaiah were contemporaries. Shortly after Amos concluded his prophesying in northern Israel, Isaiah, Hosea and then Micah began in southern Judah.

For reasons known only to God and Hosea, and about which we can only conjecture, and that it was an extended metaphor, a parable, of God's choice of the Hebrew nation, God told Hosea, "Go, take yourself a wife of harlotry and children of harlotry, for the land has committed great harlotry by departing from the Lord. So he went and took Gomer...and she conceived and bore him a son." In the Bible only two people are named Gomer, this woman and a man way back in Genesis. There are very few baby girls, or boys, named Gomer any more. Remember that name, Gomer, and thereby remember this prophecy.

In addition to that boy, Gomer also bore a daughter and another son, which we are not told were the children of Hosea, as the plot begins. The first son was named Jezreel, which means "God sows." The names Jezreel and Israel sound something alike, and it may mean that God will sow the people of Israel like seeds across other lands, as Hosea says the end of northern Israel is at hand. The name of the daughter was Lo-Ruhamah, which means "not pitied", because God would longer have pity for the people of Israel. The name of the third child, a boy, was Lo-Ammi, which means "you are not my people", because God was no longer their God. The Land, the Seed and the Blessing are moving, from the nation of Israel to the remnant of faithful believers.

Gomer, the harlot wife of Hosea, left him to be with other men. Just as had Israel to be with other gods. She enjoyed, or so she thought, wine and attention. Hosea had given her everything, she was an adulterous prostitute, and yet he sought after her. He found her as a slave to prostitution and brought her home. God then said he would sow Jezreel for himself and would pity those not pitied and would call as his people those who are not his people. All God asks is that we turn and return, nothing more. The L-S-B will move.

The words adult, adultery, adolescence and idolatry are interesting words all having the same meaning. The "u-l-t" means "another" and appears in words like alternate and ulterior. The prefix "a-d" means "toward" or to "add". Adolescence is the time one becomes another, as a child becomes a man or a woman, an adult. Adultery and adulteration mean to "add another" to a relationship where that other does not belong. That is why the word "adultery" is so often used in the old Hebrew scriptures, as the people add other gods. When a nation eliminates adultery as a societal sin and calls it "choice", "freedom", "rights" or an "affair", that society has encultarated the death of the family and of itself.

In chapter five Hosea places most of the blame for the collapse squarely on the backs of the leaders, especially the priests. In chapters six and seven Hosea gives five metaphors for Israel. Their love is like a morning cloud that goes away quickly. They are like a half-baked cake. They are as those with gray hair who have lost their strength. They are as unstable as a silly dove. They are like a deceitful bow whose arrow is aimless. They have sown the wind and shall reap the whirlwind. "Their glory shall fly away like a bird--no birth, no pregnancy and no conception." They will be "a miscarrying in the womb and dry breasts." The Hebrews spoke in words of the world and the earth.

In the concluding chapters Hosea speaks of a coming restoration, as God had brought them out of Egypt. In chapter thirteen verse fourteen are those words which Paul would later modify slightly as he wrote to the Corinthians and which many Christians hear on Resurrection Sunday and at funerals. "O Death, where are your plagues! O Grave, where is your destruction." "Who is wise? Let him understand these things. Who is prudent? Let him know them." Here end the prophets to Israel. The total collapse and captivity have arrived in the form of the Assyrian army.

And here begins, about thirty pages over in most Bibles, the story of Micah.

****

MICAH (737-690 B.C.)

The name Micah means "who is like Jehovah". The first verse sets the stage as Micah names Jotham, Ahaz and Hezekiah, three kings of Judah. With the help of the notes in most Bibles, we take a quick look back to Second Kings chapter sixteen. Amos had recently concluded prophesying in northern Israel. Micah and Isaiah had begun in southern Judah and would continue in Judah as Israel collapsed into exile, its ten tribes being lost forever to history.

Micah gives three sermons. In chapter four he speaks of the "latter day" of the end times, and in verse three are words reversed by Joel and later to be used by Isaiah, words of the Messianic age. "They shall beat their swords into plowshares, and their spears into pruning hooks. Nation shall not lift up sword against nation. Neither shall they learn war anymore."

In chapter five verse two is that great Messianic prophecy. He prophesies that from Bethlehem "shall come forth to me the one to be ruler in Israel." This was 700 years before the birth of Jesus the Christ, who for most Christians is the Messiah.

In chapter six verse eight is a great summary. God has given them the Ten Commandments and so many simple rules. They still ask, "With what shall I come before the Lord?" To this Micah says simply, "He has shown you, O man, what is good: What does the Lord require of you but to do justly, to love mercy, and to walk humbly with your God."

And here begin, about 300 pages forward in most Bibles, the story and prophesies of Isaiah.

753BC
Rome/
Jonah

722BC
Israel falls

600BC
Jeremiah

550BC

(Judah falls)

750BC
Middle
Iron

722BC
Isaiah/Mi-
cah

586BC
Ezekiel
Daniel

CHAPTER 18

ISAIAH 1-39

SPEECHES OF POLITICAL, SOCIAL AND ETHICAL JUDGMENTS

How you are fallen from heaven, cut down to the ground; For you have said in your heart, "I will exalt my throne above the stars of God;" Yet you shall be brought down to the lowest depths of the Pit. Isa. 14:12-15

The name "Isaiah" means "the salvation of Jehovah", and the word salvation is repeated many times in this book. The prophet Amos was a shepherd called to prophesy. Hosea probably came from the family of a small town merchant. Micah was a peasant. All three were men of the soil, not of the city. Isaiah was quite different from those three. He was a man of the city. He was of aristocratic heritage, and was probably a priest. Thirteen times he is called "the son of Amoz", indicating his father was a man of some prominence. According to Rabbinic tradition, but not in the Bible, Isaiah was the grandson of King Joash and the nephew of King Uzziah. Isaiah was at home working in the temple and was comfortable in the company of the kings.

The first thirty-nine chapters of Isaiah deal with the judgment, condemnation and punishment of the politically and socially elite of southern Judah. Chapters forty through sixty-six deal with the consolation, comfort and redemption of the Jewish people after the judgment and fall and during the exile in Babylon. The book is somewhat like a condensed Bible, with the first part, of thirty-nine chapters, being the old Hebrew scriptures and the latter part, of twenty-seven chapters, being the new Christian scriptures. This change of emphasis, coupled with the fact that the second part deals with prophecies much further into the future, is a natural division of this long book. The division is so natural that some students of the Bible think the second part was written by a different person about 200 years later. Many students call these "First Isaiah" and "Second (Deutero) Isaiah"; and some even refer to the final eleven chapters as "Third (Trito) Isaiah". However, if the writer of that second part could prophesy the coming of the Christ, the Messiah, 500 years later, he could just as easily have done it as to 700 years later. The mark of a liberal scholar is to weaken all prophecy, and the easiest way is to move all prophecy to the latest date conceivable.

As did Amos, Hosea and Micah, Isaiah also begins by naming the kings of his years or prophecy. He names the same kings as did Hosea, and also includes those of Amos and Micah. All four of these prophets were contemporaries. Isaiah begins with, "The vision of Isaiah the son of Amoz, which he saw concerning Judah and Jerusalem in the days of Uzziah, Jotham, Ahaz, and Hezekiah, kings of Judah." For the times of these four kings, we turn back to the books of Second Kings, chapters fifteen through twenty, and Second Chronicles, chapters twenty-six through thirty-two. The period of Isaiah's active prophesying was about seventy years.

We hear a great deal about kings, nations and wars as we read these books, especially Isaiah. Due to the period and length of Isaiah, this is the place to discuss some of this history. Let's take a brief look at what was going on. There was indeed a lot of movement. It was a period of great wars between and defeats of competing kingdoms, as the power of their weapons grew. As we look at these, focus on three kingdoms, Assyria, Babylonia and Persia. They are the ones of these prophets, as the collapse of the very small kingdoms, really princedoms, of Israel, Judah, Edom, Moab, Amorite, and others occur. As we briefly hear of time of history remember that these events cover about 275 years of very active action. One really needs a chart to keep track of these events and people, so do not feel like it is too much or too complicated. Also, remember that God did not want his people to have kings, and allowed them to do so only because humans have free will, freedom to choose. God is pro-choice, with consequences.

About 700 years before the time of Isaiah, Moses had appointed Joshua to lead the people across the River Jordan into the hill country of its West Bank. The iron age was just beginning, and the kingdoms with implements of iron were more powerful, and sea-faring Greek warriors had landed on the coast of Palestine. Eventually God blessed David and Solomon with mastery of iron, and the kingdom expanded, but only as to a small fraction of the size of the empires that would later surround them and crush them. Isaiah began his vocation about the year 745 B.C. This was also the time the larger nations surrounding the small princedoms of Israel and Judah were struggling against each other to build their empires. They would begin a swinging sweeping across this land of Israel, Judah and Palestine, some form of which may be occurring at the beginning of the twenty-first century A.D.

The kingdoms of which we read in the days of Second Kings and most of the canonical prophets, especially Isaiah, are Egypt, Amorite, Hittite, Aramea, Syria, Assyria, Babylonia, Media and Persia. That order is west to east, and except for Egypt, the order in which they were defeated. For some, it is easier to remember them in order of east to west. Persia is now Iran. Media is the western part of Persia/Iran, next to Iraq. Babylonia, with its city of Babylon near modern Baghdad, is southern Iraq and Kuwait, where the Euphrates and Tigris Rivers empty into the Persian Gulf. Assyria is northern Iraq, between the Euphrates and Tigris, the Mesopotamia, into the land of the Kurds and western Syria. Aramea is modern Syria. Amorite is the land of Syria, but by the time of Isaiah it had been greatly reduced as Syria became a nation. Hittite is eastern Turkey. The Kittim sea peoples, early Greeks, occupied most of the coastline of the Mediterranean Sea, and their empire was yet 400 years into the far horizon, with the Romans 750 years over the far horizon.

The time of the prophets was a time of overturning of kings and kingdoms in the ancient mid-east, kings of Israel and Judah and of the surrounding lands. The dominant kingdom of these surrounding groups moved from Turkey eastward down the Euphrates and Tigris into Persia. These were mainly the Hittites, the first to discover the use of iron. However, the Hittites and Amorites were conquered by Syria and then by the aggressively expanding Assyrians, who began the spread of the iron age. It was the time of Amos, Hosea, Micah and Isaiah. Tiglath-pileser III, king of Assyria, would defeat Syria, then capture most of the northern kingdom of Israel, destroying forty-six walled cities and deporting 200,000 Jews. The next king of Assyria, Shalmaneser V, would finish the conquest of Israel and capture Samaria, its capital, and continue the transportation of the ten northern tribes to the land of the Kurds, which exile would be concluded by his successor, Sargon II. Sargon would be followed by Sennacherib, who furthered the conquest into southern Judah, putting a siege around Jerusalem. King Hezekiah of Judah paid tribute of all the silver and gold in the temple and the treasury. Isaiah told him to look to God, who answered Hezekiah's prayer by slaying 185,000 Assyrian soldiers causing them to withdraw. There was a period of 160 years, as four kings of Assyria, Tiglath-pileser, Shalmaneser, Sargon and Sennacherib, pounded Jerusalem of Judah, leaving it to Nebuchadnezzar of Babylon to capture and destroy it.

This was an important time as the Assyrians remove the ten tribes from Israel and move in their own people from Iraq, very much as the Soviet Union would do in Poland and East Germany after World War II. Those are the lost ten tribes of Hebrews, never again heard from. The people of Samaria would no longer be Jews, not even backslidden Jews. They were "Iraqis", and would be disliked for centuries, as Jesus would speak of a rare Good Samaritan.

Isaiah prophesied for about seventy years, during the ever-present threat of the Assyrian and Babylonian armies. That threat would continue another seventy years after the death of Isaiah, until the time of Josiah, king of Judah. In 609 B.C. Babylonia, southern Iraq, would push northward up the Euphrates and Tigris pinching Assyria, northern Iraq, into the area of Carchemish, a city north of Lebanon, where Babylonia, with the help of growing Persia, would defeat Assyria. Egypt had come to the aid of Assyria and a great world war waged between the two armies for five years. Nineveh, capital of

Assyria was taken nearly overnight. The victorious king of Babylonia, one Nebuchadnezzar, already had taken Daniel to Babylon, where the Babylonian prophet Zoroaster was prominent. Nebuchadnezzar would then begin to harass Jerusalem, which would fall in 586 B.C. Many of these Jews would be transported to the area of Baghdad, southern Iraq, as their cousins had been transported to the area of the Kurds, northern Iraq. Two different empires. Two different exiles. Two different locations. One thousand years after Moses' exodus from Egypt the Jews were dispersed, and have so remained for nearly 2,600 years.

Just twenty-four years later, in 555 B.C., 130 years after Isaiah, the power of Nebuchadnezzar's Babylonia would end as Persia and Media arose under King Cyrus, who, in 539, would allow all Jews to return home. Isaiah prophesied as to all of these events. He also prophesied as to the coming of Jesus the Christ. The Greeks were on the near horizon, needing one more century to be ready to rise against the Persians, and the Romans were on the distant horizon needing four more centuries to be ready to rise against the Greeks. Upon the fall of Rome, Turkey arose. Each would in turn engulf Palestine.

As do most of the prophets, Isaiah uses the phrase and thought of Amos, and then of Micah, his two older contemporaries, of the "day of the Lord". There will be a day of God's judgment and decision and righteous punishment for those who disobey. Another phrase and thought used by Amos, and then by Micah, and now by Isaiah, is "remnant", a remnant of faithful believers, of Israel, of Joseph, of God's chosen, will be saved. A remnant, no longer a nation or kingdom. Isaiah's favorite title for God is "Lord of Hosts", which means "Lord of Armies". He uses this phrase sixty-five times. His second favorite title is "the Holy One of Israel," which he uses thirty-five times. "Lord of Hosts" and "the Holy One of Israel". Isaiah holds God in the very highest of esteem and worship.

We now look at this book. The first five chapters of Isaiah are sermons itemizing the sins of both Israel and Judah, which sins were essentially the same and condemned a falling away from God. In chapter one at verse nine, as he speaks of the ingratitude and rebellion of Israel, Isaiah says God has so far left only a "very small remnant" of faithful believers in Judah just before its collapse. This is a very important concept throughout the Bible, from Genesis to Jesus. There was a separation and saving of a group from Sodom and Gomorrah, and there will be a separation and a saving at the time of the "day of the Lord", of the separation of the sheep and the goats of which Jesus will speak in Matthew chapter twenty-five.

In verse eleven, Isaiah follows the comments of Amos and Micah as to worshipping God. "'To what purpose is the multitude of your sacrifices to me?' Says the Lord. 'I have had enough of burnt offerings of rams and the fat of fed cattle. I do not delight in the blood of bulls, or of lambs or goats.'" In verse seventeen, he further follows Amos and Micah in saying, "Cease to do evil; Learn to do good; Seek justice; Rebuke the oppressor." In verse eighteen is the sentence so often quoted by Lyndon B. Johnson when President. "Come now, and let us reason together."

In chapter two, verse four, he repeats a phrase of Micah, which Joel reversed. "They shall beat their swords into plow-shares, and their spears into pruning hooks." He continues Micah, "Nation shall not lift up sword against nation; neither shall they learn war anymore." In chapter three, verse twelve, Isaiah makes a statement which is extremely accurate today in those churches among us liberated from the scriptures. "O my people! Those who lead you cause you to err, and destroy the way of your paths."

Chapter six is important enough to repeat entirely. Many words and phrases of this chapter are in many hymns of the church. "In the year that King Uzziah died, I saw the Lord sitting on a throne, high and lifted up, and the train of his robe filled the temple. Above it stood seraphim; each one had six wings: with two he covered his face, with two he covered his feet, and with two he flew. And one cried to another and said: 'Holy, holy, holy is the Lord of hosts; The whole earth is full of his glory!' And the posts of the door were shaken by the voice of him who cried out, and the house was filled with smoke. So I said: 'Woe is me, for I am undone! Because I am a man of unclean lips, and I dwell in the midst of a people of unclean lips; For my eyes have seen the King, the Lord of Hosts.' Then one of the seraphim flew to me, having in his hand a live coal which he had taken with the tongs from the altar. And he touched my mouth with it, and said: 'Behold, this has touched your lips; Your iniquity is taken away, and your sin purged.' Also I heard the voice of the Lord, saying, 'Whom shall I send, and who will go for Us?' Then I said, 'Here am I! Send me.' And he said, 'Go, and tell this people: "Keep on hearing, but do not understand; Keep on seeing, but do not perceive.' Make the heart of this people dull, and their ears heavy, and shut their eyes; Lest they see with their eyes, and hear with their ears and understand with their heart, and return and be healed." Then I said, 'Lord, how long?' and he answered: 'Until the cities are laid waste and without inhabitant, the houses are without a man, the land is utterly desolate, the Lord has removed men far away, and the forsaken places are many in the midst of the land. But yet a tenth will be in it, and will return and be for consuming, as a terebinth tree or as an oak, whose stump remains when it is cut down. So the holy seed shall be its stump.'" Decimated with only a remnant stump remaining.

"Sitting on a throne, high and lifted up, and the train of his robe filled the temple." "Above it stood seraphim." "The posts of the door were shaken by the voice of him who cried out, and the house was filled with smoke." "I am a man of unclean lips, and I dwell in the midst of people of unclean lips." Those unclean lips were cleansed and purged by the touch of a burning coal from the altar, held in tongs by a seraphim. The voice of the Lord said, "Whom shall I send?" Almost without thinking, Isaiah blurted out, "Here am I! Send me." And God said, "Go." Isaiah thought a moment on that, and said, "Lord, how long?" This is the paradigm of the powerful call by God, of a prophet, and of you and of me.

In chapter seven, we begin to hear of some of these many kings and nations. Ahaz was king of Judah. Weakened Syria and collapsing Israel pressured him to join them against powerful Assyria. Isaiah's first assignment was to go speak to king Ahaz to tell him not to cut a deal with Assyria nor to fear Syria and Israel. Isaiah was to take one of his sons with him, the one named Shear-jashub, which means "a remnant shall return". Ahaz had sacrificed his own son to pagan gods and would now give himself and the treasures of the temple. As a sign, Isaiah prophesies of a young virgin giving birth to one named Immanuel. In chapter eight God names the second son of Isaiah. The name is Maher-shalal-hash-baz, which means the "the spoil speed; the prey hastes". Assyria will conquer Judah.

As Isaiah tells of the coming disasters he begins to speak of consolation and redemption for the people. Hope in faith. In chapter nine, verse six, is that great Messianic prophesy. "For unto us a Child is born, Unto us a Son is given; And the government will be upon His shoulder. And His name will be called Wonderful, Counselor, Mighty God, Everlasting Father, Prince of Peace." In the second part of Isaiah is the Messianic section of Isaiah.

In chapter ten at verse twenty, Isaiah speaks of the "day of the Lord", and three times says a "remnant" will be saved. "In that day the remnant of Israel, and such as have escaped of the house of Jacob, will never again depend on him who defeated them, but will depend on the Lord, the Holy One of Israel, in truth. The remnant will return, the remnant of Jacob, to the Mighty God. For though your people, O Israel, be as the sand of the sea, a remnant of them will return."

At the beginning of chapter eleven we have the prophecy that the Messiah will come from the son of Jesse, meaning David, and the attributes of an ideal king. "There shall come forth a Rod from the stem of Jesse, and a Branch shall grow out of his roots. The Spirit of the Lord shall rest upon Him, the Spirit of wisdom and understanding, the Spirit of counsel and might, the Spirit of knowledge and of the fear of the Lord." The ideal leader will be blessed with seven spirits, which also are mentioned in chapters four and five of the Book of Revelation, and being of the Lord, of Wisdom, Understanding, Counsel, Might, Knowledge and the Fear of the Lord. In verse six, "The wolf also shall dwell with the lamb, the leopard shall lie down with the young goat, the calf and the young lion and the fatling together; and a little child shall lead them."

Chapters thirteen through twenty-three are the "oracles against the nations," of the burdens of judgment on the surrounding nations. First there are judgments against Babylon, Assyria, Philistia, Moab, Egypt, Edom and Phoenicia, followed by sayings of thanksgiving, then judgments against Moab again and Israel and Judah. Chapters twenty-four through twenty-seven prophesy as to the purposes of God's judgment and the future glory for the nation. Chapters twenty-eight through thirty-five are of the woes against the sins of the people and of false hopes.

Chapters thirty-six through thirty-nine, the final four chapters of this first part of Isaiah, are a fairly detailed report of Judah's weakened King Hezekiah successfully negotiating with the envoys of Assyrian King Sennacherib to buy more time for Judah. In chapter thirty-eight we have the event also recorded in Second Kings chapter twenty of God answering Isaiah's cry to move the shadow of the sun backward ten degrees as a sign to King Hezekiah. These envoys gave several reasons why Judah should just capitulate, one of them was that they may be sent by God to destroy Judah as punishment. They withdrew to Nineveh, capital of Assyria, which was then shortly defeated by Nebuchadnezzar of Babylonia, whose envoys told Judah the end was at hand, and captured Judah and its capital of Jerusalem and removed many of its residents into exile near Babylon.

And here continues, as follows on the next pages, the rest of the story and prophecies of Isaiah.

CHAPTER 19

ISAIAH 40-66
WORDS OF COMFORT

"Comfort, yes, comfort my people!" says your God. "Behold, I will do a new thing. Now it shall spring forth; Shall you not know it?" Isa. 40:1; 43:19

We are reminded that the name Isaiah means "the salvation of Jehovah", and the word salvation is repeated many times in this book. Like Moses, and unlike most of the other prophets, Isaiah grew up among the aristocratic leaders of his nation. Isaiah, and Hosea and Micah, lived and spoke about the time that Homer was writing his Greek epics, *The Illiad* and *The Odyssey*.

Thirty-nine and twenty-seven total sixty-six. The Hebrew scriptures, the Old Testament, contain thirty-nine books and makes clear the judgment of God. The first part of Isaiah contains thirty-nine chapters and deals with the judgment, condemnation and punishment of God. The Christian scriptures, the New Testament, contain twenty-seven books and makes clear the saving grace of God. This second part of Isaiah contains twenty-seven chapters and makes clear the consolation, comfort and redemption of God. This change of emphasis coupled with the fact that the second part deals with prophecies much further into the future, is a natural division of this long book.

Isaiah prophesied in Judah for about sixty years, from about 745 to 685 B.C. Early in this long period, but after about twenty-four years of prophecy, he witnessed the loss into captivity of the small northern kingdom of Israel, his home. A man at the exuberant age of twenty, full of fire and vinegar and crying for change, speaks and writes very differently than he will at the age of eighty, consoling his defeated people. However, due to some differences in linguistic style and that Isaiah is not mentioned after chapter thirty-nine, and neglecting the overwhelming similarities, many scholars, since about 1800, have taught their students that this second part was written by an entirely different person about 150 years later. Their students call these "First Isaiah" and "Second (Deutero) Isaiah"; some refer to the final eleven chapters, which deal with the coming glorious kingdom of God, as "Third (Trito) Isaiah". The mark of a liberal scholar is to weaken all of the Bible, especially prophecy. The easiest way to weaken prophecy is to move it to the latest time conceivable, even after the event, so it becomes a reporting of history rather than a prophecy.

For the times of Isaiah, we turn to the Book of Second Kings chapters fifteen through twenty-one, where Isaiah is mentioned twelve times, and to Second Chronicles chapters twenty-six through thirty-two. This second part of Isaiah, no doubt was written after the fall of his Israel in 721 B.C., with the impending fall of Judah on the horizon a century into the future, as in Second Kings chapters eighteen through twenty-one. By the time of chapter forty, Tiglath-pileser III, king of Assyria, had captured most of the northern kingdom of Israel, destroying forty-six walled cities and killing possibly 200,000 Jews and deporting possibly 150,000 to northern Iraq, the land of the Kurds, his successor, Shalmaneser V, had conquered the rest of Israel and its capitol, Samaria, and removed virtually all of the Jews, possibly another 100,000, to the land of the Kurds, which exile would be continued by his successor, Sargon II. These ten tribes were never more heard from. The foreseeable fall of Judah was but a few decades into the future.

About eighty years after Isaiah, around 605 B.C., following four years of world war around Carchemish, Assyria, northern Iraq, would be defeated and conquered by Babylon, southern Iraq, and Nebuchadnezzar would be its new king. Nebuchadnezzar would then march south, harassing Judah and Jerusalem and ordering Daniel, a youth of maybe fifteen years, taken to his court in Babylon. This was the beginning of a period of about 180 years of the rise and fall of empires. It would be the time of prophets Jeremiah, Zephaniah, Habakkuk, Ezekiel and Daniel. Twenty years later, in 586 B.C., Babylon would completely capture and deport the Jews of Judah and Jerusalem. These Jews would be transported to the area of Babylon, near modern Baghdad, as their cousins had been transported to the area of the Kurds. Two different empires. Two different exiles. Two different locations. The Jews would be dispersed, and just twenty-four years later, in 555 B.C., the power of Nebuchadnezzar's Babylon would end as Persia, and then the Medes, arose under King Cyrus, who, in 539 B.C., would allow all Jews to return home. Isaiah prophesied as to all of these events. Christians believe he also prophesied as to the coming of Jesus, the Christ, the Messiah. Scholars liberated from constraints of the Bible teach that Isaiah simply could not have prophesied so many events so far into the future.

In the first part of Isaiah, he spoke of judgment and "the day of the Lord", and also of a "remnant", a remnant of Israel, of Joseph, of God, which will be saved. Now, in this second part, he emphasizes the saving of the "remnant". That is what good parents, good teachers and good counselors do, they use a different approach for different situations. They afflict the comfortable, to push them onward, and comfort the afflicted to pull them onward. Same counselor, same Isaiah, no "deutero", no "trito", just different facts and problems, handled by a man no longer in his youth and well past his maturity.

The prophets spoke to nations, and except for very rare cases not to individuals, and individual kings meant the entire nation. Their message was both for their time and for our time, as the nature and condition of humans is unchanging. They spoke of opposites, of threat and consolation, of judgment and redemption, of punishment and pardon. They asserted the monotheism of one sovereign, transcendent God, the moral standard of that one God from whom sin separates, and the coming of the saving Messiah. Their prophecies are tested two ways: agreement with other biblical teachings and actual fulfillment. There are many prophets in addition to those whose books are canonized in the Bible. They tell us that material prosperity may be granted to a person, but that virtue and holiness are the true rewards. The story of Solomon is of a man who had been given abundant worldly goods but who worshipped false gods and squandered it all.

Chapters forty through forty-three, these first four chapters, deal with the consoling comfort of an imminent God. They begin with those verses copied by Handel into his *Messiah*, sung at the time of Resurrection Sunday, as Isaiah speaks of the person of God. "Comfort, yes, comfort My people!" and includes those verses quoted by John the Baptist, "The voice of one crying in the wilderness: 'Prepare the way of the Lord; make straight in the desert a highway for our God. Every valley shall be exalted and every mountain and hill brought low." The voice said, "Cry out!" And he said, "What shall I cry?" "All flesh is grass, and all its loveliness is like the flower of the field....The grass withers, the flower fades, because the breath of the Lord blows upon it; Surely the people are grass. The grass withers, the flower fades, But the word of our God stands forever....Who has directed the Spirit of the Lord, or as his counselor has taught him? With whom did he take counsel, and who instructed him, and taught him in the path of justice? Who taught him knowledge, and showed him the way of understanding?" There is no response to that question, because the Spirit of God is God and nobody counsels him.

Isaiah continues as to the person of God and with those verses we love to hear. "Have you not known? Have you not heard? The everlasting God, the Lord, the Creator of the ends of the earth, neither faints nor is weary. His understanding is unsearchable. He gives power to the weak, and to those who have no might he increases strength. Even the youths shall faint and be weary, and the young men shall utterly fall, but those who wait on the Lord shall renew their strength; they shall mount up with wings like eagles; they shall run and not be weary; they shall walk and not faint." Here is an interesting reversal. Rather than walk, run, fly, it is fly, run, walk.

In chapter forty-one verses two and twenty-five are the first hints of this king Cyrus of Persia freeing the captive Jews to return to their homeland.

Isaiah probably wrote this prophecy around 690 B.C., being about 100 years before the fall of Judah and about 150 years before Cyrus of Persia granted permission for the Jews, who so desired, to return to Jerusalem. In verses fourteen and fifteen he calls the Jewish people a worm, which he will make into a threshing machine. This metaphor of a "worm" is used frequently in the old Hebrew scriptures, four times by both Job and Isaiah. The worm is found universally around the earth, including in the waters and the garbage heaps, where they devour and recirculate our waste. We consider them among the lowest of all living creatures, but we need them for soil conditioning.

In chapters forty-two and forty-three Isaiah speaks of the pardon of God, of forgiveness. He begins in verse one, with the first mention of the coming of a "servant," which some think could be Israel, others one of the prophets, and others the Messiah, and Christians Jesus the Christ. "Behold! My Servant whom I uphold, my Elect One in whom my soul delights! I have put my Spirit upon him; He will bring forth justice to the Gentiles. He will not cry out, nor raise his voice, nor cause his voice to be heard in the street. A bruised reed he will not break, and smoking flax he will not quench; He will bring forth justice for truth." There are no threats of judgment as in the first part. The people are in defeat and need to be lifted.

In chapters forty-four and forty-five Isaiah speaks of the great promises of God and, in verses nine through twelve, of the emptiness of idols. He begins with a promise that the children of Jacob, of Israel, are still his chosen. "Yet hear now, O Jacob my servant, and Israel whom I have chosen. Thus says the Lord who made you and formed you from the womb, who will help you: 'Fear not, O Jacob my servant; And you, Jeshurun, whom I have chosen.'" Jeshurun means "upright one," as Isaiah calls them by a name to which they will hopefully rise. It is the name used for many modern synagogues. In verse six God says, "I am the first and the last." In Hebrew, I am the *ri'shon* and the *acharon*." In the Greek of Revelation it becomes, "I am the *alpha* and the *omega*." Twice God is spoken of as the one who formed them from the womb. In verse three God will pour water on thirsty land and pour his Spirit on their descendants. The Spirit is always poured, and therein is the reason for pouring at baptism, as a symbol of total immersion in the Spirit, not in water.

In chapter forty-five verse seven is an interesting quote of God. "I form the light and create darkness, I make peace and create calamity; I, the Lord, do all these things." This is to say that God creates everything, that there is no equal, and there is no philosophical dualism as to God. We are given some degree of polar opposites in life, as one defines the other: Light and darkness; Peace and calamity; Blessing and disaster. A broad comprehension of the Ten Commandments, the plumb line rule for good, defines both right and wrong, good and evil. One must become familiar with the scriptures to reconcile these facts, as to "Why Bad Things Happen to Good People."

Chapters forty-six through forty-eight speak of God's power. A remnant, a residue, a portion of Israelites, but not a nation, will be saved from the present destruction. Assyria and Babylon, the empires which God allowed to destroy a disobedient Israel, and Judah, will themselves be humiliated as disaster and ruin befall them. Indeed, history shows that Babylon, which conquered the ancient empire of Assyria, lasted but seventy years. In chapter forty-eight we are reminded that God is the creator and the redeemer.

We then hear another mention of the coming servant, and the bringing home of the children of Zion. God assures his remnant of faithful that he will not forget them. "Can a woman forget her nursing child, and not have compassion on the son of her womb? Surely they may forget, yet I will not forget you. See, I have inscribed you on the palms of my hands." In chapter fifty we are given another brief mention of the coming servant, who will be first humiliated then vindicated.

Beginning at chapter fifty-two verse thirteen and continuing through chapter fifty-three, is the primary section on the coming servant, the suffering servant, one of the greatest and most important sections in the Bible. God's servant will be rejected. "He is despised and rejected by men, a man of sorrows and acquainted with grief." For Christians these are strong inferences the servant will be Jesus the Christ. There is the suffering of Jesus on the cross: "Surely he has borne our griefs and carried our sorrows;...Smitten by God, and afflicted." There is the gospel: "But he was wounded for our transgressions; he was bruised for our iniquities." There is redemption through propitiation: "The chastisement for our peace was upon him, and by his stripes we are healed." "All we like sheep have gone astray; we have turned, every one, to his own way....He was oppressed and he was afflicted, yet he opened not his mouth; He was led as a lamb to the slaughter....He had done no violence, nor was any deceit in his mouth."

Chapters fifty-six through sixty-six are referred to by many scholars as "Third" or "Trito" Isaiah, due again to change of focus and thought of the prophet. Verses six through eight of chapter fifty-six are the first clear mention of the religion of the Hebrew scriptures being a universal and international religion for all peoples, specifically foreigners, Gentiles, *goyim*. "And also the sons of the foreigner who join themselves to the Lord, to serve him, and to love the name of the Lord, to be his servants--Everyone who keeps from defiling the Sabbath, and holds fast my covenant-- Even them I will bring to my holy mountain, and make them joyful in my house of prayer....For my house shall be called a house of prayer for all nations...I will gather to him others besides those who are gathered to him." The sons of the foreigner, everyone who keeps the Sabbath and the commandments, shall be joyful in the temple of God, and others will be gathered. The Land, the Seed and the Blessing move from the nation of Israel to the faithful believers, which for Christians is the followers of Christ.

In the final seven chapters of Isaiah some version of the word "glory" is used twenty-three times. We hear of the coming glory, in the future. In the first verse of chapter sixty-one are the words which will be read by Jesus in the synagogue in Nazareth. "The Spirit of the Lord God is upon me. Because the Lord has anointed me to preach good tidings to the poor; He has sent me to heal the brokenhearted, to proclaim liberty to the captives, and the opening of the prison to those who are bound; to proclaim the acceptable year of the Lord."

Here ends the book of Isaiah and here begin the books of Zephaniah, Nahum and Habakkuk, which immediately follow in time but between which the organizers of our Bible insert ten other books.

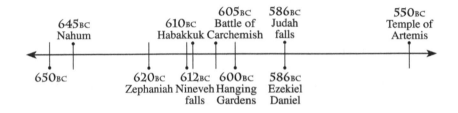

CHAPTER 20

ZEPHANIAH, NAHUM
AND HABAKKUK

JUDGMENT ON NINEVEH AND JUDAH; FAITH

The day of the Lord is at hand; the righteous shall live by faith. Zep 1:7;
Hab 2:4

We will first look at the times of these three prophets, Zephaniah,
Nahum and Habakkuk, then briefly at each of the three. They are three of the
final prophets to the divided kingdoms, just before Jeremiah. The northern
kingdom of Israel had been captured by Assyria and those ten tribes dispersed
roughly eighty years prior. The southern kingdom of Judah was destined to
be captured by Babylon in roughly fifty years. These three prophesied during
these waning years. Understand, this was a time of great tragedy, and these
men spoke heavy and depressing words. There is a glimmer of hope, but only
for a remnant of faithful believers. It is just too late for the Jewish kingdoms.
These prophets make you squirm and exhaust you. Each of these three books
is but five or six pages long.

These three spoke out mostly during the reign of King Josiah, the last
true and decent king of Judah, the one killed by the Egyptians en route north
to Carchemish. The problem was the damage of the final breaches of the
covenant had been so severe that God was determined to bring an end to this
little kingdom of Judah. In the book of Second Kings chapter eighteen, we are
told that King Hezekiah, the first king after the northern kingdom had fallen
to Assyria, furthered his predecessor's sacking and nailing closed the doors of
the Temple as he gave more gold to the Assyrians. Hezekiah was the one who
had called in Isaiah and asked for a sign from God that he would live awhile
longer, and the sign given was that the shadow of the sun moved backward.
Hezekiah was essentially a good ruler who ruled twenty-nine years.

Between Hezekiah and the good Josiah came fifty-five years of rule
by King Manasseh. In Second Kings chapter twenty-one we are told that
Manasseh was very evil. He rebuilt the altars to false gods and burned his
own son as a sacrifice to them. There were probably no prophets speaking

during the time of Manasseh. Due to his actions, God decided to bring the end to Judah and to Jerusalem and cast off the remnant of his heritage into the hands of the enemy. The situation was as bleak as it could get.

Manasseh was followed by King Josiah, the last true king of Judah. Zephaniah, Nahum and Habakkuk prophesied during the reign of Josiah. Jeremiah also began his sixty years of prophecy at this time. Manasseh had been so evil that the time of the end was near at hand, and God would not delay the judgment any longer. Josiah was a good king, but he could not reverse the trend. God had said the people simply had continued to move further and further from him ever since Moses returned them to the land.

The time of Josiah was a time of religious revival, and the religious leader was most certainly the prophet Zephaniah. In Second Kings chapter twenty-two we are told of King Josiah and that he did what was right in the eyes of the Lord. We are also told that the high priest at the time was Hilkiah, the father of the prophet Jeremiah. Hilkiah found a book of the law hidden away in the closed temple. It was certainly the Book of Deuteronomy, but may have been the entire Pentateuch, the first five books of our Bible. It is believed to have been concealed in the cornerstone of the temple, and had been so lost and not followed for decades, for many decades, probably for centuries. When the young King Josiah read this he tore his clothes and ordered a full-scale revival. He had the temple cleansed of false idols and false priests.

The people had lived for so long under evil rulers, especially Manasseh, that the rule of God had been totally forgotten. We are told that the primary Mosaic festival of the Passover, commemorating the Exodus, had not been observed for over 500 years. It could logically be presumed that the other Mosaic festivals had also been ignored, being the Pentecost, to commemorate the giving of the law to Moses on Mount Sinai, and *Yom Kippur*, the day of Atonement for sins.

Josiah strove to bring an end to the worship of Asherah, later to be known in the British Isles as Eoster, the mother-goddess of fertility, love and sex, from which we get the English word "Easter". It is good to pray to God for his grace of fertility, love and sex, but not to weave and wave fabrics for and pray to some idol. Josiah also strove to bring down the houses of the male cult of prostitution. Both of these were condemned in Deuteronomy chapter twenty-three verse seventeen, and other verses. In the late twentieth century, these are the two leading discussions of the liberal churches, as the world takes over those churches. This is what had become of the people of the Exodus, the people of Joshua and David, a collapse begun by Solomon. During a 275-year period they had allowed kings to lead them into total decadence.

We are told in Second Kings 23:29, that in 609 B.C. King Josiah would ride down from the West Bank to try to stop the armies of Egypt from going north to help Assyria in its final battle against Babylon. He would be killed, and Egypt and then Babylon, after defeating Assyria and Egypt at

Carchemish, would put pawns in as the final four kings of Judah. This is a time of tremendous upheaval and turmoil. It is a time of an explosion of prophets. Zephaniah, Nahum and Habakkuk spoke out.

****

ZEPHANIAH (640-621)

Now, let's take a brief look at Zephaniah. Zephaniah means "hidden in Jehovah". In verse one we are told Zephaniah was the great-great grandson of King Hezekiah, the king of Judah about 100 years previously, and that the present king was Josiah.

About 100 years before Zephaniah, Amos, and before that Joel, had spoken of "the day of the Lord". Zephaniah will now use that phrase seven times, and rephrase it twelve more times. In scripture there are essentially two periods of "the day of the Lord". The first was this period of cleansing judgment at the time of the collapse and captivity. The second will be greater and will be at the end times, the second coming of Christ.

Because Zephaniah speaks so strongly of that Day, many believe he passes over the first and imminent Day and speaks of the second coming. This is primarily due to the second and third verses. God said, "I will utterly consume everything from the face of the land. I will consume man and beast; I will consume the birds of the heavens, the fish of the sea, and the stumbling blocks along with the wicked. I will cut off man from the face of the land." But he did do this with the removal of Israel and Judah. Uncommitted lukewarm people, whether sitting on the pews or otherwise idling away a day of worship, are an abomination to God.

Amos had described "the day of the Lord". Beginning at verse fourteen Zephaniah does also, with the words wrath, trouble, distress, devastation, desolation, darkness, gloom, clouds and thick darkness.

In chapter two Zephaniah makes his call for the people to repent, saying, "Before the decree is issued...before the Lord's fierce anger comes...before the day of the Lord." He pleads with them, "Seek the Lord, all you meek of the earth, who have upheld his justice. Seek righteousness, seek humility. It may be that you will be hidden in the day of the Lord's anger." He then goes on to prophesy what will happen to the five surrounding heathen nations of Philistia, Moab, Ammon, Ethiopia and Assyria. As do many of these prophets, he uses that word "remnant" as he speaks of the small group of faithful believers who will be saved through it all.

In verse thirteen he prophesies as to Nineveh, the capitol of the powerful empire of Assyria. He "shall destroy Assyria, and make Nineveh a desolation, as dry as the wilderness. The herds shall lie down in her midst." A fact of history is that about a decade later Assyria would be defeated by the rising empire of Babylon and its King Nebuchadnezzar, and Nineveh would disappear not to be discovered for over 2,000 years, in 1842 A.D. After conquering Nineveh, Nebuchadnezzar would then turn his eyes and armies toward Judah and capture it.

Chapter three concludes this book with God's promise of redemption and a coming day of hope. In verse thirteen he again refers to that remnant, not a nation, of faithful believers who will remain on the land. They will do no wrong as they wait for God to complete the execution of his judgment.

****

NAHUM   (662-608; 615)

Now, let's take a brief look at Nahum. Nahum means "comfort", he speaks of the Lord being a stronghold in time of trouble. Nahum was a contemporary of Zephaniah, and it is debatable as to whether his prophesies came before or after Zephaniah. For this discussion, he comes after Zephaniah.

We are told he was from the town of Elkosh, but scholars cannot determine whether that was in Galilee or near Nineveh. The town of Capernaum means "village of Nahum", "village of comfort". In either event, he moved or escaped into Judah.

Nahum speaks of Nineveh, of Assyria, and of its terrifying armies and its evil ways. The fall of Nineveh is in fact the theme of this book. Nahum prophesied sometime around 615 B.C., during the reign of King Josiah. About 150 years before Nahum, God had called Jonah to go to Nineveh to preach. At that time the empire was much smaller, but growing. At that time they repented in sackcloth and ashes, and God did not punish them. Nahum is a sequel to Jonah, and God will now punish Assyria for not following through with their conversion. Jonah was a call to repentance. Nahum is a statement of judgment.

Nahum opens up with, "God is jealous, and the Lord avenges. The Lord avenges and is furious. The Lord will take vengeance on his adversaries, and he reserves wrath for his enemies. The Lord is slow to anger and great in power, and will not at all acquit the wicked." The meaning of the word "jealous" has become somewhat distorted for us today. It is a derivative of the word "zealous", which can be substituted in nearly every case in the Bible. With great zeal God zealously protects what is his and carries out his judgments.

In chapter one verse fifteen we read, "Behold, on the mountains the feet of him who brings good tidings, who proclaims peace!" These are nearly the same words used previously by Isaiah and later quoted by Paul in his letter to the Romans.

It was next to impossible for anyone to believe the great power of Assyria, which had been continually increasing from 1300 B.C. to 600 B.C. and from a small area around Nineveh to cover everything south to what is today Kuwait to the southeast and down the Nile River to the southwest. The city of Nineveh was thirty miles long and ten miles wide, with five walls 100 feet high and forty feet thick with a moat outside which was 140 feet wide and sixty feet deep, all protected by a powerful and ferocious army. It sat beside the upper waters of the Euphrates River where the Khoser River flowed into it. At the time of Jonah, Nineveh had a population of nearly one million people.

In verse seven, Nahum says, "The Lord is good, a stronghold in the day of trouble, and he knows those who trust him." The stronghold is God, not the walls and weapons of men. In verse eight, Nahum continues, "With an overflowing flood he will make an utter end of its place and darkness will pursue his enemies." He again repeats this in chapter two verse six, and in chapter three tells of the pursuit and complete defeat.

That is exactly what would happen to Nineveh in 612 B.C. King Nebuchadnezzar was enlarging his city of Babylon and his empire. His armies would move north to Nineveh. Either a great flood of the Euphrates occurred or the Babylonians destroyed a dam, either way a great overflowing flood as predicted by Nahum, knocked down the walls of Nineveh, and it was captured. In chapter two Nahum even describes the uniforms of the Babylonians. The Babylonians would continue to pursue the Assyrians northwestward to Carchemish where they would finally defeat them in 605 B.C. and promptly turn south to capture tiny Judah.

****

HABAKKUK (612-589; 603)

Now, let's take a brief look at Habakkuk. Habakkuk means "God is our salvation". This is a sequel to the Book of Job, and the continuing faith in God though one wonders why the innocent suffer while the evil seem to thrive. Habakkuk's time was the very end and collapse into captivity of Judah.

Habakkuk begins with, "O Lord, how long shall I cry, and you will not hear?" He begs God not just to stand there, but to do something. God answers his cry by telling him that he used Assyria to punish Israel and was destroying them and was going to use Babylon for awhile as his instrument to carry out his judgment against Judah. Habakkuk complains that such is just not fair.

However, at the beginning of chapter two, Habakkuk decides, "I will stand my watch and set myself on the rampart, and watch to see what he will say to me, and what I will answer when I am corrected." God immediately tells him to record a vision. In verse four he says, "The just shall live by his faith." Herewith, hidden in this little book, are two very powerful concepts, standing watch and living by faith. Six centuries later, Paul will quote the fourth verse in his letter to the Romans, and fifteen centuries after that Martin Luther would read the letter and begin the great Reformation of the church. It is faith alone and not some indulgences or payments to the men of the worldly church. Luther would set forth his theology in his hymn, "A Mighty Fortress Is Our God," as he sang of a fortress, a bulwark, a helper, a flood, Christ Jesus, it is he.

In chapter two God answers as to faith being rewarded. He lists five woes of the nation of Judah which must be punished. These are greed and covetousness, gain by evil violence, gain by murder, drunken orgies and idolatry. The chapter concludes with those words heard so frequently in many churches. "The Lord is in his holy temple; let all the earth keep silence before him."

In chapter three is the great poetic prayer of Habakkuk, as concluded in the same manner as Job, by submitting to and praising God. Even in his frustration, Habakkuk prays that God remember mercy in his time of wrath. "Though the fig tree may not blossom, nor fruit be on the vines, though the labor of the olive may fail...Yet I will rejoice in the Lord....The Lord God is my strength."

And here begin, as follows on the next pages, the story and prophesies of Jeremiah, as printed about 175 pages earlier in our Bibles.

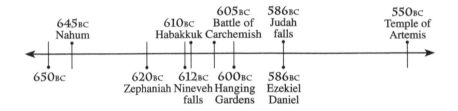

CHAPTER 21

JEREMIAH 1-12
UTTER FAITHLESSNESS OF JUDAH/ISRAEL

Because your fathers,...have walked after other gods and have served them and worshiped them, and have forsaken me and not kept my law,...I will cast you out of this land...(and) not show you favor. Jer. 16:11, 13

Jeremiah means "Jehovah will lift up". First, let's recall to mind the stage, the scene, for this book of Jeremiah, as to what was going on in his world, and why his words are so depressing and exhausting. Without a concept of the events of that world a person just cannot understand this man and his book. Among the books of the Bible this may be the most neglected. Just saying his name tends to make people slump and go into a trance. Nobody ever enjoys hearing the words of these outspoken men at the time of the collapse of the kingdoms. In addition the prophets require some working knowledge of history, ancient and present. About the best people can say to one who preaches on these is, "You must have put a lot of work into that talk." Jeremiah is a "watershed" as to time, person and book, in that it marks the end of all that had gone before. The Land, the Seed and the Blessing move. Syncretism, the mixing and toleration of other gods, is the sin begun by Solomon and the cause of collapse.

In the preceding chapter we heard of the history and scene at the time of the final four prophets to the collapsing southern kingdom of Judah. Zephaniah, Nahum, Habakkuk and Jeremiah were these final four. They all four prophesied during the latter years of the reign of the good King Josiah, but Jeremiah also continued well past Josiah and past the time of the capture and disappearance of the small kingdom of Judah into captivity and exile. Understand, this was a time of great tragedy, and these men spoke heavy and depressing words. The slight glimmer of hope of the other three for a remnant of faithful believers is essentially gone in Jeremiah. It is just too late for this Jewish kingdom.

Jeremiah may have been born around 642 B.C., eighty years after the fall of northern Israel and fifty-six years before the fall of southern Judah. There is some debate as to whether he was appointed as priest by King Josiah, at the age of fifteen years. In the book of Second Kings chapters twenty-two and twenty-three, we are told of King Josiah, who reigned over Judah for thirty-one years. He was a good king, but could not overcome the evil damage done in the eyes of God by his predecessor, King Manasseh, who rebuilt the altars to false gods and burned his own son as a sacrifice to them. Manasseh had ruled fifty-four years, and kept the doors of the temple nailed shut as he gave away the gold inside.

The names in the family tree of Jeremiah and the family tree of King Josiah and his descendants, the final four kings of Judah, can lead to some confusion. Jeremiah the canonized prophet is not the Jeremiah who was the father of King Josiah, and so not the grandfather of the other kings. Two simple, but hard to find, facts, clear this confusion. First, Jeremiah the prophet was about six years younger than King Josiah, and not the Jeremiah who was Josiah's father-in-law. Second, the fathers of the two Jeremiahs were born in different towns. In the book of Jeremiah, we are told in the first verse that he was the son of Hilkiah of the priestly family of the town of Anathoth, two miles north of Jerusalem in the land of Benjamin. In the first verse of the last chapter of Jeremiah, and in 2nd Kings 24:18, we are told that Zedekiah, the last king of Judah, was the son of Josiah and the grandson of Jeremiah of Libnah, twenty miles southwest of Jerusalem in the land of Judah. Two different Jeremiahs, born in two different towns, both with fathers named Hilkiah who were priests.

We are reminded that Josiah's high priest, Hilkiah, the father of the prophet Jeremiah, found a book of the law hidden away in the closed temple. It was certainly the Book of Deuteronomy, but may have been the entire Pentateuch, the first five books of our Bible. The primary Mosaic festival of the Passover, commemorating the Exodus, had not been observed for over 500 years. This is what had become of the people of the Exodus, the people of Joshua and David, a collapse begun by Solomon. When the young King Josiah read this he tore his clothes and ordered a full-scale revival. He had the temple cleansed of false idols and false priests. In its early stages the revival was probably led by Jeremiah.

Now we look at some very important history, of which all hear in Sunday School classes but never assimilate. Assyria and Babylon and Nebuchadnezzar. In 609 B.C. Nabopolasar, Nebuchadnezzar's father, pushed his armies of Babylon, southern Iraq, northward up the Euphrates and Tigris to Nineveh. He pursued the expiring Assyrian army due west, across Mesopotamia, and northwest Syria, to the Syrian boundary with Turkey and the city of Carchemish. Neco, the Pharaoh of Egypt, did not want Babylonia to become a great power, and began his march northward along the Mediterranean coast. For four years a great world war raged.

In Second Kings chapter twenty-three, we are told that at the start of this war, for some reason, probably because he did not want any person or nation to help Assyria, or maybe at the request of Babylon, Josiah, the king of little

Judah, up on the mountains of the West Bank, decided to bring his small army down to the valley at Megiddo and stop Neco of Egypt. Josiah was killed by the Egyptians at the Mount of Megiddo, at Armageddon. Pharaoh Neco immediately took charge of Judah, removing one of Josiah's sons as king and appointing another son as a puppet ruler for Egypt. Between verses thirty and thirty-one is one huge omission of the battle of Carchemish and the change of empire from Assyria to Babylon. The end of Judah was on the immediate horizon for all to see. Jeremiah would begin to prophesy of coming collapse and captivity, seventy years of captivity. The kingdom of Babylon lasted only seventy years.

In 607 B.C. Nebuchadnezzar's father backed up and captured the Assyrian capitol of Nineveh. In 605 B.C. he defeated Assyria. His Babylonian army then looked south toward Judah and Jerusalem. Nebuchadnezzar took over at the death of his father, and promptly completed the first of three invasions of Judah and Jerusalem. The puppet king of Egypt became the puppet king of Babylon. His name was Jehoiakim. This puppet king of Egypt then of Babylon was the king of Judah against which Jeremiah contested and prophesied. Jeremiah was not at all liked by these rulers, the princes and priests of Judah. He suffered for it.

King Josiah had struggled in vain to bring his kingdom back to God. As recorded in the first twelve chapters of Jeremiah we are told that the prophet supported Josiah with his exhortations to the people to repent and his threats of defeat and captivity if they did not repent. Josiah wanted to save his people, save them from Assyria, from Babylon and from Egypt. However, God had set a course of strong discipline, of judgment, with Babylon as the instrument. When the people walk down a road by which they lose the concept that God is totally sovereign, they likely continue to the end and perish.

It was at the first invasion by Nebuchadnezzar that he carried off the cream of the crop of Judah. He selected from the royal family and the nobility, youths without blemish, handsome and skillful. One of those youths was a lad named Daniel, who came of age in Babylon during the final twenty years of Jeremiah and Judah. Ten years later Ezekiel would also be taken to Babylon where he began to prophesy. Daniel and Ezekiel no doubt knew Jeremiah. Jeremiah indeed lived and spoke during violent and treacherous times. This was the end times of the diminished kingdom of David and Solomon. This first invasion of Jerusalem by Nebuchadnezzar in 606 B.C. was the date from which the seventy years of captivity and exile spoken of by Jeremiah commenced, though it would be another twenty years before a more complete end of Jerusalem would occur. Babylon lasted only seventy years, until Cyrus of Persia defeated it.

We are reminded, at this time young Daniel over in Babylon will interpret the meaning of the colossal statue in a dream of King Nebuchadnezzar. He will tell the king that the head of gold is his Babylonian empire which defeated the Assyrian empire, the chest and arms of silver is the Medo-Persian empire of Cyrus, the belly and thighs of brass is the Greek empire, and its legs of iron and feet of clay is the Roman empire. Assyria, Babylon and Persia are the changing empires of Jeremiah and Daniel. Persia will conclude the old Hebrew scriptures with the rise of the Greek empire being a part of the Book of Esther, and then Rome rising at the start of the new Christian scriptures.

At this date of 606 B.C., according to the first verses of chapter thirty-six, God told Jeremiah, "Take a scroll of a book and write on it all the words that I have spoken to you....Then Jeremiah called Baruch" as his scribe for his dictation. At that date Jeremiah was thirty-six years old and had been preaching his prophecies for twenty-one years, and he was still very active. He began to dictate as things came to mind, so this book of Jeremiah is not in chronological order, some of which is fairly obvious, most of which is not. Also, chapter thirty-six tells us the scroll was read to the puppet king Jehoiakim who cut it all up and burned it in his cooking fire. God told Jeremiah and Baruch to do it again. Many students of the Bible have their ideas as to how this book should be rearranged to put it all in sequence as to time.

In reading this book it is most important, or helpful, at least to be aware of four time periods. First, is the period during the reign of the good King Josiah. The first twelve chapters cover this period. Second, is the tumultuous period following the death of Josiah and the defeat of Assyria and Egypt by Babylon at Carchemish. Third is the period between the first invasion and the final third invasion of Babylon upon Jerusalem, the time of the puppet king Jehoiakim, which is the period of most of Jeremiah's harshest sermons. Fourth, is the period of the final exile out of Judah, which is brief in this book of Jeremiah.

The writer's computer indicates that the phrase, "thus says the Lord" is used 149 times by Jeremiah. Of these, the longer version, "thus says the Lord of hosts, the God of Israel," is used twenty-nine times. He is very emphatic that he is not a false prophet.

Jeremiah begins with telling us of his ancestors. He then, in verse four, tells us of his call by God, which begins, "Before I formed you in the womb I knew you; Before you were born I sanctified you." Those words are very similar to words of Isaiah some eighty years earlier; "The Lord has called me from the womb; from the matrix of my mother he has made mention of my name....(He) formed me from the womb to be his servant." These are words of two of the greatest prophets, spoken as their nation was in moral and physical collapse, which words the majority of the people did not hear then and will not hear today. Most of those who do not hear them simply stay out of the churches, especially one where they might hear these words.

Moses had resisted his call by telling God, " I am not eloquent...but am slow of speech and slow of tongue." Isaiah, as smoke filled the temple, told God, "I am a man of unclean lips." Jeremiah tells God, "I cannot speak, for I am a youth." These are the standard excuses people have used to this very day.

These are the excuses for resisting a call and not speaking of God at work, at play, or at a small gathering, or for boldly inviting another to church.

Six hundred years after Jeremiah, Jesus would tell little stories to make his point, very short ones as metaphors or similes and longer ones as parables. Jeremiah did likewise, and at times even acted them out to get the attention of the people. Jeremiah uses twelve such little stories, the first two of which are in chapter one, as God asks Jeremiah, "What do you see?" He responded, "I see a branch of an almond tree." The Hebrew word for almond and for watching sound alike. God told Jeremiah he was watching over his word, which Jeremiah was to speak.

God again asked, "What do you see?" to which Jeremiah responded, "I see a boiling pot, and it is facing away from the north." Here begin the prophecies. For Judah, the seething turmoil would pour over from the north, as Babylon under Nebuchadnezzar would invade from that direction. God explains that this will be his judgment upon these people who "have forsaken me, burned incense to other gods, and worshiped the works of their own hands."

In chapter two verse thirteen, God rephrases the apostasies of forsaking God and looking to themselves as he says, "They have forsaken me, the fountain of living waters, and hewn themselves cisterns, broken cisterns that can hold no water." In that country water is most precious, especially the flowing living fresh water of a stream. Here we have a reference to the Christ. But the people look to the stagnant water of their cisterns. In verse twenty-seven, God says of the people who worship man-made gods, they say "to a tree, 'You are my father,' and to a stone, 'You gave birth to me'."

In chapter three God instructs Jeremiah to make final pleas for the people of Judah to repent, as he compares them to a faithless wife and to one who commits adultery with a tree and a stone. He says that if they repent and return from their horrendous backsliding he will give them shepherds according to his own heart who will feed them with true knowledge and understanding.

This call is continued in chapter four, but with the threat of judgment if they do not repent. In verse six Jeremiah speaks of disaster and great destruction coming from the north. They will come in chariots like the whirlwind, with horses swifter than an eagle, to plunder the people of Judah. He continues in chapter five as he gets somewhat stronger, saying the people "have lied about the Lord, and said, 'It is not He. Neither will evil come upon us, nor shall we see sword or famine." Jeremiah attacks the prophets and says of the people they are a "foolish people without understanding, who have eyes and see not, and who have ears and hear not."

The crescendo continues in chapter six. In verse six he predicts the siege which Nebuchadnezzar will place around Jerusalem. Beginning at verse thirteen he attacks the priests and the false prophets. "From the least of them even to the greatest of them, everyone is given to covetousness, and from the prophet even to the priest, everyone deals falsely. They have healed the hurt of my people slightly, saying, 'Peace, peace!' When there is no peace." In verse sixteen is a repeat of a thought of Job, that the people remove the landmarks of society. "Ask for the old paths, where the good way is, and walk in it....But they say, 'We will not walk in it.'" Today our people remove the ancient landmarks, and refuse to walk along that way.

In the British colonies of America in March 1775, at St. John's church in Richmond, Virginia, Patrick Henry recalled these verses of Jeremiah, which were writ large upon his heart. He spoke of a threat taking place in the north. "There is a just God who presides over the destinies of Nations...Our chains are forged! Their clanking may be heard on the plains of Boston...It is vain, sir, to extenuate the matter. Gentlemen may cry, 'Peace, Peace'--but there is no peace. The war is actually begun. The next gale that sweeps from the North will bring to our ears the clash of resounding arms!...I know not what course others may take; but as for me, give me liberty or give me death."

In chapter seven, Jeremiah continues to call for repentance as the crescendo moves on to judgment. He tells them not to trust the priests, the prophets nor the corruptions of the temple. He says, "If you thoroughly amend your ways, then I will cause you to dwell in this...land that I gave to your fathers." If, then...but if not, then. In verse eleven he speaks of the corruption of the temple, which verse Jesus will later quote. "Has this house, which is called by my name, become a den of thieves in your eyes?" At verse eighteen he says of the people of Jerusalem that, "The children gather wood, the fathers kindle the fire, and the women knead dough, to make cakes for the queen of heaven." The whole family works to worship this queen of heaven. This is a twisted and distorted worship of the true God for the continuation and maintenance of the species, of mankind. We are to pray to God for healthy and abundant provisions, provisions of both food and of children. Even today churches liberated from the scriptures debate the invasion of the worship of this queen of heaven, known as Astarte, Oester, Diana, Minerva, Mother-earth, and now probably some new name.

In chapters eight, nine, ten and eleven he continues his laments over the backsliding of the people and their hard refusal to return to God. In chapter eleven he personalizes the message as he relates it more to himself. The period of the reign of the good King Josiah is coming to an end. He recalls that for years he has been speaking to a people who just refuse to listen. They even turned on Jeremiah as he says, "I was like a docile lamb brought to the slaughter; and I did not know that they had devised schemes against me." He finishes chapter twelve with, "If they do not obey, I will utterly pluck up and destroy that nation, says the Lord." It is the time of Josiah's death and the beginning of twenty years of foreign control, briefly by Egypt then by Babylon. The preaching of Jeremiah will now explode in the faces of the leaders.

And here continues, as follows on the next pages, the rest of the story and prophecies of Jeremiah.

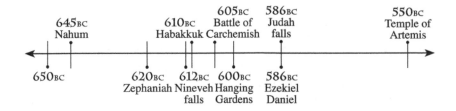

645BC Nahum		610BC Habakkuk	605BC Battle of Carchemish	586BC Judah falls		550BC Temple of Artemis

650BC   620BC   612BC   600BC   586BC
Zephaniah Nineveh Hanging   Ezekiel
falls   Gardens   Daniel

CHAPTER 22

JEREMIAH 13-52
JUDGMENT AND CONSOLATIONS

I will make a new covenant with the house of Israel...not according to the covenant that I made with their fathers...which they broke....I will put my law in their minds and write it on their hearts. Jer. 31:31-33

We are reminded that among the books of the Bible Jeremiah may be the most neglected. Just saying his name tends to make people slump and go into a trance. Nobody ever enjoys hearing the words of these outspoken men at the time of the collapse of the kingdoms. In addition the prophets require some working knowledge of history, ancient and present. About the best people can say to one who preaches on these is, "You must have put a lot of work into that talk." Jeremiah is a "watershed" as to time, person and book, in that it marks the end of all that had gone before. The Land, the Seed and the Blessing move.

In his last comedy, *The Tempest*, Shakespeare wrote, "What is past is prologue." There is a proverb, which being unable to locate, may here be quoted imprecisely. "Those who do not know history are doomed to repeat it." Each of us must know history, and especially biblical history. In an attempt to avoid serious inquiry and in-depth discussion, some pastors deny that the Bible is history. But the Bible is history, and it shows repetitive cycles. A person who denies this history denies the value of prayer itself, for "surely God would not intrude into history." Gerhard von Rad, a German theologian of the mid-twentieth century coined the phrase *heilige gesschichte*, which is "holy history" or "salvation history". Today, most of us do not learn history, particularly biblical history. It is somewhat difficult, and since about 1960, less and less valued. That may be because we are repeating the history of these prophets when the people and their leaders turned away from God.

Our encyclopedias of history tell a tale. Karl Marx, the mid-nineteenth century German atheistic philosopher of dialectic materialism, was followed closely in time and on the charts of philosophy by Friedrich Nietzsche. Nietzsche, the atheistic existentialist philosopher of naturalism and nihilism of the latter nineteenth century wrote, "History is nothing more than the belief in the senses, the belief in falsehood." He was followed closely in time and on the charts of philosophy by Sigmund Freud, another atheistic materialist and the German father of our modern psychiatry. Freud was followed closely in time and on the charts of philosophy by John Dewey, an atheistic professor at Columbia U. in New York City. From his prestigious position, Dewey began the teachers' union and spread his belief that history and truth evolve and depend upon a person's personal experience. This invasion into our public schools began about 1930 and was completed about 1990. We live in a world of total confusion. Our federal laws require students to be taught there are no absolutes as to history and truth, but require bankers to believe absolutely a person's history of credit.

Let's continue this story of the working of God in the history of this world, as Jeremiah lived it, interpreted it and recorded it. As previously stated, it is most important at least to be aware of four time periods as in the last four chapters of Second Kings. First, is the period during the reign of the good King Josiah. Jeremiah's first twelve chapters cover this period. Second, is the tumultuous period of the death of Josiah followed by the defeat of Assyria and Egypt by Babylon at Carchemish. Third, is the period between the first invasion and the final third invasion of Babylon upon Jerusalem, the time of the puppet king Jehoiakim, which is the period of most of Jeremiah's harshest sermons. Fourth, is the period of the final exile out of Judah, which is brief in this book of Jeremiah.

The first twelve chapters took place during the reign of the good King Josiah. During this period Jeremiah strongly called the people of Judah and Jerusalem to repent. Then in rapid succession, the world around Jerusalem began changing and Jeremiah with each change. As predicted by Nahum, Nineveh, the capitol of the mighty Assyrian empire, was captured by the rising Babylonian empire. King Josiah was killed by the Egyptian army, which took control of Jerusalem during a three-year period as it joined the expiring army of the dying Assyrian empire in its losing world war with the rising Babylonian empire. Jeremiah's oracles took a minor change as he spoke with more warnings and judgments and some weeping laments. We are reminded, at this time young Daniel over in Babylon will interpret the meaning of the colossal statue in a dream of King Nebuchadnezzar.

In chapter thirteen are two physical actions Jeremiah may have actually performed, except that the first may have been a vision, as the Euphrates was some 400 miles to the northeast. God told him to buy a linen waist cloth and wrap it around his loins, then to hike to the Euphrates and hide the loin cloth in a cleft in the rock. After many days God told him to go get the loin cloth. He did and found the cloth spoiled and good for nothing. God told him that so is the pride of Judah. God then told Jeremiah to tell the people that every jar will be filled with wine and that he will fill all of the people with drunkenness and then dash them one against the other without pity. God told Jeremiah that he doubted whether the people could change, as their culture was so decadent and their habits so fixed. "Can the Ethiopian change his skin or the leopard its spots?" Their free will seemed hopelessly misdirected to allow for any repentance.

Chapter fourteen begins with the word of the Lord telling Jeremiah that the land of Judah is as though a severe drought had come upon it. The people, the animals and the plants could find no water, no matter where they searched. As a last resort, taking God for granted, they call upon him for water. He says he will not accept them and will punish their sins. At verse eleven, God tells Jeremiah not even to pray for the welfare of the people, who continued to listen to false prophets who told them they were fine doing what they were doing. God was going to severely discipline the people, and there would not be much delay.

Something is happening concerning the Land, the Seed and the Blessing, the L-S-B. In chapter sixteen God tells Jeremiah, "You shall not take a wife, nor shall you have sons or daughters in this place....The sons and daughters who are born in this place...shall die gruesome deaths...I have taken away my peace from this people...lovingkindness and mercies." With all of that, Jeremiah says, "O Lord, my strength and my fortress, my refuge in the day of affliction." We have free will. We can choose to turn our back to God. He can choose to walk away.

In chapter seventeen God speaks through Jeremiah as to the human heart, meaning the seat of everything that is real to a person. He says, "The sin of Judah is written with a pen of iron, with the point of a diamond, it is engraved on the tablet of their heart." That is somewhat more powerful than being written in stone. He begins what he will finish in chapter thirty-one, that the people need a new heart, a new covenant. "The heart is deceitful above all things, and desperately wicked; Who can know it?" This recalls Psalm 51, written by David when caught in sin concerning Bathsheba, 400 years earlier. "Create in me a clean heart, O God, and renew a steadfast spirit within me. Do not cast me away from your presence, and do not take your Holy Spirit from me." One must know the boring history surrounding Jeremiah to know the depressing depth of his pit. Down deep in the bottom, in this land, was planted a new seed, a renewed blessing.

Jeremiah, and God, conclude chapter seventeen and begin eighteen with what may be the final appeal to repentance, which is wrapped in a reminder of conditions to receiving the blessing. One after another comes "if...but... then." "If you heed me carefully, to bring no burden through the gates of this city on the Sabbath day, but hallow the Sabbath day, to do no work in it, then shall enter the gates of this city kings and princes sitting on the throne of David....But if you will not heed me...then I will kindle a fire in its gates... and it shall not be quenched." In our nation, it is estimated that four out of five people carry burdens on the Sabbath day and do take no time to worship God.

These conditions are continued in eighteen with the parable of the potter's wheel, a parable of the absolute sovereignty of God, that primary absolute truth which the followers of Sigmund Freud and John Dewey, from 1930 to 1990, cast out of our state-run public schools. God directed Jeremiah to go down to the potter's house. He did and observed the potter at his wheel molding some clay into a vessel which was going badly. The potter simply took that clay into his hands, mushed it around and began again. The faulty vessel never came into existence, and in its place was a good vessel. God explained that humans are as clay in the hands of the great potter, and spoke more "if...but...thens." This time the words apply not to an individual but to a nation. At this depth of depression is another seed change. A change is coming for his chosen nation, which has repeatedly said, "We will walk according to our own plans, and we will every one obey the dictates of his evil heart." Predecessors to Nietzsche, Marx, Freud and Dewey, as their individualism now runs rampant through our nation.

Of course, the pronouncements involved the people listening to false prophets and false priests, who told them everything was fine. So they determined to attack Jeremiah with their tongues, to slander him, to bear false witness, and to keep their power. This caused Jeremiah bitterly to ask God to punish them, which was in accordance with God's announced plans. It was now probably about the time the Babylonian armies fully defeated the Assyrians and the Egyptians at Carchemish and turned south toward Jerusalem under the rule of Nebuchadnezzar.

In chapter nineteen we have another living parable, as Jeremiah acts out a teaching. It again involves a potter's vessel, as Jeremiah is directed to go buy an earthen flask. "Then you shall break the flask in the sight of the men who go with you....Even so I will break this people and this city... which cannot be made whole again." It was a Mid-Eastern custom to write the names of one's enemies on a clay tablet and then to smash it, somewhat like burning an effigy.

The chief priest heard of these preachings of Jeremiah and increased the attack on Jeremiah from words to actually having him beaten and put into stocks. God did not help much, as he told Jeremiah, "I will make you a terror to yourself and to all your friends....I will give all Judah into the hand of the king of Babylon." This sent Jeremiah into a fit of depression as bad as the one in which Job had been when he had cursed the day he was born. After first conceding the power of God, and mentioning his vigorous sermons, Jeremiah does likewise as he laments his birth. "Cursed be the day in which I was born! Let the day not be blessed in which my mother bore me! Let the man be cursed...(who) did not kill me from the womb." That is some serious depression.

Some reason for this depression was that following its victory, the Babylonian army, under Nebuchadnezzar, conducted its first of three invasions of Jerusalem, taking control and captives. Jehoaikim, Josiah's son, who had given Jeremiah so much grief, was still king, but now switched from puppet for Egypt to puppet for Babylon. In chapter twenty-one God has Jeremiah speak that God has "set my face against this city....It shall be given into the hand of the king of Babylon, and he shall burn it with fire....I will punish you according to the fruit of your doings." These sayings were directed primarily at the leaders, just as Jesus will do.

In chapter twenty-three he severely attacks the shepherds of the flock, the prophets and priests. He says the shepherds have scattered the flock. He has previously said he would disperse the people. In verse three is, "I will gather the remnant of my flock out of all countries where I have driven them, and bring them back to their folds." Of course, this refers to the recovery of the remnant of faithful believers, as individuals and not as a nation, and of the dispersion of that time. Many erroneously quote this as a return to the land of Palestine as a nation in 1948 A.D. and the years following, which is terribly out of time frames, except that God is constantly gathering believers into the fold.

This is followed by a prophesy of a Branch of David, which picks up on the words of Isaiah some 100 years earlier. "Behold, the days are coming,.. that I will raise to David a branch of righteousness; a king shall reign and prosper, and execute judgment and righteousness in the earth. In his days Judah will be saved, and Israel will dwell safely. Now this is his name by which he will be called, 'The Lord our righteousness.'" Jeremiah did not knowingly speak of the second coming and end times, but in later years, the words of Isaiah and of Jeremiah took on greater significance as messianic sayings, especially as there would be no records of any descendants of David beyond the time of Christ Jesus.

In chapter twenty-four we have another short parable, that of the good figs and the bad figs. Jeremiah's nemesis, King Jehoiakim, has died and an even weaker king sat on the throne. God showed Jeremiah a vision of two baskets of figs placed before the temple, one of very good figs and one of very bad figs. As with the rod of almond and the boiling pot of chapter one, God asks, "What do you see?" God then explains that the good figs are those who leave Judah to go into exile in Babylon, and the bad figs are those who remain. He will bring the exiles back and replant them. The fact is that all figs are sinners and follow other gods, but those who at least get out of the terribly evil culture of Jerusalem will stand another chance, while those who remain will not. This is very applicable today for those who are in a bad culture, a bad group of friends, even a bad religious body. Make the break; leave that culture, that group, that false religious body.

In chapter twenty-five Jeremiah prophesies that the Israelites will be an "everlasting reproach," but then says the nations of the land shall serve Babylon seventy years, at which time the king of Babylon shall be punished.

Here is the prophesy of seventy years of captivity. To get a full seventy years one must begin counting from the first invasion by Nebuchadnezzar in 606 B.C., not from the final invasion of 587 B.C. and continue to the return in 536 B.C., following the decree of Cyrus of Persia. Many think the number seventy simply refers to the period of a lifetime, of three-score-ten, a long time. Chapter twenty-five concludes with a list of nations which must drink of "the cup of the wine of the wrath of God."

In chapters twenty-six through twenty-nine Jeremiah recounts various events in his life, including his recent conflict with Hananiah, a leader of the false prophets who continued to say everything was just fine in the land. God told Jeremiah to wear a wooden yoke around town to show the people will be under the yoke of Babylon. Hananiah broke the yoke off, but Jeremiah said the true yoke would be iron. Jeremiah was imprisoned for his prophesies that God sent Babylon to punish Judah and that they must simply give in to that punishment. In chapter twenty-nine Jeremiah, from prison, sends a letter to those in exile in Babylon, telling them to build houses and plant gardens as the exile will last seventy years, of which about sixty yet remained.

As Isaiah had modified his tone and message to fit the circumstances after the exile to Assyria, Jeremiah changes his. Chapters thirty and thirty-one comprise a short "Book of Comfort." He tells them this "day of the Lord", this "time of distress of Jacob", this "storm of the Lord" will pass, that God has loved them with an everlasting love. At this time Daniel is coming of age in Babylon, and Ezekiel is on his way. Verse eight of chapter thirty-one says, "I will bring them from the north country, and gather them from the ends of the earth." Of course, at that time the north country was Assyria and the route to and from Babylon. Many erroneously quote this as referring to the situation of the Mid-East after 1948 A.D., though God always gathers believers.

The Bible is replete with paradox and balance. We have a seeming paradox in chapter thirty-one beginning at verse thirty-one. At the very depths of the pit God says, "Behold, the days are coming when I will make a new covenant with the house of Israel...not according to the covenant that I made with their fathers...which they broke....I will put my law in their minds and write it on their hearts, and I will be their God, and they shall be my people. No more shall every man teach his neighbor, and every man his brother...for they all shall know me, from the least of them to the greatest." The change was not to occur at that time, but in days yet to come. At that time, God will change the covenant from external to internal. It will be written, not on tablets of stone but on the tablet of the heart. The L-S-B is moving, while remaining on target.

In the book of Leviticus God directed that every seventh year the land lie fallow and that every fiftieth year, the jubilee year, all slaves be set free and all debts forgiven. There is no evidence in scripture that the Israelites ever obeyed either of these two directions. In chapter thirty-four God chastises them for that, as sort of an after thought, an "and furthermore." Some mathematical students calculate that the seventy years of exile is to make up for those lost Jubilee years since the days of Joshua.

In chapter thirty-two, while in prison, Jeremiah purchased a piece of land in Judah, an indication that he did believe the people would return to the land after seventy years and the land would have value. In chapter thirty-three verses fourteen through twenty-six, we have a repetition of what is written in chapter twenty-three as to the coming days of a branch of righteousness springing from the house of David. These verses are not in the Hebrew scriptures as translated into Greek around 250 B.C. and known as the *Septuagint* or "LXX". They seem to have begun to appear about 100 A.D. with the development of the Jewish Masoretic text. These verses are "messianic" in that they speak of the righteous branch of David arising to be both king and priest.

In chapter thirty-six Jeremiah recounts the direction of God to him in 606 B.C. when Jehoiakim was king, to write down all he had said during the past twenty-one years of prophesying. Jeremiah employs Baruch as his scribe. It takes one year to get it all down. Then Baruch is told to go read it aloud in public. The religious leaders reach their final breaking point with Jeremiah, who is still in prison. They have the scroll read to King Jehoiakim who cuts it up with his table knife and throws it into his cooking fire. God tells Jeremiah and Baruch to write it again.

In chapter thirty-seven Jeremiah tells of the final fall of Jerusalem, and of his being thrown into a cistern which has little water but a lot of mire. He has no food and the weak king allowed him to be hauled back out. The remaining chapters tell of Jeremiah being forcibly taken to Egypt, where he presumably dies. Chapters forty-six through fifty-one are oracles against the surrounding foreign nations. Chapter fifty-two is an appendix restating some of this history.

With the complete capture of Judah in 587 B.C. and the removal of the sons of Josiah from the throne, there would be no more lineal descendant of David sitting upon such throne. Such records are simply non-existent. Except for the lineage of Jesus the Christ as given by Matthew and Luke, there is no proof of any descendant of David from that day to the present to sit upon such throne. Upon the return allowed by Cyrus of Persia, Zerubbabel, a descendant, would serve as high commissioner, but not as king. There was some record of the descendants of Levi to serve as priests, *kohanim*, to conduct altar services; and these men conducted services in the replacement temples until about 100 A.D., but from that time to the present there is no record of any lineal descendants of Levi to conduct the services, no men to approach the altar in some modern temple in Jerusalem. For Christians, Jesus the Christ is the "high priest", the *Kohen Gadol*.

****

LAMENTATIONS

The book of Lamentations is a funeral dirge for the city of Jerusalem. It also mentions the mental depression and physical ailments Jeremiah suffered. Chapter three is a personal prayer and lament. Verse twenty-two has those oft heard words of the Revised Standard Version, "The steadfast love of the Lord never ceases, his mercies never come to an end; they are new every morning; great is thy faithfulness."

And here begin, on the following pages, the story and prophecies of Ezekiel.

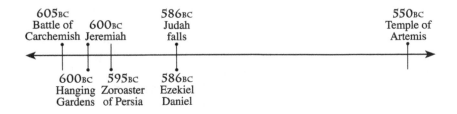

605BC
Battle of   600BC
Carchemish Jeremiah

586BC
Judah
falls

550BC
Temple of
Artemis

600BC   595BC
Hanging   Zoroaster
Gardens   of Persia

586BC
Ezekiel
Daniel

CHAPTER 23

EZEKIEL 1-14
JUDGMENT ON JUDAH/JERUSALEM

The end has come upon the four corners of the land....I will repay them for all their abominations....Their silver and gold will not be able to deliver them. Ezk. 7:2,3,19

The name Ezekiel means "God strengthens". Of all of the books of the Bible, Ezekiel probably mentions the most dates and with the most accuracy. Even with that, the dates cannot always be set with true accuracy. This problem of fixing these dates is of no real importance to the book. In the very first verse we begin with what appears to be a specific date, but we find a problem. It says "in the thirtieth year", but that is not anchored to any specific beginning date. Most scholars take it to mean the thirtieth year of Ezekiel's life, which could make it July 31, 593 B.C., if the date of the next verse meant the same date.

We are told the place was on the river Chebar, which was actually a large canal southeast of Babylon, near modern Kuwait, and that it had been five years since Jehoiachin, king of Judah, had been taken captive by Nebuchadnezzar, king of Babylonia. That was in 598 B.C. during the second of three invasions of Jerusalem. At that time 10,000 people had been force-marched about 500 miles to Babylon. These first two verses also will send us into a look at the history of the world at that time.

Jeremiah had received his call and begun preaching in Jerusalem in 627 B.C. Four years later, in 623, Ezekiel had been born near Jerusalem. Three years later, in 620, Daniel had been born. In 605 Ezekiel was studying for the priesthood, possibly under Jeremiah, when Nebuchadnezzar defeated the Assyrian armies and then first invaded Jerusalem. At that time Daniel, a fifteen-year old lad without blemish was carried away in the first wave of exiles to Babylon. In 598 when Ezekiel was force-marched to Babylon to remain among the prisoners, Daniel was working in Nebuchadnezzar's palace and had been for seven years. Ezekiel and Daniel most certainly knew one another well.

We are reminded, with Jeremiah came the end of the kingdoms, and of any descendant sitting on any throne in the land. The temple was destroyed and the *kohanim,* the priestly descendants of Levi, had no temple and no altar. It is most certainly during the exile period of Ezekiel and Daniel that the synagogue system of a place to study and pray began.

Jeremiah, Ezekiel and Daniel spoke in obscure words and symbols. About seven centuries later John would receive and write the book of the Revelation in such obscure words and symbols. These revelations are more veiled than unveiled, more "vealed" than revealed. They are called "apocalyptic" writings, as the four horsemen of the apocalypse, the Revelation. Jeremiah did not veil his prophesies as much as did Ezekiel and Daniel. The reason for this may well be that Ezekiel and Daniel were younger and lived in Babylon decades later.

Many people say all religions are alike, or so similar as to be virtually the same. Indeed, the Israelites had so found things. In the name of "tolerance", the sin of syncretism, they slipped easily from praying to the one true God for a fertile produce of food and children to praying to some wooden or stone idols, the gods of their Canaanite neighbors, for rain and to another for free-sex. That can and will happen if the pastors, the shepherds, do not lead the people correctly. Many Judeo-Christians say there are only two religions, two ways; the way of Jesus and all of the other ways. At the time and place of Ezekiel and Daniel, there was just such another religion, very close in thought and very close in geography. It is appropriate to mention this religion so as to avoid it.

Babylon was located on the Euphrates River about 300 miles north of the Persian Gulf and modern Kuwait. In that area the Tigris River is but twenty-five miles to the east, and about 100 miles east of that is Persia, modern Iran. It was the age of the prophets. A contemporary of Ezekiel and Daniel was Zarathustra, a Persian prophet and founder of a new form of religion. Zoroaster was his name in Greek. Many of us have heard the phrase of the book "Thus Spake Zarathustra", which is a book of his numerous prophecies. He lived and worked in the same land as did Ezekiel and Daniel, but on the east side of the Tigris River. He strove to join various religions as one monotheistic religion. He taught Pythagoras and other Greeks, who carried much of his philosophies back to Greece. His teachings became the major religion of Persia centuries before the Muslim conquest brought Islam. Many of the philosophies of Zoroaster and of the Greeks would later have to be distinguished from Christianity. A slight change of the compass will lead eventually to a sea change of thought and religion.

It was also a time of changing of empires, of world war. Jeremiah, and Ezekiel, spoke during the very active time of Assyria being replaced by Babylonia and of the disappearance of the kingdom of the tribes of Israel. Ezekiel spoke during the very active time of the consolidation of the empire of

Babylonia under Nebuchadnezzar, and as the Persian empire began to grow. Daniel would speak as the Persian empire, with its religion of Zoroaster, took Babylon. About 100 years later, the Persian empire would begin its fall to the Greek empire, with its religious concepts and thoughts. All of this worldly history is mentioned, or alluded to, in our Bible, and needs to be examined from the first two verses of Ezekiel's book.

Ezekiel's first task was to explain to the Israelites the causes of their exile into Babylonia. Ezekiel does this with stories of many visions and of many directions from God to speak frankly to the exiles in Babylonia. God chooses a person to speak to people as one of them, as a level equal. Moses turned from adopted son of the pharaoh to be a Hebrew slave to speak to the Hebrew slaves. Joshua was a soldier for God to lead the soldiers of God. Ezekiel, trained as a priest, became an exile slave to preach to the slaves. Daniel lived as a prince to speak to the princes. Jesus would meet the woman at the well to speak of living water. We also see among these prophets that each has a special message. One might say that Jeremiah focused on God the Father, Isaiah on God the Messiah and Ezekiel on God the Holy Spirit.

In the first twenty-four chapters, Ezekiel tells of the judgment of God on Judah and Jerusalem, its capitol. For Ezekiel these are essentially events of the past, of which he prophesies, "tells forth", the reasons for this punishment. In chapters twenty-five through thirty-two he prophesies as to the surrounding nations, both "forth telling" the reasons for their punishment past, and "foretelling" their punishment future. In chapters thirty-three through forty-eight he prophesies by foretelling of the future restoration of the people. In all of this there are numerous visions, symbols and allegories. This is the prophet of imagery, and one is required to read and reread and look at pictures and maps. For these reasons Ezekiel is normally avoided and frequently taught and preached with error, which it is trusted is not the case here.

Ezekiel uses five phrases time and again. According to my computer disc, the most used, at 127 times, is "thus says the Lord God." Next, at 93 times, is "son of man". Next, at about 61 times, is "they shall know that I am God". Next, at 50 times, is "the word of the Lord came unto me". "The glory of God", the *shekinah*, is used twelve times, mostly in the first few chapters. A summary of Ezekiel would be that Ezekiel was nothing great, just "a son of man", but "the word of the Lord came to him" directing him to tell the exiles, "thus says the Lord God", "the glory of God" has moved away from Jerusalem, and the Israelites are being disciplined so that "you shall know that I am God."

Now we look at the beginning of this book. Ezekiel begins with a vision of the throne and chariot of God with its four living creatures. God had led the people of Moses by a pillar of fire at night and a pillar of cloud, a thick and bright cloud, during the day. Throughout the old Hebrew scriptures, that cloud represents the presence and glory of God, the *shekinah*. Such a cloud appeared to Ezekiel. It is very difficult to describe in words such a vision. Ezekiel repeatedly qualifies his descriptions with the words "like", "likeness", "seem," and "appearance". He tells us that within that cloud were four living creatures with the form of a man. Each had four wings and four faces, which were like the face of a man to the front, the face of a lion to the right, the face of an ox to the left and the face of an eagle to the rear. Two of their wings covered the body while two wings stayed straight out. Beside each creature was a wheel, which had a wheel within it, a wheel within a wheel. The rims of the wheels were full of eyes. Over their heads was a dome above which was something like a throne, from which came a voice.

The face of man represents intelligence, and for Christians the gospel of Luke with Jesus as man. The face of the lion represents dignity and holiness, and for Christians the gospel of Matthew with Jesus as king. The face of the ox represents strength and faithfulness, and for Christians the gospel of Mark with Jesus as servant. The face of the eagle represents speed and heavenliness, and for Christians the gospel of John with Jesus as God. These four creatures will be mentioned again in chapter four of John's book of Revelation.

This was the call of Ezekiel. This was the glory of God, the *shekinah*. God was simultaneously ministering both in the region of Babylon and also with Jeremiah and his people 500 air-miles to the west in Jerusalem. This is an example of one of the attributes of God. He is omnipresent, in all places at all time. He is a transcendent God.

In the first verse of chapter two, the voice calls Ezekiel by the title "Son of man", the first of 93 times. This is not a demeaning title. It sets the space between God and man. The phrase had been used a dozen times previously in the Bible, but only as the general fact that humans are sons of humans. Here it is a title from God. Six hundred years later, Jesus would take it for a title of himself to emphasize that he is both deity and human.

In chapters two and three Ezekiel is commissioned five times. He is to go to the people in exile, who will reject him and seem like scorpions. He is also handed a scroll and directed to eat it, words and all, to "inwardly digest" that the heart's blood may carry it to every cell in the body. He did so, and it was sweet as honey in his mouth. In chapter ten of the Revelation, John will have a similar experience. The Spirit of God then lifted Ezekiel and took him to the exiles at Telabib, where he was overwhelmed for seven days. The name of this town was chosen for the name of the town of Telaviv in modern Israel.

In chapter three at verse sixteen, is the fourth commission of Ezekiel, that of a watchman, a sentry. About 150 years earlier, as the northern kingdom of Israel was collapsing, the prophet Hosea had used this metaphor in saying "the prophet is the watchman of Israel". The prophet Habakkuk, a contemporary of Jeremiah, working back in Jerusalem, had used it as he said he would take his stand to watch from the tower as he waited on God's response to his cry. Jeremiah has also used the metaphor as God said he had set watchmen over the people to give warning. The watchman is the first line of defensive warning. His duty is to stay awake, alert and sound the call of alarm should the enemy attack. These have been the prophets of God. These verses make clear that if the people do not heed the warning their blood is their fault, but if the watchman does not give the warning, their blood is on his hands. This is a clear call to evangelism, to spread the word, not to sit back and say all religions are the same and then tolerate a syncretic mixing of theology.

In chapter four we have an apocalyptic story of God telling Ezekiel to take a brick which will represent Jerusalem and to build a siege and ramparts around it. He is then to lie on his left side for thirteen months, 390 days (in the Greek, 190 days in Hebrew) and then turn and lie on his right side forty days. God would even tie him up with cords so he had to stay in position. Each day represented one year. During this time of almost fifteen months he was limited daily to twenty-two ounces of water and eight ounces of a mixture of grain and beans. The people of Jerusalem were being starved out during the siege. Students of the Bible have difficulty placing the two time periods, but it seems that both end when the people will be allowed to return. The 390 years would begin at the of death of Solomon and the division of the kingdom, indicating they had been dying of starvation since Solomon. The forty years would begin at the final collapse of Judah.

In chapter five Ezekiel is to tell the exiles of burning in fire, striking with the sword and being scattered to the winds, and of cannibalism during the siege. The four plagues of pestilence, famine, sword and wild beasts will be repeatedly brought on the people. He also says God has set the city of Jerusalem in the center of the nations. Which even seems true to this day, with the insoluble problems of the Near-East focused on Jerusalem.

From the days of Solomon, nearly 400 years earlier, the people had built altars to other gods on what have been called "high places". In chapter six God tells Ezekiel to tell the people of the condemnation of the mountains of Judah. Of these problems he is to tell them that this is all to get their attention and begins to say it is so "they will know that I am the Lord." In chapter seven is the telling of the coming end for Judah and Jerusalem, which may be occurring at the very moment God speaks of it to the people in exile. Again in verse fifteen are the four plagues, and in verse nineteen is described extreme inflation by which gold and silver are worthless. In verse twenty-six God places much of the blame on the priests and elders, from whom the law of God has perished.

Chapters eight through eleven depict the exit of the glory of God, the *shekinah*, from the temple and from Jerusalem, from the north gate, the entrance, the south gate, the east gate and finally the Mount of Olives. In chapter eight is described a vision of something like a man whose loins were on fire and whose upper torso gleamed like bronze. With what appeared to be a hand, this man grabbed Ezekiel by the hair of his head and lifted him to a point between earth and heaven where he saw a vision of the temple of Jerusalem. There he saw seated an image of jealousy, probably a statue of the sex goddess Astarte, Queen of Heaven, which provoked the glory of God, the *shekinah*. Abominations were seated upon the throne of God. Images of creepy things and idols were on the walls, and there were seventy elders waving smoke censers to them. Women were weeping for their fertility goddess. On the porch were twenty-five men with their backs to the temple as they faced the sun to worship it.

In chapter nine he saw that the glory of God, the *shekinah*, had moved from the throne and the *cherubim* to the doorway. The exit would continue. He saw six men, executioners, who were to go through the city slaughtering every person. With them was a man dressed in linen, who was to place a mark, which was the sign of the cross, the last letter of the Hebrew alphabet, on the forehead of those not to be slaughtered, the faithful remnant. The day for repentance had come and gone. Their deeds would be upon their heads.

In chapter ten is the continued exit of the glory of God, the *shekinah*, from the temple. Ezekiel saw the re-enactment of the glory, the bright cloud, moving from the *cherubim* to the threshold. The man dressed in linen participated. Again Ezekiel sees the wheels within wheels and the four living creatures with their four faces, but the face of the ox has been replaced by that of a *cherubim*. The glory of God moves further away. The ox is replaced by the *cherubim* which carry the *shekinah* from the threshold to the east gate in preparation to leave the area.

In chapter eleven God gives the hope of the restoration of the people to the land but with a new heart. He again sees those twenty-five men praying to other gods as God tells him he will gather them from this exile. At verse nineteen he picks up on the very thing Jeremiah tells the people back in Jerusalem, maybe even at the same time. God says, "I will give them one heart, and I will put a new spirit within them, and take the stony heart out of their flesh, and give them a heart of flesh, that they may walk in my statutes and keep my commandments; and they shall be my people, and I will be their God. But as for those whose hearts follow the desire for their detestable things and their abominations, I will recompense their deeds on their own heads." Still and again is that everlasting free-will to choose and that condition to the promise. Then "the *cherubim* lifted up their wings, with the wheels beside them, and the glory of the God of Israel was high above them. And the glory of the Lord went up from the midst of the city and stood on the mountain." Humans have free will to turn their back on God. God has free will to walk away from such a person.

For Ezekiel, he now has come fully to the time of the exile. In chapter twelve God tells him of the symbols of the dismay of exile and of the natural fear of the people. This is all so that "they will know that I am the Lord." In chapter thirteen God again lays much of the blame on the heads of the false prophets, both male and female. They had spoken for their own personal profit, telling of the personal visions, and not of visions from God. He tells of the prophets telling the people that all is peace and fine, just as Jeremiah was warning, when in fact it was horrible. The elements of the weather will bring the final destruction of the temple.

In chapter fourteen God again tells of the idolatrous worship of other gods. He mentions the strong men of Noah, Job, and even of Daniel, who is now beginning his work in the palace in Babylon. He alludes to the new covenant as a change from the old, as he cautions that the righteousness of one man does not serve to save another, not even that person's child. There is no more inheritance of salvation. Again he calls up the four acts of judgment, being sword, famine, evil beasts and pestilence. All of the Hebrews were not worthless by nature. There was a remnant of faithful believers who would be saved as all others would be consumed.

And here continues, as follows on the next pages, the rest of the story of Ezekiel.

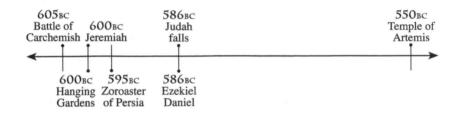

605ʙᴄ | 586ʙᴄ | 550ʙᴄ
Battle of | 600ʙᴄ | Judah | Temple of
Carchemish | Jeremiah | falls | Artemis

600ʙᴄ | 595ʙᴄ | 586ʙᴄ
Hanging | Zoroaster | Ezekiel
Gardens | of Persia | Daniel

CHAPTER 24

EZEKIEL 15-48
APOSTASY AND RESTORATION OF ISRAEL

I will give you a new heart and put a new spirit within you; I will take the heart of stone out of your flesh and give you a heart of flesh. I will put my Spirit within you. Ezk. 36:26-27

Jeremiah, Ezekiel and Daniel all prophesied at the time of the collapse of Judah, the second and final of the two small city-state princedoms, of the end of the kingdom of David and Solomon. We are reminded that Jeremiah had received his call and had begun preaching in Jerusalem in 627 B.C. Four years later, in 623, Ezekiel had been born near Jerusalem. Three years later, in 620, Daniel had been born. In 605, when Nebuchadnezzar defeated the Assyrian armies and then first invaded Judah and Jerusalem, Ezekiel was studying for the priesthood. At that time Daniel, a fifteen-year old lad without blemish was carried away in the first wave of exiles to Babylon. In 598 when Ezekiel was force-marched to Babylon to remain among the exiles, Daniel was already working in Nebuchadnezzar's palace, and had been for seven years. Ezekiel and Daniel most certainly knew one another and Jeremiah well.

This was a time of changing of empires, of world war. Ezekiel spoke during the very active time of the consolidation of the empire of Babylonia under Nebuchadnezzar, and as the Persian empire began to grow. Daniel would speak as the Persian empire, with its religion of Zoroaster, conquered Babylon. About 100 years later, the Persian empire would begin its fall to the rising Greek empire, with its religious concepts and thoughts. All of this worldly history is the stage for these men.

Jeremiah and Ezekiel are the prophets of the new covenant, of God's word and commandments being written on the hearts of humans, and not upon stone as in the past. Here was the colossal seed change of the relationship of God to his people. It was about 585 years before the birth of Jesus the Christ, who for many who call themselves Christians is the Messiah, and the actuality of that new covenant. The stage is here being set. That is the single, solitary big event in the history of mankind.

It is of the utmost importance for a person to impress upon his or her mind, and heart, that the time of Jeremiah, Ezekiel and Daniel was not just a time of tremendous changing world empires. Of greater importance, it was a time of changing theology by the unchanging God. The first temple, that built by Solomon, of which we see many drawings, is forever changed. In about fifty years Cyrus of Persia will free the exiles to return home. Not all will return, and those who do will reluctantly rebuild the walls and a very small temple of Jerusalem. There will never again be a descendant of David to sit on any earthly throne. For about 650 years, until shortly after the crucifixion of Jesus, there would be descendants of Levi to serve as *kohanim*, priests, at the temple altar, but there would never again be services and sacrifices as previously. As Ezekiel observed, the glory of God, the *shekinah*, had moved out of the temple, never to return, because the Hebrews had placed other gods on the throne in the temple. Jesus would even refer to Herod's temple as a "den of thieves".

We humans have determined there are two lines of thought, two theologies, as to how God has dealt with his people. One line is called "Covenantal" and one is called "Dispensational". Each divide human history into seven, or maybe eight, sections, which fairly match each other as to time periods in human history. The eight covenants God has made are titled Edenic, Adamic, Noahic, Abrahamic, Mosaic, Davidic, Palestine and New. The eight dispensations are Innocence in Eden, Conscience with Adam, Human-government with Noah, Promise with Abraham, Law with Moses, Grace with the First Coming, Kingdom with the Second Coming, and Righteousness in Eternity.

A comparative study of these two is a long-term study. As to which one you or your local church ascribe, a few points will give an indication. As to the old Hebrew scriptures, "covenantal" belief is that people are to accept all unless specifically rejected in the new Christian scriptures, whereas "dispensational" belief is that people are to reject all of the old unless specifically accepted in the new. As to the old prophecy, covenantal belief is that it deals with the people as church, whereas dispensational is that it deals with ethnic Israel. As to the millennium, that 1,000-year period at the end times, covenantal belief is that it is most likely symbolic and could apply to various times in relation to the second coming, whereas dispensational is that it is literal, earthly and has not yet begun.

During the late nineteenth century, after the American war between the states, there was a surge of study of the Bible. One branch began as a fine analysis but eventually drifted off into a belief that the Bible was essentially just another book written by some men. That wagon-load was pulled by what may be called "liberal churches", churches liberated from the scriptures. To counter that drift there began what may be called "fundamentalism", which published certain foundational beliefs for Christians, and led to the movements called "Pentecostal" and "Holiness." In the early twentieth century, these separate views and emphases gave rise to church splits and new denominations, such as the Assembly of God, which may be a modern third wagon somewhere between "pentecostal-conservative" and "liberal-progressive."

Part of the biblical research which started these wagons was an interest in biblical prophecy, primarily Isaiah, Jeremiah, Ezekiel, Daniel and Revelation. Depending upon how one defines these, there was the Second Great Awakening of 1790-1860 A.D. and the Great Revival of 1870-1890. The great disseminators of Dispensational, as opposed to Covenantal, theology spoke and wrote in the late nineteenth and early twentieth centuries. Some of the dispensationalists were John N. Darby, Cyrus I. Scofield and Charles Larkin. In 1909 and 1917, Scofield published his thoughts and notes on many passages of the Bible, in what was the first "study Bible" and known as the Scofield Reference Bible. His opinions introduced a somewhat new and different view as to Israel and a Jewish nation, elevating the prophecies of the Bible to the point of beginning new denominations, probably particularly out of those of the Methodist and Baptist groups.

As people were increasingly reading Scofield's notes as to prophecy, there were two men active in Austria. A Jewish man, Theodor Herzl, was publicizing his views that the Jews must return to and occupy Jerusalem, views later termed "Zionism." A struggling artist and architect, Adolph Hitler, was developing his views that the Jews should not move to Jerusalem, to Zion. Whenever a person drifts from reading the scripture with the faith of a child, to understand simply what God says, a problem breeds. In his second letter to Timothy, Paul cautioned us all to "rightly divide the word of truth." The truth is planted and grows according to Jews, Gentiles and the Church; as to times and seasons; as to covenants and dispensations; and as to earth and heaven. Jesus tells us to watch and believe and that there will be signs, but we will not know the hour.

And now we continue and conclude our overview of this book of Ezekiel. Ezekiel's first task was to explain to the Israelites the causes of their exile into Babylon. Ezekiel does this in the first twenty-four chapters with stories of many visions and of many directions from God to speak frankly to the exiles in Babylon. For Ezekiel these are essentially events of the past, of which he prophesies, "tells forth", the reasons for this punishment. In chapters twenty-five through thirty-two he prophesies as to the surrounding nations, both forth telling the reasons for their punishment past, and foretelling their punishment future. In chapters thirty-three through forty-eight he prophesies by foretelling of the future restoration of the people and of a mythical, or millennial, temple, practically too large to be built by human hands. This is the prophet of imagery, and one is required to read and reread and look at pictures and maps. For these reasons Ezekiel is normally avoided and frequently taught and preached with error, which it is trusted is not the case here.

Recall that Ezekiel uses five phrases time and again. These are "thus says the Lord God", twenty-seven times; "son of man", ninety-three times; "they shall know that I am God", fifty-seven times; "the word of the Lord came unto me", fifty times; and "the glory of God", twelve times, mostly in the first few chapters. Recall that a summary of Ezekiel would be that Ezekiel was nothing great, just "a son of man", but "the word of the Lord came to him" directing him to tell the exiles, "thus says the Lord God," "the glory of God" has moved away from Jerusalem, and the Israelites are being disciplined so that "you shall know that I am God."

In chapter fifteen we have an allegory of the vine and its branches but not in the way in which Jesus will speak. God refers to this as evil which he brought upon Jerusalem comparing the people to the wood of a vine which is worth nothing except burning in the fire. Ezekiel continues to tell the people their punishment is their own doing. In chapter sixteen Ezekiel tells them they were a motherless child whom God picked up and raised to womanhood. She was well raised, but turned into a harlot who sacrificed her own children as she paraded around as an adulterous wife. God will gather up her lovers, those surrounding nations, and destroy them all together. He says those nations and their gods are the mother of this girl, and quotes an old proverb, "Like mother, like daughter."

In chapter seventeen he speaks another allegory. There was a tall cedar of Lebanon among the topmost branches of which nested an eagle. This was Nebuchadnezzar, who was the instrument of God. However, the people, as a vine, reached out to another eagle, that of Egypt to save her. God then says he will take a branch from the very top of that cedar and plant it on the high place in Judah to save the people. For many Christians, this saving branch is Jesus the Christ, but the interpretation may depend upon whether such Christian is "covenantal" or "dispensational".

Chapter eighteen is the place of huge change in the covenant of God with his people. Mark it well. It is another part of the beginning of the New Covenant. The concept of writing on their hearts is expanded along a new branch. He quotes a proverb. "The fathers have eaten sour grapes, and the children's teeth are set on edge." This is very true. Not only is the child an inheritor of genes from the parent but also "genes" of the environment. The parent is extremely important to a child. The second commandment given to Moses as to having no graven images, goes on to say God will visit "the iniquity of the fathers upon the children to the third and fourth generations." The father eats sour grapes, and the teeth of his children have an awful taste.

God tells the people that one will neither be punished for the sins of another nor saved by the righteousness of another. Simply being a descendant of Adolph Hitler is no guarantee of being a lost soul and being a descendant of Abraham is no guarantee of salvation. Even during a person's own individual life span, a person can gain or can lose personal salvation. Here is personal, individual accountability and responsibility. This is not a New Testament concept. The entire eighteenth chapter explains this to those people, and to each of us. Being a citizen of a certain nation will not effect a person's salvation. Ezekiel takes Jeremiah's new covenant a step further. Mark this well.

Following on this individual accountability, in chapter twenty God and Ezekiel continue to emphasize that the people themselves are responsible and that only each person alone and nothing and nobody else can now save or lose any person. This theme continues through chapter twenty-four. In chapters twenty-five through thirty-two Ezekiel speaks of the nations surrounding the fallen kingdom of Solomon. They also will suffer, but above all "they will know that I am God," and God has not failed to save the people of the fallen kingdom but is disciplining them, as he will each of those nations and peoples.

In chapter thirty-four Ezekiel prophesies against the shepherds, the priests, the *kohanim*, of Israel. "Woe to the shepherds of Israel who feed themselves! Should not the shepherds feed the flocks? You eat the fat and clothe yourselves with the wool; you slaughter the fatlings, but you do not feed the flock. The weak you have not strengthened, nor have you healed those who were sick, nor bound up the broken, nor brought back what was driven away, nor sought what was lost; but with force and cruelty you have ruled them. So they were scattered because there was no shepherd....Behold, I am against the shepherds, and I will require my flock at their hand...I myself will search for my sheep and seek them out."

In chapter thirty-six Ezekiel prophesies that God says to the Israelites in exile, "I will take you from among the nations, gather you out of all countries, and bring you into your own land....I will give you a new heart and put a new spirit within you; I will take the heart of stone out of your flesh and give you a heart of flesh. I will put my Spirit within you and cause you to walk in my statutes, and you will keep my judgments and do them. Then you shall dwell in the land that I gave to your fathers; you shall be my people, and I shall be your God."

These verses certainly speak of a time fifty years later when the Hebrews will be allowed to return and also of the coming messianic age when many Hebrews are truly faithful believers. However, many people disconnect the foregoing as the following verses are quoted out of time context by modern "Zionists" and applied regularly to events in modern Palestine. "I will multiply the fruit or your trees and the increase of your fields....The desolate land shall be tilled instead of lying desolate in the sight of all who pass by."

Chapter thirty-seven has two   allegorical prophesies. In the first the Spirit of the Lord set Ezekiel down in the "valley of the dry bones". To these disconnected bones, God directed Ezekiel to prophesy. He did, and there was a noise, a rattling, as the dry bones came together, bone to bone. Then sinew, flesh and skin covered them. Then came the four winds and a breath, and the bones lived and stood up on their feet. Ezekiel explained that thus would God raise the exiled Hebrews and bring them back home from this exile in Babylon.

In the second allegory, God tells Ezekiel to take two sticks. He is to write on one the name "Judah" and on the other "Joseph and Israel". He was then to join the two sticks together as one stick. Ezekiel is to explain to the people that they will no longer be two separate people but only one, known as Israel. This was a time specific prophecy, that the two small kingdoms were one. However, many people disconnect and omit the foregoing and quote only the following, verse twenty-one, out of time context and apply it regularly to events in modern Israel-Palestine. "Surely I will take the children of Israel from among the nations, wherever they have gone, and will gather them from every side and bring them into their own land:" Verse twenty-two continues the concept and context of the Babylonian exile. "I will make them one people in the land, on the mountains of Israel; and one king shall be king over them all; they shall no longer be two nations." About forty years later King Cyrus of Persia would allow the captive Israelites to return to the mountains of Palestine.

Chapters thirty-eight and thirty-nine speak of Gog, Magog, Meshech and Tubal. Gog is a person who rules over the areas of Magog, Meshech and Tubal. This is a symbolic use of an unknown leader of unknown lands who and which would attack the area known as Israel, Judah and Palestine from the north. All attacks, except from Egypt, come from the north and not from the Sea to the west or the desert to the east. In this highly apocalyptically hidden prophesy it is impossible to determine who Gog may be nor where the lands are from which specific attack will come. In the early twentieth century C.I. Scofield took the position that the land was Russia, and so many so believe, though numerous other commentaries disagree.

The final nine chapters are prophesies as to the restored people and a restored temple. This vision came to Ezekiel in 573 B.C., thirty-five years before the people would be free to return. It is a plan, a blueprint, for the religious and political rehabilitation of the people of Israel. In chapters forty through forty-two we are told of the temple. When the people do return, they will not even attempt a serious endeavor to follow the blueprint, and such a temple will not be built. The reason may be that it is not a plan for the return and rebuilding by Zerubbabel. In addition to the problem of animal sacrifices, most read this as a symbolic plan for the true and pure worship of God or the future eternal reign of God, or the millenial reign of Christ. At verse one of chapter forty-three the vision was of the return of the glory of God, the *shekinah*, to the temple. At verse seven God sets some of the usual conditions on his return, including not defiling his name nor indulging in idolatry.

Because they had participated in desecrating the former temple, in chapter forty-four the Levitical priests are generally demoted to lesser functions in the visionary temple. Only the descendants of Zadok will serve as priests, *kohanim*, in the sanctuary and at the altar. Chapter forty-seven tells of a river which flows from the threshold of the altar, the center of the temple. It is not normal water but is a healing and nurturing water which gets deeper as it flows, though there are no tributary in-flows. Chapter forty-eight tells of a visionary or symbolic division of the land as held at the time of David.

And here begin, as on the following pages, the story and prophecies of Daniel.

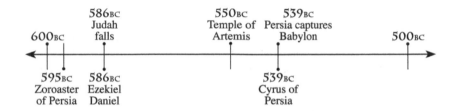

586ʙᴄ
Judah
600ʙᴄ   falls

550ʙᴄ   539ʙᴄ
Temple of Persia captures
Artemis   Babylon   500ʙᴄ

595ʙᴄ   586ʙᴄ
Zoroaster Ezekiel
of Persia Daniel

539ʙᴄ
Cyrus of
Persia

CHAPTER 25

DANIEL

DANIEL, NEBUCHADNEZZAR, VISIONS, CYRUS, PERSIA

A stone was cut out of the mountain, without hands, and it smote the image on its feet of iron and clay, and broke them in pieces, and also the bronze, the silver, and the gold. Dan. 2:34, 45

Daniel means "judgment of God". With Daniel we awake to a drastic change in the history of Israel, of the Jewish nation and people. Jeremiah was at the rising face a vast watershed, and Daniel was at the falling face of that watershed. An immeasurable change of the environment and life of the Hebrews had occurred. Suddenly they were captives among a people whose prosperity they had never imagined. Forever altered are the concepts of Abraham, of Moses, of Joshua, of the land promised, of Kings David and Solomon and the Temple. There was no Moses. The Temple was burned to a heap of ashes. Unlike the people of the South after the U.S. War Between the States and the Japanese after World War II, but like the East Germans of WWII, the Jews were deported, scattered and dispersed across the Mid-East.

Jeremiah, Ezekiel and Daniel were all contemporaries, with Jeremiah being about twenty-five years older than the other two. Jeremiah had begun prophesying in Judah several years before Nebuchadnezzar first invaded in 605 B.C., and took away young Daniel. Seven years later, Nebuchadnezzar invaded again and took away Ezekiel, who shortly began prophesying in captivity to the exiles. For many years Jeremiah spoke at home in Judah and Ezekiel spoke hundreds of miles to the east, yet they both said very similar things and possibly on the same days. Daniel is somewhat different. His whole story is told from the palace of Nebuchadnezzar and does not relate directly to his fellow Israelites living in exile. The people taken away by Nebuchadnezzar totaled about 5,000 to 10,000. The number taken about 140 years earlier by Assyria may have numbered 50,000 to 100,000.

To fully understand the books of Kings, and their complement of Chronicles, and the books of the prophets coming at the time of the latter portion of those books, one should study other books to become familiar with the surrounding countries of Egypt, Assyria, Babylon and Persia. One should have a working knowledge of that period of 900 B.C. to 600 B.C. Daniel, who lived to be about ninety, moves us further along in time and in geography, not just with his own era but with his visions and prophecies. To attempt to understand Daniel's prophecies, one should have more than a superficial knowledge of the period from 600 B.C. to the time of Christ, and many believe even beyond that to about 1800 A.D. One certainly should have a book or two handy to explain the Babylonian empire of Nebuchadnezzar, the Medo-Persian empire of Cyrus and those Xerxes successors, the Egyptians, the rise and decay of Alexander's Greek empire and its successor the Roman empire. These twenty-one pages of Daniel are packed with words as to all of these empires. Without some knowledge of history and geography it is futile to participate in a discussion as to Daniel.

An indication of the historical depth of this book, is that the Babylon of Daniel's day is referred to by reference books as neo-Babylon. The old Babylon existed some 1,200 years prior, right after the time of Abraham. The best known ruler of old Babylon was Hammurabi, who is credited with writing the early civil codes, some of which basic human rules would appear in the code of Moses. The glory of both old Babylon and new Babylon is that which Saddam Hussein of Iraq claimed to be rebuilding in the late twentieth century.

The first six chapters, half of the book, of Daniel are historical and include two dreams of Nebuchadnezzar. When a teenager, three of Daniel's friends were put into a fiery furnace. When a man in his early eighties, Daniel was put into the lions' den. The second half is of Daniel's four visionary dreams. They are of the dream of the four beasts, very similar to those later in Revelation; his vision of the ram and the he-goat; the prophecy of seventy weeks; and the vision of the days to come, of the Greek empire and possibly the Roman empire.

A contemporary of Daniel was Zoroaster, whose name in Greek was Zarathustra, as in "Thus Spake Zarathustra". He was a religious teacher and prophet of ancient Persia, modern Iran, to the east of Babylon, "Iraq". Zoroaster was born about seven years before Daniel was born. As his religious teachings were of the peaceful and sedentary life, many of his teachings can cause confusion with some of the teachings of the new Christian scriptures.

Daniel is not some outdated book of mystical fortune telling. Many have wasted countless days trying to figure out the numbers and dates given by Daniel in his explanations of these dreams and visions. The message of Daniel is that God is in control, is sovereign, has a plan and is always with those who believe and faithfully persevere in that belief regardless of seeming defeat, as on a cross. This book does have a connection to John's book of Revelation. In Revelation Babylon is the evil empire, but Daniel depicts Nebuchadnezzar and his people to be much like many people attending many churches today. They are basically good people, though not particularly religious or believers.

The book of Daniel begins at chapter twenty-four of Second Kings, after the death of Josiah, the good king of Judah, who took his army down from the hill country to attempt to stop Neco, the Pharaoh of Egypt, from passing on north to war against rising Babylon at Carchemish. After four years of war, Babylon defeated Egypt and Assyria and turned south toward Judah. The first verse of chapter twenty-four says simply that Nebuchadnezzar made Judah's King Jehoiakim submit to him. The book of Daniel begins by telling us that at that time Daniel, a youth without blemish, was taken as a captive back to Babylon.

Nebuchadnezzar ordered that the captive young men in his palace eat the same food and drink the same wine as the king, and that they be well educated, for three years. Daniel and his three friends were to be given new names, for their new lives. Daniel was renamed Belteshazzar; Hananiah was renamed Shadrach; Mishael was renamed Meshach; and Azariah was renamed Abed-Nego. The youths did not rebel against their new names, but Daniel did object to the rich diet and wine. He requested that the four of them eat only vegetables and drink water for ten days. His request was granted. After the ten days it was observed that the four were healthier than the others, so their diet was continued, and their education.

In chapter two, when Daniel was about eighteen, we have the first of two dreams of Nebuchadnezzar. The dream troubled the king, and he could not sleep. He told no one the contents of his dream. He called before him his magicians and sorcerers to tell him the meaning of the dream. They protested that they could not interpret the dream if he would not tell them what he had dreamed. The king became angry and furious and directed that all the wise men be destroyed. They sought out Daniel to help them. Daniel went to the king to plead that he be given time to tell the king as to the dream. Time was given.

Daniel went to his three friends, Hananiah, Mishael and Azariah, and asked them to seek the mercy of God for him. The dream of the king was then revealed to Daniel. At verse twenty we have Daniel's hymn of praise to God. Daniel returned to seek an audience with the king. Daniel told him he was not able to make known the dream but that God in heaven was able and began to tell of the dream.

The king had dreamed of a great image of human form. Its "head was of fine gold, its chest and arms of silver, its belly and thighs of bronze, its legs of iron, its feet partly of iron and partly of clay." In verses thirty-four and forty-five Daniel reports a fact which is seldom reported, except among what today may be called "fundamentalist" churches. "A stone was cut out of the mountain, without hands, and it smote the image on its feet of iron and clay, and broke them in pieces, and also the bronze, the silver, and the gold."

He continues, from foot to head. "Then the iron, the clay, the bronze, the silver, and the gold were crushed together, and became like chaff from the summer threshing floors: the wind carried them away so that no trace of them was found. And the stone that smote the image became a great mountain and filled the whole earth." This is the "smiting stone," which is rarely to never preached in the more liberal churches. "In the days of these (final ten) kings the God of heaven will set up a kingdom which shall never be destroyed." Many Christians see this stone as Jesus the Christ.

Daniel explains that the head of gold represents Nebuchadnezzar himself. He explains that "the God of heaven has given (the king) a kingdom, power, strength and glory." As to the chest and arms of silver, Daniel only says that such is another kingdom which shall arise and be inferior. As to the belly and thighs of bronze, he says only that a third kingdom then shall rule over all the earth. As to the legs of iron, there shall be a fourth kingdom which shall break and crush all of the others. As to the feet and toes partly of clay and partly of iron, there shall be yet another kingdom, a divided kingdom, which shall break apart.

Upon hearing this interpretation, this powerful king "fell on his face, prostrate before Daniel" and answered, "Truly your God is the God of gods, the Lord of kings." He promoted Daniel on the spot and made him ruler over the whole province of Babylon and chief administrator over all the wise men, a position he would hold for about seventy years. This is very similar to the promotion of Joseph back in Egypt, about 800 years earlier. This book of Daniel depicts Nebuchadnezzar quite favorably, as he was the agent of God to discipline the people of Israel.

From this simple explanation of the dream has come a great deal of speculation over the centuries. All agree the head of gold is Nebuchadnezzar, as Daniel makes clear, whose kingdom will end in 539 B.C. As to the rest of the image, speculation scatters and seems to depend upon one's view of the church of Rome, for or against. This division also applies to the vision of four beasts in chapter seven, the vision of the ram and the he-goat in chapter eight and to the vision of the end times in chapter eleven. This division of two different interpretations causes great confusion, especially to a person not aware of the two interpretations.

As to the great image, the point of disagreement and separation begins with the chest and arms of silver. The two separate views are whether the chest and arms of silver are the combined Medo-Persian kingdom, modern Iran, which kingdom ended in 331 B.C., or that of the Medes only with the Persian empire then dropping to be the belly and thighs of bronze. This is purely human speculation as Daniel gives no guidance.

The view that the chest and arms of silver is the combined Medo-Persian kingdom is somewhat anti-Roman as it allows the bronze belly and thighs to be the Greek empire, which will end in 146 B.C., and the legs and feet of iron and clay to be the Roman empire, which will finally end in 476 A.D. This is probably the more realistic view as the Roman empire was a coming reality, but need not necessarily extend to and include the Roman church, though many take it to that level.

The other view, that the chest and arms are the Medes only, drops the Persian empire to be the belly and thighs of bronze and the Greek empire to being the legs and feet. This seems to be a very pro-Roman view as neither the Roman empire nor church are smote into pieces. Both the Greek and the Roman empires divided into what can be counted as ten kingdoms and did horrible things to the Jews just before and after the birth of Christ. Proponents of each view can very neatly prove out the dates and persons to support their respective view.

In chapter three we are told that Nebuchadnezzar made a statue nearly ninety feet tall, very skinny and over-laid with gold. He ordered that upon the sound of many musical instruments, including the horn and the bagpipe, everybody was to fall down in worship of this statue. Certain wise men, being jealous of Daniel and his people, had the king also order that any one who did not so bow down would be cast into the furnace. Then certain men came to the king and maliciously accused Daniel's three friends of not so bowing down. Calling them by their Babylonian names, Shadrach, Meshach and Abed-Nego were brought before the king, questioned and ordered cast into the furnace. To hold these men it would have been a large furnace, no doubt a smelting furnace, which was heated to seven times normal. The three were fully clothed, bound and put into the furnace. The heat was so great that the men who ushered them into the furnace were burned to death.

When the king looked upon the three, he saw with them a fourth man. They were all four just walking around in the furnace. The fourth was like the Son of God. He ordered them to come before him. The three came, but we are not told about the fourth. The cords which bound them were burnt away, but not a hair or piece of clothing was harmed or even smelled of smoke. Nebuchadnezzar exclaimed, "Blessed be the God of Shadrach, Meshach and Abed-Nego," and he decreed that nobody would speak against that God.

In the Apocrypha, several short books used in the Roman Bible, we find two hymns of praise the three young men recited while in the furnace. One is attributed only to Azariah, known as Abed-Nego, and the other by all three and is used in the Morning Prayer service in most Anglican prayer books as the *Benedicite, omnia*, "O all ye works, of the Lord, bless ye the Lord."

In chapter four we have Nebuchadnezzar's second dream, which is probably decades after that first dream. Nebuchadnezzar is about sixty years old and Daniel about fifty. He dreamed of a great and strong tree in the midst of the earth. It reached to the heavens, and all of the birds nested in its branches and the beasts found shade and all flesh fed from it. Then a watcher came down from heaven and ordered the tree cut down and cut apart. The stump was to remain and be bound with iron. The stump was personified, and its mind was changed from that of a man to that of a beast for a period of seven times. He reveals this dream to the wise men, who can not explain it, so he calls in Daniel, who came.

Daniel is at first alarmed, but he explains. The tree is Nebuchadnezzar who provides for all his people. He is to lose his mind for seven years and wander among the beasts of the field, and made to eat grass like an ox. Twelve months later this illness and experience will indeed come upon the king. At the end of seven years he just as suddenly recovers, and again praises the God of heaven.

At the date of this dream of Nebuchadnezzar, probably 570 B.C., Daniel is about fifty years old. Zoroaster, the Persian religious philosopher, is fifty-seven. Pythagoras, the Greek philosopher and mathematician, is twelve years old. Buddha will be born in India in about seven years. Confucius will be born in China in about nineteen years.

Chapters seven and eight compose a flashback between chapters four and five. Daniel has one dream in which he has four visions. In chapter seven is the first vision, in which he sees four great beasts, each beast different from the other, come up out of the sea. The first is like a lion with two eagle's wings. The second is like a bear which lies on its side with three ribs in its mouth. The third is like a leopard with four bird's wings. The fourth is a dreadful beast with ten horns, with a little horn. We are not told what these four beasts represent. Scholars say these four correspond to the four parts of the great image in Nebuchadnezzar's dream in chapter two and present the same two divergent views, as to whether or not the Medo-Persian kingdom was combined thereby setting up the third stage as Greece and the fourth as Rome. Today most agree the lion corresponds to the image's head of gold and represents Babylon. The bear corresponds to the chest and arms of silver, and here we have the same disagreement. Those who think chest and arms of silver is the combined Medo-Persian kingdom also think the bear is the Medes and Persians, a somewhat anti-Roman empire and church view. Those who believe the dream ceases with the bad times just before the birth of Jesus, say the bear represents the Medes, and then the leopard the Persians and the dreadful beast the end of the Greek empire as Antiochus Epiphanes. Those who believe the dream extends on to cover the church of Rome, say the bear is the combined Medo-Persian empire, the leopard the Greeks, and the beast the Romans. Both sides admirably defend their view.

In verse twenty-five we have the first of four times given. "A time, two times and half a time." This is three-and-a-half, which is half of seven. A "time" is deemed a "year", which is probably the prophetic year of 360 days, which may then be further confused with each prophetic day representing a year for 1,260 years. The hopeless confusion as to numbers begins.

Chapter eight is Daniel's third vision, that of a ram and a he-goat. The he-goat, with a pointed horn on its forehead, came out of the west and attacked the ram. The scripture tells us the ram represents Medo-Persia, successor to Babylon, and also that the goat is the Greek empire, which rapidly will bring an end to the Persian empire in 331 B.C. In verse nine we are told of a little horn coming out of the goat, and the modern interpretation begins as to whether this is Antiochus Epiphanes of about 170 B.C., or is the church of Rome, centuries after Christ. Both sides give good debate. In verse fourteen we have the second of four times given. There are to be 2,300 evenings and mornings, which may be 1,150 days, or 2,300 days or 2,300 years, which can get one to about the time of the American War of Independence. There is no specific starting date for the days or years and much modern confusion as to interpretation.

After putting the preceding flash-back in place, we now go to chapter five and the story of the feast of King Belshazzar with the handwriting on the wall. This takes place about 539 B. C. when Daniel is eighty-two years old, and near the end of his life. Nebuchadnezzar has died and been succeeded by Belshazzar, who holds a great feast for which he uses the vessels taken from the temple. A finger appears and writes on the wall in an unknown language. Daniel, who had been renamed Belteshazzar, is called to explain the writing to Belshazzar. He explains that the king and kingdom has been weighed in the balance and found wanting and are to be given over to the Medes and the Persians. The next verse, the last in the chapter, tells us that very night the Persians capture the city of Babylon. The first verse and last verses are an interesting combination, the kingdom is lost during a night of revelry, as the watchmen fail to watch. As in Nebuchadnezzar's dream, the Babylonian kingdom, the head of gold, lasted only as long as the seventy years of exile, and was replaced by the chest and arms of silver.

Seventy years earlier the Assyrian city of Nineveh had been captured by the Babylonians by causing a flooding of the Khambar River, a tributary of the Tigris River which ran through it. Now the city of Babylon is captured by the Medes and Persians, as the inhabitants party, by diverting the Euphrates River which runs through it, to allow the invaders to come through the water tunnels. In both situations the watchmen on the tower fail to observe and to warn.

The victorious Medes and Persians also keep Daniel in his position of authority. The king of the Medes decrees that no one will worship any god except him for thirty days, upon penalty of being thrown to the lions. Daniel, then about seventy-two years old, is spied upon as he prays openly to God. Much to his own regret the king has Daniel thrown into the lion's den. The king can not sleep that night. The next morning he rushes to check on Daniel, finds him alive and well and promptly orders him released. This chapter six concludes by telling us Daniel continues to serve King Cyrus of Persia, and is no doubt responsible for the decree of return, as he very likely tells the king that Isaiah had prophesied about a century earlier of a ruler named Cyrus who would set the captives free.

Chapter nine begins with mention of Daniel reading of Jeremiah's prophecy of seventy years of exile and captivity of the Jews, which period is at the time about concluded. Then we have twenty-one verses of Daniel's prayer. At verse twenty-four is the prophecy of seventy "sevens," translated in many Bibles as seventy "weeks of years", as brought to him by the angel Gabriel, and not to be confused with the preceding seventy years of captivity. This "seventy sevens" could be 490 days but is most likely the prophetic 490 years, which years are probably short years of 360 days. Gregorian calendar years would be 483, which would put the end of the "seven sevens" at the crucifixion of Christ. The seventy is 7-62-1, with no gap, however, some interpretations separate that final seven year period with an ever enlarging elastic gap, now some 2,000 years long.

Chapter ten sets the stage for chapter eleven. Again Gabriel, or some believe Christ of the Christian scriptures, appears to Daniel, and explains that he has been delayed three weeks because of problems contesting with the bad angel of Persia. As for understanding chapter eleven we look to Gabriel's advise to Daniel in verses four and nine of chapter twelve. In chapter twelve, Daniel is twice told to close up and seal the book of this vision until the end of time. We are not to understand chapter eleven until the end. However, countless people have wasted countless hours vainly attempting to decipher it.

Chapter eleven is of the wars between the kingdom of the north and the kingdom of the south. All agree that until verse fourteen, all applies to the last two divisions of the Greek empire, the Seleucids of Syria and the Ptolemies of Egypt. The disagreement begins at verse fourteen. Those who believe the end is with Antiochus Epiphanes just before the birth of Jesus, continue the dates in tight succession. Those who believe the problem is the church of Rome, add some elastic gap and jump at verse fourteen from about 200 B.C. to the take over by Rome of Palestine beginning in 65 B.C. These dates are great for learning and discussion, but we are not to understand until the end times. In chapter twelve Daniel is told twice to "shut up the words and seal the book until the time of the end...for the words are closed up and sealed till the time of the end."

And here begin, as follows on the next pages, the stories of Ezra and Haggai. In most Bibles, Ezra is about 475 pages preceding Daniel, and Haggai is about 75 pages following.

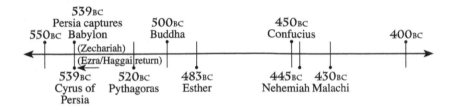

539BC
Persia captures
550BC Babylon
(Zechariah)
(Ezra/Haggai return)
539BC 520BC
Cyrus of Pythagoras
Persia

500BC
Buddha

483BC
Esther

450BC
Confucius

445BC 430BC
Nehemiah Malachi

400BC

CHAPTER 26

EZRA AND HAGGAI

RETURN OF EXILES AND REPEAT OF SYNCRETISM

Make confession to the Lord God of our fathers, and do his will; separate yourselves from the people of the land, and from marrying pagans. Ezr. 10:11

Chapter five of Daniel tells us of the feast of Belshazzar, king of Babylon, and of the handwriting on the wall, which Daniel, at the age of eighty-two, interpreted. The last verse of that chapter tells us that Belshazzar died that very night as the Medes, and Persians, captured Babylon. Daniel, one of the many exiles, was among those captured, and he remained active in the palace of the new rulers, the Medo-Persians. The kingdom of Babylon, of Nebuchadnezzar, had lasted a short time, just barely long enough to take and contain the captives for seventy years.

Daniel was most certainly quite familiar with the book of Isaiah, which had been written about 150 years earlier, though some more liberated scholars think the second part was written by someone else about the time Cyrus released the exiles. Isaiah chapter forty-four verse twenty-eight and chapter forty-five verse one state that one Cyrus shall fulfill God's purpose that the temple be rebuilt and that God will open the way for Cyrus to do that. Tradition and logic are that Daniel was instrumental in motivating the decision of Cyrus to decree the release of the Hebrews as he pointed out to King Cyrus that prophecy from Isaiah. The Persian empire which Cyrus had founded, of the Achaemenid kings, was sympathetically tolerant of the religions of those they governed, including the Jews.

****

EZRA

Ezra, a scribe and student of the Mosaic law, gives day, month and year for many of these events. He begins this restoration of the community of exiles to Jerusalem with such a supporting statement. Cyrus of Persia states that the God of heaven has commanded him to rebuild the temple in Jerusalem. He decrees, in 538 B.C., that the exiles be allowed to return and build the temple in Jerusalem, and further that the people of the place where any exile lives help with silver, gold, goods, cattle and free-will offerings. Further, Cyrus brings forth the silver and gold vessels which Nebuchadnezzar had removed from the temple and gives them to the exiles to take back with them. It seems God used Babylon not only to punish and remove the disobedient Hebrews, but also to keep both the exiles and the vessels until the time of return to their homeland.

In chapter two Ezra itemizes those returning to Jerusalem in the first release, which is by far the largest group. He tallies 42,360 plus 7,337 servants for a total of nearly 50,000. This was not all of the exiles, some think it was a fairly small part, as many chose to remain where they were having done as Jeremiah had directed and built homes and livelihoods. The leader of this caravan and the new government of the returnees is Zerubbabel, a descendant of David. The head priest is Jeshua. Ezra himself does not go with this first group but remains behind in Persia, where he records the events occurring in Jerusalem in the first six chapters of his book. About eighty years later, at chapter seven, he will lead the second, much smaller group, and continue his record as an on-site participant.

With the collapse of the kingdom of David and Solomon, the destruction of their temple and the deportation of the Jews, a dramatic change in the lives and lifestyle of the Hebrew people occurred. They were no longer identifiable as an independent nation. The cult of animal sacrifices was terminated. According to tradition Ezra, the student of the law, is credited with the beginning of the formation of the Hebrew Bible, the scripture canon, which will be finalized shortly before the time of Christ. He is credited also with the beginning of the "synagogue" style of worship, which is teaching and Bible studies, which will take on full form about the time of Christ. From this synagogue style will come the Christian form of church worship.

In chapter three we are told of the people rebuilding the temple. They are settled in Jerusalem by October 537 B.C. These first six chapters of temple building cover twenty-one years. After unpacking the first thing the returning exiles do is build the altar, to offer burnt offerings according to the law of Moses. It is the time of year for the civil New Year and the Day of Atonement (*Yom Kippur*), followed by the Feast of Tabernacles (Booths), to commemorate living in tents during the exodus from Egypt. Certainly many of those returning exiles are living in tents around Jerusalem.

In verse seven, we are told that King Cyrus gave them a grant of money for the venture, and from this they pay the workers. The foundation of the temple is laid. The priests are given their assignments and their vestments. They praise God and sing some psalms responsively. Some of the older people who had seen the former temple weep, no doubt because this temple is so much less in size and grandeur. However, others shout for joy, and their sounds merge as one. This was not to be the temple of David and Solomon nor will it be the one described by Ezekiel thirty-five years earlier.

There is no work of God which is not opposed by the people of the world. This restoration is no exception to such a challenge. In chapter four we are told of these. Along the top ridges of the mountain range, some fifty miles north of Jerusalem, the capitol of the former southern kingdom of Judah, lies Samaria, the capitol of the former northern kingdom of Israel. The last of the ten tribes of Hebrews living to the north had been removed nearly 200 years earlier and replaced by a mixture of immigrants. Those transplanted inhabitants of Samaria had fought with those of Jerusalem then, and now it was much more extreme. And this animosity between the descendants of those transplanted into Samaria and the returnees will continue another five centuries to the time of Christ.

In chapter four Ezra tells us of the strong resistance of the Samaritans to any rebuilding by the returned exiles in Jerusalem. First they use fake friendship to attempt to infiltrate the returnees, as they offer to help with construction. This offer is turned down. Then they hire counselors to frustrate the construction. This technique of intimidation works. Construction of the temple stops, but construction of personal homes picks up. As in the past, the returned Jews are again disobeying and joining the world around them. This intimidation and neglect of the temple continues until 530 B.C. and the death of King Cyrus, and even through the reign of King Cambyses and also the reign of King Darius. In verse six we are told the Samaritans continue their harassment well after that by writing a letter to King Ahasuerus, who succeeded Darius. Their letter to Ahasuerus is to complain that the Jews were considering building a wall around the city and would then cease paying taxes and rebel. Ahasuerus then orders that all construction cease. Ahasuerus (Xerxes) is the king in the book of Esther.

In chapter four we find many names which should be identified. These are some of the rulers of the kingdom of the silver chest and arms of Nebuchadnezzar's dream interpreted by Daniel, as they are repelled by the early rulers of the belly and thighs of bronze. In verse five is Darius. This is the king who extended the Persian empire westward across modern Turkey to the area of modern Greece. After four years of planning, Darius unsuccessfully invaded ancient Greece but was defeated in the battle of Marathon in 490 B.C. A Greek named Pheidippides ran with the news of victory to Athens twenty-one (six?) miles away, and died from exhaustion. The Greek empire was being born. In verse six we hear of Ahasuerus who succeeded Darius. That was his Persian name; the Greeks called him Xerxes. This is the king in the book of Esther. He also planned an invasion of Greece, which he began in 480 B.C. with five million troops and supporting navy. He was forced from Thermopolae and in 479, lured into a trap at Salamis, lost his fleet to the Greek trimere ramming ships. The Macedonians and Greeks would struggle among themselves for 150 years until Philip II, father of Alexander, consolidated the empire. In verse seven is mentioned King Artaxerxes, who permitted the building of the wall around Jerusalem, and was the last ruler in the old Hebrew scriptures. In verse twelve the people are referred to as "Jews" to begin that title as the name by which they will be called. It is a nickname for those who live in Jerusalem in Judah.

****

HAGGAI

Work on the temple, mostly the altar, lasted less than two years, ceasing in 535 B.C. Ezra chapter five begins by telling that the prophets Haggai and Zechariah speak to the Jews to encourage them to continue rebuilding the temple. Here we insert the book of the prophet Haggai, only two pages long, and which we now discuss. We also could insert the first six chapters of the book of the prophet Zechariah, but we will discuss him in the next section. These are two of the three very short books at the very end of the old Hebrew scriptures. Haggai is a practical prophet, as he tells the Jews simply to finish the temple. Zechariah is a visionary prophet who will give them hope. The pre-exilic prophets spoke of punishment. The exilic prophets spoke of consolation. Now the three post-exilic prophets speak of restoration.

Between chapters five and six of Ezra, which tell of the rebuilding of the temple, is a fifteen-year gap. God then sends Haggai to encourage the disheartened people. Haggai tells us in his first verse that the time is August 520 B.C., during the reign of King Darius, seventeen years after the first return. Haggai delivered four brief prophetic sermons. Chapter one is the first, as he tells them they have been distracted by too many personal matters. The Lord tells Haggai that the people are stalling and saying it is not yet time to complete the temple. He challenges the people, asking, "Is it time for you yourselves to dwell in your paneled houses, and this temple to lie in ruins?" He asks them to consider that during the time they were not working on the temple, their crops have been small, their drink has not satisfied them, their clothes have not kept them warm, and their wages are "put into a bag with holes." Haggai tells them God directs that they to go to the mountains to get wood for the temple, and God will blow away whatever else they may do, and repeats the fact that they wrongly busy themselves with their own house and neglect the house of God. Zerubbabel, their civil leader, has the people obey. Haggai gives them God's message, "I am with you, says the Lord." The people begin to work on the temple.

The first third of chapter two is Haggai's second sermon as he gives encouragement to those of riper years who had seen the temple of Solomon and were disappointed with this one. He tells them that the God who brought the people out of Egypt is still with them, and further nudges that prophecy of Jeremiah and Ezekiel as to writing the law on their hearts, to which Ezekiel added that a new spirit will be put within them. "My Spirit remains among you: Do not fear." There is a very definite movement in the increasing illumination of the revelation of God. From the presence of his *shekinah* glory comes the presence of his Holy Spirit, which for many Christians is yet some five centuries into the future.

In the middle third, Haggai admonishes them as to the syncretism of mixing the faith of God with other religions. This is an ancient complication, which, at the end of the twentieth century, will be known as multiculturalism or new tolerance as to all religions being equal, which leads to no religion except that which each individual may conjure. He asks whether something holy can make holy an unholy thing merely by touching it, to which they reply in the negative. He asks whether something unholy can make unholy a holy thing merely by touching it, to which they reply in the affirmative. By this he tells them by associating and marrying with the unholy Samaritans and their gods, they do not make the Samaritans holy, but rather they themselves become unholy.

In the final third of chapter two, Haggai closes with again assuring them God will be with them if they follow and obey him. He tells Zerubbabel, whom God has chosen to govern and lead the people, that God will destroy the kingdoms around. Zechariah then speaks the first part of his message, which also is of rebuilding and restoration, but not so much of the building as of the morality of the people.

****

EZRA (CONTINUED)

The Samaritans continue their efforts to defeat the construction. Chapter five of Ezra at verse three continues with their obstruction. It has been about twenty-one years since Cyrus decreed the rebuilding. During that time Cyrus was succeeded by Cambyses, who was in turn succeeded by Darius. The Samaritans write to King Darius questioning the authority of the Jews to build. In chapter six, Darius orders a search of the records, and finds the decree of Cyrus in the Ecbatana in the treasury where such rolls are kept. Darius promptly renews the decree to rebuild the temple, and further orders that all those "beyond the river," being west of the Euphrates, will not only not interfere on pain of death but will contribute both financially and with goods to the project. After fifteen years of neglect, in 520 B.C. the people resume work on the temple and complete it in four years. They celebrate with the feast of the Passover, the Unleavened Bread, commemorating the exodus of Moses from Egypt.

At chapter six verse fifteen, we could insert the second half of Zechariah. At this point also goes the book of Esther and her being appointed queen to King Ahasuerus, mentioned in chapter four of Ezra, as he now moves into the period covered by Ahasuerus' successor, Artaxerxes. It is now 486 B.C., fifty-three years after the return, and only the foundation and altar have been built, but no small temple and no walls.

In Ezra chapter seven we are finally officially introduced to Ezra. We are told he is the great- grandson of Hilkiah, the priest who had found the scrolls of Deuteronomy in the temple and lead the revival of King Josiah, as reported in Second Kings chapter twenty-two. He is a scribe skilled in the law of Moses. "He had prepared his heart to seek the Law of the Lord, and to do it, and to teach statutes and ordinances in Israel." He requests King Artaxerses to allow him to take an entourage back to Jerusalem. His request is granted, and in 458, about eighty years after the first group of 50,000 had returned with Zerubbabel, Ezra, the priest, leaves with about 1,758 men, including thirty-eight Levitical priests. His mission is to rebuild and restore the morals and religious life of the Jews.

In chapter eight we are told of Ezra's preparations and departure. In chapter nine Ezra discovers that these adult grandchildren of those King Cyrus had allowed to return were doing the same thing their great-great-great-great-great grandparents did that caused God to remove them from the land promised and into captivity. The people and the priests are intermarrying with the idol worshipers of the land and not keeping the commandments of God and have built only the temple foundation and altar but not the temple nor the walls. Of course, they are a relatively small number of refugees and without the kingdom and wealth of David and Solomon. Ezra preaches the scripture to them and many repent.

And here begin, as on the following pages, the story of Esther and the prophecies of Zechariah, which are contemporaries but written about 600 pages apart in most Bibles.

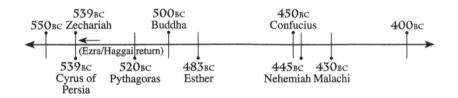

CHAPTER 27

ZECHARIAH AND ESTHER
SLOW REBUILDING AT JERUSALEM; A JEWISH GIRL IS
EMPLOYED TO SAVE HER PEOPLE

*Thus says the Lord of hosts: "Return to me, and I will return to you....
Turn now from your evil ways and your evil deeds." Zch. 1:3-4*

There are six books which make up the chronological conclusion of the
old Hebrew scriptures, being the period following the allowed return, about
105 years. These are three history books, Ezra, Esther and Nehemiah, and three
prophecy books, Haggai, Zechariah and Malachi. Ezra began by reporting on
the first eighty years of the return of the exiles to the area of Jerusalem. From
there all six actually lived and cover a period of about twenty-five years.
Some of the dates are a bit confusing and uncertain, but the fact is that all six
were of the same time and overlapped each other. Esther and the second part
of Zechariah may be inserted at the end of chapter six of Ezra.

One fairly needs a time chart as to the times of which five of these
writers speak. Ezra reports on sections of the first eighty years of the return
of the exiles to the area of Jerusalem. Esther covers about ten years near the
middle of those eighty years, and deals not with the minority who returned
to Jerusalem but with the majority who remained back in Persia. Nehemiah
mentions briefly the first years but primarily deals with the end of those
eighty years and then the rebuilding of the wall. Haggai and Zechariah
prophesied in the early years of the return, though the second half of
Zechariah was probably written much later. Malachi prophesied about ten
years after these other five and independently of them, as he brought to an
end the old Hebrew scriptures.

The period covered by these six books are of the first five kings of the
Persian empire, being Cyrus, Cambyses, Darius, Ahasuerus (Xerxes), and
Artaxerxes. Only Ezra, as he reports events prior to his own involvement,
mentions Cyrus, who decreed the return of 539 B.C., probably with the
counsel of Daniel. None of them mentions Cambyses, whose nine-year
reign came during the fifteen-year period the exiles failed to complete the
rebuilding of the temple, the gap between chapters four and five of Ezra.

Cambyses was succeeded by Darius who reigned during the time both Haggai and Zechariah prophesied and the temple was completed. He was succeeded by Ahasuerus (Xerxes), the king at the time of Esther. Ahasuerus was succeeded by Artaxerxes, the last king mentioned in the old Hebrew scriptures, who reigned at the time of the actual return of Ezra and Nehemiah and of the prophet Malachi. These men ruled over an empire nearly the size of the Greek empire and the Roman empire, all three of which dwarfed the much smaller kingdom of David and Solomon.

We are reminded of some contemporaries of Zechariah, Esther and Ezra. Pythagoras, the Greek philosopher and mathematician (582-500), is in the last days of his life. Buddha, of India (563-483), and Confucius, of China (551-479), are at the peak of their lives. Socrates, the Greek philosopher (469-399), is just into the near future.

****

ZECHARIAH

Between chapters five and six of Ezra, which tell of the completion of the temple, is a fifteen year gap. At the end of those fifteen years, about 520 B.C., God sends Zechariah and Haggai to encourage the disheartened people. These two prophesy after the exile (post-exilic) and speak beyond consolation to a restoration of the people. Haggai speaks to them of the immediate concerns, of completing the temple, which they will do within four years, and of syncretism, mixing with other gods. Zechariah speaks in a much more visionary fashion, of the near and distant future for the Jews. Scholars attribute the first eight chapters of this book to Zechariah, but most consider the last six chapters to have been written by someone else, decades or centuries later. For us these messages are timeless.

Seventeen years earlier, this group of some 50,000 Jews had left decades of captivity in Persia and returned to Jerusalem. King Cyrus had agreed to assist them, but he had been succeeded by Cambyses who is now succeeded by Darius. Assistance has faded, and the Jewish refugees are greatly discouraged. They have built houses for themselves but have not rebuilt the temple. They have begun, as had their ancestors, to look to the false gods of the people around them.

Zechariah begins with a call to repentance and then records his eight visions of encouragement. Beginning at verse eight is his vision of four horsemen among the myrtle trees. These messengers of God report back to him that the surrounding nations are oppressing the Jews, who wonder why God allows such. They are told that they have disobeyed by not completing the temple.

Beginning at verse eighteen is his second vision. He sees four horns, representing the nations that scattered the Jews, and four blacksmiths, who will take down those horns after the chastisement of the Jews is complete.

Beginning at chapter two is his third vision. He sees a young surveyor with a measuring line and an angel. Jerusalem is being measured to be occupied with God as its protective wall. God's angel then calls all of the exiles back from Babylon.

Beginning at chapter three is his fourth vision. He sees Satan accusing Joshua, the high priest, dressed in filthy clothes, of sin. God forgives Joshua and dresses him in clean linens.

Beginning at chapter four is his fifth vision. He sees a gold lampstand with seven candles and an unending supply of oil, representing the constant Spirit of God. "Not by might nor by power, but by my Spirit, says the Lord of hosts."

Beginning at chapter five is his sixth vision. He sees a flying scroll, which represents God's judgment on individual sin.

Beginning at verse five is his seventh vision. He sees an evil woman in a basket, representing the wickedness of all the nations. She is sent back to Babylon and sin is removed.

Beginning at chapter six is his eighth vision. He sees four war chariots with horses, representing God's judgment coming upon those who oppress God's people.

The concluding five chapters are two oracles. The first is a judgment on the people. One must remember the people are slowly and indifferently rebuilding a very small replacement temple; the old Hebrew scriptures with their Old Testament are coming to an end. The comparison to Solomon's temple and to the one to be built by Herod at the time of Christ, is like comparing a large cathedral in New York City or Washington D.C. to a small church in a small rural community. In chapter eleven God says he will no longer have pity on the inhabitants of the land promised. God takes two staffs, one named Grace and one Union. He then takes the staff of Grace and breaks it, annulling the old covenant with the Jewish people. He then breaks the staff of Union, annulling the brotherhood between Judah and Israel.

****

ESTHER

The book of Esther reads like a three-act play organized around three pairs of banquets. It sets the event for one of the seven feasts of the Jews, being one of the two which were not established by Moses. This is the Feast of Purim, pronounced Pur-eem.

Esther could be inserted in the book of Ezra right behind Zechariah and before Ezra chapter seven. The name Esther means "star", and she is the star of this short story about her, which is one of two books in the Bible named for a woman. God is not mentioned in this book, neither by name nor by reference, but his worship is obvious. This book begins by telling us about King Ahasuerus, also known as Xerxes in Greek, and that his huge Persian empire contains 127 provinces and extends from India to Ethiopia. It also includes all of Palestine and modern Turkey, being larger than either the Assyrian or the Babylonian empires. We are told that in 483 B.C., during a six-month period while he convenes his military leaders, and gives a great banquet which lasts seven days. This convocation of his leaders is to organize an army that may have totaled 5,000,000 men. A large military excursion is being planned.

This book has nothing to do with the remnant of Hebrews who had returned to Jerusalem in 538 B.C., about sixty-five years prior to this story of Esther. A remnant of about 50,000 had returned as recorded in Ezra and about 75,000 remained in Persia. Esther has to do with saving those 75,000 who chose to remain in Persia from an ethnic cleansing, not the 50,000 over in Jerusalem.

Ahasuerus (Xerxes) was the fourth king of Persia, third after Cyrus. He was the son of Darius, who had quelled an uprising in Babylon and knocked down the wall around that city from 300 feet to 75 feet, in what was the beginning of fifty years of fruitless war with the Greeks. Darius also had attempted to extend his empire westward from what is today western Turkey across the Dardenelles, the Hellespont and the Aegean Sea into what we know as Greece. At that time the people we know as Greeks, occupied not only Greece but also southern Italy and the sea coast of southern France, Libya, most of the Black Sea and of modern Turkey in the Mediterranean. In 490 B.C. his army had crossed into Greece proper, but his contingent of 60,000 men was defeated by 10,000 Athenians on the plain of Marathon. The runner Pheidippides had run the twenty-one miles to Athens with the news of victory. Darius' son, Ahasuerus (Xerxes), now planned to do what his father could not do, conquer the Greeks.

About 483 B.C., as Ahasuerus (Xerxes) gave this banquet for his military leaders, his Queen, Vashti, gives a banquet for the women. The men consume ample wine and after seven days are quite merry. The king directs that his queen come into the banquet to show her beauty. She refuses to come. The king is enraged, and his princes are concerned that her disobedience will cause all wives to refuse to obey their husbands. The king decrees that Vashti will no longer be queen and that a beauty pageant be held for her replacement. He also decreed that every man be lord of his own house. He does not order that wives be abused slaves; however, any movement of women's liberation is put on hold.

Between chapters one and two Ahasuerus (Xerxes) sends his army of 5,000,000 men with ships, to the Aegean Sea to invade Greece. In 479 B.C. a contingent of Persians lands on the Athenian peninsula, and forces the Greeks to move down the peninsula to the island of Salamis off the coast of Athens. There they wait with their new trimeres, ramming-style ships, in the narrow strait of water. They encourage the Persians to think they are completely defeated and lure the many Persian ships into the confined waters where they ram and board the ships, thereby destroying the Persian fleet of Ahasuerus (Xerxes).

The defeat of Darius at Marathon ten years earlier and this defeat of Ahasuerus at Salamis in 479 B.C. marked the beginning of the fall of Persia and the beginning of the rise of Greece. However, it would be another 150 years before the Greek empire defeated and replaced the Persian empire. This change of empires had been Nebuchadnezzar's dream interpreted by Daniel about 125 years earlier. Persia was the breast and arms of silver in that dream and also the bear and ram of Daniel's visions. Greece would be the belly and thighs of bronze in that dream and the winged leopard and the he-goat of Daniel's visions.

Chapter two begins, in 479 B.C., by saying, "after these things, when the anger of King Asahuerus had abated," with no mention of two years of fruitless warfare in "Greece," leading the reader to think only of his disapproval of Queen Vashti. The king had returned home to rest. The search for and training of the beautiful virgins for the beauty pageant had lasted two years. At verse six we are told of Esther, a young Jewish girl who had been adopted by Mordecai, her older first cousin, upon the death of her parents. Esther is selected for the competition and wins great favor in the eyes of the pageant manager who takes special care of her during her year of training. She also wins the favor of King Ahasuerus, who directs that she be his new queen. Upon the advice of her cousin Mordecai she does not tell anyone that she is Jewish. Neither does she nor Mordecai tell the king that Mordecai is the one who had reported to her that two of the king's guards planned to harm the king.

In chapter three, about five years later, we are told of a man named Haman being promoted to a position second only to the king, a prime minister. All are then to bow down to Haman; however, Mordecai refuses to bow. Haman becomes furious! However, he can do nothing to Mordecai so he seeks to destroy all of the Jews in the kingdom. It has been sixty-four years since 50,000 Jews had returned to Jerusalem with Zerubbabel. About 75,000 Jews chose not to return and remained in the area of modern Iraq and Iran. Haman now wants to have a genocide as to all of those. He agrees to pay the king 10,000 talents, 375 tons, of silver to decree the genocide. This anti-Semitism is no doubt to be funded by confiscating the assets of the Jews, just as would be done 2,400 years later by Hitler's nazis. The king authorizes Haman to do as he deems required, and Haman issues an edict of death to all Jews.

In chapter four, Mordecai learns of the decree and tears his clothes and puts on sackcloth and ashes. Queen Esther has her servant go to Mordecai to inquire of his problem. When she learns of the decree and of Mordecai's direction that she go speak to the king, she informs Mordecai that upon penalty of death no one can go to the king unless first called by him. Mordecai tells her this intercession may be the very reason for her existence. She agrees to go, even if she perish for it.

In chapter five, Esther goes to the king in his inner court. He asks of her request. She invites him and Haman to a dinner. The king orders Haman to join him at the dinner. At that dinner he again asks of her request, and she says she will tell him at another dinner for the two the next day. On his way home, Haman sees Mordecai, who will not bow and seems unafraid, and Haman becomes enraged. At home he brags to his wife of his new wealth and that the queen is preparing a second dinner for only the king and himself. She tells him to build a gallows 75 feet high for Mordecai, which he does.

In chapter six we are told, that night the king can not sleep. He directs that the chronicles of deeds be brought to him for reading. There he learns that Mordecai had been the one who reported on the two guards who planned to kill the king. He asks what honor had been bestowed upon Mordecai and was told none. The king then asks who is waiting in the outer court and is told Haman waited. He directs that Haman come in to see him. The king asks Haman what should be done to honor a man in whom the king so delights. Haman wrongly presumes he spoke of himself and says the man should be given the king's robes and ride the king's horse as all are told to honor this man. The king then orders Haman to do just that and informs the man is Mordecai. It was so done by Haman himself. Haman then returns to his home and is reminded to be at the dinner prepared by Queen Esther.

In chapter seven the king and Haman join Esther for dinner. After enjoying some wine, the king again asks of her request. She asks that he grant her life as she would not make her request except that she is his queen. However, she and her people are being sold as slaves to be slaughtered. She does not directly tell the king that she is a Jewess, but that someone has ordered her death. As Haman and not the king has issued the edict, the king becomes incensed and asks who would order such a thing. She informs him it was Haman. The king storms out. Haman becomes terror-stricken, and begins to beg Esther for his own life. The king returns to see Haman at the couch with Esther and accuses him of assaulting his wife and orders that he be hung on the very gallows he had built for Mordecai. It is done. A version of the Golden Rule: Do unto me as I would do unto others.

In chapter eight, the king promptly promotes Mordecai to the position previously held by Haman, that of prime minister, second to the king in command. Esther also gives to Mordecai the residence of Haman. She then intercedes with the king as to his existing decree to exterminate all Jews in the kingdom. The edict can not be revoked, but the king has the power to overrule it, which he does. It is now July, and the death sentence is to take effect in February. The messengers have six months to spread the word throughout the very large kingdom. They succeed.

In chapter nine Mordecai rises to even more power. The Jews rise to smite those who are their enemies, doing as they please to those they hate, killing more than 75,000. The next day they rest and feast. These days are on the thirteenth and fourteenth days of the Jewish month of Adar, which is about the first two days of March. The two days are declared by Mordecai and Esther to be forever feast days for all Jews. To decide the day to begin his planned genocide, Haman had cast lots, thrown the dice. The Hebrew word for "casting lots" is purim (pur-eem). It is declared that these two feast days henceforth be called Purim, and be a time for sending gifts to one another.

And here begin the stories of Nehemiah and Malachi, the last books in the old Hebrew scriptures, which are contemporaries but written about 550 pages apart in most Bibles.

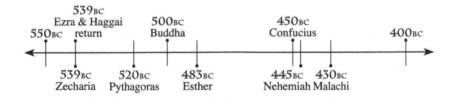

CHAPTER 28

NEHEMIAH AND MALACHI

JERUSALEM WALL REBUILT; PRAYER;
JUDGMENT OF THE WICKED

*From the days of your fathers you have gone away from my ordinances
and have not kept them. Return to me, and I will return to you.* Mal. 3:7

Nehemiah means "the Lord has comforted," and is shortened at times
to Nahum. Most of the dates in the Bible can be fairly well established as
to our modern calendar. However, there are some dates which are difficult
for us to fix. Understandably most of those are during the periods of the
two times of exile, slavery and returning. There is no record in the Bible of
most of the period of bondage in Egypt, so the dates as to the exodus are
uncertain. Likewise, there is not much record in the Bible of the period of
bondage in Babylon, so the dates as to that exodus and return are uncertain.
Socrates (469-399 B.C.), teaching in Greece, to the west, as that empire
began to consolidate, was a contemporary of Nehemiah. Buddha of India and
Confucius of China had died and Plato of Greece was in the near future.

The books of Ezra and of Nehemiah were early on one book. It is probably
better to separate them. The book of Ezra and the book of Nehemiah, and the
other four books of the period, Haggai, Zechariah, Esther and Malachi, read
nicely until they are closely examined as to dates, then some conflicts arise.
Most scholars place Ezra before Nehemiah and many after. Students of these
books fall into four groups, which may be spread across a graph shaped like
the curvature of a bell. The problem with dates makes no difference in the
story, and the vast majority of students are totally unconcerned as to these
dates. First there are those on the left side of the curve who consider the Bible
as fictional mythology, and therefore are unconcerned. Next there are those
on the right side of the curve who consider many matters in the Bible to be
unrevealed until later days. The bulk of that bell curve is made up of those
who are simply unaware of any conflict of dates and also a much smaller
group who continue to try to figure them out.

In 538 B.C. Cyrus, King of Persia, decreed that all Jews who so desired
were free to return to Jerusalem. One year later the return, the much smaller

second exodus, began. About 75,000 Jews chose to remain in the land of their captors, in modern Iraq and Iran. About 50,000 exiles began the march of about 700 miles from the area of Babylon, near modern Baghdad, back to Jerusalem. This group was led by Zerubbabel. This band of lowly, defenseless, unorganized refugees returned to a city destroyed by the invading Babylonians during years of war.

The return applied to all Jews; however, it was effective only to those of the two tribes that made up the former southern kingdom of Judah. Those Jews of the former northern kingdom, of Israel, and its ten tribes, had been captured 183 years previously and were never again heard from. Those captives had been disbursed across the area of the upper parts of the Euphrates and Tigris Rivers, that land today occupied generally by the Kurds in northern Iraq, parts of Syria and eastern Turkey. They are those of "ten lost tribes." Those displaced were replaced mostly by relocated Assyrians, who occupied the area around Samaria.

The first and primary objective of the returnees was to rebuild their temple, which had been built by Solomon 440 years earlier and then destroyed by the Babylonians some sixty years earlier. The replacement building would not be nearly as great as the former one. Ezra tells us they first built their altar and the temple foundation, then quit for fifteen years until the prophets Haggai and Zechariah arrived to fire them back up. They then completed the rebuilding of their much smaller temple in four-and-a-half years.

However, the people began increasingly to neglect the worship and laws of God. So fifty-two years after that temple was completed, Ezra himself was given permission to lead a small group back to Jerusalem. He was a priest well-versed in the law of Moses. His task was to rebuild the people themselves and to restore them to the law and worship of God. He worked at this for several years. The book of Nehemiah begins after Ezra had been at his work for fourteen years and ninety-four years since the return.

****

NEHEMIAH

At the end of chapter one we are told that Nehemiah was a cupbearer to King Artaxerxes in the Persian winter capital in Susa. A cupbearer was head steward of the king's private quarters and on close terms with the king. Artaxerxes was the son of King Xerxes (Ahasuerus), who had chosen the Jewess Esther to be his queen. She was the step-mother of the King Artaxerxes, and very likely still alive and active and speaking to the king about the Jews and Nehemiah. We soon learn that Nehemiah had more abilities than that of steward of wines or of living quarters. He had extensive organizational and leadership skills.

At the beginning of chapter one we are told that Nehemiah learns that the Jews in Jerusalem, though they long ago rebuilt the temple, still have no protective walls around their city. We quickly learn at verse five that Nehemiah is a man of prayer, and hear his first of ten prayers. This is the longest of his ten reported prayers. Seven times we are given short prayers of one or two sentences, and twice we are told simply that Nehemiah prayed. Here he prays before asking the king to allow him to leave his duties and go to Jerusalem. He asks God to remember his words to Moses that if the people faithfully obey he will restore them to the land, but if they do not obey he will scatter them. He then prays for success in his request to the king.

Nehemiah was a man of prayer. Many students call this habit of regularly going to God in prayer the "Nehemiah Principle." Nehemiah had a personal relationship with God as he spoke regularly of "our (your, my) God." He took nearly everything to God. When one calls on God to remember, as Nehemiah did, one actually may be moreso reminding oneself. In verse nine, we first hear the Greek word *diaspora*, which means "across sew" or "be scattered". It has become a word of art and refers to the "dispersion" of the Jews away from Jerusalem.

In chapter two Nehemiah speaks to King Artaxerxes, who is depicted as being friendly and understanding toward his people and the Jews. The king asks Nehemiah why such a sad face. Nehemiah fires up a bullet prayer to God before answering. Then, in the courtly manner of inferiors to superiors, Nehemiah speaks without mentioning Jerusalem. The king asks how long it will take. We are not told the response as to time. The request is granted, along with letters to pass through various areas. In verse ten we first hear of Sanballat of Samaria, and Tobiah, a servant to the ruler of "Jordan". Both of whom are likely descendants of those transplanted long ago into the area, and who will cause Nehemiah trouble.

At verse eleven, Nehemiah arrives in Jerusalem. The city now being very gradually rebuilt and repopulated is smaller than in days of yore and much smaller than in coming centuries. It's crumbled walls are in the outline of a right footprint. He rests for three days, then at night, certainly with a full moon, begins to examine the wall. He starts at the area of the southern part of the old west wall, where the print of the heel meets the arch of the foot. He walks the wall in a counter-clockwise direction. He then tells the people that the wall must be rebuilt. At the end of chapter two we again meet Sanballat and Tobiah, as they mock and ridicule the Jews as to thinking they can build a great wall around the city.

Chapter three sets out the assignments of those to build the wall. Starting at the northeast corner, the area of the print of the right little toe, and again going around in a counter-clockwise direction, Nehemiah assigns families sections of the wall and various gates.

At chapter four we again meet Sanballat, the Samaritan. This conflict between those transplanted into the area of Samaria and the Jews of Jerusalem, about thirty miles apart, will still exist 450 years later at the time of Christ. Sanballat continues his mockery as he tells his troops that these feeble Jews are trying to build a wall out of rubbish and that a fox could knock down their wall. In verses four and five Nehemiah prays to God that the Samaritans be given over to captors. Work on the wall is then begun, because the people have a mind to work.

Again in verse seven Sanballat becomes angry and plots confusion among the Jews. Again Nehemiah, and his people, pray to God for a wall of protection. As work continues the people begin to complain of their weakness and of the great amount of rubbish to be removed. Also the Samaritans are beginning physically to threaten the workers. Nehemiah has half of the people carry spears, swords and bows to protect the workers. They labor from dawn till dark, from star to star. They even sleep in their clothes and keep a weapon beside them.

In chapter five the people begin to complain about economic problems. Work on the wall no doubt contributes to the problems, but the main cause is most likely a sustained drought over that summer of 444 B.C., as it is now probably around August. Their land and fields are their very lifelines, for food and borrowing. They have mortgaged their lands and borrowed to pay the king's taxes. They have even sold many of their children, sons and daughters into slavery. In verse six we are told Nehemiah becomes angry and then seeks his own counsel. He brings charges against the officials and leaders for charging usurious interest, their greed and selfishness. He directs that no more interest be collected on loans, and he himself lends them money.

At verse fourteen he states his primary principles as to governing, which he would follow during his twelve years of administration. As a "governor" he, and each of his assistants, would make no profits, acquire no land, do the job at hand, feed himself, and not lord it over the people. He then sends another one-sentence bullet prayer to God.

At chapter six, as work on the wall continues, we again see Sanballat and more conflict. The Samaritans ask five times for Nehemiah to come talk with them. He refuses as it is only a plot, similar to the one used against Ezra, that of accusing the Jews of sedition and rebellion against the king, that they build a wall for such purpose. Nehemiah replies that such thought is an invention of their own minds, and in verse nine prays that God strengthen his hand. He is told they plot to kill him, but he refuses to hide and again prays to God to remember these people and their schemes. In verse fifteen we are told the wall was completed, in fifty-two days, making the time early October. The wall will not be dedicated immediately.

In chapter seven, a repeat of Ezra chapter two, a census is taken as the people are numbered. First Nehemiah posts guards to the temple. Unlike the situation ninety years earlier, he is concerned that the people are not paying sufficient attention to their private homes, probably meaning their families.

In chapter eight they have Ezra read the law aloud to the people. This is likely that reading mentioned in chapter eight of Ezra's book. Ezra is the scribe well-learned in the law of Moses, as in the first five books of the Bible. The people stand for the reading, as the people do today in many churches for the reading of the Gospel. They weep as they recall their personal sins. In verse fourteen the people are surprised to learn that the Feast of Tabernacles, commemorating the living in tents during the exodus of Moses, has not been observed since the time of Joshua, over 900 years earlier. They prepare to observe the feast for its required seven days.

Chapter nine begins with the people fasting in garments of sackcloth and separating themselves from foreigners, no doubt including a separation from such marriages. They confess their sins and the iniquities of their fathers. From verse six to the end is a long penitential psalm reciting the history of the relationship with God from creation, through the exodus, to the return, to removal from the land due to disobedience, and to this return from exile. At verse eight Nehemiah says, as had Joshua, that all the promises of God as to the land have been fulfilled.

Chapter ten begins with the preparation of a covenant with God to obey and a list of those who signed the covenant, leaders, priests, Levites and the rest. At verse twenty-nine begins a summary, an abstract, of that covenant. There will be no mixed marriages, the Sabbath will be observed, the temple tax paid, the wood offering made, and that of the first-fruits, tithes and offerings will be paid over and the temple will be supported.

Chapter eleven sets out those who will live inside the city walls and those outside. As in Esther, lots are drawn, the Purim, as one out of ten will live inside the wall. Chapter twelve contains the genealogies of the religious leaders, the priests and the Levites. Beginning at verse twenty-seven the wall is finally dedicated, probably a month after it was completed. The Levites are purified. A procession is made around the top of the wall, half in one direction and half in the other.

Chapter thirteen sets out the reforms instituted by Nehemiah. After twelve years Nehemiah returns to the king and receives permission then to return again to Jerusalem. Upon his second return he finds that during his absence the priest in charge has put Tobiah, the Samaritan associate of Sanballat, into quarters in the courts of the temple. Nehemiah throws him out, then again purifies the Levites. That done, at verse fourteen he prays for himself, that God remember his good deeds. He goes back to his task, as the people are working on the Sabbath, mainly in the winepresses. He brings an end to that. Again he prays to God to remember him. Then he promptly reminds the people that they are not to marry with the surrounding people, having children who do not even speak their own language. He curses the men, beats some of them and pulls out most of their hair as a badge of dishonor. The final verse is a bullet prayer for God to remember him.

****

MALACHI

Malachi is the last book in the old Hebrew scriptures. He was a prophet but also a bit of a historian as he writes of what the Jews were doing at that time. He wrote around 434 B.C., which was about 100 years after the first group of exiles returned to Jerusalem with Zerubbabel to rebuild the temple. It had been ten years since Nehemiah returned to rebuild the walls around Jerusalem. Socrates, teaching over in Greece as that empire begins to consolidate, is a contemporary of Malachi. There will be 428 years of biblical silence, from Malachi until the time of Jesus and the new Christian scriptures. A time of silence about 100 years longer than that between the books of Genesis and Exodus.

The people, mainly the priests, question and challenge Malachi, and God, at every turn, as they deny that they have done anything wrong and that God is unfair. Malachi answers them to the effect that God is righteous and just. There are seven categories of challenges, which intensify and aggravate from doubt through relative morality to total separation from the faith, a gradual progression to spiritual death. The clergy are to lead the people in the true faith, but frequently, rather than lead they follow, as the ways and philosophies of the world win over the clergy. The people and the clergy had simply gotten tired of and bored with the statutes and commandments of God and of the rebuilt temple.

The first of the challenges is at the second verse, as the Lord tells the people, "I have loved you," to which he gets a childish response, "In what way have you loved us?" They begin by questioning and doubting the love of God for Israel. They are told that they need only look at the troubles of their cousins in neighboring Edom to see the relatively greater love God has had for the Jews. Searching and inquiring is a way of growth in the faith, but the Jews simply doubted God, an early sign of a developing leaving of the faith.

The second challenge is at verse six, as God itemizes some of the sins of the priests, the clergy, and presents his indictment against them. They ask, "In what way have we despised your name?" He tells them, "You offer defiled food on my altar." Again the third challenge is a childish denial: "In what way have we defiled you?" God tells them that they offer blemished offerings, not the first and best, as they cheat God in a meaningless spirit of worship. If that were not true then go put that food on the governor's table. He goes on to tell them that divorce between husband's and wives is rampant as they break their covenants to each other in faithlessness.

The fourth challenge is at chapter two verse seventeen, as the people ask, "In what way have we wearied the Lord?" They are told that they say, "Everyone who does evil is good in the sight of the Lord, and he delights in them," as they also question God's justice. This is a form of the relative morality of Second Kings and of the late twentieth century. Everybody just does as he or she pleases, and makes up their own rules.

The fifth challenge is at verse seven. They are told, "From the days of your fathers you have gone away from my ordinances and have not kept them. Return to me, and I will return to you." After being told of their waywardness in a fairly specific manner, the people immaturely ask, "In what way shall we return?" By this they deny their sin.

The sixth challenge is at verse eight. The people ask, "In what way have we robbed you?" They are informed, "In tithes and offerings...you have robbed me. Bring all of the tithes into the storehouse." A default in the giving of alms for the poor and oblations for worship is another whisper of coming spiritual death.

The seventh challenge is at verse thirteen. The people are told that their words have been harsh against God. They ask, "In what way have we spoken against you?" They are told specifically, "You have said, 'It is useless to serve God; what profit is it...? So now we call the proud blessed, for those who do wickedness are raised up.'"

Malachi concludes with a prophesy that the day of judgment is coming. The book of Malachi is the last book of the old Hebrew scriptures, both in fact of chronology and in the organization of the Bible. The old Hebrew scriptures end on an extremely low note of the continual fallings and failings of the Hebrews, far from the high hopes of the beginning, of Abraham, Isaac and Jacob, and also of Moses and then David.

And here begin, as follows in that 400-year gap between the old Hebrew scriptures and the new Christian scriptures, the stories of the Greek Empire, the Maccabees, the Roman Empire and the Herods.

CHAPTER 29

GREEKS AND MACCABEES
JEWS UNDER GREEK EMPIRE THEN ROMAN

This is the dream….You are this head of gold. After you shall rise another kingdom…, then another, a third kingdom of bronze….And the fourth kingdom shall be as strong as iron. Dan. 2:36-40

We now come to the 428-year period of biblical silence between the end of the old Hebrew scriptures and the beginning of the new Christian scriptures. The old Hebrew scriptures ended around 434 B.C. with Malachi's prophecies concerning the corruption of the people and especially of the priests. In First Kings we heard of the division of the Hebrew kingdom established by David and Solomon around 930 B.C. In Second Kings we heard of the capture of the northern kingdom by the Assyrian empire, and a century later the capture of the southern kingdom by the Babylonian empire. Then we heard of Cyrus, the king of the Medo-Persian empire, allowing the Hebrews to return to Jerusalem. At the time of Esther the embryonic Greek empire was causing the Persian empire some problems. Then the old Hebrew scriptures close with the Hebrews again not following the statutes and commandments of God. Silence, cold, hard silence for four centuries.

Suddenly, the new Christian scriptures begin. They begin with the birth, the incarnation, of Jesus, believed by many Christians to be the Christ. The geography is still the same, but not much else. Long gone is the Medo-Persian empire. Long gone are the prophets. The Roman empire is in control, but the people speak neither Latin nor Hebrew but rather Greek, and the Bible is written in Greek in the land of Hebrews and Romans. There are regular and serious problems between the Romans and the Jews. The small makeshift temple erected by the returning exiles over 500 years earlier is now described as quite large and extravagant. We hear of Sadducees, Pharisees, Sanhedrin, Zealots, Essenes and Herods, and even evil Samaritans. Instead of just the Torah, the first five books, there seems to be a large collection of books, an entire collection of thirty-nine books of old Hebrew scriptures. What has happened? Who are these people? What are these things?

At the end of the Old, the Persian empire ruled, and at the beginning of the New the Roman empire ruled. Simply stated, in between was the fall of the Persian empire, the rise and the fall of the Greek empire and the rise of the Roman empire. These empires successively ruled and controlled the Jews.

In music there are rests, places where a silent pause is placed. At times this is for emphasis and at times to mark a change in the movement of the music. In our Bible, there are three rests, three places of silence. These are both for emphasis and to mark a change in the movement of God.

Regardless of the depth of their study, except for those who have researched deeply into the period, there is usually a wide and dark chasm between the old Hebrew scriptures and the new Christian scriptures. The gap is not just in theology but also in lost history. Nearly everybody in the world has heard something of the birth of Jesus Christ and of his crucifixion and resurrection. Those who attend church only at Christmas and Easter have heard something of Herod, evil Samaritans and Pontius Pilate, but most know nothing of who they were. They hear of Rome and Roman soldiers but, except in the Roman Church, nothing of Latin words and very little of Hebrew or Greek words. Too many churches have thrown out teachings of this history. Their members will never get this work of God in secular schools or the news media. Let us now meet and know some connective tissue.

In most Protestant Bibles there is nothing of that 428-year period in between the Old and the New. Most Roman Catholic, Greek Orthodox and recently the National Council of Churches U.S., Bibles include two or four books of Maccabees from the apocrypha to cover about forty-five of those years, being from about 175 B.C. to about 130 B.C. There is no doubt that some emphatic change had occurred during those years.

In the Bible there are three fairly large gaps filled only with silence. These are decades and even centuries when the Hebrews were essentially doing nothing but existing. The first is that period between Genesis and Exodus, from Joseph to Moses, about 300 years of bondage. The second is that period of wandering in the wilderness as a generation of mumblers perished, a period of thirty-eight years missing between chapters nineteen and twenty of the book of Numbers. The third is that period between the books of Malachi and Matthew, 428 years of silence, as the Hebrews again existed in their own wilderness and bondage on the west bank of the River Jordan, around Jerusalem.

The word that describes this period between the Old and the New is "Intertestamental". It is indeed a very "biblical" era. It is the time mentioned at length in the book of Daniel. In chapter two Daniel interpreted Nebuchadnezzar's dream of a large statue. The statue's chest and arms of silver are usually taken to mean the Medo-Persian empire, the belly and thighs of bronze taken to mean the Greek empire and the legs of iron to be the Roman empire. In chapter seven Daniel envisioned four beasts. In chapter eleven he envisioned conflict between the north and the south. Nearly all students of the Bible agree that the Greek empire of Alexander was part of each of those chapters. The "intertestamental" years are essentially of the Greek empire, as Alexander, in a *blitzkrieg*, swept across the Medo-Persian empire. The period closes with the Roman empire, the legs of iron, taking over the western and Near-East part of the Greek empire.

There is another view of these events in Daniel. Regarding chapter two, many, mostly Roman Catholic, believe the Greeks were the legs of iron. Regarding chapter seven, as to the four beasts, probably most believe the Greek empire was the third beast, the leopard with four wings and the he-goat. However, many, mostly Roman Catholic, believe the Greeks were the fourth, the dreadful one with iron teeth and ten horns. Regarding chapter eleven, as to the conflict between north and south, probably most believe the Roman empire and church of the dark ages was involved in most of that conflict. However, many, mostly Roman Catholic, believe the Greeks continued in the violence from Daniel's verse fourteen to the end.

At the conclusion of the old Hebrew scriptures we read of Ezra returning to Jerusalem to encourage the Hebrews to rebuild a small temple. He was followed by Nehemiah who was allowed by the Persian king Artaxerxes to return to Jerusalem where he encouraged the returned exiles to rebuild the wall around Jerusalem. Those scriptures close, about 434 B.C., with the prophet Malachi very bluntly telling those returned refugees, especially the priests, that they are rapidly slipping into a spiritual death as to God. Then, silence.

At the conclusion of the old Hebrew scriptures, the Persian empire established by Cyrus in the days of Daniel, controlled the territory from India westward to the area of modern central Turkey and southward to Egypt. Cyrus permitted the Hebrews to return to Palestine. In the area of Palestine the Jews faded into disobedient apostasy. There was nothing remarkable to be written about them. God was preparing another movement. The area of Palestine remained under the rule of Persia, some 700 miles to its east. As centuries later there would be the peace of Rome, the *pax Romana*, there was a *pax Persias*. Some 800 miles to the west of Palestine around the Aegean Sea, the Greek peoples were fighting through their divisions to a consolidation.

Greek peoples, the "Sea People" of Phoenicia and Gaza, for centuries had occupied and controlled most of the coast line of Italy, Greece, the Aegean Sea, the Black Sea and the Mediterranean Sea, and the entire perimeter of modern Turkey. As the Jews began to return, Pythagoras moved from the Greek island of Samos off the coast of Turkey to the area of southern Italy where he taught mathematics and of the Transmigration of Souls. As Nehemiah and Malachi were beginning to finish their work, Socrates was speaking and teaching in Athens, Greece. The city-states of Athens and Sparta then began in 431

B.C. and concluded in 404 B.C., their war in southern Greece around what is essentially that large island of Peloponnesia, their Peloponnesian Wars.

Plato, forty-three years younger than Socrates and his student, then reigned supreme in the philosophies of Athens. He was followed by Aristotle, forty-three years younger than Plato and his student. Many young men from Rome journeyed to Athens to be taught by Socrates, Plato and Aristotle. Phillip II of Macedonia, the northeastern area of modern Greece, adjoining the area of the southern Balkans, was keeping the Persians at home as he maneuvered to consolidate all power and control over Greece. Phillip II had Aristotle tutor his young son Alexander. The Greek empire envisioned by Daniel was germinating. Our Bibles are filled with a 428-year gap of hard silence as God's movement changed. As Jeremiah and Ezekiel had prophesied, God prepared the world for a new covenant as he would put his "law in their minds, and write it on their hearts." He will give them a "new heart and a new spirit." He himself will be their shepherd as a branch will arise from the line of David. For Jews and Christians this refers to some messianic prophet. They disagree as to his identity.

As the Greeks warred among themselves, Persia continued to meddle but not seriously to invade. Phillip II of Macedonia consolidated the Greek peoples and was preparing to push eastward across the lands controlled by Persia. In 336 B.C. he was assassinated in Peeler, near his home province of Macedonia. The throne of power passed to his twenty-year old son, Alexander. The young king wasted no time. With 35,000 troops, he promptly rolled eastward, crossing the Dardanelles, the Hellespont, the bridge from Greece to Turkey, from Europe to Asia, then to wind through modern Turkey as he relieved Persia of it. He defeated the Persian army at Issus, at the northeast Mediterranean, reportedly killing 110,000 Persians. The Persians retreated eastward to northern Persia. Alexander turned south to relieve Persia of Palestine and of Egypt. It was 332 B.C. During the next 300 years Greek would be the language of the Near- and Mid-East, even to the point of eliminating Aramaic and Hebrew.

Alexander would continue to sweep up the territories of the collapsing Persian empire. He turned eastward to cross Syria, then south to Babylon. His army totally razed and leveled Babylon. The Greek empire was rapidly replacing the Persian empire as the primary central world power. At Susa, the winter palace of the Persian kings, where Daniel had spent his final years and where Nehemiah had been a cupbearer, in one grand ceremony, 10,000 Greek soldiers took Persian wives. They then continued eastward to take Persia and kill its king. Alexander then wound eastward to take modern Afghanistan and Pakistan, where his soldiers rebelled causing him to stop at the Indus river before entering India and begin a return westward to Greece. In 323 B.C., during a drunken orgy in the ruins of Babylon, Alexander died at the age of thirty-three. His four generals began to fight over control.

Alexander had looked only eastward, and a little southward. His successors would sit on their divided spoils. They would not look westward across the Adriatic Sea to watch the consolidation and growth of Rome. The territory of Alexander was divided among his four generals, but two promptly gained control over all of the territory. Seleucus I Nicator, "the victor", took control of the northern territories from Turkey across Syria and Persia to India. Ptolemy I Soter, "the savior", took control of Egypt, Libya, Arabia and Palestine. The Seleucids and Ptolemies would fight over and across Palestine for 150 years. During this time, just to the west of Greece, Rome continued to consolidate. Eventually Rome would move eastward over Greece but not over Persia, and then turn westward aound the Mediterranean and across Europe.

Daniel chapter eleven prophesies the conflict between north and south, conflict between the Seleucids of Syria and the Ptolemies of Egypt across Palestine. These are the eastern two large quarters of the Greek empire. At about verse sixteen many think the embryonic Roman empire enters into the prophecy. And some then even carry the events near into our twentieth century.

In 285 B.C., promptly upon assuming the throne of Egypt, King Ptolemy II called together in Alexandria, Egypt, named for young Alexander the Great, seventy-two scholars of the old Hebrew scriptures, and of Hebrew and Greek. He called six scholars from each of the twelve tribes, though it is somewhat difficult to understand how he identified sixty from those ten lost tribes deported by the Assyrians from Israel nearly 450 years prior. These seventy-two men, gathered at the great library in Alexandria, were both to assemble the old Hebrew scriptures, increasing them from just the first five books, and accurately to translate them into the Greek language of the empire. Legend has it that the project was completed in seventy-two days, but actually these men probably labored forty to 150 years at the task. They produced the old Hebrew scriptures, what would become "the Bible" until centuries after Christ, when it became for Christians the "Old Testament." The book took the name "Seventy", which in Greek is *Septuagint*, abbreviated "LXX".

Included in that Bible were thirteen Hebrew writings, being additions to Jeremiah, Ezra, Esther and Daniel, and two wisdom books, and two books relating to the history of the rebellion of the Jews in Jerusalem against the Seleucid heresies around 166 B.C. Centuries later the Greek church would retain these books in their Bible, but the Roman church would remove them for awhile but then gradually begin reinserting them, though not as true scripture. At the Protestant Reformation Martin Luther gave them the title of "Apocrypha", which means "encrypted" or "concealed", as their message was not clear. Most Protestants removed the Apocrypha from their Bibles. The Anglicans and Lutherans retained some readings in their lectionaries. Toward the end of the twentieth century the National Council of Churches U.S. began to include it in their New Revised Standard Version.

The two primarily historical books concerned the revolt of the Jewish Maccabees against the Seleucids, the remnant of the Greek empire to the north of Palestine which encompassed modern Syria, Iraq, eastern Turkey and eventually western Turkey and Greece. Egypt and Libya were controlled by the Ptolemy portion of the Greek empire remnant. The period of First Maccabees covers a forty-year period from 175 B.C. to 134 B.C. Second Maccabees covers the same period as the first seven chapters of First Maccabees, with some historical conflict. The entire Apocrypha was written in Hebrew by a Jewish author about 100 B.C. but is not included in the official Jewish scriptures and has come to us only in the Greek.

In 198 B.C. the Seleucid portion of the Greek empire took control of Palestine from the Ptolemy portion, and for about twenty years continued the tolerance of the Ptolemies toward the Jews. In 175 B.C. Antiochus IV Epiphanes became king of the Seleucid portion, and that tolerance began gradually to change. The empire, including the Seleucid kingdom, was dissipating and Antiochus Epiphanes determined radically to Hellenize all of and in his portion of the empire. This especially included the Jews and their temple worship, which was to be eradicated. This meant destroying all copies of the Torah and desecrating the temple by erecting in it, in early December 167 B.C., a statue of Zeus to be worshipped.

It was during this early part of the second century B.C. that four Jewish parties or sects arose. First were the Sadducees, which party contained the aristocrats, political intellectualists, Hellenistic sympathizers, temple people, those who controlled the high priest, those who believed only in the Torah, and not in angels, demons or any form of resurrection. Second were the Pharisees who were just the opposite, and mostly highly educated believers in all of the Jewish Hebrew scriptures and in angels, demons and a resurrection, who were of the synagogue as developed during the exile and believed God could be worshipped any place the Torah could be carried. Third were the Essenes, a pious sect of fundamental Judaists, those of whom John the Baptist would be a part. Fourth were the Maccabeans, those who arose in military and political opposition to Antiochus Epiphanes and the Seleucid rule.

The Maccabees, known as the Hasmonean dynasty, led a revolt and war against the Seleucids and after several victories restored a fairly independent rule by the Jews over most of Palestine. They cleansed the temple, rebuilt the altar and sanctuary, and on the 25th of Kislev (early December) 164 B.C. burned incense, lighted the official lamp stand in the temple, and re-dedicated the temple. Thus began the Jewish feast of Ha-Nukkah, the dedication. Antiochus Epiphanes died shortly thereafter. The Maccabean party would last until about 40 B.C.

During the intertestamental period, between the Old and the New, the Greek empire arose and declined, and during its decline the Roman empire was arising. By 168 B.C. Rome had conquered Spain, Carthage, parts of North

Africa, and Macedonia (northern Greece). In 71 B.C. Spartacus and his slave revolt had been put down by Pompey. Critical to Palestine, in 63 B.C. the Jews, led by the weakening Maccabean leaders, invited Pompey into Palestine to protect them from the declining Seleceud-Greeks of Syria. In 60 B.C. Pompey allied with Julius Caesar and Crassus for the triumvirate leadership of the new Roman empire. In 44 B.C. Julius Caesar was assassinated. In 31 B.C. Augustus defeated Antony and Cleopatra and the empire became united under one leader.

The land to the south and east of the Dead Sea, modern Jordan, was occupied by the Idumeans, also known as Edomites. In 104 B.C. the Maccabees forcibly converted the Idumeans to Judasism. By 55 B.C. members of the Herod family were centrally involved in the government of Idumea and of Judea to the west, in Palestine. In 47 B.C., for his assistance, the Romans appointed Herod procurator of Judea. In 40 B.C., though he was not from Judea but was an Idumean, he was appointed King of the Jews. He was hated by the Jews. In 37 B.C., with the aid of Mark Antony, Herod and the Romans officially captured Jerusalem. Along with his political abilities, Herod also was noted for his grandiose building programs, which included the port city of Caesarea, a string of fortresses of which Masada was one, and the new and third temple in Jerusalem, the construction of which was begun in 20 B.C. Jesus the Christ was born in 6 B.C.. Herod died in 4 B.C. and his kingdom was divided into four parts, for his sons, Herod Phillip I, Archelaus, Herod Antipas and Herod Phillip II.

Herod's temple was to replace the dilapidated small temple remaining from the one built by the exiles at the time of Ezra and Nehemiah, some 500 years earlier. It was both to placate the Jews and to meet his grandiose building plans. The construction process would last 82 years, with a completion date of 62 A.D. It was larger than but not as richly ornate as the temple built by Solomon. The temple built by Solomon took seven years to build and was ninety feet long, thirty feet wide and forty-five feet high. Herod's temple was also ninety by thirty but was 150 ft. high, fifteen stories. This temple, in the construction process, was the one known by Jesus and his disciples and was the one destroyed by the Romans in 70 A.D.

At the end of the old Hebrew scriptures, Persia was the central world power, and there was a small unimposing temple in Jerusalem. During the approximately four centuries before the start of the new Christian scriptures, the Greek empire arose to replace the Persian and was in turn replaced by the Roman. The Maccabees arose and declined. The Sadducees, Pharisees and Essenes arose, as did the Sanhedrin and the Synagogue type of worship. Under the auspices of the Romans, Herod came to rule all of Judea. A large temple was under construction.

And here begins, as follows on the next pages, the story of the birth, life and crucifixion of Jesus the Christ.

CHAPTER 30
THE GOSPELS
INCARNATION, BAPTISM, MINISTRY,
CRUCIFIXION AND RESURRECTION

In the beginning was the Word, and the Word was with God, and the Word was God. He was in the beginning with God. All things were made through him, and without him nothing was made that was made. Jhn. 1:1-3

The first four books of the new Christian scriptures, Matthew, Mark, Luke and John, are frequently thought of as the biographies of Jesus the Christ. They are indeed much like a biography, but they do not record the complete life of Jesus and are not in completely accurate order as to days and years. Students of the Bible are of the opinion that Mark, which is the shortest and most concise, was written prior to the others. These scholars say that then Matthew and Luke used Mark and one other source as an outline to write their record of events. Therefore, all three of these books are quite similar but not identical. They are called "synoptic" as they take the "same view" of events. John, on the other hand, wrote somewhat more independently and on a more theological level than a simple record of events.

All four gospels were written by humans inspired by the Holy Spirit some forty to sixty years after the crucifixion and resurrection. Each wrote for a different group and for a different purpose. In these more recent centuries several scholars have endeavored to put the four gospels together in a compatible order, in "parallel" as a "synopsis", a "harmony" between them. Where they appear to us, in our limited knowledge, to be in disagreement, biblical students have done an excellent job of closing nearly all gaps.

Matthew was a Jewish tax collector for the Romans when called. He wrote his book to the Jews of the Near-East. He wrote of Jesus as King of the Jews. He wrote of the Son of David, the Son of Abraham. Centuries later a lion would become the symbol for Matthew. Mark was a very young man when called to be a helper to Peter and to Paul. He wrote his book to the gentile Romans. He wrote of Jesus as the suffering servant of God. He wrote of the Son of Man as servant. Centuries later an ox would become the symbol for Mark. Luke was a physician, a gentile, the only non-Jew, a Syrian Greek, when called. He wrote his book to the Greeks. He wrote of Jesus as perfect man. He too wrote of the Son of David. Centuries later a man would become the symbol for Luke. John, the brother of James Zebedee, was a Jewish fisherman when called. He wrote his book to the Ephesians on the west coast of Turkey. He wrote of Jesus as the Messiah, the Deity. He wrote of the Son of God. Centuries later an eagle would become the symbol for John. These four men focused on the four groups involved at the time, the Jew, the Greek, the Roman and the crowd of people, being each and everyone of us.

The purpose and mission of Jesus the Christ, the Messiah, the Anointed One, was to suffer on the cross, to die as a human being for the sins of humanity and to be resurrected by God the Father in final victory over sin and Satan. As difficult as that may be for us fully to comprehend, such was the reason for his being as a human. Except as the instruments of God the Father, neither the Jewish leaders nor the Roman officials put Christ on the cross. God did that for the offer of salvation to mankind.

As evidence of the importance of the various events in the life of Jesus, there is a weight as to the number of chapters. In these four books there is a total of eighty-nine chapters. Only four cover the first thirty years of his life, including his birth, those Christmas chapters. The remaining eighty-five chapters cover the last three years of his life. Fifty-eight of those cover his ministry and twenty-seven cover the final week of his life. Neither the gospel of Mark nor of John even mention the actual birth. Except for John's majestic prologue as to the Logos, the "Word", the "Logic", both begin their records with John the Baptist and Jesus at thirty years of age. Nearly one-third of these four books is dedicated to the last week, the crucifixion, resurrection and ascension, the very purpose of his life as a human.

There are thirty-five miracles reported in these gospels. Miracles are not the primary purpose of Jesus, but only signs of his being and power to reconcile humans to God. Nine are miracles of nature and twenty-six are miracles of healing. Some of the nature miracles are turning water into wine, large catches of fish, feeding the multitudes and calming the sea. Some of the healing miracles are the restoration of wholeness to the lepers and the paralytic, restoration of life to two dead men, sight to the blind and hearing to the deaf, and of the exorcism of demons. The healings each usually involved some type of a touching followed by acting on faith. The exorcisms were done by his command over the demons to leave. Some students of the Bible think miracles may be an alteration of God's natural laws, but most think they are rather a supernatural knowledge and use of those laws.

There are some thirty-two parables told by Jesus reported in these gospels. A parable is a short story, usually fictitious, "thrown alongside", parallel to a set of true facts to illustrate a moral or religious concept. Matthew, who writes of the King, in his thirteenth chapter, records eight parables to teach of the kingdom of God, of Heaven. These include those of the four soils, of weeds, of a mustard seed, of yeast, of a hidden treasure and of a pearl of great price. Luke, who writes of the perfect man, records parables of service, prayer, humility and concern for our fellow man. He reports of unworthy servants, the prayer of the tax collector, a good Samaritan, and of lost sheep and the lost prodigal son. Mark reports a few parables, but John reports none.

At the time Jesus became man, the Greek empire had ruled the Near- and Mid-East for over 300 years, and Greek was the primary language of the area. Romans, with their growing empire, had only recently displaced the Greeks, but Latin had not replaced Greek. Hebrew as a language had essentially disappeared, as had Aramaic, the language of many native in the area. The four gospels, and all of the other books of the new Christian scriptures, come to us in the Greek.

Of course, Jesus was born as man. He became incarnate. However, he had always been, always existed. That fact is so beautifully expressed by John. "In the beginning was the Word, and the Word was with God, and the Word was God. He was in the beginning with God. All things were made through him, and without him nothing was made that was made."

In Greek the word John wrote which is translated into English as "Word" was "Logos". Logos means both the word itself and also the logic or thought carried by that word. When John writes that "the Word became flesh", he wrote the "Logos", meaning the logic, thought, reasoning, intellect and the spoken word of God the Father became flesh, just as had Adam and Eve, but also now as God and man.

Matthew and Luke give us the genealogy, the pedigree, of Jesus as a man. Matthew, a Jew who wrote to the Jews, in keeping with the ancient Hebrew custom of naming male descent, lists the legal ancestry beginning with Abraham, the first Hebrew, through David to Joseph. Luke, a Syrian Greek wrote to the Greeks of Mary and the humanity of Jesus, lists the ancestry from Mary back through David to Adam, the first human, as he too names the males, but includes two females, Rahab and Ruth.

There are three announcements, three annunciations, by angels as to coming births. Angels would have an aura of awesome power and would regularly begin by telling the person, "Do not be afraid." The first two births are announced by Gabriel to women and recorded by Luke. The birth of John the Baptist to Elizabeth is announced to her husband Zechariah, a priest. He is told he will lose his voice until that day of birth. Six months later, when Mary visits her older cousin Elizabeth, Gabriel announces to young Mary the coming birth to her of Jesus. Mary first responds by saying she has been with no man, a virgin, and is told it will be by the Holy Spirit. Mary's next response is complete submission and the wonderful words which came to be known by the Latin as the *magnificat*: "My soul doth magnify the Lord." The third annunciation is to Joseph as he is told of the coming birth to his betrothed and not to fear to marry the young girl Mary.

Luke and Matthew record the events surrounding the birth of Jesus, the nativity, the incarnation. Luke introduces us to the fact that Palestine was then controlled by the growing Roman empire. About sixty years earlier the

Jews had invited Pompey to come assist them in their struggles against the fading remnant of the Greek empire. Matthew introduces us to the fact that, about thirty years earlier, Rome had installed Herod, who was not a Jew but an Idumean, and Edomite, to have the title "King of the Jews" and to rule Palestine.

Luke tells us a decree went out from Caesar Augustus that all were to report to their home of record to be polled for taxes. Joseph and his pregnant wife Mary began the forty-mile journey south from Nazareth to Bethlehem. As there were many people returning to Bethlehem, there were no rooms for Joseph and Mary. They spent the night in a shelter for a family's livestock. Luke then gives us his phrases so often heard at the time of the Christ Mass. "She brought forth her firstborn son, and wrapped him in swaddling clothes, and laid him in a manger....There were in the same country shepherds living out in the field, keeping watch over their flock by night....An angel of the Lord stood before them....Do not be afraid...I bring you good tidings of great joy....Glory to God in the highest." At the direction of the angel, the shepherds promptly ran to Bethlehem and to that manger.

These four gospels are not exact biographies of Jesus but rather records of his teachings and events around his life. Scholars have difficulties fixing the exact date of the events of his life, which has nothing to do with the message. Just to take a position, a good date for the incarnate birth of Jesus is either December 6 B.C. or April 5 B.C.

Again, as to dates, scholars have difficulties fixing the inclusive dates of the public earthly ministry of Jesus. Most agree his baptism by his cousin John and the beginning of his ministry was about April 26 A.D., at the earthly age of thirty. There is a meaningless debate as to whether the crucifixion was three or four years later. Either way, his ministry may be divided and described two ways. One is according to his teachings. The first six months, after his baptism was a quiet family time and may be described as his time of Inauguration. The next eight months he did some healings and acceptable teachings and may be described as his time of Popularity. Crowds love a winner. At the end of this period, Jesus began to challenge the Jewish leaders and his own disciples. This is well described as his time of Opposition and lasted for either two or three years, setting the crucifixion at either April 29 A.D. or 30 A.D.

Luke tells us that on the eighth day, the baby was taken to the temple in Jerusalem to be presented to God. It was also the time for circumcision. Upon entering the temple, the elderly Simeon saw the child and said those words so often used in churches as one surrenders to God, as at evening prayer. "Lord, now you are letting your servant depart in peace...for my eyes have seen your salvation."

Matthew then introduces us to Herod the Great, that Edomite ruler of the Jews as appointed by the Romans. He had built up cities to honor the emperors and himself. About fifteen years before the incarnate birth of Jesus he had begun the grand scale improvements to the temple which construction would continue for yet another seventy years, only to be torn down by the Romans eight years after such completion. Wise men, magi, bearing gifts for this child-king had journeyed from the east. Herod tried to trick them into returning to inform him when they located this child king. They followed the star to Bethlehem, but were told by an angel not to return to Herod. Herod issued a decree that all male children under the age of two years were to be killed. No doubt using the wealth given by the wise men, Joseph and Mary took the baby and fled to Egypt where they would remain until the death of Herod two years later.

Luke then gives us the only information as to Jesus until he is thirty years old. He simply tells us "the child grew, and waxed strong in spirit, filled with wisdom, and the grace of God was upon him." He tells us that at the age of twelve, Jesus was taken by his parents to Jerusalem where he astonishes the teachers and all who hear him with his understanding and answers. Mary and Joseph, wrongly presuming he was with their group, leave and have to return to find him after three days. His mother mildly chastises him, to which he responds, "Did you not know that I must be about my Father's business?"

Eighteen years later, when Jesus and his cousin John the Baptist are thirty years old, Matthew and Luke resume their narratives and Mark and John begin theirs. Within a year, Herod Antipas, one of the sons of Herod the Great, has John the Baptist beheaded and three or four years later Jesus crucified. Luke again sets the new political scene by telling us it was in the fifteenth year of Tiberius Caesar, that Pontius Pilate was the Roman governor, Herod Antipas was the local ruler and his brother Herod Phillip II ruler of the area east of the Sea of Galilee.

John the Baptist was living in the countryside and preaching strong words against those who did not follow the word of God. He is a voice crying in the wilderness. He is also baptizing many in the River Jordan. He preaches that he baptizes with water but that one is coming who will baptize with the Holy Spirit and with fire, one whose sandal he is not worthy to loosen. As he preached, Jesus came to him to be baptized. As Jesus came up out of the water a voice from heaven said, "This is my beloved Son, in whom I am well pleased." Naturally, the religious leaders, the Sanhedrin, promptly sent a delegation to inquire as to John's credentials as clergy.

Promptly thereafter Jesus is led by the Holy Spirit into the desert wilderness to be tempted by Satan, the devil himself. Jesus fasted forty days, then while hungry and tired, Satan tempts him with some of the primary temptations common to each of us. He tested Jesus, who did not fail, as to his need for emotional security, as to his psychological need for power and significance. As he had done with Adam and Eve, Satan slightly misquotes scripture, the word of God, just little distortions.

It is at this point that the gospel of John begins. John the Apostle, does not report the events of the incarnation, baptism and testing of Jesus, but the other three do. He records the calling by Jesus of the first two of his twelve apostles, two fishermen, Andrew who goes to bring his brother Peter. The next day he calls Philip. With each of his apostles the call was usually simply, "Follow me," and each promptly does so. Philip brings in Nathanael. Jesus goes to a wedding party in the small village of Cana. He shows up with his apostles. The host runs out of wine. Jesus turns the water in several very large vessels into wine. His first miracle, a nature miracle.

It was springtime and time for the Passover, the first of maybe three for Jesus during these years. The last would be a "last supper" on the evening of his arrest in the garden. He becomes outraged at the corrupt financial activities in the temple court and makes a cord whip with which he drives the cattle and sheep out, and then knocks over the tables. His first cleansing of the temple. Jesus is then questioned as to his credentials. He replies that should the temple be destroyed he would raise it in three days. The questioners are confused, as the temple of Herod had already been under construction for about forty-six years.

It is at this Passover that Nicodemus, a ruler of the Jews, a Pharisee, a professor at the school, comes to Jesus by night. John regularly uses the metaphor, the comparison, of night and light for wrong and right. He asks how one could be born again, a second time, from above. Jesus explains, or tries. Then comes that great quote. "For God so loved the world, that he gave his only begotten Son, that whosoever believeth on him should not perish, but have eternal life." In addition to night and light, John also writes of the world, of being the flesh, and of giving.

Jesus returns from Jerusalem by way of the province of Samaria, the area where 700 years before the Assyrians had removed the Jews and replaced them with people from the area of modern Iraq. Even to the day of Jesus the Samaritans were considered unholy and dangerous. In Samaria he meets a woman of some ill-repute drawing water at a time of day when other women would not be around. He speaks to her of living waters.

Jesus arrives back in Nazareth in the province of Galilee, and begins what is termed his great Galilean ministry and the year of his popularity. It starts on a down note. After healing the son of a nobleman, he reads in the synagogue in Nazareth from the book of Isaiah and then receives his first rejection, there in his hometown. His townspeople even lead him to a hill to stone him, but he walks right through the crowd and leaves.

He walks down the hill to Capernaum at the north end of the Sea of Galilee. There he calls four more fishermen. It is the entire fishing crew of Mr. Zebedee, which is his sons James and John Zebedee, and Peter and Andrew. This is promptly followed by several healings in the area. He then calls Matthew, also known as Levi, a hated collector of taxes. He teaches using several parables. He does some more healings. He then again confronts the religious leaders, the Pharisees, as to their teachings. He prays all night and calls the rest of his apostles, Bartholomew, Thomas, another James, Simon the zealot and Judas Iscariot. Jesus chose Judas.

After this he teaches a crowd sitting on the grassy hillside by the sea. This becomes known as the Sermon on the Mount. He speaks of blessings, the beatitudes, of responsibility, of God's law and Kingdom, of hypocrites and harsh judgments and gives the golden rule of one to another. He is indeed very popular. This is all part of the training of the twelve, and the first of five discourses reported by Matthew. He continues with his brief discourse on the commissioning of his twelve disciples and then several parables as to what the kingdom of God would be like.

During most of the first two years of his ministry, as he teaches and heals, and before he begins to challenge the Jewish leaders, Jesus makes two walking tours around the vicinity of Galilee. During his third tour around Galilee he begins to issue challenges. He feeds the 4,000 and the 5,000, and he also rebukes the Pharisees. Then, as reported mostly by Luke, he walks through Judea and Perea ministering to many whom he meets along the way, including an adulterous woman and ten lepers. He teaches of lost sheep and lost sons, and of his second coming. Luke reports that, "when the time had come for him to be received up, that he steadfastly set his face to go to Jerusalem." Several months over the horizon, a Good Friday and a cross wait for him. From here on he will walk alone. His disciples will not fully understand. Everything begins changing rapidly.

On the Sabbath Jesus rides a donkey into Jerusalem. The crowds call him king and wave palm branches. Christians celebrate this as Palm Sunday, but it actually would have been on Saturday. On Monday he again goes into the temple courtyard and chases out the money changers. He quotes a phrase from both Isaiah, about 740 years earlier, and enlarged by Jeremiah about 650 years earlier. "My house shall be called a house of prayer, but you have made it a den of thieves." Isaiah had prophesied the temple shall be "for all nations", not just for Hebrews. Jeremiah, as had nearly every prophet of the old Hebrew scriptures, was chastising the Hebrew priests and leaders for their apostasy in the temple. Malachi, 460 years earlier, had strongly indicted the priests for their teaching. Matthew, a Jew who wrote to the Jews, quoted Jesus, a Jew, using a phrase that says both that the temple is for all nations to worship and that the leaders still continue to misuse the temple.

Tuesday and Wednesday Jesus speaks and mainly teaches his disciples as to the end of the ages. Thursday they prepare for the Passover meal, the "last supper" in the "upper room". He washes the feet of his disciples and tells them of the true vine as they walk about a mile to the Garden of Gethsemane, where he prays for them and is then arrested, being identified by his disciple Judas.

During the late hours Thursday Jesus is moved from one location in the city to another as the Jewish leaders fabricate charges against him. He is moved between Herod Antipas and Pontius Pilate. During the early hours Friday he is illegally tried and convicted. He is stripped, scourged and made to carry the large cross to the site of crucifixion, a horrible method of execution. There, between two criminals, he is placed on the cross at 9:00 a.m. He is mocked by the crowd and speaks three sayings of concern for others. At noon darkness comes over the whole land. As he hangs on the cross after the noon-hour he speaks the four sayings of concern for himself, the last being at 3:00 p.m. as he yields up his spirit. The earth quakes, graves open, and the foot-thick curtain in the temple tears across the weave, from top to bottom.

During the next three hours, before 6:00 p.m. or sunset, Joseph of Arimethea and Nicodemus, two of the Sanhedrin, request permission to take the body down from the cross and bury it in a new tomb. Permission is granted, and he is placed in the tomb and a huge stone rolled across to seal the doorway. The Jews request Roman guards and are told to place their own, which they do. The tomb is sealed and guarded from sundown Friday to sunrise Sunday.

Sunday, resurrection Sunday, at dawn Joanna, Mary Magdalene and Mary, the mother of James, go out to the tomb. An angel has rolled aside the huge wheel shaped stone from the tomb and is sitting on it, leaving the tomb open. Two men appear in shining robes and tell them Jesus has risen and is not there. The women are both frightened and filled with joy. They rush to tell the others. Peter and John also go to the tomb and see that it is empty. The tomb guards go to tell their Jewish superiors what has happened and are given moral and financial support to tell people that they had fallen asleep, and the friends of Jesus came and removed the body.

The resurrected Jesus makes many appearances to many people. That same Sunday he walks, talks and breaks bread with two of his followers along the road to Emmaus. Later he meets with his disciples in the same upper room of the last supper and allows them to touch him and eats with them. Days later he meets with them again and has Thomas touch the place of his wounds. During the forty-day period from the resurrection to his ascension to heaven, Jesus, in his glorified body, appears a reported ten times. He appears to Mary Magdalene, to the women, to Peter, to the two men near Emmaus, to the ten disciples, to the ten plus Thomas, to seven disciples fishing, to over 500 at once, to James, to the eleven disciples at the commissioning, and finally at his ascension to heaven. Months later he appears to Paul on the road to Damascus.

And here begins, as follows on the next pages, the story of the Acts of the Holy Spirit as the apostles spread the word and the church.

CHAPTER 31
ACTS
ACTS OF THE SPIRIT TO USE PETER AND PAUL
TO SPREAD THE CHURCH

We will give ourselves continually to prayer and to the ministry of the word. Acts 6:4

In the gospels, especially Luke's, which cover thirty-three years, and in Acts, which covers another thirty-two years, there is a succession of rulers, which can be somewhat confusing, especially when both volumes together cover about sixty-five years. There are four offices which have successive holders. The big one is that of emperor of the Roman Empire, then the Roman ruler or king of Palestine, then the Jewish ruler of Palestine, then the High Priest.

The Roman emperors begin with Mark Antony, then Octavia Augustus, then Tiberius, Caligula, who was insane, Claudius, who was an imbecile, and Nero, a hopeless egomaniac. The local Palestinian kings begin with Herod the Great, who died when Jesus was eight years old and still with Joseph and Mary in Egypt. His kingdom was divided into four parts, each termed a tetrarch, meaning "of four primates". Three of his sons ruled these four. Archelaus ruled Samaria, Judea and Idumea, the native area of the Herods. Herod Antipas ruled Galilee and Perea. Herod Phillip II ruled Traconitis and Iturea. One can see where the confusion as to just who is meant by "King Herod."

Archelaus was so violent, killing 3,000 Jews upon assuming his position, that he was deposed just about the time the twelve-year old Jesus was teaching at the temple. Archelaus was replaced by a Procurator, a governor in our parlance. Years later Pontius Pilate would hold that office. Then thirty years later, in the latter chapters of Acts, the office is held by Felix and then by Festus. Paul will be tried by these local governors before being sent to Rome. The High Priests are fairly well identified.

The story of the gospels, the life of Jesus, takes place during the time of Emperors Octavia Augustus and Tiberius, the time of five Roman procurators or prefects, of which we hear only of the fifth, Pontius Pilate, and the time of Herod the Great then of his three sons, the tetrarchs, Archelaus, Herod Antipas and Herod Phillip II. The story of the Acts, takes place during the time of Emperors Caligula, Claudius and Nero, the time of procurators Pilate, Felix and Festus, and the time of King Herod Agrippa I and Herod Agrippa II.

Luke, the gentile physician from Syria, wrote one story, one book, in two volumes, and they should be read together as such, one continuous treatise. We tend to lose sight of the fact, as teachers simply speak of the first volume as one of the four gospels. Luke continues his gospel in Acts. He begins his gospel by informing us that he writes an orderly account, a narrative, to Theophilus, "lover of God". He begins the volume on Acts much the same way, then covers the thirty-two years from the resurrection to the end of Paul's work. Acts, with its historical teaching, should be read monthly.

As originally written by Luke, neither of his two volumes had a title. When the New Testament was being officially canonized Luke's two volumes were kept in sequence and the second given the title "Acts" as it was the action of the Holy Spirit through various men. This volume, together with Luke's first volume, are the primary writings about the acts of the Holy Spirit. In some of his letters Paul will write to describe the Holy Spirit.

The first eleven verses of Acts reiterate some high points of his gospel, including the ascension, as it bridges over into this second volume. Chapter three concludes with the selection by lot, by *purim*, of Matthias to be an apostle to replace Judas Iscariot, who had hung himself.

Chapters two through twelve are primarily about Peter, one of the original twelve apostles, and his ministry. Chapters thirteen through twenty-eight are about Paul and his ministry. Peter had met Jesus while a fisherman. Peter met Paul while persecuted by him. This volume also mentions John as a companion to Peter. It is not about the acts of the apostles, but about the acts of the Holy Spirit. This entire volume is tightly packed, mainly with historical facts. The first few chapters also have much as to religion, so we will look at them more extensively.

Jesus was twelve years old when he joined the teachers at the court of the temple and astonished them with his understanding and answers. Three years later, in 10 A.D., when he was fifteen, a boy was born in Tarsus, in what we call Turkey. He was named Saul, and would be renamed Paul. In Jerusalem, Herod the Great, who had ordered the killing of the male babies at the time of the birth of Jesus had been dead fourteen years. His project of enlarging the small 500 year-old temple, was in its twentieth year. When Saul was fourteen years old, he was sent to Jerusalem to study under Gamaliel, to become a Pharisee. It was 24 A.D., the year Jesus was baptized by John the Baptist in the River Jordan and began his public ministry, an insert between chapters two and three of Matthew. During his teenage years Paul most certainly witnessed the three-year ministry of Jesus, the cleansing of the temple and the crucifixion.

Following the resurrection, Jesus walked the earth forty days, then ascended, was lifted up, to heaven. Ten days later, on the day of Pentecost, the

Holy Spirit promised by Jesus came. Chapter two opens with Pentecost, the beginning, the birth date, of the Church of Jesus Christ, of latter day saints, if you will. On this day the apostles were gathered together when a sound, like a rushing wind, came from heaven. Something like tongues of fire touched each of the men. They were filled with the Holy Spirit. A crowd of people from different areas and languages gathered around them. The apostles began to speak. The crowd heard in their own language, their own tongue. Tongues of fire and tongues of language. The Holy Spirit.

In chapter two, Peter gives his first sermon. He tells the group that the men are not drunk as it was only nine o'clock in the morning. Peter and Paul both tell us we are to preach Jesus Christ and him resurrected. Billy Graham the great evangelist of the latter twentieth century followed this pattern. Peter set a five-part pattern to be followed in all sermons, or witness talks. First, what did Jesus do? In verse twenty-two, the answer is works, wonders and signs. Second, what did you do? Crucified him. Third, what did God do? Raised him from the dead. Fourth, what are you doing now? Telling people about this, witnessing. Fifth, what more can you do? Repent, be baptized and receive the Holy Spirit. On that very day 3,000 souls did just that.

In verse forty-two are the five visible signs of a church, the right hand of the Spirit. Look at your hand. Not listed is what the apostles did, Evangelism, the thumb. Teaching, *kerygma*, is the index finger pointing the way. Fellowship is the middle finger, the central part, *koinonia*. Breaking bread is the ring finger, the marriage to Jesus, *diakonia*. Prayer is the little finger, so often neglected.

The chapter ends with fellowship taken to its ultimate, the ideal communal living. All owned their own property but were to sell as necessary for the good of the group. This is not the concept of Communism. First, Communism is not governed by Jesus Christ. Second, these people owned their real estate and personal possessions. Third, all sharing was purely voluntary.

Chapter three is another miracle of nine o'clock in the morning followed by the second sermon of Peter, a miracle and a message. As Peter and John enter the temple to pray a lame man asks for a donation. Peter responds, "Silver and gold I do not have, but what I do have I give to you. In the name of Jesus Christ rise up and walk." The man is healed. As the three stand there, Peter preaches to the astonished crowd. He assures them that both they and their leaders crucified Jesus out of ignorance, and again invites them to repent, and again arouses the leaders.

In chapter four is the first of the renewed clashes with the Jewish authorities. That evening Peter and John are arrested and jailed overnight, but 5,000 are converted to believers. The next day they are called before Ananias, the retired high priest, and Caiphas, his son-in-law and current high priest, the same two who about two months before had sponsored the crucifixion. Peter, whose name in both Hebrew and Greek means stone or rock, tells them Jesus was and is the stone, recalling Nebuchadnezzar's dream of the large image in Daniel chapter two, and its smiting stone which crushed those feet of clay and iron. The two high priests order them to cease such preaching and releases them. The preaching has not ceased to this very day, though many authorities still try to contain it.

In chapter five we have the story of Ananias, not to be confused with Annas the high priest, and his wife Sapphira. In the communal life-style Ananias sold some possessions but did not turn all of the proceeds over to the community, then both lie about it. They lied, and they died. Led by Peter, the apostles do great healings right at the temple, and multitudes come to believe. This time the high priests arrest all twelve of the apostles, but an angel opens the prison doors and directs them to return to the temple and preach. Again they are all arrested and brought before the council, being mostly Sadducees, but also Pharisees and other leaders, to whom they explain, "We must obey God rather than men."

A member of that council is Gamaliel, a highly respected Pharisee and teacher. During the past seven years he had been instructing Saul from Tarsus, who is now twenty-one years old and himself a Pharisee. Gamaliel directs that the apostles be removed from the room. He then cautions the council as to these apostles, telling them that, "If this plan or this work is of men it will come to nothing; but if it is of God you can not overthrow it--lest you even be found to fight against God." They beat the apostles, order them to cease preaching and release them. The apostles immediately return to their preaching.

In chapter six the murmurings of the people within the church begin, and will continue to this day. The Greek Jews complain that they are not being treated fairly by the Hebrew Jews. The twelve direct that seven, of good repute and full of the Spirit and wisdom, be chosen as deacons, to serve the group. Stephen is the first among the seven. A group of freed slaves who had formed their own synagogue complain of Stephen's preaching and have him haled before that council. Chapter seven is the speech of Stephen, the story of the Jews from Abraham through Moses to Jesus. The council orders that he be stoned to death. They appoint Saul, the young Pharisee, to oversee the stoning and the closing of the house-churches.

Chapter eight opens with the campaign of Saul to lay waste and ravage the churches and the men and women involved, which actually forces the spreading of the church from Jerusalem to all of Judea and into Samaria. A man named Philip, not the apostle, sees an Ethiopian eunuch reading the old Hebrew scriptures. The Spirit tells Philip to go to the man, and ask if he understands. The man tells him, "How can I unless someone guides me?" So Philip teaches him of the good news.

In chapter nine Luke tells us of the experience of Saul the Pharisee, now twenty-five years old, as he travels to Damascus, Syria, 175 miles northeasterly from Jerusalem, in search of Christians to kill. A light from heaven flashes about him, and he falls to the ground. A voice says, "Saul, Saul, why are you persecuting me?" "Who are you, Lord?" "I am Jesus, whom you are persecuting....Arise and go into the city, and you will be told what you must do." Saul arises, but is blind. He goes to Damascus where another man named Ananias, at the direction of Jesus, takes in this most feared Pharisee. While staying there, the Jews hear of Saul's conversion and seek him out, but his friends lower him in secret from a window. A man named Barnabas takes him, and will be his primary traveling companion from then on. Saul remains in hiding and maturation for a total of three years before returning to Jerusalem.

As the Spirit incubates in Saul for three years, Luke resumes his narrative of Peter from verse thirty-two through the next three chapters. In chapter ten, at noon, Peter becomes hungry and sees a vision with all kinds of animals, reptiles and birds from which he is to eat. He refuses, but a voice tells him that all foods cleansed by God may be eaten. We are told of Cornelius, a commander of 100 Roman troops, whom Peter visited. Cornelius receives the Holy Spirit, and Peter baptizes him. The first baptism of a non-Jew, a Gentile.

In chapter eleven, Peter returns to Jerusalem to report on his new ministry to the Gentiles. God has also given the Holy Spirit to Gentiles. He compares this to his vision of the meats, that what God has cleansed is good. We are told that the dispersion of the people of the Word has now reached into Turkey, Syria and Cyprus. Barnabas is sent to Antioch, then into Turkey to look for his friend Saul, where he finds him, back in his hometown of Tarsus. Barnabas brings Saul to Antioch where the two work to build the church. This is the first time and place that the people are called Christians. Saul's ministry has begun.

In chapter twelve we are told of the King Herod. It is now about 44 A.D., fifteen years after the crucifixion. This is Herod Agrippa I, who continued the actions of his grandfather and uncles, as he now rules all of Palestine. It was his sister Herodias who had married her two uncles, first Phillip II then his half-brother Herod Antipas, and had John the Baptist beheaded. Agrippa I now orders James, the brother of John Zebedee, put to death. He then arrests Peter, the third time, but again an angel opens the doors and Peter walks out. Agrippa refuses to give God the glory and is struck by worms and dies. Barnabas and Saul return from Jerusalem, taking young John Mark with them. It is at this time that James, the brother of Jesus, writes his short book, his epistle, his letter to the churches.

The first twelve chapters are about Peter. Chapter thirteen through the end of Acts, are about Paul as Luke narrates a travelogue of Paul, including his arrest. During these travels Paul wrote his letters, his epistles, of the New Testament, being twenty-five percent of our Christian scriptures. Let's hear a rapid litany of this sequence as Paul travels around the areas of modern Turkey, Greece and Rome. Saul is his Jewish name, Paul his Latin.

Through the middle of chapter fifteen is the time of Paul's First Journey. In chapter thirteen Barnabas and Paul are set apart by the Holy Spirit, Bar-Jesus is blinded by the word of Paul, Paul preaches at Pisidian, Antioch and becomes the missionary to the Gentiles. Chapter fourteen tells of Paul's first journey, around southeastern modern Turkey. Paul and Barnabas do a healing and were thought of as gods, but the Jews turn the people against them and Paul is stoned and left for dead. He heals and continues his teachings.

Chapter fifteen tells of Paul returning to Jerusalem to settle with the other apostles the issues as to whether a person must first become a Jew to be a follower of Christ. They decide that one need not first become a Jew and that circumcision is not required, but that one must abstain from idols, unchastity and from eating or drinking blood. Paul confronts Peter on several issues. This is the first church council. It is 49 A.D., and Paul is 39 years old.

Paul leaves Jerusalem to begin his Second Journey which takes him around the Aegean Sea, the west coast of Turkey and the east coast of Greece, about 1,500 miles one-way. It lasts a little over three years, from 50 A.D. to 54 A.D. and is reported from the middle of chapter fifteen to the middle of chapter eighteen. Near the end of this journey he begins to write those letters to churches which make up so much of the new Christian scriptures of the Bible.

Paul is a Jew and a Pharisee and for these reasons his practice is to go to the synagogue of places he visits and to teach. This usually gets him into trouble with the local Jewish leaders. In chapter sixteen we are told that Paul goes to Philippi in Macedonia, Greece, where he casts a demon out of a woman, and the Jewish leaders turn the people against him. Paul and Silas are thrown in jail. An earthquake causes the jail doors to open, but Paul does not walk out, to the great relief of the jailer who is then converted. The authorities decide to release Paul. He goes to Thessalonica, where he is again forced to leave.

Paul goes on to Athens where he debates Greek philosophy and the new Christian teachings. There are monuments all over the city to every god a person could imagine and even one monument to an unnamed god. Paul picks up on that to discuss Jesus as this as yet unnamed god. As usual he is asked to leave and goes on to Corinth, a most sinful and cosmopolitan city, where he remains with Aquila and Priscilla for eighteen months. While in Corinth he writes his two letters back to the church in Thessalonica, in which he explains some things of the second coming of Christ and gives them encouragement. He then concludes this second journey as he sails back to Jerusalem. It is 54 A.D. and Nero is enthroned as Roman emperor. Life is going to get much worse for the followers of Christ.

At the end of chapter eighteen Paul promptly begins his Third Journey, which nearly retraces his second trip and also lasts about three years, from 54

A.D. to 58 A.D. During this time he works with most of the "seven churches" of which we read at the beginning of John's book of Revelation, either starting or enlarging them. While in Ephesus he writes his First and Second epistles to the church in Corinth. Timothy is with him and remains for a while in Ephesus. From there Paul goes on to Corinth where he writes his epistle back to the church in Galatia. There were Judaizers following in behind Paul, and he writes to refute their teachings that one need (should) first become a Jew in order to become a Christian. While in Corinth he also writes his epistle to the church in Rome, to prepare them for his intended visit as he hopes to go on to Spain. However, he retraces his path back to Jerusalem.

Chapters twenty-one through twenty-eight record Paul's return to Jerusalem, his arrest and transportation to house arrest in Rome, where he writes four of his epistolary books back to his churches. These concluding chapters begin about 58 A.D., about twenty-eight years after the crucifixion of Jesus. Paul concludes his third and, except for transportation as a prisoner, his final journey. Upon arriving at the coast of Palestine he is cautioned by his friends not to go on to Jerusalem for fear for his life. He does travel to Jerusalem, where Jews from the area of modern Turkey accuse him falsely, and he is initially arrested by the Romans as protective custody.

Paul is taken before the Roman tribunal, a local judge, and reiterates his personal history and the events of his conversion on the road to Damascus. He tells the court that he is a good Jew and also a natural born Roman citizen, and can not be bound up, and so is bound on a lenient arrest for the governor. He is then also sent before the Jewish Sanhedrin, where the council splits over the issues, particularly as to the resurrection, as the Sadducee members do not but the Pharisee members do believe in a resurrection. Paul and his case are then referred to the governor.

Paul is officially accused by the Jews of being a pestilent agitator among all the Jews. Governor Felix holds Paul as a prisoner for two years and will call him before him at times in hopes of being paid a bribe. Festus replaces Felix as governor, and when Festus calls Paul up he exercises his right to appeal on up to Caesar, who at the time was Nero. Festus refers the matter of Paul on to Herod Agrippa II, king of the Jews and great-grandson of Herod the Great, king at the birth of Christ Jesus. Agrippa calls before him Paul, who again reiterates his personal history and the events of his conversion on the road to Damascus. In the saddest statement ever, Agrippa said he "was almost persuaded" by Paul to be a Christian. Agrippa also says he would have set Paul free had he not previously appealed to Caesar. Paul is directed to be transported to Rome.

En route a violent storm comes up, threatening the ship and all 276 aboard. Paul assures them that they will all be safe. The ship does sink but all live and spend time on the island of Malta. Paul finally arrives at Rome and is given quarters as house arrest while awaiting an audience with the emperor.

He is confined there for two years, during which he has many visitors and continues to preach Christ resurrected.

Here the book of Acts ends. We know from other books that Paul wrote four epistolary books during that time, his prison letters. These were Philemon, Colossians, Ephesians and Philippians. Apparently Paul was released from prison. During his release he wrote his three pastoral epistles, being First and Second Timothy and Titus. However, a few years later he was again arrested and executed, as tradition has it by beheading.

And here begin, as on the following pages, the two letters to the Thessalonians.

CHAPTER 32

THESSALONIANS I AND II
FAITH AND THE SECOND COMING

God from the beginning chose you for salvation through sanctification by the Spirit and belief in the truth, to which he called you by our gospel. 2 Ths. 2:13-14

We are reminded that Paul was born in what is today Turkey, in the city of Tarsus. It was about 10 A.D., about three years after the young Jesus, at the age of twelve, taught in the temple. In his youth Paul migrated to Jerusalem and was brought up as a disciple of Gamaliel I, an honored Pharisee and teacher of the law. Paul was a highly educated Hebrew of Hebrews, a Jew of Jews. He was both a Jew and a Roman citizen, which gave him various political privileges. He was extremely proud and fervent about both. He was at home in the Graeco-Roman world. His trade, his occupation, was a tent-maker and leatherworker.

During the three years of the ministry of Jesus, as he walked to the cross in Jerusalem, Paul lived in this Jerusalem, as a late teenager, training to be a Pharisee. Paul would have been very aware of this Jesus person. One can imagine that as a nineteen year-old diligent student he was at the temple as Jesus threw out the money-changers, and that he followed the entourage throughout the night of the arrest, trial and torture and then stood on the hill to observe the crucifixion. When Paul was about twenty-three years old, upon authority from the high priest, he was an official persecutor of the followers of Jesus. In chapter seven of Acts, he stood with the high priest to listen to that wonderful summary of Jewish history given by Stephen, then held the coats of those who threw the stones to kill Stephen. He ravaged the churches, dragged off men and women, pursued others to foreign countries and imprisoned them.

Paul pursued the followers of Christ, which made him a follower of Christ, an acolyte. On one pursuit from Jerusalem to Damascus, Syria, 150 miles to the northeast, Jesus came to Paul, on the road, in a blinding light. Paul's spiritual eyes were opened as for days his physical eyes were blinded. Paul was converted. His brilliant mind and his enthusiasm were totally and completely turned to Christ. On the spot, he became a fanatical, right-wing, evangelical, radical Christian. He withdrew for about three years, among the Apostles, to sort it all out, then he visited Damascus and later began carrying the word to the Gentiles, this Jew, to the Gentiles, of Turkey, Greece and Rome.

Paul left Jerusalem to begin his Second Journey which took him around the Aegean Sea, the west coast of Turkey and the east coast of Greece, about 1,500 miles one-way. The journey lasted a little over three years, from 50 A.D. to 54 A.D. and is reported in Acts from the middle of chapter fifteen to the middle of chapter eighteen. Near the end of this journey he began to write those letters to churches which make up so much of the Christian scriptures of the Bible. His first two letters were back to the struggling church in Thessalonica. It was apparently to respond to some questions brought to him from Thessalonica by Timothy.

During a thirty year period Paul set up home churches. These groups had every problem of people trying to sort it out and work together. An evangelist or church planter generally does not hang around long. He goes to the next planting leaving the plant to a pastor to nurture and develop. What would frequently happen when Paul left is that the Jews would be looked to by the newcomers as the authorities. The Jews would begin to slip back into their old ways of laws, customs and rituals. They would insist on everybody becoming a good true Jew before they could be considered Christians. They would insist on circumcision and other things of the old law. They would then explain that Paul was not one with full authority and knowledge, but that they knew more. They would say Paul did not personally know Jesus and was not even one of the twelve, or thirteen, apostles. They would tear and rip at the minister's teachings and sermons over lunch. They would call Paul a fool. The old Hebrew scriptures call them mumblers. The new Christian scriptures calls them Judaizers. Others are called false teachers.

All of Paul's letters focus on his conversion and the stark difference between his before and his after, the law and grace, death and life. The concerns to which Paul responded in his preserved letters were and are: to Thessalonica as to jealousy of the Jews toward Paul but primarily the when and how of the Second Coming of Christ; to Corinth as to division over sex, marriage, conscience, order, spiritual gifts, and attacks on Paul; to Galatia as to requiring all to first become Jews; to Rome as to just what Christianity is in relation to history, the Old Testament, the law and grace; to Philemon as to blooming where you are planted, even as a slave; to Colossae as to false teachers; to Ephesus as to God's plan for perseverance in unity; to Timothy as to false teachings and what is required of church leaders; and to Titus as to church leaders and conduct. These are not simply theories to be discussed but truths to be lived.

Paul was in Corinth when he wrote back to Thessalonica. He stayed in Corinth about eighteen months before setting sail back to Palestine. During the early months of his stay, he wrote the first of his canonized letters, these two to Thessalonica, the only ones he wrote during his second journey, a total of less than six pages. Paul had been shamelessly chased out of Thessalonica and to Corinth by angry and jealous Jews. As we will be told in chapter three, Paul sent his assistant Timothy back to check on the people. Timothy returned to inform Paul that the church still was strong but that those Jews continued to persecute the church-people back in Thessalonica It was so vicious that the followers began to think that the "day of the Lord", that period of end times judgment and wrath, was upon them. They wondered when Jesus would really come again. Some of them, thinking Jesus would never come, lost hope. Some of them, thinking his coming was at hand, quit working and sat idle.

The primary and central teaching of both of these letters, particularly the second, is the second coming of Christ. In both combined there are twenty references to the second coming. In Greek the name of this second coming, this "showing forth", is *parousia*, from which our liturgical churches get the name "parish" for the area a particular church is charged with showing Jesus. Each of the five chapters of the first letter end with a reference to the second coming. A concern of those in Thessalonica was when and how the second coming would occur, including what would happen to those who die before the coming.

The secondary teaching of these two letters is "faith, hope and love", a timeless and timely teaching. Paul begins this first letter by commending them with words he will use in the letter he will write next, four years later to the church in Corinth, "faith, hope and charity". In verse two he commends and in verse nine he specifies. In the past they had exhibited a "work of faith, labor of love, and patience of hope." By this they "turned to God from idols", indicating they had been pagans, and "serve the living and true God". Into the future, they are to maintain a steadfast hope as they "wait for his Son from heaven."

First Thessalonians has much of the teachings, the doctrines, of the church. In verses four and five Paul suggests both the doctrine of the Trinity, of the one, unified Godhead, and also of salvation. He tells them they are beloved by God who has chosen them. He tells them, and us, that the gospel came not only by the spoken word but also in power and in the Holy Spirit. In all he speaks of the Lord Jesus Christ. He writes of being saved. God the Father saved a person when he chose them, elected them, in Christ before the world began. God the Son, when he physically died on the cross, offered salvation to any and all who faithfully believed in him. God the Holy Spirit saved a person on some specific hour in that person's life, between birth and death, when the person became convinced and convicted.

In chapter two Paul tells them, and us, of his practices as an evangelical missionary. Paul writes that they, and we, are not to listen to false teachings as the gospel does not come from error, uncleanness or guile. They are not to use flattery to convince people nor as a cloak for greed, as many do yet today. He writes that they are to do as he does, to be like a mother and a father to those they bring in and along. A mother nurses, feeds and cares for her young. A father exhorts, calls his young out and encourages and charges them to lead a life worthy of God. He concludes chapter two by saying that at the second coming one will be able to boast only of those he has brought to Christ. It is estimated that ninety percent of those in any church were, in some manner, physically brought into that church by an active member. If they are not brought and then nurtured the pews and chairs are empty. Paul is first an evangelist and second a pastor.

Chapter three begins with reminding the people of his assistant Timothy, whom he had sent back to them and who has now returned to inform Paul and to bring their questions. In verse thirteen he states that Jesus will return "with all his saints". He speaks of "saints" and of "holy ones" more than eighty times in his letters, without always defining whether he means humans or angels. Here he probably means both as he refers to the archangel, Michael. Again, he concludes with another reference to the second coming. They, and we, are to understand that there will in fact be a second coming, of which Jesus himself spoke at length, as primarily reported in chapter twenty-four of the gospel of Matthew.

Chapters one through three are concerned with thanksgivings and receiving the gospel. In chapter four he speaks more of instructions and teachings. About eleven years after writing these two short letters, Paul will write to the church at Ephesus. He will write that letter during his two-year stay in prison in Rome. That will be one of his finest letters, both as to grammar and as to a refined concept of his teachings, as he will then have plenty of time to proofread, revise and correct. In chapters four and five of that letter he will write of three walks, which walks he touches on in chapter four of this first letter.

In the first eight verses of chapter four Paul writes of walking in holiness. In the next two verses he writes of walking in harmony, and in verses eleven and twelve he writes of walking in honesty. To Ephesus he will ask them to "walk worthy of the vocation." Here, each is to walk in holiness, to sanctification, another church doctrine, to do the will of God. Each is to abstain from immorality. At verse four, each is to "possess his vessel," which some English Bibles translate as to care for the vessel of one's wife, but which more likely means to care first that the vessel of yourself be holy. Paul will ask the Ephesians to "walk not as other Gentiles, in vanity." Here, in verses nine and ten, we are to walk in love and harmony with all the brethren. He will ask the Ephesians to "walk in love...as children of the light." Here in verses eleven and twelve he writes that each is to "live quietly, mind your own affairs, and work with your own hands." People are not to sit idly waiting but to work and prepare for the coming visit.

Verses thirteen through eighteen of chapter four speak of the second coming. Paul strives to answer two questions of the Thessalonians, and of nearly every person as he or she begins to settle into being a new Christian: the when and how of the second coming and what happens to those who have already died. In verse fifteen he writes that those who have died in the faith will be raised at the time of the coming, the advent. The coming will be as was the ascension but in reverse. "The Lord himself will descend from heaven with a shout, with the voice of an archangel, and with the trumpet of God."

Verse seventeen is the verse of which we hear a lot, but very few people know where it is in the Bible and what it really says. It is the verse on what is known as the "rapture". In the original Greek the word is *harpazo*, which means seize, snatch, carry away forcibly. About 400 A.D. Jerome translated the Hebrew and Christian scriptures into the common, or vulgar, Latin of the people, and it became known as the Vulgate. He used the Latin word *rapio*, as *rapiemur*, which has the meaning of "forcibly taken". From this word the English word "rapture" was derived. Most English translations use the phrase "caught up". Rapture means simply "wrapped up and taken away." Paul tells us that the faithful will be wrapped up and taken to meet Christ in the air. However, he states it in such a way as to allow and cause the Thessalonians to think the coming may very likely be very soon, and he has to correct that fixed thought in his second letter.

Chapter five opens with Paul writing that people are not to be concerned as to the season and time of this Second Coming as it will come as a "thief in the night". He uses the Hebrew phrase of "Day of the Lord", for these days of judgment in the end times. For Christians this is the introduction of the period of "Tribulation". Later John will write in chapter twenty of his book on Revelation that at the second coming there will be a 1,000-year period, a millennium, during which Satan will be bound in chains. In chapter twenty-four of Matthew is recorded the discourse of Jesus to his disciples as to these end times. Jesus speaks of this great tribulation, following wars, rumors of wars, famines and earthquakes, and tells them, and us, "that day and hour no one knows, not even the angels of heaven." Daniel was told as to his vision of the end times to "shut up the words, and seal the book until the time of the end."

It is beyond the scope of this present writing to discuss the several, basically four, different views on matters of the Second Coming. It may border on sacrilegious heresy even to attempt futilely to figure the end times, yet volumes are written and videos made on the subject. Nearly all agree there may be some 1,000-year reign of Christ. One needs a chart to keep track of the various "pre-" and "post-" opinions. In the latter twentieth-century and early twenty-first, those who choose to think the tribulation will come before this millennium, "pre-millennialists", have been the most outspoken, and sold the most books and videos. Those who choose to think the tribulation will come after the millennium, "post-millennialists", have been less outspoken and sold less books and videos. There are also those who think the millennium is some period between Christ's ascension and second coming, "amillennialists". There are also those who choose to think the rapture comes before the tribulation, "pre-tribulation", by which some will be left behind. There are also those who think the rapture comes after the tribulation, "post-tribulation". All of this seems to have nothing to do with living a life as exemplified by Jesus the Christ. It is probably best to be a "pan-millennialist" believing it will all "pan out" in the end times.

****

SECOND THESSALONIANS

Second Thessalonians is only two pages long. In chapter two Paul strives further to explain the events of the Second Coming, specifically that the coming may not be so very soon. He specifies that before that coming there will be a rebellion and falling away, a great apostasy, but we are not told any details of this rebellion. We are told there will be revealed a man described as the "man of lawlessness," "son of sin" and "son of perdition", and that he will oppose and exalt himself above God and sit as God in the temple of God. Most students of the Bible agree this is the "anti-christ" later mentioned by John in verse eighteen of chapter two of his first letter. Neither are we to attempt to figure out who this man of lawlessness, this anti-christ, is, as his identity will be revealed at the end times. We are not to surmise that it is some Nero or Hitler or Pope or some other rising world leader. Also, when Paul wrote this the Jerusalem temple had not yet been demolished. Paul is not saying some temple in Jerusalem must be rebuilt. Today temples of God may include St. Peter's in Rome, St. Paul's in London and the National Cathedral in Washington, D.C., or some rebuilt temple in Jerusalem, as possible locations for the anti-christ, so imaginations run wild with predictions.

Paul concludes with telling the congregation they are chosen by God to be saved, and set apart by the Holy Spirit to believe the truth. People are to stand firm and hold to the traditions taught by Paul. They are to continue to work for their livelihood and to keep away from any one who is idle, as any one who will not work will not eat.

And here begins, as on the following pages, Paul's first letter to the church at Corinth.

CHAPTER 33

FIRST CORINTHIANS
DIVISIONS, DISORDERS, IMMORALITY,
MARRIAGE AND SPIRITUAL GIFTS

No one speaking by the Spirit of God calls Jesus accursed, and no one can say that Jesus is Lord except by the Holy Spirit. 1 Cor. 12:3

The books of the prophets in the old Hebrew scriptures have three organizational similarities to the books of the new Christian scriptures. The books of the prophets are grouped together and not in order as they were written, and the same is true for the epistles. The books of the prophets are arranged according to length, and the same is true for Paul's thirteen epistles. Most of the prophets worked during the book of Second Kings, and most of the epistles were written during the time of the latter part of the book of Acts.

We are reminded that Jesus was about fifteen years old when Paul was born in Tarsus, in the south-eastern part of modern Turkey. Paul was born a Jew and a Roman citizen. As a teenager, he moved to Jerusalem where he was taught by Gamaliel I and where he lived during the three-year earthly ministry of Jesus. At the age of nineteen he most certainly watched the events of Calvary. Six years later, as a young Pharisee, as reported in chapters seven through nine of Acts, his task was hunting down Christians, which he was doing when the risen Christ came to him as he traveled to Damascus, in one of the greatest conversion experiences in the Bible and in history. Paul became a born-again, radical, right-wing, conservative, evangelical, pentecostal Christian.

Following his conversion Paul went into seclusion for three years, which would later become the customary instructional period for new Christians. Within a short time he went on the first of his three journeys, as he traveled around his home area of south-eastern Turkey. He returned to Jerusalem and shortly began his second journey, a trip of about 1,500 miles one-way across Turkey, around the coastline of the Aegean Sea and down to Corinth, Greece, where he established a church before sailing back to Jerusalem. During these first two trips Claudius I, an unstable and vicious man, was emperor in Rome, which controlled Greece and Palestine. In Palestine Herod Agrippa II was in the early years of his fifty-six year reign.

Paul, now in his mid-forties, did not stay long in Palestine before beginning his third journey, virtually a retracing of his second. About this time Claudius I was replaced as emperor by Nero, who would rule for the remaining fourteen years of Paul's life. In chapter nineteen of Acts we are told of a man named Apollos, who had learned much of Christ in Ephesus and then crossed the Aegean Sea to southern Greece. Paul will mention this Apollos in the first chapter of this First Corinthians. While in Corinth some questions as to some problems in the Corinthian church came to Paul. In chapter twenty of Acts we are told that when Paul left Corinth he sailed due east across the Aegean Sea to Ephesus, on the western coast of modern Turkey, where he paused to write some answers back to Corinth. This is the epistle of First Corinthians. Later he journeyed on to Thessalonica, or Philippi, where he paused to write the epistle of Second Corinthians.

Corinth was truly a very pagan city. Due to its location, the area of Corinth had been an ancient location of various communities. Greece is about the size of the U.S. state of Florida. Like Florida it is a peninsula, jutting out into the Mediterranean Sea, with the Aegean Sea to its east and the small Ionian sea to its west at the heel of Italy. At the southernmost part of Greece is Peloponnesia, which is a large island about the size of the western panhandle of Florida, connected to the mainland by an isthmus, a short strip of land about six miles wide. The city of Corinth has occupied its place at the strip of connector land since about 900 B.C.

Above all other cultures, the Greeks loved their athletic events. In 776 B.C., the time of the divided kingdoms of Israel and Judah as recorded in Second Kings, in the city of Olympia, fifty miles southwest of Corinth, on this Peloponnesia, they began the Olympic games, mostly running events. These were to commemorate Zeus, as did the Statue of Zeus, one of the Seven Wonders of the Ancient World. Two centuries later, in 581 B.C., the time of the exile of the Jews to Assyria and of Daniel, in Corinth they began the Isthmian Games, a smaller version of the Olympics. The Isthmian games were to honor Poseidon. About this time a temple was built sixty miles from Corinth, being ten miles up the isthmus and fifty miles to the west. This was the temple to the goddess Gaea, known to the Romans as Cybele, to the Canaanites of old as Astarte, mother-earth, the mother and nourisher of all things. The temple was to be known as the Oracle at Delphi.

About a century later, around 490 B.C., the time of the return of the Jews from exile in Babylonia toward the end of the old Hebrew scriptures and the Persian empire, the embryonic Greek empire had repelled the Persians at the city of Marathon, twenty-six miles northeast of Athens. A runner ran those miles to inform Athens of the victory. From 431 to 404 B.C. Athens fought with Sparta, to the south, for control of the area in their Peloponnesian war. About a century later, Greece would boast Socrates, Aristotle and Plato. Shortly after that Philip of Macedonia had begun, and years later his son Alexandria completed, the sweep of the Greek empire across all that Persia controlled. Shortly after that, in 290 B.C., across the Aegean Sea near Turkey, the Seleucid Greeks built a colossal 100-foot bronze statue to Apollo, called Helios by the Romans, another of the Seven Wonders. Forty years later they rebuilt another of the Seven Wonders, the temple to Artemis the goddess of fertility, known to the Romans as Diana. In 146 B.C. the Romans destroyed Corinth due to a rebellion, and 100 years later Julius Caesar rebuilt it. It then had more than a dozen pagan temples and over 1,000 temple prostitutes. Greece indeed was in its pagan glory, and Rome, Christ and Paul were yet centuries into the future.

For centuries, rather than make the long sail around the southern tip of Peloponnesia, ships would come along the natural canal between the mainland and Peloponnesia and anchor at the connecting isthmus at Corinth. They would have their cargo moved across the six-mile wide isthmus on greased tracks then loaded on other ships. Over 2,000 years later, about the time the canal was dug across the isthmus of Panama, a similar canal was dug across the isthmus of Corinth.

This is all to say that Corinth was not some little farming community near Palestine. It was a prosperous, cosmopolitan, swaggering, sensual, hedonistic, pagan, immoral seaport. The people were into philosophies and the intellect and extremely skeptical of any supernatural phenomena. They had no idea of the "God of Abraham, Isaac and Jacob". Into this environment, on his second journey, Paul planted a small home church, probably a mixture of pagans and Jews. When he returned on his third journey he found them divided as to whom to follow, as to sexual problems and marriage situations, as to rank and orders in the church and as to various gifts of the Spirit and the resurrection. Paul's first two letters, to the Thessalonians, as to the Second Coming and the raising of the dead, and now this letter to the Corinthians, as divisions, sex, marriage, church hierarchy and Spiritual gifts, are questions debated, sometimes heatedly, in the churches today, and even in the same order.

As usual, Paul begins this letter with his salutation of praise and grace to the people. However, they have failed to follow Jesus the Christ and have begun to divide into followers of certain humans, factions as we have with denominations. In the first four chapters Paul warns against factions. Some are following Chloe, some Apollos, the man who had come over from Ephesus, and some Peter. Some claim to follow Christ. He tells them that Jesus of the cross is the only guide to follow. The cross is folly to those who will not be saved. Jews demand signs; Greeks demand wisdom; and the cross was folly to both. The one calling for believers is to follow the cross. In chapter two Paul adds that he does not preach in lofty words or high wisdom but only as to Jesus Christ and him crucified. From this example preachers are not to stray.

In chapter three Paul writes of the progression of the growth of a believer in the local church. Growth in Christ under different nurturers is not factions. First they are fed only with milk, and later with solid food. First the seed is planted by one person and then watered and nurtured by another. God will give the growth. One person lays the foundation and another finishes the building. There is no foundation other than Christ. In chapter four he writes that believers are not to puff up themselves as compared to other believers, as it will be for Christ so to judge. In verse ten, with some hyperbole, he writes that the ministers are fools for Christ's sake, weak and at times disreputable, whereas the new believers are wise in Christ, strong and held in honor. However, they are still not to judge harshly any believing leaders.

Beginning at chapter five through eight, Paul changes the subject to church order and disorder and standards of conduct for the Christian life. He begins by charging that some with that Corinthian church are more immoral than the sexually amoral pagans around them. One man is living with the wife of his father. Such people are to be removed from the body of the church. In verse seven is the sentence appropriate to the Holy Communion Table. "Christ, our paschal lamb, has been sacrificed for us. Therefore, let us keep the feast." We are not to go backward to the old leaven but forward to the new leaven of Christ. Again he writes that, though believers are to minister to the pagan heathen, they are not even to associate with one who calls himself a believer yet is guilty of immorality. The church would certainly not appoint or retain such a person as an ordained leader.

In chapter six he writes that believers are not to go to the court of an unbelieving judge. At the time of Paul, the Roman empire allowed Jews to try civil matters in their Jewish courts, criminal matters were tried in Roman courts. At that time believers were still considered to be Jews. If the matter were between two believers they are to present it to a believing judge. In modern times such may be still permitted and should be followed, as in arbitration, or the choice of a state judge.

At verse nine Paul discusses standards as to the kingdom of God. He lists those who will not inherit the kingdom, being the immoral, idolaters, adulterers, homosexuals, thieves, the greedy, drunkards and revilers. We heard much at the end of the twentieth century, still hear it in the twenty-first, as to this word "homosexual", or more accurately, "homoerotic", including debates that it is not explicitly in the Christian scriptures. Paul coined the Greek word *arsenokoitos*, which means "two lustful men on a couch". Paul had an extensive vocabulary and did not restrict his meaning to "catamite", "pederasite" or "sodomite", though those may be included, nor to "bestiality", nor did he mean "effeminate". Of course, the word also would include two women so improperly acting. He goes on to explain that our bodies are the temple of God and not meant for immorality or prostitution. This ancient and modern debate also relativizes and mocks "morals", which is simply the customary standards of any specific society.

Chapter seven is the marriage chapter, more specifically Christian marriage. Paul later writes that it may be well for a person to remain unmarried, but to refrain from sexual immorality, remain truly celibate. Here he says each man should have his own wife and each wife her own husband. Each should give to the other his or her conjugal rights, except by agreement for a time for prayer. Neither rules over his or her own body but shares with the other. Otherwise, Satan enters the relationship.

He continues that one should not divorce the other, and if they do then not to marry another. If one is or becomes a strong and true believer in Christ and the other is not, that is not a ground for divorce and the one should remain in the marriage and by example bring the other to Christ. Everyone is to lead the life God gives them and grow in Christ.

In chapters eight through ten Paul writes of the true freedom and liberty of following Christ. Each of us, especially the Greeks in Corinth in Paul's day, values his or her freedom and liberty. In Corinth the people had a lot of temples and places to honor their many gods. He begins in chapter eight by discussing the food the people would leave in these places for the god, and for the priests. With all of their philosophies, Paul first takes their reliance on special knowledge down a peg or two and substitutes love of the true God. Since an idol has no real existence it is okay to eat food dedicated to some idol; however, consideration must be given to a weak Christian who would be confused by such action. One should not act on his liberty if such would cause a fellow Christian to stumble. We are told in scripture that a glass of wine may be good for the stomach. It is not hypocritical to refrain from drinking an alcoholic beverage in the presence of one who might be confused by seeing a Christian so drink, but it is being sensitive.

In chapters nine and ten Paul writes of self-discipline offsetting and controlling a Christian's freedom and liberty. He begins with examples of his own life. Though he does not have a wife, others are free to be accompanied by their wife. One who preaches the gospel is free, free to meet each person right where that person is at the time, to be a slave to slaves, a Jew to Jews, a weak person to the weak, a strong person to the strong, all things to all men in order to bring them to Christ. We are to be as disciplined in going after our crown as is the athlete going after his crown. He then gives them warnings and lessons from Hebrew history that the Hebrews were offered everything but did not have the self-discipline to follow God's commandments and failed.

In chapter eleven Paul writes of decorum in worship, of women and of the Lord's Supper. He begins with a thought on which he will write again in chapter five of Ephesians, the relationship of a man and a woman, specifically a husband and a wife. He tells us the head of a man is to be Jesus Christ, and then the head of the woman is the man. The other side of this coin is that if the head of the husband is not Jesus Christ then the husband may not necessarily be the head of the woman. Very few men have Jesus Christ as their head, and Satan comes into the family.

At verse twenty-three are the verses historically used by the churches during the Lord's Supper. During the twentieth century many churches left these words and only later to search in vain for a replacement. Let's hear some of these words as in the majestic King James Version. "The same night in which he was betrayed, he took bread: And when he had given thanks, he brake it, and said, 'Take, eat; this is my body, which is broken for you: this do in remembrance of me.' After the same manner also he took the cup, when he had supped, saying, 'This cup is the new testament in my blood: this do ye, as oft as ye drink it, in remembrance of me.'" Paul then gives the exhortative warning not to partake unless first examining yourself and faithfully believing.

In chapter twelve Paul names nine gifts of the Holy Spirit. Depending upon how one counts them and how one overlaps them, Paul identifies in three epistles a total of twenty-one Spiritual Gifts. In addition to those here, he names eight more in Romans and five more in Ephesians. The gifts named here are the more inspired gifts and the more difficult for many to comprehend. Here he names Prophecy, Faith, Discernment of Spirits, Healings, Word of Knowledge, Word of Wisdom, speaking in Tongues, Interpretation of Tongues and Miracles. Faith means a supernatural faith, beyond a lower level of general faith. Word of knowledge is receiving just one word or phrase, not the whole book, of some fact that is unknowable to that person at that time from general knowledge. Word of wisdom is a similar special wisdom. Interpretation is the gift to interpret what another says in an unknowable language.

Paul follows his naming of these gifts with the love chapter. In essence he says that none of these gifts are valid without love. The concluding part of this chapter is read at many weddings. "Though I speak with the tongues of men and of angels, but have not love, I have become sounding brass or a clanging symbol. And though I have the gift of prophecy, and understand all mysteries and all knowledge, and though I have all faith, so that I could remove mountains, but have not love, I am nothing." He concludes this chapter with, "And now abide faith, hope, and love, these three; but the greatest of these is love." Faith and hope are both in the present, but faith is confidence in God today and hope is expectation of future good.

In chapter fourteen Paul explains that the gift of speaking in tongues is, as with all the gifts, a good gift from God but is one that builds up only the speaker as he or she speaks to God. All of the gifts are for the good of the community, but to reach the community, "tongues" must be interpreted for the rest of the group. The gift of prophecy is similar to tongues, but the speaker prophesies in a language known to the hearers, unlike tongues. A person unfamiliar with these gifts or not a believer erroneously may think Paul is here castigating the gift of tongues, whereas he is explaining by contrast how it is to be used. Within the church we are to, "Let all things be done decently and in good order."

As he prepares to conclude, Paul writes of the resurrection of Christ Jesus. "Christ died for our sins according to the Scriptures, and...He was buried, and...He rose again the third day." At the time Paul wrote, the "scriptures" meant only the old Hebrew scriptures as there were not yet any new Christian scriptures. "If Christ is not risen, then our preaching is empty and your faith is also empty....And if Christ is not risen, your faith is futile; you are still in your sins!" The concluding part of this chapter is read comfortingly at many funerals. "How are the dead raised up? And with what body do they come?...What you sow is not made alive unless it dies....It is sown a natural body; it is raised a spiritual body....O death, where is your victory? O death, where is your sting?"

He concludes this first letter with an exhortation to good stewardship and offerings to the church.

And here begins, as follows on the next pages, Paul's Second letter to the Corinthians.

CHAPTER 34

SECOND CORINTHIANS
PAUL'S TESTIMONY AND APPEAL TO RECONCILIATION

If anyone is in Christ, he is a new creation; old things have passed away; all things have become new. Now all things are of God, who has reconciled us to himself through Jesus Christ, and has given us the ministry of reconciliation. Therefore, we are ambassadors for Christ. 2 Cor. 5:17-18, 20

Let's recall briefly some facts about Paul, and Corinth. Paul was a well-trained Pharisee, who at the age of twenty-three was assigned to persecute the followers of the risen Christ. The risen Christ came to Paul on the road north to Damascus, Syria. After a three-year incubation period he began a seven-year period of teaching around Damascus and Palestine. Paul the Pharisee had become a born-again, radical, right-wing, conservative, evangelical, pentecostal Christian. He was now the target of those Pharisees whom he had left and, while living in exquisite joy, would suffer physically for his change. Twice he lists some of those sufferings in this second letter to the Corinthians.

Paul made three journeys, as we see in the maps in the back of our Bibles. At the age of thirty-four he went on that short first journey, which took him only to the island of Cyprus, then into what is today central Turkey and back to Palestine. His second journey, in his early forties, took him about 1,500 miles westward, as he traveled the coast line of the Aegean Sea, going northward, then westward, then southward to Athens and Corinth, from where he later sailed back to Palestine. While in Corinth, Greece he wrote his first two letters, those back to Thessalonica. His third trip was much like his second, across Turkey and around the Aegean Sea. He began it at the age of forty-four.

On this third trip he arrived at Ephesus, on the western coast of modern Turkey, an important port-city, due east across the Aegean from Corinth and Athens, about 300 miles by water. At Acts 20:1 Paul was visiting and working in Ephesus, when he received news from Corinth. Corinth was the center of the pagan worship of fertility goddesses and was but sixty miles southerly of Athens, the center of the worship of many gods and human intellect. Ephesus was nearly as immoral as Corinth. Paul may have written at least four letters over to Corinth, but the first and third of these are lost to us. In what we call the first letter, he responded to Corinth as to their internal problems with divisions, sexual promiscuity, rank and order in the church, gifts of the Spirit and the fact of the resurrection. Paul then went north to Philippi and there wrote our second letter to Corinth, about eighteen months after the first. This time he wrote a much more personal letter, as to his coming to Christ, his sufferings and the personal attacks against him by false teachers. The church in Philippi was a model of encouragement. The church in Corinth was a model of discouragement.

Neither of these two letters is a tightly structured theological treatise as both are personal letters to friends and fairly difficult to outline. Second Corinthians differs from First Corinthians in several respects. The First focuses on the church and its people, the Second on the person of Paul and his ministry. The First deals with those questions of sex, marriage and such; the Second deals with false teachers who attack Paul and deliver a wrong message. The First gives practical instructions; the Second gives the personal testimony of Paul, an autobiographical sketch, a witness talk.

Paul begins this letter with greetings and salutations according to his form in his letters. From there the first seven chapters are what may be termed an *apologia*, which means "away logic or words". In literature *apologia* means "explanation" or "defense", and is somewhat different from an apology. Without directly teaching or lecturing Paul simply explains who he is and some of his experiences that have molded him, an earthen vessel with flaws and cracks but all very real and honest, a man of integrity. From his experiences and his knowing Christ, comes his authority. The tone and tenor of this letter is the progressive training of a minister and of his task, resources, adversities and triumphs. Though Paul's first letter to Timothy, written nine years later while in a prison in Rome, will be for ministers, from this letter are derived many ordination sermons and lectures to ministers. As ministers do not like to preach as to themselves, most congregations do not hear many sermons on this letter.

In verses three through eleven Paul gives thanks for the divine comfort of God. To the ancient Hebrew, the word "father" meant the one who originates something, a concept we were told to deny in the late twentieth century. Paul writes that God the Father is the origin of all mercies and of all comfort. Eleven times here, Paul uses the Greek compound verb *parakaleo*, which means "call beside". In his gospel, John uses the same word as a noun, *parakletos*, "one called beside", to mean the Holy Spirit. In John's gospel it is translated as "Comforter", and here it is translated as "comfort". The Holy Spirit, the Comforter, is called to stand beside us. The English word "comfort" means "with strength". Paul gives thanks that God the Holy Spirit is his source of strength in time of trouble. He then concludes this chapter with an explanation of his travel plans.

The first part of chapter two deals with personal relationships. Hurt and pain are most frequently caused by one friend to another. Paul mentions a letter he had written which was very stern, being one of the two letters which are lost to us. Evidently the group had responded to that letter by making changes and had even punished one of those who participated in the attacks on Paul. Evidently this person also made amends and remained. Paul says he should now be forgiven. At verse fourteen he concludes this chapter with an allusion to the Trinity, the source of strength. God, who is in Christ, leads us to triumph as we spread the fragrance of the knowledge of Christ. This aroma, the Holy Spirit, is the perfume of life to those who believe but the perfume of death to those who do not believe, and perish. Paul refers to those who twist the word of God as being those who perish.

With that allusion to the Holy Spirit, Paul also begins his thoughts on the transformation of an apostolic minister, an evangelical teacher. In many ventures in life we have constantly to list our credentials, our resume. Paul does that beginning at chapter three. His primary letter of reference is the people themselves, a letter written not on tablets of stone but on the hearts of the people of the church. Remember, Paul was and is a converted Pharisee, well-versed in the old Hebrew scriptures, which at the time of Christ was that translation into Greek called the Septuagint. Writing on stone and on hearts is a reference to both the law of Moses and the prophesies of Jeremiah and Ezekiel to those of the collapsing kingdom of Judah, some 600 years earlier. God told them that he would make a new covenant with the houses of Israel and Judah, which would not be written on stone tablets but in their hearts. People who attend church, you and I, are the only letter, the only book, the only word, of God and Christ that many people will ever read.

We must lean on God, as we of ourselves are insufficient but our sufficiency is in God. Jesus had said that he had come not to cast away the old law but to fulfill it. Paul explains it is impossible to follow the old law to the letter and that to try to do so will kill a person. In faith and love we are to follow the spirit of the law, which will give new life. The glory and splendor of God shines in the old law, but it was of rules which tended to condemn a person. The new law is of righteousness and convinces and far exceeds the old. In verse seventeen he again alludes to the Trinity, as he writes that, "the Lord is the Spirit, and where the Spirit of the Lord is, there is freedom."

In chapter four Paul continues with the source of strength of the minister. Not only are ministers to renounce underhanded ways and deceitfulness, but they are not to tamper with God's word. Because Satan, the god of this world, has placed a veil over the eyes and minds of many people, they will not see the light and will remain unbelievers living in darkness and perishing. At verse seven he writes of our human frailty and the hope that sustains us. We are only pots of clay, earthen vessels, which are afflicted and perplexed in this life but never forsaken or destroyed. We have a treasure within us, which is the knowledge and hope of being raised to be with God. In English we are called both "humans" and *homo sapiens*; both are theological words from

Latin. The word "human" means that we were formed from the "humus", the soil. From that comes the Latin word "homo", not to be confused with the Greek word which means "same". "Sapien" is from the Latin for "wise". *Homo sapien* means "wise dirt-ball," and refers to the fact that God breathed life and wisdom into this humus soil.

From verse thirteen through verse ten of chapter five, Paul writes of the resurrection, a sequel to chapter fifteen in his first letter to Corinth. "Though our outer nature is wasting away, our inner nature is being renewed every day." "Things that are seen are transient, but the things that are unseen are eternal." Paul the tentmaker writes of our bodies, our earthen vessels, as being earthly tents, which are being destroyed, probably beginning at the age of about twenty years. We ourselves will move from these present tents into future tents, "a house not made with hands, eternal in the heavens." "We walk by faith, not by sight."

In verse ten he writes, "We must all appear before the judgment seat of Christ." Only here and in Romans 14:10 do we hear of this judgment. Most students think that in scripture there are five judgments, though many think eight and many think only one. Here Paul wrote to those in Corinth, Greece as to the *bema*, that raised platform at the Olympic and the Isthmian games where the judges sat and handed down awards, the rewards podium. This judgment is probably for believers only; they will receive judgment based upon what they did while in the earthly body, being punishment or crowns and rewards. Paul tells of these matters so the people will be confident boldly to answer those who attack Paul and the teachings of Jesus. We are not to pride a person on his position but on his heart. To those who accused Paul of being somewhat crazy, they are to respond that indeed they are all beside themselves for God.

Chapter five from verse sixteen to the end well may be the heart of the new covenant, the New Testament, the Bible and forgiveness. Paul refers to all he has just written as he begins with, "Therefore, from now on we regard no one according to the flesh. Even though we have known Christ according to the flesh, yet now we know Him thus no longer....We implore you on Christ's behalf, be reconciled to God. For he made Him who knew no sin to be sin for us, that we might become the righteousness of God in Him."

Paul uses two words here which are critical: reconciliation and ambassador. The word reconciliation in English, and in the Greek from which it is translated, is most interesting. The basic part of the English word is "cilia", which means the hairs of the eyelid. The eyebrow, above the cilia, is the "supercilia". A supercilious person is one who raises the eyebrow in a condescending manner. The prefix "con-" means "with". "Concilia" means with the eyelashes of one person directly in front of the eyelashes of another person. From this we get our words "conciliatory" and "counselor". The prefix "re-," means "back" or "again". Reconciliation means back again eye lashes to eye lashes. The Greek word used, *katalloso,* is equally descriptive. It is two words combined. *Kata* means "deep-down", as in cata-lyst and cata-strophe. *Alloso* means "change" or "exchange". *Katalloso* means a "deep-down exchange," an exchange of our worldly values for those of Christ. That is the ministry of Christ given to Christians, for themselves and others, to experience a deep-down change and return eyelash to eyelash with the loving and forgiving God.

With that one will be an ambassador for Christ. An ambassador is one who re-presents the master. An ambassador carries the exact message without changes, without deletions, without additions, without amendments and without distortions. Those who change the word or water it down will meet Christ at the *bema* judgment seat.

In chapters six and seven Paul continues his *apologia,* his explanation of his ministry. He begins by cautioning us not to accept the grace of God in emptiness, in vanity, taking it for granted. At verse four he lists some of the adversities he has suffered, including beatings, imprisonment and hunger. In chapter eleven at verse twenty-three he will list more. We are each put through the wringer of life, though not quite to the extent Paul suffered. In verse five he tells what carried him through, being purity, knowledge, forbearance and kindness. He then writes what was the source of these, being the Holy Spirit, genuine love, the word of truth, the power of God and the weapons of righteousness. He then lists the result, the paradoxes as seen by humans and as seen by God.

He concludes chapter seven with thoughts that are very much out of synch with the modern concept of a "new tolerance" with its commitment to non-commitment. A believer is not to be yoked to an unbeliever, but once into such a marriage the believer is to stay. There is no partnership, no fellowship between light and darkness, righteousness and iniquity. The U.S. Declaration of Independence states that all men are created equal. We know that from there inequality begins. Paul writes of this inequality. Therefore, believers must make a judgment, not a prejudicial pre-judgment but by the use of the God-given heart and intellect. Believers are to judge through the love and example of Jesus. Believers are to be separate, that is to be segregated from non-believers, which is not to say they are not to evangelize. Believers are not to be indiscriminate but rather are to be discriminating people. Unbelievers would have the concepts of these words be distorted and deconstructed.

In the concluding chapters Paul first speaks of good stewardship and liberal giving and then speaks of his severe problems of life in living for Christ Jesus. He tells them that the small church at Philippi has given to build the church in Corinth. The Philippians have given both out of their abundance of joy and their extreme poverty. He reminds them that "our Lord Jesus Christ, that though he was rich, yet for your sakes he became poor, that you through his poverty might become rich." For the service of Christ we are to give according to what we have and not according to what we do not have. This is Christian liberality. "He who sows sparingly will also reap sparingly, and he who sows bountifully will also reap bountifully....For God loves a cheerful giver."

He then speaks of his severe problems of life in living for Christ Jesus. "For though we walk in the flesh, we do not war according to the flesh. For the weapons of our warfare are not carnal but mighty in God for pulling down strongholds." Somebody evidently accused Paul of being a fool because he then speaks of himself as a fool for Christ. He mentions twice that he may be a knowledgeable and weighty writer but in person is a poor public speaker. He fears that when he is away from the church in Corinth that, like Eve was misled by the serpent, the people are misled by false teachers. Even Satan disguises himself as an angel of light and righteousness. He confirms his credentials by telling them that he is a Hebrew of Hebrews, an Israelite of Israelites and a descendant of Abraham, a good Jew.

Toward the end of chapter eleven he itemizes some of his sufferings. "From the Jews five times I received forty stripes minus one. Three times I was beaten with rods; once I was stoned; three times I was shipwrecked; a night and a day I have been in the deep; in journeys often, in perils of waters, in perils of robbers, in perils of my own countrymen, in perils of the Gentiles, in perils in the city, in perils in the wilderness, in perils in the sea, in perils among false brethren; in weariness and toil, in sleeplessness often, in hunger and thirst; in fastings often, in cold and nakedness--besides the other things, what comes upon me daily: my deep concern for all the churches." After writing this he will further be arrested and imprisoned in Rome, shipwrecked again and finally executed.

Paul concludes this letter with that benediction which is repeated so often in our church gatherings. "Finally, brethren, farewell. Be perfect, be of good comfort, be of one mind, live in peace and the God of love and peace shall be with you. Greet one another with a holy kiss. All the saints greet you. The grace of the Lord Jesus Christ and the love of God and the fellowship of the Holy Spirit be with you all." All of this from the man who wrote one-fourth of the new Christian scriptures.

And here begins, as follows on the next pages, Paul's letter to the people of the church at Galatia, the central part of modern Turkey.

CHAPTER 35

GALATIANS
SAVED BY GRACE AND FAITH AND NOT BY LAW

A man is not justified by works of the law but through faith in Jesus Christ. Gal. 2:16

Let's first look at this place called Galatia and at Paul's method of writing. Today Galatia is the central part of Turkey. In the more ancient days of Abraham and Moses it was occupied by the Hittites. There is some evidence that these Hittites began the iron age. About the time of Moses, early Greek tribes moved into the area. Around 1,200 B.C. the expanding Assyrian empire grew westward and began to move the Hittites out, and later the Babylonians and then the Persians ruled the area of modern Turkey. About 300 B.C., the period of the end of our old Hebrew scriptures and before the Greek empire of Alexander, many Celtic Gauls from the area of modern France moved in and settled into the mountainous area of central Asia Minor, of modern Turkey. These people from Gaul were called Galatians.

All three of Paul's journeys took him through Galatia, central Turkey. On his brief first journey he went into Galatia and returned. On his next two trips he spent much time traveling across Galatia. Scholars cannot determine to which Galatians Paul wrote this letter, to those in the North or to those in the South. Neither can they determine the exact date of the letter. Some think it was in 49 A.D. after that brief first trip, making it his first letter. Some think it was in 57 A.D. near the end of his third trip, and for our purposes it is placed at that date. It makes absolutely no difference when or whether Paul wrote which letters. They are indeed the inspired word of God.

About seven years after Paul's letter to the Galatians, Peter wrote his first letter, to all of the Jews dispersed throughout central Turkey, including Galatia. Let us remember that the book of Acts covered the actions of the Holy Spirit as the apostles spread the church during a period of about thirty-eight years. In Acts chapter eleven we are told that Peter ministered also to non-Jews and in chapter fifteen of the first church council, at which Peter supported Paul, that a person need not first become a Jew and be under bondage to the law in order to be free under Christ.

During his third journey, as he slowly circled the Aegean Sea from Ephesus, Turkey to Corinth, Greece, Paul wrote four of our letters. From Ephesus he wrote two back to Corinth, one back to Galatia and one forward to Rome. Writing these four letters during a two-year period to churches which had been in existence about four years, it is understandable that he discussed about five or six of the same subjects in each letter, and followed a similar writing style in each. Some of such subjects were humble but assertive defenses of his authority and apostleship, a defense of the Gospel against all attacks, of the universal offer of faith in Christ, and the unity of all human relationships in Jesus Christ. His style is replete, mostly, with contrasts but also with many comparisons. His primary contrast in this letter is between Law and Grace, between bondage and freedom. Law versus Grace, and Works versus Faith also will be primary topics in his next letter, the one to Romans, in which his arguments will be a lot more formal.

In this letter to the Galatians one can find answers to many of the great questions as to the Christian faith. Probably the biggest is freedom from the laws and sacramental traditions of the old Hebrew scriptures, and that this freedom comes with an equal measure of personal responsibility. Paul explains, as he will emphasize in his next letter, the one to the Romans, that the old law of Moses is not wrong or evil but simply incomplete and insufficient when compared and contrasted to the example and the teachings of Jesus. Trying to live by the letter of law and tradition is totally inadequate compared to a personal experience of biblical scripture. The law of Moses, such as the Ten Commandments, are still alive and well as guides and boundaries. Humans cannot live a life in complete agreement with these laws, and we are to understand them as plumb lines. Also, in modern times we hear much of "personal experiences", usually meaning that each person can come freely to Christ by some touchy-feely personal warm fuzzy. However, the personal experience is with Christ Jesus of the holy scriptures.

As with all of his letters, Paul begins with his salutation, in which he usually refers to the grace of God as presented through Jesus the Christ. He then denounces any teachings other than what he has taught of Jesus and him alone. He tells them that even if an angel preached any word contrary to what Paul taught then the angel is to be accursed. From verse eleven well into chapter two he explains what he did during the seventeen years from the time the resurrected Jesus came to him on the road to Damascus and to the time he visited this area of Galatia on his first journey. About three times he points out that he received his authority from Jesus himself and does not need to go to any other person, including the other apostles in and around Jerusalem. In chapter two verses three and seven he refers to circumcision as he points out that one need not first be a Jew in order to be a follower of Christ.

Beginning at verse eleven Paul points out both his independence from the other apostles and also the agreement between all of them. In Acts we are told of three church councils in Jerusalem, with the one of chapter fifteen being the most critical. The date was about 50 A.D. as Paul was preparing for his second and longer journey. At this council Paul and Peter led the way in the decision that a person need not first become a member of some Jewish nation to be a follower of Christ. They need not be circumcised nor adhere to all of the dietary laws. Following that council, Paul and Peter met in Antioch, and Paul chastised Peter for being at home with Gentiles while on his trips but changing and avoiding them when Jews from Jerusalem came on the scene. He pointed out Peter's hypocritical ways. Now, in this letter to the Galatians, Paul points out that this independent confrontation with Peter is evidence of his authority from Christ.

In chapters three and four Paul sets out the teachings, the doctrine, of the primacy of faith and of faith alone and only. He connects the faith to true freedom, and emphasizes that with freedom comes a commensurate responsibility. This faith comes from a personal experience with the living scriptures of Christ which and who is not some warm fuzzy feeling, but the basics of a disciplined life. Those concepts presented problems, then and now, to us humans, who do not readily accept responsibility or discipline and so are prone to relinquish freedoms to some human ruler, to some state authority, who will both care for them and control them. Humans, from birth to death, will choose a warm fuzzy without responsible discipline.

Paul begins this third chapter by calling these Galatians fools who have been bewitched into turning from the course of freedom back to enslavement. At verse six he states the simple teaching of "justification by faith". He refers to Genesis chapter fifteen verse six where Abraham moved out from northern modern Iraq with his large family and herds to go to some as yet unidentified lands. He did this on faith, and God simply reckoned that was all he required and thereby deemed Abraham to be righteous. God justified Abraham solely on his faith. About 1,200 years later, as the southern kingdom of Judah was collapsing, the prophet Habakkuk would also refer to this in saying that "the righteous shall live by faith" and thereby be saved. Paul so states here in Galatians and will again in his seventeenth verse to the Romans. In 1520 A.D., Martin Luther will pick up on these words and begin the Reformation of the church. Faith alone, *sola fide*.

In verse ten Paul explains that we are not saved by doing good deeds, not by good works, and that it is a curse to think one can be saved by vainly trying to keep the laws and traditions. That is not to say that a Christian is to do no good works. In his book James will explain that truly good works will come out of and be evidence of a person's true faith. Good works will literally explode out of such a person. However, for a person to think that doing a good deed or giving a big donation will save them is a cursed error, and will even prevent the faith that saves.

Paul then explains the use and purpose of the ancient laws. It is not at cross purposes to Jesus. It is just not the final end. Over the following centuries theologians such as Augustine, Luther and Calvin would further enunciate the uses of the law. First there is the Civil use to restrain evil, as enforced by the police. Second there is the Theological use to show where a person falls short, to accuse, and to encourage self-restraint. Third is to Guide and reorient a person. Whether we like it or not the Civil use will be enforced by the police, even though we may at times rebel. We each rebel to some degree against the Theological use, and either ignore most of the broad scope of the Ten Commandments or rationalize around and away from the matter. Paul says the law is good, but it does not give true freedom and salvation.

He concludes the third chapter writing that "through faith in Christ Jesus, the Son of God, we each become a child, a son or daughter, of God." We do so in full equality, as it makes no difference whether one is Jew or Greek (Gentile), nor slave or free, nor male or female. We all are united in faith in Christ. Christ is the central hub of all human relationships, the church, the family, husband and wife. That is not to say there is a united, universal one-world government and brotherhood, nor that any of us is to do other than "love thy neighbor as thyself," which presumes each person respects and loves him or her self. With that the person becomes an inheritor of the promises made by God to faithful believers of Abraham and his descendants, and without first or thereafter becoming a Jew.

In chapter four Paul begins with pointing out that a young child is much like a slave in the lack of freedom and with tight control, until the child matures. He explains that this was and is necessary because the undisciplined human nature invariably over time will take a freedom to some harmful extreme. He discusses the responsibility that comes with this new freedom in Christ. Freedom quietly to abort a recently fertilized egg in the fallopian tube or uterus will become license to murder a baby exiting the womb at full term. As with the heedless yelling of the pro- and con-abortionists, Paul asks in verse sixteen, "Have I become your enemy by telling you the truth?"

At verse twenty-one he allegorizes the story of the two mothers of the two sons of Abraham, of Sarah and Hagar and their sons Isaac and Ishmael, as told in Genesis chapters sixteen through eighteen and in twenty-one. Abraham had a son, Ishmael, by Hagar the slave girl. In due time he had a son, Isaac, born to his wife Sarah. Ishmael was born of the ordinary human impulses of the flesh; Isaac was born because of God's promise. Sarah was a free woman, while Hagar was a slave girl.

Paul uses about a dozen polar opposites in these verses. Law and Promise. Hagar and Sarah. Ishmael and Isaac. Persecutor and Persecutee. Old covenant and New covenant. Jerusalem now and Jerusalem above. Bond woman and free woman. Flesh and Promise. Flesh and Spirit. Sinai and Free. Mother of slaves and Mother of freemen. Children of slavery and Children of promise. These are the two covenants: the one from Mount Sinai, on the Arabian peninsula, which gives birth to bondage, which is Hagar and corresponds to Jerusalem which now is, and is in bondage with her children; the other of Jerusalem above which is free, the mother of us all. The Jerusalem of the now, the present, of which Paul wrote was full of injustice, violence, murder and subject to cruel and wicked rulers. The Jerusalem above already exists in heaven and also in the Church on earth, whose members are colonists sent to prepare the way for God's kingdom on earth at the second coming. It is of both worlds, heaven and earth, and of both ages, the present and the future. If eternity is the endless absence of time then each of us right now, and from conception, already is in eternity.

In chapter five Paul gives some practical advise on the actual practice of the life of liberty and faith. In the first twelve verses he admonishes the people of Galatia that they have fallen from this grace of God by listening to Judaizers, people who would erroneously convince them that in addition to faith in Jesus they need the old law and traditions. They say that Jesus is not sufficient, and that erroneous contention holds true today with many people.

To follow the remaining remarks it would be helpful to have your Bible open to verse seventeen of this chapter five, as Paul lists and compares life in the flesh and life in the Spirit. Paul is speaking of spiritual warfare, of two opposing sides. One side will prevent you from doing what the other side does. In verses nineteen through twenty-one Paul lists sixteen "works of the flesh". These are what the ancients call sin, which the New Age congregations call tolerant alternatives. This is what theologians call depravity, as we deprive ourselves of the grace and love of God. These works are progressive, as they move from being purely personal to being one-on-one then to being group actions. Paul says these works are plain, evident and manifest. Like the fruit on the tree or the end of the hose. He begins at verse seventeen with "sexual immorality", what one does in the privacy of the bedroom or the back seat of a car. Some texts translate this as "fornication" or adultery. In the late twentieth-century, we began to hear there is no such thing as sexual immorality. We do have control over our own body. Paul and God are very pro-choice. Each person, each society and each nation has free will to choose what and whom they will serve, and then to reap the rewards or pay the price of the choice.

A person then moves from the purely private and personal, outward to the uncleanness of "impurity", then outward to the lasciviousness of "lewdness", riding a reckless disregard, and a license to be licentious from their bedroom into our streets. As one works his, or her, way into the streets he follows the god, the "idol", into whom he has plugged. Our English Bibles then use words like "sorcery" and witch craft. The Greek uses *pharmo*, which includes drugs and which gives us the English word pharmacy. Two thousand years ago Paul wrote that what begins in the bedroom as sexual immorality passes into the streets with drugs. Many in our society and in positions of power and leadership, under the banner of "new tolerance" and "political correctness", frequently openly support and permit this list up to and through this final item and on through the selfish ambitions of politics.

Paul writes that a person then moves further outward, from relatively private and personal acts toward others, to thoughts which are directed against and do impact on one's fellow man. We're out on the street now, but remember, it started in the privacy of the heart and then the bedroom. The works of the flesh will produce the fruit of hatred, which is "enmity" and a characteristic of hostility toward others. From this comes "contentions", which is simply ongoing discord and strife. Then we have "jealousy". In the old Hebrew scriptures jealousy was a good word, and meant zealous and protective. In the intervening centuries it came to be used only in the negative, and then as aggressively to desire what is someone else's, as the envy and covetousness of the tenth commandment.

Paul continues that a person then moves yet further outward, from thoughts and acts toward others, from hatred, contentions and jealousy, to direct public attacks on others. We humans in the flesh then have "outbursts of wrath". This is not a long-lasting anger, but a temporary outburst of temper. From there we have the planning and conniving of "selfish ambitions". The Greek word Paul used here, *eritheia*, refers to public figures who are selfishly open to bribes; those who canvass for power over the public for selfish gain. For this, one needs to enlist others of the same ilk and breed. This begins with Paul's dissensions, which is a separation and parting into parties. What is the next natural step? We choose our factions, divisions and political parties. Paul used the word "heresy", which means to choose, to pick your sect, which then is a hardening and crystallization of those dissensions.

Then, sort of stuck in here all alone, is "envy". This is what Euripides called "the greatest of all diseases among men". The word Paul used here is different from jealousy and covetousness. Now that simple, inward jealousy has moved outward as it has joined with hate. This differs from a desire to have what the other person has. This is a desire that the other person not have what he, or she, has. It is not that one wants another person's ice skating ability but that the one will break the other's knees so she or he can no longer skate so well. Then Paul moves on, into public, wide open acts, "drunkenness", "revelries" and "the like". We cannot overcome these on our own. But, we are not alone.

People love to hear and recite verses twenty-two and twenty-three as to "love, joy, peace, patience" and on, without understanding the preceding verses. We can have the "fruit of the Spirit". This is just one fruit. It is in the singular, with nine facets. This is not our fruit. It is the Spirit's. This is faith, hope and love. "Love" is that *agape* love, a love in spirit as contrasted to the flesh, the eros. "Joy" is founded in God, and in *chara* as in "charismatic," "character" and "eucharist." Luke and Paul write many, many times of joy. "Peace" is not an absence of strife or some time of inactive sitting back. This is a deep tranquility of soul, from God. Peace on earth, good will to men. When we "pass the peace" in church, it is not a time for simple "hellos", "good to see you" or "nice dress". It is a serious prayerful word and time, this peace, *agape* and *shalom*. "Long-suffering" is a type of patience, a waiting in God. "Kindness" means being helpful. Paul's word for "goodness", or generosity, also means beneficence. It is *agathosune* and is found in Greek literature only in four of Paul's letters. It carries with it a sense of a power, an energy, not to be mellow or passive, but to be active in a righteous indignation and attack, rebuke and correction of untruth. "Faithfulness" means sticking to and with the faith. We can have faith but desert it, leave it and abandon it as a derelict on the sands of political correctness, sensitivity, tolerance and fear. "Gentleness" means a submission to God. It is that meekness by which the meek shall inherit the earth. It is having a teachable spirit, not being too proud to learn. "Self-control" is mastery of your self, through Jesus the Christ.

Verse twenty-three ends with, "Against these there is no law." At first reading this seems very confusing, but read on and see that Paul means there is no law of God. However, there is a law of the world, of the flesh, which tells us that we will not do these things. We will not have love and joy and peace. We will not be patient and kind and good. We will not be faithful and gentle and control our selves.

In verse twenty-four, he writes that those who belong to Jesus Christ have crucified the flesh with its passions and desires. This crucifixion is what the theologians, and many churches, refer to as mortification, the death of the control of the flesh and a new life in Christ.

In the first part of chapter six Paul says that we in the church of Jesus Christ are to associate with and listen to trusted and proven fellow pilgrims for mutual help. If we are unevenly yoked with unbelievers we are simply asking for trouble and problems. He then concludes with a summary and repetition of his plea.

And here begins, on the following pages, Paul's letter to the church in Rome.

CHAPTER 36

ROMANS
JUSTIFICATION AND SANCTIFICATION

Those who live according to the flesh set their minds on the things of the flesh, but those who live according to the Spirit set their minds on the things of the Spirit Rom. 8:5-6

This book, this letter, to the Romans, may be more studied and have more commentaries written about it than any other book of the Bible. It is somewhat like the gospel of John in that both have a surface beauty easily appreciated and understood upon the lightest reading and a bottomless depth for the deepest scholar. Both have a timeless application for all ages and many in every age work to cast them aside rather than believe. After an overview of this letter, we will look at some of the depth of the first chapter, to have a taste of the depth. We will then skim the remaining chapters. This is but an overview of a very packed and extensive long letter. Simply hear, or read, some of the basic concepts presented as embedded in key words.

This letter was written by Paul, probably at the age of forty-eight years, during the third of his three journeys, while in Corinth, Greece, shortly before beginning his 1,600-mile return to Palestine. About six years earlier, during his second journey, Paul had stayed in Corinth for eighteen months and written back to those in Thessalonica, Greece. Now he is again in this most cosmopolitan of cities, this seaport city in the vicinity of the ancient Olympic and Isthmian games, of the Peloponnesian Wars and of so many temples to fertility goddesses. The church in Corinth by now may have worked its way through most of those earlier problems as to sex, marriage, factions, gifts of the Spirit and the resurrection.

There is no record of Paul, nor of Peter, having already been to Rome, nor of who may have established the church in Rome. In Acts chapter two we are told that people from Rome were among the crowd at that Pentecost when the Holy Spirit came upon the people. Those people may have returned to Rome and established that church on their own. Paul now writes this letter to them telling of his plans to come visit. He was writing to those in the political, military and economic capital of that part of the world, the Roman Empire. He writes to these people of history, of the sweep of history. He begins with Adam and the fall in the garden. He tells of sin entering into human life on earth in various forms and aspects. He tells of Abraham and his faith and of Moses and his laws. He then tells them of Jesus the Christ, the new Adam. He tells of the Holy Spirit and the struggle each of us has with sin. He tells that God is faithful and will grant salvation to each and every faithful believer who comes to him.

As with much of the Bible, this letter is based on ancient Hebrew thought and language. It was written to the Romans, with their consideration of government and language of Latin. These then were transposed into Greek thought and language. Now we have that translated into English thought and language. We are to learn and to rise to the level of that work, penetrating into the Greek and the Hebrew, and not to walk away from it nor try to change the words to our lowest English vocabulary. Let's look at some words as used by Paul, many of which are disputed in modern psychology, one being the very word "psychology" itself.

We get our English word "psychology" from the Greek word *psuche*, which means "soul". "Psuchology" is the study of the soul, but psychology does not recognize the soul. "Soul" is the force or power which animates a human. "Sin" is more than just "missing the mark;" it is a fact, a real and separate entity. "Flesh" is the physical matter of a human; it is neutral but is the port of entry for sin into a human, and is therefore at times considered the evil opposite of the good. "Spirit" is a separate divine entity, a person of the Holy Trinity. Humans also have a human spirit, which distinguishes them from the baser beasts of the field. God's Holy Spirit reinforces the human spirit. The spirit of a human is also at times referred to as "inner man", or "heart" or "mind". "Body" means the organization of a group of members into some unified form, as the human body or the church body, and is not the same as "flesh". "Wrath" of God is as always the certain eradicating vengeance of perfect holiness against unholiness. "Peace" is tranquility of soul, that reconciliation of which Paul wrote in Second Corinthians chapter five.

As with his other letters this is technically not a theological treatise, but it comes pretty close. It is not a child's simple bed-time story. Actually, probably no part of the Bible is for relaxing bed-time reading, as it is to cause one to change. This letter-book is in the form of a formal argument as presented to the judge in an open courtroom. It presents a highly organized argument as to God's plan for the salvation of humans in and through Jesus the Christ. It is about Jesus Christ, about Christology. It is not so much about the person of Jesus Christ, but about the work of Jesus Christ. At the moment of the Cross the price was paid for all human guilt, and at the moment of the Resurrection the work of victorious salvation became effective and offered to all of humanity, only believe and receive. In the early chapters we find a discussion on two related teachings of the church. These two sound like four concepts but are really only two phases of one concept: "Justification by faith," which is imputed righteousness, and "Sanctification," which is imparted righteousness. In other words, as a result of a person's faith God "puts" righteousness upon a person, and it eventually becomes "part" of the person.

Overall and throughout this letter, this book, deals with the grace as found in the gospel of Jesus the Christ. The letter may be divided into three (or four) sections. The first section, chapters one through eight, has a definite flow or movement as Paul covers the sinfulness of the world from the distant past through his and our present. This flow of history may be subdivided into about three subparts. In the first three chapters Paul, the one-time Pharisee, writes of the sinfulness of all the world, of all humanity. Most people think humans are sinners because they sin, but we sin because we are sinners. This unrighteousness brings on the wrath of God, wrath against sin, as humans live in a hell instead of a heaven. He explains that God has always offered humans a way out if they only believe, as by this belief God will simply deem or reckon that person to be righteous, to be justified. Upon growing in that condition the believer will become sanctified, and move from a hell to heavenly holiness. In this section we meet those Hebrew concepts written in Greek and transposed into English as "sin", "flesh", "wrath", "spirit" and "soul".

The second and shorter middle section, chapters nine through eleven, is a look into the future and God's plan for grace and the church as they relate to Israel. It deals with the fact of the Jewish rejection of the Gospel of Christ. Do not forget that Paul was a highly educated Pharisee, out of that Jewish group which hounded Jesus the most during his earthly ministry. Here are three chapters, four pages, which expound and explain the grace of God toward those who first heard and rejected God's plan of salvation.

The third and final section, chapters twelve through sixteen, consists of practical guidelines and ethics for believers in their daily lives to attain a heavenly holiness. It tells of righteousness practiced, in the church, the body of Christ, that group of separate members organized into some unified form, as is the human body. These individual members, and this organized body, this church, included both weak and strong Christians who live in this world of temptation to sin. How are we to live in this quaqmire? Let's look through this argument written as a plea for each of us, a plea to understand, believe and follow God's plan for salvation.

Paul seems so anxious to teach that he writes the first six verses about being "set apart" for God and does not give his greeting until verse seven. He is so excited that the first six verses are one sentence, which problem for the reader continues throughout the letter. The very first verse is a first prime example of the surface beauty with and underlying bottomless depth of this letter. He defines his service to God as being a total servant, a slave, an English word which we are told to avoid to be politically correct and ultra-sensitive. Pause on that: Paul says repeatedly that one is to be a slave to God.

He then says he is called, which is the base word for church, which gives us our words, "ecclesiology" and "ecclesiastic" as believers are called, called vocally by the voice of God, to a vocation and not to some job. He says he is "set apart" which is the phrase from which came the word "Pharisee". Paul is a Pharisee for God. Paul writes of the gospel of Jesus. Many like the English word "gospel" and others the phrase "good news" and still others "word of God", while some avoid the word "evangelical" and others love it. They are all the same, the same word. The Greek word Paul uses is *euangelion*, which means "good message of God", and from which comes "evangelic". The English word "gospel" is from the Anglo-Saxon, or German, word *gut spiel* which means "good speak". Notice how much is packed into just that first verse, and you will begin to understand the cause of so many commentaries on this letter to Rome. It is not our purpose here to dig that deeply.

In verses two through four, or five, Paul writes of the nature of Christ and sets out the overall scope, the theme, of this letter. God promised this salvation in the books of the old Hebrew scriptures. His son would be born of the flesh of the line of David. By the Spirit of God, due to the resurrection of Christ, shall a person receive this saving grace. In verse seventeen we have the key verse upon which most students see the focus of this letter. "For in (the Gospel) is the righteousness of God revealed from faith to faith; as it is written, 'The just shall live by faith.'" We readily see from notations in most Bibles that this is a reference to Genesis 15:6, where Abraham, a fairly well-to-do man, gathered his large extended family, his herds and workers, and left his land in what is northern Iraq, and began his journey to some distant land as yet unidentified to him, later to be known as Palestine, and did so on a blind faith in God. For that God declared this worldly sinner to be set right. "He believed in the Lord, and he reckoned him as righteous." The prophet Habakkuk spoke of this in saying, "The righteous shall live by faith." Martin Luther was struck by this and began the Reformation. This verse seventeen also may state the sections of this letter. The first four chapters emphasize "faith". Chapters five through eight emphasize the word "just" or "righteous". The final five chapters emphasize the word "live".

Paul writes of Grace, and there is but one Grace of God. However, for teaching purposes, the church teachers like to break it into three, four or five phases. For our purposes we settle on three. There is the first phase of which a person is totally unaware until the subsequent phases impact a person and the earlier phases then become evident to him or her. This first phase, which goes before, is usually termed Prevenient Grace. God's graceful calling is always out there for each of us to receive. God makes the first move. It is error to believe, as many do, that the human makes the first move. The second phase is when the human responds and grace enters the person, and God welcomes them home. This is the grace of which Paul here writes as to Abraham. This is usually termed Justifying Grace, or Actual Grace. It is still the same one Grace. This grace is simply put into a person by God; it is imputed. As the person continues to respond and grow and makes a habit of striving to salvation, this grace enters the third phase and becomes a part of the person and is now imparted grace, and is termed Sanctifying Grace, or Habitual Grace. All is still the same one Grace. This is the flow of which Paul writes to the Romans.

The body of the church extends this Grace, these graces, to the people as best it can by various means as what may be termed sacraments, rites and ordinances. Of these means are the two basic ones of Baptism and Holy Communion. There is also Forgiveness, which is also termed Confession, Reconciliation or Penance; there may be included Confirmation; there is Ordination; and Marriage; and Final Unction, which is also a form of Healing; and Burial, the service for the departed, which is in reality a service for the living, as the burden of grief is shared among the community.

From verse eighteen through thirty-two, Paul writes of the nature of mankind, of human nature, of what we are by nature, of man without God. Notice how current and up-to-date are these verses. Humans suppress the truth of God. They know God but neither honor him nor give him thanks and credit. They consider themselves wise but are fools. People like to think God will always be there for them, but three times Paul writes that God will give people that for which they desperately strive. Notice that Paul does not say God will "give up on" the person but that God will "give the person over" to what they choose. God is pro-choice. He will give them up to lusts of the flesh should they worship the flesh of creatures. He will give them up to dishonorable passions should men have sex with men or women with women. Those who say perversion is not perversion will be given up. He will give them up to any of a series of a depraved mind.

In chapter two and part of three, Paul speaks of the Jewish community to which he writes. He reminds them that they also are fallen and in need of the saving grace of God. He writes of their temples, idols and law, and that circumcision should be applied to the heart and not just to the flesh. In chapter three at verse twenty-five Paul uses a Hebrew word, *hilasterion*, modified into Greek. John will use the word in his First Letter. It refers to the "sacrificial atonement" of Christ for all humans and can cause some theological debate. Translations of that word, following the Reformation of the sixteenth century, in the King James Bible and the English Prayer Books through 1928, were invariably as "propitiation" for sins. That is to say Christ goes before us for one's salvation and piety. The Revised Standard Version changed that to "expiation", which is to say that one's salvation and piety comes from Christ. Paul concludes chapter three emphasizing that Jews, and all humans, are not saved by good works, nor by claiming to follow the law of Moses but only by faith in God through Jesus the Christ.

This leads directly into chapter four. After having stated the principle of justification by faith, he begins to give examples. Using the example of Abraham he discusses the fact that the law only serves to point out where a person goes wrong. It cannot save a person. Circumcision is merely a sign, as God looks on the heart. It is faith in Jesus which allows God to put, to impute, the righteousness of Jesus into us. Here Paul is telling us how to become a Christian, how God saves a sinner. It is simply by faith. In chapter five he gives examples of the fruit of this faith and reconciliation to God. At verse twelve he states that sin entered into humans of this world through Adam and from him to all of succeeding humanity. Here again is a theological concept, that of Federalism, that things flow both from the root and down from the pinnacle, as in the U.S. system of government. These verses may be the foundational statement upon which others about "works" may be read. We are incapable of saving ourselves. He then summarizes man's righteousness contrasted with God's gift of righteousness.

Beginning with chapter six and through eight, Paul discusses the second phase of grace. First God simply puts it into or on a believer, "imputed" grace or righteousness. Then as the person strives to live with it, the grace becomes a part of the person's life, and is "imparted" grace or righteousness. The person is in that stage of being set apart, of being sanctified. In chapter six Paul sets out the freedom from the tyranny of sin which this gives to a person. "For the wages of sin is death, but the free gift of God is eternal life in Christ Jesus our Lord."

Chapter seven tells of gaining freedom from the Law's condemnation. The law of the old Hebrew scriptures was for a temporary time of testing, from the time of Moses to the time of Christ. The law was good as it showed what was good and what was not. But the law did not show how not to sin nor how to make amends for any sin. Paul uses the first person pronoun "I" thirty-eight times in this chapter as he explains that neither he, nor any person, can avoid sin as it dwells within each of us. Without God and his grace there is a total failure of the self, the first person pronoun, the "I." "I serve the law of God with my mind, but with my flesh I serve the law of sin." In chapter eight he tells us not to set our minds on any law but to set and keep our minds on the Spirit.

Paul expounds upon verses twenty-nine and thirty of chapter eight. "Whom God foreknew (already chosen), he also predestined (set apart) to be conformed to the image of his Son....Whom he predestined, he also called; whom he called, he also justified (set right with God); and whom he justified, he also glorified (shared the glory)." In chapters nine through eleven we are told of God's dealing with the Jews. These are the central verses involved in the predestination and election of Augustine (4th century A.D.) and John Calvin (16th century A.D.).

In chapter nine we are told the Israelites are descendants of the covenants and promises. However, not all who descended from Abraham and Jacob are true descendants as to them, or Israel or these covenants, as it is not a matter of the flesh but of God's mercy. In his mercy, through Christ Jesus, God has now both rejected the sons of Israel and reached out and offered these covenants to all, Gentiles and others, who will believe.

Beginning at verse thirty through chapter ten, we are told that the basis of the covenants is faith in God through Christ Jesus, whom most descendants of Israel in the flesh have rejected. They have also rejected God's purpose, laws and works and stumbled over this stumbling block. They sought to establish their own system and did not submit to God. "Faith comes by hearing, and hearing by the word of God." These people have heard as the words "have gone out to all the earth…to the ends of the world."

As to this rejection of the descendants of Israel in the flesh, we are told in the first ten verses of chapter eleven that the rejection is not total and in verses eleven through twenty-four that the rejection is not final. The concluding verses tell us that God's ultimate purpose is mercy and not rejection. The hardening upon the heart of part of Israel will last until the full number of Gentiles is attained.

Chapters twelve through fourteen are a series of practical ethics for living the Christian life. We are to "present our bodies a living sacrifice, holy, acceptable to God." We each have gifts which differ from that of others and are to use them, such as prophecy, ministry, teaching, exhortation, giving, leading, mercy and cheerfulness. "Abhor what is evil. Cling to what is good." "Be constant in prayer." "Do not avenge yourselves, but leave it to the wrath of God." "Be subject to the governing authorities." "Owe no one anything except to love one another." Do not do anything which will cause another Christian to stumble.

And here begin, on the following pages, the letter of James and Paul's letter to Philemon.

CHAPTER 37

JAMES AND PHILEMON
ACTION FROM FAITH; SLAVE AS BROTHER

If anyone is a hearer of the word and not a doer, he is like a man observing his natural face in a mirror; for he observes himself, goes away, and immediately forgets what kind of man he was. Jas. 1:23-24

****

JAMES

It is fairly certain that the letter of James was written by the brother of Jesus, and not by either of the two James' who were of the twelve disciples. There is a bit of uncertainty as to the date the letter was written. It may have been the first written of the books of the new Christian scriptures, at 49 A.D. before the judaizing problem within the church. Due to references in Peter's first letter and many verses on the same subjects in Paul's letters to Galatia and Rome, it may have been written around 58 A.D. For our purposes, the date of 58 A.D. is chosen. There is some thought it was written about 80 A.D. None of this debate has any effect on its inspiration or importance to us.

This letter is one of five general or universal or catholic letters, including Peter's two and Jude. It is a sermonic letter, and not very personal. It is the book of proverbs of the new Christian scriptures. It is based on the wisdom, the sapiential, literature of the old Hebrew scriptures, as the light of the gospel of Jesus passes through it. It contains many expressions characteristic of Jesus, though not always a direct quote.

Without getting into the debate of what is meant by and who was "a brother of Jesus", we simply agree that this James was a brother of Jesus. During the earthly ministry of Jesus, those named as brothers of Jesus did not see him as a deity or follow him but rather questioned his authority as much as anybody. Neither James nor Paul were one of the twelve original apostles of Jesus. In his first letter to Corinth chapter fifteen verse seven, Paul writes that after the resurrection the risen Christ appeared to James. This miraculous evidence of the resurrection no doubt had the same effect on James as that Damascus Road experience had on Paul, and James was converted on the spot, but time had to distill his soul. James became the recognized leader of the church in Jerusalem. Tradition has it that the Jewish leaders cast James down from the pinnacle of the temple in 70 A.D., and a crowd below then stoned him to death, and for this reason God promptly used the soldiers of Rome to destroy that temple.

In Hebrew the Greek name James is *Jacob*. He begins by writing that this letter is of *Jacob* to the twelve tribes in dispersion. There is some thought that the letter corresponds to chapter forty-nine of Genesis where Jacob describes the characteristics of his sons. It is a practical letter on Christian ethics from the standpoint of a devout Jew. It takes for granted the moral authority of the Mosaic law. This is a letter of developing spiritual maturity.

The books of James, Hebrews and Matthew are written primarily to Jews. Throughout this letter James writes of actual deeds or works. Hebrews has much as to doctrine. Paul also writes much of doctrine and largely of faith. Paul and James both write of a saving faith. James emphasizes that this faith will produce the fruit of deeds, but these deeds do not save a person; the faith does. Paul and James write of the edifice of Christianity, Paul of its foundation and James of the upper structure. Neither they nor their books are in conflict, as some who lack a full understanding of the various writings and purposes would think.

In chapter one, the first twelve verses speak of trials from the outside. We are to view these as tests which prove and improve us. We are to pray to God for wisdom, and this is to be done in faith with no doubt that we will receive it. James then uses one of his many metaphors. A doubter is like a wave on the ocean which is tossed about by every changing wind. He is double-minded, unstable and has a half-hearted allegiance and will not receive. James cautions that worldly wealth will not save a person who will perish as does the grass in the heat. To endure is to win the crown of life.

Beginning at verse thirteen, through verse twenty-seven, he writes of temptations on the inside and sets out the stages of sin. We are tested by God, but we are tempted by Satan. Mixing some metaphors, James says we see a temptation, a lure which entices, the first look. That is not sin. Even Jesus was tempted. It is to be stopped at that stage. We are to flee from such temptation. If not, then comes the desire, the lust of the heart, the second look. Sin is given birth. The struggle then becomes much more difficult. It is the third stage, the actual acting on the sin that is sin. At verse twenty-three James writes, "If anyone is a hearer of the word and not a doer, he is like a man observing his natural face in a mirror; for he observes himself, goes away, and immediately forgets what kind of man he was."

In chapter two, we are to practice the truth, as our faith produces good deeds and good works. Ushers in the church are to treat and seat all people equally and not according to the clothes on their backs or the rings on their fingers. If a person is ill-clad or lacking food it does no good simply to tell them, "Go in peace and be warmed and filled." You must give them food and clothing. Faith without good works is dead, but the faith saves and not the good works. Faith alone can save, but faith is never alone.

In the first verses of chapter three we are told that those who teach are held to a higher standard. We are to control our tongue. It is but a very small part of our body, but it is as a lighted match to a dry forest, as a bit in a horse's mouth, as the rudder on a ship. With one and the same tongue a person curses another person then worships God. The same spring does not give both fresh water and salt water as the salt water ruins the fresh.

In chapter four James writes of three threes, three phases of wars, three enemies and three admonitions. Three phases of wars are those between a person's lusts for pleasures, as these lusts cause one to kill and even if a lustful person asks, such asking is wrong because it is based on lust. In verses four through seven are stated the three enemies to humans, as are also stated in most baptismal services, the world, the flesh and the devil. In verses eight through seventeen are three admonitions, being to draw near to God, not to speak evil of one another and not arrogantly to boast of some control over tomorrow.

James concludes with telling us to remain steadfast in faith, as a farmer patiently awaits the fruition to harvest. If Christians suffer they are to pray. If they are cheerful they are to sing praise. If they are sick they are to call for the elders of the church to pray over them and anoint them with oil. They are to confess their sins to one another.

****

PHILEMON

As told by Luke in the twenty-first chapter of Acts, about 57 A.D. Paul completed his third and final journey and sailed back to Palestine. Several months later, not having yet gone on to Jerusalem, he was told not to go as he would most certainly be arrested. Called by God, he went on to Jerusalem. He was told by many messianic Jews that his teachings that the old law did not save a person and that one need not be circumcised to be saved, caused the Jewish leaders to complain about him. Not wanting to cause problems, he agreed to endure the rites of purification before entering the temple.

Some Jews from Asia minor, that is modern Turkey, where Paul had traveled during each of his three journeys, stirred up the crowd against him. They began to beat him. The Roman soldiers came to prevent further problems and arrested Paul. This arrest, trial and the transportation to Rome for his court appeal would cover two years and the last eight chapters of Acts. Much of this arrest would be a house-arrest by which he could freely teach and have visitors, one of whom was Onesimus from Colossae. Toward the end of this arrest, at the time of the last chapter of Acts, Paul would write his four prison letters, Philemon, Colossians, Ephesians and Philippians.

This letter to Philemon is a very short letter, being but one page long, only twenty-five verses. Only the second and third letters of John are shorter, with that of Jude being only slightly longer. Philemon was a man who participated in a small house-church in Colossae, in modern Turkey, a place near Paul's travels but there is no record of his having visited. Onesimus was his slave who had been unprofitable to his master, and possibly stole something, and ran away, ending up in Rome where he met Paul. A runaway slave, when caught, would be flogged and possibly killed. Paul wrote this letter to request that the runaway be received back as a brother in Christ. This letter is personal but is also intended for all in that church group. It is not deep theology but rather Christianity applied in social service. It speaks of walking the talk, of accepting all as a brother in Christ.

Our English word "slave" derives from "Slav", the ethnic name for the people of eastern, southeastern and central Europe. In the middle of the ninth century, these people were primarily Muslim and were enslaved under Charles I of France. Jews "were essential suppliers of exotic commodities from the Muslim world and of slaves from Eastern Europe....and could trade and own" these slaves. (*Heritage: Civilization and the Jews*. Abba Eban. Summit Books, New York. 1984, p. 121)

Onesimus returned carrying this letter with him. Paul begins it with great tact writing of his love and thanksgiving for the people of the house-church. At the opening he refers to himself as a prisoner locked in prison. In verse twenty-three he refers to himself as a prisoner of war. At verse eight he begins to intercede on behalf of Onesimus whose name in Greek means "profitable" or "useful". This runaway named "Profitable" previously may have been unprofitable but will now be profitable, as he has come to the Lord Jesus. Paul even indicates he would like to have Onesimus returned to him as a freed man to be with him. In verse sixteen is the key verse and plea for the people to accept this runaway, as they are to accept all people, as a brother, not as a slave.

Many say Paul was not a strong advocate against the practice of slavery, but they do not read all of Paul nor all of the scriptures which Paul loved. There were many forms of slavery, from indentured servants who essentially sold themselves for some benefit, to bond-servants who were bound for some crime or debt, to war captives. Onesimus was a bond-servant, the lowest of all slaves. Paul's letters indicate he was opposed to slavery but did not attack this widely accepted practice head-on, choosing rather to spread the brotherly love of Christ. We must recall that Paul was a Pharisee, deeply versed in the first five books of our Bible. One of the most misinterpreted and anti-slavery verses in all of scripture is verse nine of chapter four of Genesis. Cain had slain Abel, and God asked Cain, "Where is Abel your brother?" Cain replied,

"I do not know; am I my brother's keeper?" Immediately God cursed Cain and evicted him from the garden. Not only had Cain murdered his brother but he was insolent toward God. Humans do not keep humans; God does. See hereinbefore page five.

The Hebrew word *amar* means to guard in the sense of possession and is translated as "keep" or "keeper". When used for humans it applies only to God. Only God keeps or possesses humans, who in turn keep or possess things or livestock. Am I, are you, a keeper of humans? The answer is an emphatic, No! I am not my brother's keeper. We are to love our neighbor and to give help in time of need, to give food or money, but we are not to own or keep our neighbor. That applies to any form of slavery, including "wage-slavery" or any welfare system whereby the person handing out money controls the recipient to the point of possessing, keeping or enslaving him or her. This is a key concept to a democratic, federal republic such as the United States.

Paul taught of Jesus the Christ, and to treat all as a brother, or sister. This was his campaign against sin, including slavery in all of its forms. About six years earlier, Paul had written in chapter seven of his first letter to Corinth that a person is to bloom where planted, even if a slave, but is to gain freedom as they can. Contemporaneously with this letter to Philemon, Paul also wrote this letter to the church at Colossae. In chapter three he wrote that a slave is to work heartily in service of the Lord, and then in full obedience to his master. This concept he would reiterate a year later in chapter six of his letter to the Ephesians. We are to bloom where we are planted and to become free in Christ. Each of us has but one major choice, to whom and to what we will be a slave. Paul teaches that we are to choose to be a slave to Jesus the Christ.

In verses eighteen and nineteen Paul calls to mind the substitutionary sacrificial atonement of Jesus on the cross. He says that whatever Onesimus owes is to be charged to Paul's account, and writes with his own hand in large letters that he will pay the debt of Onesimus. There is some evidence that this young slave did gain his freedom and some decades later became the bishop of Ephesus. This may be the reason this letter became part of our new Christian scriptures.

And here begins, as on the following pages, Paul's letter to the church at Colossae, the home of Philemon and Onesimus.

CHAPTER 38

COLOSSIANS

FALSE TEACHINGS OF FALSE PHILOSOPHIES

Beware lest anyone cheat you through philosophy and empty deceit, according to the tradition of men, according to the basic principles of the world, and not according to Christ. Col. 2:8

As told by Luke in the twenty-first chapter of Acts, about 57 A.D. Paul completed his third and final journey and sailed back to Palestine. Several months later, not having yet gone on to Jerusalem, he was told not to go as he would most certainly be arrested. Called by God, he went on to Jerusalem. He was told by many Messianic Jews that his teachings that the old law did not save a person and that one need not be circumcised to be saved, caused the Jewish leaders to complain about him. Not wanting to cause problems, he became a Jew to Jews and agreed to endure the rites of purification before entering the temple.

As previously stated, Jews from Asia minor (modern Turkey), where Paul had traveled during each of his three journeys, stirred up crowds which would beat him. Roman soldiers had come to prevent further problems and arrested Paul. It was about mid-way in the twelve-year reign of Nero. Recall that much of Paul's arrest was a house-arrest which gave him freedom to teach and have visitors. One of whom was Onesimus the slave of Philemon from Colossae. Recall that toward the end of his arrest, at the time of the last chapter of Acts, Paul would write his four prison letters, Philemon, Colossians, Ephesians and Philippians. He probably wrote this letter to Colossae shortly after his letter to Philemon and about the end of the book of Acts, around 61 A.D.

This letter is a companion letter to that to Philemon. It goes from prison to that same church group in Colossae. Understandably it mentions some of the same people. It is also a companion letter to the next letter, the one to the Ephesians, which Paul will write several months later. Both letters are about nine pages long. Both speak of the body of the Church, of Jesus the Christ. To Colossae he writes of the head of the body, of Jesus himself, of what scholars call Christology. To Ephesus he will write of the body itself, of the church congregation, of what scholars call Ecclesiology. About six years earlier, in his first letter to the Corinthians and then to the Romans, chapter twelve of each, Paul had made mention of the body of the church but as separate

279

members, as the foot, the hand or the eye. In Colossians and Ephesians he writes of the body as one living unified organism.

Like most of his letters, including those to the Corinthians, Paul writes to a specific congregation in response to problems or questions they had. As with those letters, we do not have the questions, but we have his answers. From Paul's answers we can fairly well come up with the problems and questions. In Colossae the primary and central problem is set out in chapter two verse eight. They were having a problem with a philosophy of an empty and vain deceit. The philosophy was a form of that Greek philosophy called "gnosticism". Our English words "know" and "knowledge" come from the Greek word *ginosko*. The gnostics were "know-it-alls" with secret cultic type rules. The city of Colossae was in Asia Minor, which is the western part of modern Turkey. They were at the meeting point of the eastern culture of Palestine and Syria and the western culture of Greece and Europe. This gnosticism is the same problem with which John would deal when he would write his gospel and letters about thirty years later. It also included a hierarchy of angels and demons from the ancient religious philosophies of Babylon and Iran. These philosophies had come to Greece some 400 years earlier when many Greek youths were sent to Babylon and Persia (Iran) to be taught.

Paul begins his letter with his greeting and then thanksgiving for them. In verses four and five he combines the three words faith, love and hope. This is the fifth and final time he combines these three words. He combined them in his letters to Thessalonica, twice in the first and once in the second, and combined them in that well known last verse of chapter thirteen of First Corinthians. Peter will do so in his first letter. Faith is always directed heavenly, toward God and salvation of the soul. Hope also is always directed heavenly, and is the two-in-one connective being a present expectation of a future joy. Love refers to that horizontal agape love for other human beings. Faith always comes first, and hope then springs simultaneously as it reaches forward. From these two then comes agape love.

In verse six Paul assumes and appropriates a catchphrase, a buzz word, of those false gnostic know-it-all teachers. He says the gospel is "bearing fruit and growing" in them. This phrase comes from that metaphor of a vine. In our human language we have a limited number of words and images. They can be misappropriated and distorted and must be established one way or the other or a culture cannot be of one mind. In modern times, in many uses, words have become distorted, such as "tolerance", "gay", "choice", "absolute" and even "love". In verse seven he mentions Epaphras, as he had in his letter to Philemon. Here he calls him a bond-servant and there a fellow prisoner, both referring to being a servant for Christ.

Verses nine through fourteen are a prayer. The Holy Spirit is not mentioned in this letter, but here Paul prays that they each be fully granted three supernatural gifts of the Holy Spirit, being knowledge, wisdom and understanding. Wisdom and knowledge are the two special gifts for which Solomon asked and received of God, but he promptly left God as he tried to mix in the gods of his hundreds of wives, a syncretism of gods and cultures. Beginning at verse twelve Paul does several things. Through verse fourteen he writes in the past tense. Through Christ God has qualified, transferred and redeemed us. It is finished. One need only to believe and accept.

In his letter to the Romans, at the end of chapter eight, Paul had mentioned things that can not separate us from the love of God. Two of those were principalities and powers. Here, at verse twelve, we find "saints of light" who have been delivered from the "dominion of darkness". In this letter and in the next, to the Ephesians, he again assumes and appropriates more buzz words and concepts of the gnostic know-it-alls. These refer to their ranking of angels and demons. There are seven of these words, being thrones, dominions, principalities (rulers), authorities, powers, world rulers and evil spirits. He will use some of these words several times in Colossians and Ephesians as he goes directly after the false know-it-alls.

At verse fifteen Paul launches into the reasoning as Christ being the head of the body and all in all, and his attack against those teachings, which today we term "heresies." He now writes in the present tense, Christ is. Christ is prime in all things, in the universe and in the Church. In Christ all things were created and he has dominion over everything, including thrones, dominions, principalities, authorities, powers, world rulers and evil spirits. Christ is the head of the Church. In verse nineteen he again takes over two of their words, fullness and pleasure. Christ is full of the pleasure of God. In verses twenty and twenty-two, as he had to the Romans, he writes of the primary and central mission of Christ, the reconciliation of humans to God through Christ. In the last five verses and the first five of chapter two Paul authenticates his own ministry by again itemizing some of his sufferings for Christ.

In chapter two verse six he again uses the metaphor of a plant, a vine, a tree, as it searches for sustenance sending its root downward, ever deeper, and its branches and leaves upward, ever outward. In English we do not much use the Greek word for root, *rhiza*, but we hear almost daily the Latin word, *radici*. A radish is a root, as is a carrot. From the center, the root, of a circle we draw a radius. Our word radical is an adjective, not a noun. A person is not a radical, but a radical as to some noun. Some people are radical workers. We are called to be rooted in Christ, to be radical Christians. There simply is no other kind. From that root we are to be built up and to build up an edifice, the superstructure.

There were two Greek philosophies which resisted the message of Christ, Stoicism and Epicureanism. Four centuries before Paul, the disciples of Socrates and Plato would sit on the porch and discuss philosophy. A century later, from *stoichos*, the Greek word for a row of masonry or people which fall in line, came "Stoic". These Stoics held to a diminished emotionalism and an impassivity to worldly circumstances. A variation of this was Cynicism, from *kyno,* the Greek word for canine, a dog, from their unfeeling attitude. Along the same line was Epicureus who formalized the debate of the relationship between God and evil, leaving God impotent to control evil. This philosophy led to the elimination of God and the giving in to physical and mental pleasures. From this, and *hedone,* the Greek word for pleasure, came the philosophy of Hedonism, that happy pleasure is the highest good.

As the philosophies of Stoicism and Epicureanism were developing, the rapid, sweeping domain of Alexander the Great destroyed the ancient Near-Eastern social orders in which a person had an established position, from which improvement could be had. After Alexander the established order was replaced by a search for the true relationship between the inner person and the cosmos. Stoicism with its self-sufficiency and Epicureanism with its detachment arose to leave people in a situation of despair. These philosophies of despair confused the people of Colossae, as they confuse the people of the streets and churches today.

Solomon fell away from God, not by a simple direct falling, apostasy, but by a continuous slippage. The name of the slippage is "syncretism" which means the mixing, or the attempt to mix, things which simply do not mix, as oil and water or as God with other gods. For the Colossians the syncretism was the mixing of human philosophies with the philosophy or theology of God. These two syncretic mixings have been with humans through eternity. In the modern U.S. they both mix under the banner of "new tolerance".

At chapter eight Paul comes down full force on the philosophy of the gnostics. In our world there are as many philosophies as there are people. Every body has his or her own view of life. Books on philosophy are endless, and the subject overlaps and convolutes so as to be virtually incomprehensible to the vast majority. Though most of these philosophies have been given a title only over the past few centuries, they have existed forever, and will continue. We have materialism, dialectic, dialectic materialism, naturalism, positivism and existentialism and today modernism, scientism and spiritualism, to mention but a few. Each of these tends to attack and seduce every person from Christ. Into which one would we place sexual diversion and perversion?

Verse eight of chapter two may be the most egregiously violated verse in scripture, especially by our colleges and universities during these modern days. "Beware, lest anyone cheat you through philosophy and empty deceit, according to the tradition of men." The principles of the world are the primary elemental teachings and spirits, as in the chemistry elements and elementary grade school. In Christ "dwells all the fullness of the Godhead bodily; and you are complete in him, who is the head of all principality and power." Christ is fullness, all in all. Christ is the ruler of all the hierarchy of angelic and demonic ranks. A Christian has been "buried with him in baptism, in which you also were raised with him through faith in the working of God." The bonds and chains of sin have been nailed to the cross, and the principalities and powers disarmed and publicly humiliated.

These philosophies had many personal rules and taboos. Pseuedo-intellectuals always have rules and taboos to be imposed. In the latter part of chapter two, Paul cautions against such rules and taboos, and concludes with, "These things indeed have an appearance of wisdom in self-imposed religion, false humility, and neglect of the body, but are of no value against the indulgence of the flesh." Many people think that Christianity has many rules and taboos to be imposed upon a person. They are wrong. The only rule is to know Christ. The only taboo is to avoid and flee from sin.

In chapter three verse two, Paul writes, "Set your mind on things above, not on things on the earth." Here mind means one's thoughts and affections. This is another phrase Paul uses in five of his letters, once to Corinth, once to Galatia, three times to Rome, once to Colossae and six times to the Philippians. We hear this phrase regularly in sports language. An athlete is to set his or her mind, to have the right mindset, to put on the game face, to focus on the required move, to visualize success. That is all a very ancient biblical and life concept from ancient days.

The rest of chapter three is an exhortation, a calling out, to live the good life. He touches on the doctrine of mortification, of putting to death what is earthly in you, such as immorality, impurity, evil desire, covetousness and idolatry. We are to put away anger, wrath, malice, slander and foul talk. We are to put on compassion, kindness, humility and patience. We are to bear with and love one another, and above all put on agape love.

At verse eighteen, he continues and applies these principles of love and respect to the family and the home. Paul will write similar words to the church in Ephesus, especially at Eph. 6:22. Peter will do so in his first letter. He speaks primarily to the man of the house, though many today take a misunderstood and heated issue with his exhortation to wives. Interestingly, it seems those who want to delete the verse as to wives also ignore the next verse as to husband loving their wives. The two simply are one. He writes of the duties between child and father. Then, perhaps thinking of Onesimus, the returned runaway slave, he writes that servants are to do their tasks and, most importantly, in the first verse of chapter four, that masters, or employers, are to treat their servants justly and fairly, being mindful that they themselves have a master in heaven to whom they are and will be accountable.

Paul concludes this letter with an exhortation to remain steadfast in prayer, to be gracious toward non-Christian pagans and mentions Philemon's runaway slave Onesimus. He also sends greetings from Mark and Luke, indicating they are with him.

And here begins, as written about ten pages earlier in most Bibles, Paul's letter to the church at Ephesus.

Chapter 39

EPHESIANS
God's Plan for Unity in Christ

God put all things under Christ's feet, and gave him to be head over all things to the Church, which is his body, the fullness of him who is all in all.
Eph. 1:22-23

In the book of Acts, the latter part of chapter twenty-one, Luke writes of Paul's arrest. The events of this arrest, the passage of Paul to Rome and his confinement there cover the remaining seven chapters of Acts. During these two years Paul wrote his four letters from prison, Philemon, Colossians, Ephesians and Philippians. The epistle Philemon was written to the church at Colossae, as was the letter to Colossians. Naturally, they had many things in common. Colossians was and is about the body of Christ, the Church, of what scholars call Ecclesiology. It has a lot in common with the epistle to Ephesus which also was and is about the body of Christ, the Church, and the congregations as the body, of what scholars call Ecclesiology. About six years earlier, in his first letter to the Corinthians and then to the Romans, chapter twelve of each, Paul had made mention of the body of the church but as separate members, as the foot, the hand or the eye. Now he writes of the body as one living unified organism.

In the latter nineteenth century A.D., the budding age of scientism, scholars began to dig at great length into the archaeology of the lands of the Bible and into the critical analysis of the words and phrases of the Bible. Archaeology is serving predominantly to prove the facts of the Bible. As to the words and phrases, many scholars decided to decide that portions of the Bible just cannot be fundamentally correct. This usually comes out of what is termed "higher criticism," which means critiquing using other materials "higher" than or outside of the Bible. Some write treatises that half of the book of Isaiah was not written by Isaiah. Much of that decision was based upon two facts. One was that the latter part of Isaiah had a lot of prophecy as to events about Jesus the Christ, some 600 years into the future, and such just could not have been written so long before it occurred. Another fact was that the words and phrases in the latter part sounded and were a bit different from those in the first part, as though a person's vocabulary and writing style could not change over the years of one's life.

Similarly, some scholars have decided that Paul did not write Ephesians, as a person's vocabulary and writing style just could not change over the years of one's life time. Paul wrote his Thessalonian and Corinthian letters five to ten years prior to Ephesians, in his early forties. He wrote Colossians at the beginning of his two-year confinement in Rome and Ephesians at the end of those two years. This highly intelligent itinerant evangelist was forced to sit and ruminate then emphasized that the Gentiles to whom he had preached were chosen of God just as were the Jews of old. The main reasons some scholars would say Paul did not write Ephesians are: Paul used about eighty words in Ephesians that he does not use in his other letters; Paul uses the word "gentiles" to include Christians with Jews as God's chosen people; in chapter twelve of First Corinthians the Spirit grants certain gifts and God appoints others, but at Ephesians chapter four verse seven some gifts come from the Christ; the usually self-deprecating Paul, who deemed himself an apostle, could not have written in chapter two verse twenty that the apostles and prophets were part of the foundation of the Church.

Let's now set the stage for Paul and this city of Ephesus. In 54 A.D., the year Paul began his third journey, Emperor Claudius I died, most certainly murdered by Agrippina, his wife and niece, so her fifteen-year old son Nero could become emperor. Five years later Nero had Agrippina killed. At the time Paul concluded his Roman imprisonment and wrote Ephesians, Nero was about half-way through his fourteen-year reign. About two years after Paul wrote Ephesians and was released Rome burned, for which many blamed Nero and others blamed the Christians and began the persecutions. Nero became a terrible despot which caused many rebellions throughout the empire. Some of this rebellion would arise in Palestine, eventually leading to the destruction of Jerusalem and the temple in 70 A.D.

Ephesus was a city in Asia Minor, the western part of modern Turkey, on the coast of the Aegean Sea. At the time it had a population of about 350,000. As reported in chapter nineteen of Acts, during his third journey, about seven years earlier, Paul had spent three years in Ephesus. He debated daily and ran a type of seminary from ten in the morning to four or five in the afternoon. Ephesus is the first church of the seven mentioned in chapters two and three of Revelation. The other six were nearby, being Smyrna, Pergamum, Thyatira, Sardis, Philadelphia and Laodicea. In the Revelation, Ephesus is referred to in terms of a good apostolic church, but fallen and in need of repentance and return.

About 250 miles due west across the Aegean Sea lay the Greek cities of Athens and Corinth. About fifty miles south of Corinth, Greece, was the Statue of Zeus, built to be honored by the Olympic games. About sixty miles north and west of Corinth, about 550 B.C., the Greeks built the grand Temple to Gaea, the goddess of mother earth, famed as the Oracle at Delphi. About the same time, under the influence of the neo-Babylonian empire, in Ephesus was built the grand Temple to Artemis, the fertility goddess Astarte. This temple was four times the size of the Parthenon in Athens. Eventually the Greek goddess Gaea and Diana, goddess of the moon, then of the hunt, also became an Astarte goddess. In the second half of chapter nineteen of Acts, Luke wrote of this Artemis. About 250 miles south of Ephesus along the coast was the island of Rhodes on which the Greeks built a statue in 290 B.C., not quite as large as the Statue of Liberty. The Statue of Zeus in Greece, and the Colossus of Rhodes and the Temple of Artemis were three of the seven wonders of the ancient world.

About 62 A.D. from confinement in the Rome of Nero, Paul writes to the people of Ephesus whose friends worship in the great Temple of Artemis, the goddess of fertility, which looms large before them. Paul writes of another building, of the temple of God as the body of Christ. He writes of foundations, cornerstones and building blocks. As in Colossae, the multitudes worshipped rulers and principalities in high places. Paul writes of the ruler of all in heavenly places. He writes in the form of a letter, but it is a theological treatise on the Church and unity in and through Christ Jesus. Like Romans and Colossians, this letter was not directed so much to specific problems in one specific congregation, but to all of the churches. As with most of his letters part is teaching doctrines and part is practical application of that doctrine. With Ephesians, the first three chapters are generally doctrine and the last three application. The letter is a strongly Trinitarian treatise.

Paul begins with his usual greetings and salutations. From there this first chapter sets the stage for the rest of the letter. Paul apparently senses the tendency of the people to fall away, of which John will write in the Revelation some thirty years later. Paul does not call on the Ephesians to do anything more, only to remember, remember what they know. This is the same we are called to do in the words of the traditional historic communion service. "Do this in remembrance of me." They will not fall away if they but keep their eyes upon Jesus. Also, in the traditional Anglican historical annual communion readings for the year are seven readings from the last three chapters of this letter, second only to the ten from the book of Romans.

What is reportedly one of the longest sentences in the Greek of the Bible are verses three through fourteen. Here he sets out the general purpose of God as to salvation and the main theme of this letter. He also states six blessings, to which may be added a dozen more to the end of chapter two. In verse four he repeats that doctrinal teaching of predestination of which he had written five years earlier to the Romans, as at chapter eight verse twenty-eight of that letter. God chose us in Christ before the foundation of the world and destined us to adoption as his children. With this Paul begins his teaching that the chosen people of God are not the Jews for being Jewish, and not as a nation, but are those who come in Christ. With this he also will redefine the concept of "Gentile" as not those who are not Jewish but those who are not "in Christ," a very significant change in that meaning of that word for Christian believers. This redemption is through the blood of Christ, a concept from which many churches drifted during the twentieth century.

The Greek word *ethnos* means a group or multitude of people, primarily with a common culture. From that we get our English word "ethnic". The Latin word for family, a large extended family, is *gentil*, from which came our English word "gentile". Both words simply refer to a large group with a common communion or culture. In the earliest old Hebrew scriptures the Jews were chosen of God, and all others had a common pagan culture and were called *goyim*, and translated "gentile" as distinguished from "chosen". With the Christ, Christian believers were no longer deemed "gentiles" but were among the "chosen". Paul also writes of a new temple of God. Paul explains these facts in this letter to Ephesus and not knowing and remembering those two facts has caused much confusion in our churches, especially during the latter twentieth century.

At verse nine we are told that God has "made known to us the mystery of his will, according to his good pleasure, which he purposed in himself." Such being the will of God, in his almighty and free choosing, and the purpose of his plan. That is, "In the dispensation of the fullness of the times he might gather together in one all things in Christ, both which are in heaven and which are on earth--in Him." That is the purposeful plan of God and the main theme of this letter. At verse eleven Paul begins to emphasize this plan in the power of the unity of the Trinity of the Father, the Son, and the Holy Spirit. Nearly every time Paul uses the word Christ in this letter it is preceded by the definite article "the", but such is omitted in our English translations. It should read "the Christ," to emphasize that there is but one.

In looking back over these first verses we see the six blessings, all of which are accomplished events of the past, existing in the present and to be fully realized in the future. In verse four is being chosen in Christ. In verse five the chosen are adopted as the sons, the children, of God, with Christ as a brother in the family of God. In verse seven the chosen are redeemed and forgiven by the fact of the cross. In verse nine the secret of the ages has been revealed in the Christ. In verse twelve the Jews were the first chosen until the coming of the Christ, and in verse thirteen also those who have heard and believed are chosen, no longer gentiles. Probably most ministers do not understand that believers are not gentiles, and that they are chosen.

At verse seventeen Paul prays that the people have a spirit of wisdom and revelation in the knowledge of the Christ, much as he had in the first chapter of Colossians. He prays that "the eyes of your hearts be enlightened," that light reach deep into your soul. This is that they and we may know the answer to the three "whats" he then lists. "What is the hope of his calling?" From the Greek word for calling comes the word for church. The hope is for the second coming of the Christ as king and our being with him in eternity, saved. "What are the riches of the glory of his inheritance in the saints?" This has an interesting twist. It is not our inheritance from the Christ but his inheritance of us. We, the church, are the glory of the Christ. "What is the exceeding greatness of his power toward us who believe, according to the working of his mighty power?" To emphasize this power, Paul uses four different Greek words for power; from one of these comes the English word "dynamite", and from the other "energy". This unimaginable power is that which raised the Christ and which comes to us through the Holy Spirit to defend us against the world, the flesh and the devil. He alludes to this in the following verses as he uses four of the words of the followers of pagan religions, being rulers, authorities, powers and dominion in high places. The Christ is ruler and authority above all.

Paul concludes this first chapter with a rephrasing of his main theme. All things are under the feet of the Christ. The Hebrew word for foot is "regal", from which it is easy to get our word for "royal", and a simile for "king", as a king has things under his feet. As in Colossians he repeats that Christ is the head of the body which is the Church. The Church is the fullness of Christ. Christ and his Church is the "all in all".

In chapter two Paul continues the theme of unity in Christ. At verse one he calls on them to remember that they were dead without God. He then tells them how not to walk, or live, but how to walk. He will again pick up on the proper walk in life in chapters four and five. Without God people walk in the way of the world, as acolytes, as followers, of the ruler of the dominion of darkness in high places. At verse five he begins to tell that believers are saved by the grace of God. In Romans he wrote that we are justified by faith, and here that we are then saved by grace, through this faith.

At verse eleven Paul further explains the movement of non-Jewish believers from the group called Gentiles to the group called Chosen. He writes of those far and those near, a reference both to the Jews dispersed far from Jerusalem, and any Gentiles far from God. He groups them all together as he explains that the Christ, the Messiah, has broken down the wall that separates people from God and that separates Jew from non-Jew, referring to the wall in the temple at Jerusalem. In 70 A.D., eight years after Paul wrote this letter that wall in Jerusalem would in fact be destroyed along with the rest of the temple. The incarnation of Christ caused the destruction of this wall of hostile separation. In verse sixteen he picks up on the reconciliation as written in Romans, Second Corinthians and Colossians, that such is through the way of the Cross. He concludes chapter two with the metaphor of a new temple built with the Christ as the cornerstone. There is no requirement for any other temple to be built.

In chapter three verse six Paul uses three words of sharing, to make it again clear that believers are among the chosen of God. As the Jews may be chosen so are those believers once termed Gentiles, who now are equal heirs, equal members of the body and equal sharers of the promise. In verse ten he writes that the Church is not restricted to earth but is a work of the Christ in all heavenlies of the universe. In verse fourteen he continues the prayer he started in chapter one, as he bows his knees. He then renews the metaphor of a plant which he had used in Colossians. We are to be rooted and grounded in the love of God. Once again, the Latin word for root is *radici*. We are to be radical Christians, as there is none but what are rooted in Christ. Paul concludes chapter three with a now familiar doxology.

Beginning at chapter four to the end, Paul gives practical applications and exhorts the people to live, to walk, in the way. He begins with the emphasis on the unity of the Church in Christ. In verse four are those much heard words, "one body and one Spirit,...one hope, one Lord, one faith, one baptism, one God and Father of all." In verse nine he writes what is called the *descensus* clause. Christ "descended into the lower parts of the earth." This is thought to have been where Christ was on that Saturday between the crucifixion and the resurrection, in the realm of Satan, facing him down and bringing hope. At verse eleven he sets forth the five-fold ministry, being that of apostles, prophets, evangelists, pastors and teachers. These are the builders of the building of the temple of the body of Christ.

Paul then gives his second exhortation, to have done with pagan ways. In verses twenty-five through the end of chapter four, is written how we are to live with and among one another. "Speak the truth....Do not let the sun go down on your wrath....Let no corrupt word come out of your mouth." This is a warm-up and a lead into the second half of chapter five. This is most important within the household, the home, where the primary relationship is between husband and wife, and secondary between parent and child. This is the way we are to walk.

Paul then gives his third exhortation, mutual subordination in the Christian household. In chapter five we are told more how to walk in the way. Walk in love. Walk as a child of the light. Walk as the wise. At verse eighteen begins another very long sentence in the Greek, as it runs through verse twenty-four. In the English it is broken into seven verses with the addition of six verbs. This causes a lot of confusion, especially at what is verse twenty-two, at which point all English Bibles even separate into paragraphs. "Wives be subject to your husbands, as to the Lord." See Col. 3:18.

Paul wrote this as one would have a double-decker sandwich, all as one unit. Each of the three slices of bread is a mystery. The first slice is verse eighteen, as he begins by setting the condition that both the husband and wife must be filled with the Holy Spirit. If they are not, then this section does not apply to them. At verse twenty-one is the middle slice, another impossible mystery. They are to be subject to one another. It is impossible for each to be subject to the other at all times in all matters. At verse thirty-one is the third slice, another mystery. Paul refers back to Genesis, that the two shall be one flesh. There is the third mystery, and another impossibility. If both the husband and wife are not filled with the Spirit, they cannot conceive either of submitting to one another or being one flesh. Such people who are not so filled will not notice that this section speaks mostly of the charge to husbands as how to love their wives.

The first verses of chapter six speak of the loving relationship between parent and child, which thought is continued in the next verses as to the relationship between master and servant. Verses ten through eighteen is the exhortation to put on the armor of God, as would a soldier of that day. The loin is to be girded with truth. The breastplate is righteousness. Your feet are to be shod with the gospel. Your shield is to be the faith. Your helmet is to be salvation, and your sword the Holy Spirit.

And here begins, as on the following pages, Paul's letter to the church at Philippi.

CHAPTER 40
PHILIPPIANS
FALSE TEACHINGS OVERCOME BY JESUS, NOT THE LAW

Whatever things are true, whatever things are noble, whatever things are just, whatever things are pure, whatever things are lovely, whatever things are of good report, if there is any virtue and there is anything praiseworthy-- meditate on these things. Php. 4:8

About 300 years before Paul, Philippi had been named by Alexander the Great for his father, Philip. It was in Greece, at the northern end of the Aegean Sea, and situated several miles inland from the coast, and not being a port city never grew to great size. In 42 B.C. it was the site of the battle between Brutus and Cassius on one side against Mark Antony and Octavia on the other. As a result of their victory, Octavia became Augustus, the first emperor of the Roman empire, the one mentioned by Luke to date the birth of Christ Jesus. "It came to pass in those days that a decree went out from Caesar Augustus that all the world should be enrolled." To honor that victory, Augustus declared Philippi to be a Roman colony with special rights and benefits, as a miniature Rome.

Two highways, built mostly before the time of the Roman Empire, crossed Italy. The well-known Appian Way crossed Italy for 360 miles north to south from Rome down to the heel of the boot. The Egnatian Way crossed about 700 miles from northern Italy eastward, around the north end of both the Adriatic and Aegean Seas, to the Bosphorus at Byzantium, modern Istanbul. About mid-way, at the northern end of the Aegean Sea, this main route from Rome to Byzantium passed through little Philippi. God was using the worldly structure of the pagan Roman Empire to spread the Gospel, just as he would two millennia later with the radio and the internet.

Luke also writes in Acts chapter sixteen that as Paul was on his second journey during which he went into the area of Asia Minor, the Aegean Sea and Greece, a man told him in a vision to come on to Macedonia, the vicinity of Philippi. Paul did so, taking with him his newly found partner Timothy, and he stayed at Philippi for several weeks. Soon after his arrival he met a woman by the name of Lydia who was a seller of purple goods, which were quite expensive. Her eyes were opened to the Lord, she was baptized and opened her home for a house-church. This was the beginning of a faithful congregation, a group which was liberal in its financial and spiritual support of Paul and conservative in its theology throughout the remainder of his days. This was the first church established in Europe. They were evangelical both in holding fast to the teachings and in missionary preaching.

It was at Philippi that Paul and Silas were arrested and jailed. While in jail they prayed and sang. An earthquake caused the doors to open, but Paul and Silas did not escape. When the jailer came in fear of severe punishment for allowing them to escape he was greatly relieved to find them still there. The jailer asked that great question, "Sirs, what must I do to be saved?" and received that simple answer, "Believe on the Lord Jesus Christ, and you will be saved, you and your household." Only believe. Only faith.

Five years later, about 52 A.D., Paul again visited Philippi during his third journey. He passed through, went on south to Corinth and then returned. On this visit he wrote his second letter to the Corinthians. He then returned to Palestine, where he was again arrested. He would not again travel freely nor visit any of his churches. At the time Paul wrote this letter to Philippi he was at the end of three years as a prisoner, the last two in Rome, as written in the last verse of Acts. The year was most likely 62 A.D. Nero was more than half-way through his fourteen-year reign as Emperor. In two years Rome would burn, the Christians would be blamed, and the persecutions would begin.

The church at Philippi did not have the theological and doctrinal problems of Galatia, Corinth and Colossae, but they did have some problems about which Paul wrote. Like most small communities and churches their problems were more of a personal nature. Some of them were beginning to think they were somewhat more perfect than others, and were the only ones going to heaven. Another problem was with the Jews, not the Jews who were becoming believers and part of the faithful but the Jewish adherents, of the type who had caused Paul to be arrested. It had been about thirty-three years since the crucifixion and resurrection of Christ, and the lines were being drawn between Jew and Christian.

In this letter Paul does not present an argument or a finely tuned and organized theological doctrine. It is more of an intimate and personal witness testimonial. He just simply and plainly tells his story, his Christian beliefs. He hints that he no longer believes that the return of Christ is imminent nor that it will occur during his lifetime, as he had when he wrote those letters to the Thessalonians ten years earlier, when he was forty-two. The words most used in this letter are "joy" and its relative "rejoice". Another much used set are "all" and its relative "always". It has been but a matter of months since he wrote his letter to the Ephesians. His thoughts of "all in all" and "unity in Christ" are still with him as he writes to the Philippians.

As irony would have it, Paul writes from incarceration in Rome to Philippi, where he was first incarcerated. As usual, he refers to himself as an apostle or as a bond-servant, a slave. As with each of his letters, Paul begins with his signature salutation of the eastern, the Hebrew, word for "peace" and the western, the Greek, word "grace". He mentions bishops and deacons, but not presbyters. When he writes of these three offices it is always in the plural, as he refers to them in the singular only when referring to Jesus the Christ, who is the shepherd, the priest, the minister.

From verse three through eleven, Paul offers a prayer of thanksgiving for these people in Philippi. He uses the word "all" six times in these verses. We do not have to rewrite the words of the Bible to make it all-inclusive. We need only teach and preach it as it is written. In verse six he mildly launches his dispute with those who superciliously deemed themselves perfected in Christ and better than others. "He who had begun a good work in you will complete it until the day of Jesus Christ." This is also his insinuation that he no longer anticipates the return of Christ to be imminent and during his lifetime. At verse nine he prays for their agape love to abound in knowledge and discernment, much the same as he had in the ninth verse in his letter to Colossae, a repeat of the request of Solomon, for a supernatural wisdom.

Beginning at verse twelve, through the end of the first chapter, Paul writes of his life in his Roman imprisonment, which was largely a house-arrest. Our word "penitentiary" is rooted in the Latin word for thinking and reflecting, for being pensive. During these times of time-out or lock-in, as a quiet time at school, work or play, a person can and should grow. As was the thrust of his letter to Philemon, Paul continued to bloom where he was planted. The gospel spread through the praetorian guard, that body of some 6,000 men who were the personal body-guards of the emperor. Further, Paul's example of preaching while under arrest served to encourage others to preach more boldly.

Here Paul continues the use of those words "joy" and "rejoice", two words which seem somewhat confusing to the world which usually sees Christianity to be a religion of hard rules which serve only to depress and suppress Epicurean delights of life. The Hebrew word for "joy" comes from the word for "leap". It is from the activity of a young lamb as it jumps and bounces around for no apparent reason. When Mary told her cousin Elizabeth that she was pregnant with a boy by the Holy Spirit, the babe John leaped with joy in the womb of Elizabeth. When the wise men saw the star they leaped with joy. In Greek the words for joy and rejoice are from the same root as the word for charisma, charismatic and grace. In Latin it comes from the word for being glad. Joy is an emotion, like love and hate, and is also related to the mind. It has to do with the immediate sense of happiness for some good and is usually outwardly and physically demonstrated. It can run from mild gladness to heightened exultation. When spiritual, it is the second of the nine fruits of the Spirit of which Paul had written five years earlier in his letter to the Galatians.

In the first eighteen verses of chapter two, Paul sets out the way of the life of a Christian. He fairly sarcastically asks, "If there is any consolation in

Christ, if any comfort of love, if any fellowship of the Spirit, if any affection and mercy," then he asks that they complete his joy. He continues his theme of unity in the body of Christ as in his letter to the Ephesians. He asks that they be "like-minded, having the same love, being of one accord, of one mind." Our English words "communion" and "community" mean "with one-mind".

The second commandment, which is like unto the first, is to "love your neighbor as yourself." You are not to love others more nor less than yourself. That can be difficult. To those who love themselves so much more than others, Paul strongly suggests in verse three that they try loving others better than themselves until they get the idea. Paul continues into verse seven, as he writes that Christ Jesus was, and is, God, but that he humbled himself by emptying himself of characteristics of God in order to become fully human. We are not told exactly what qualities Christ emptied, but we know it included omnipresence, the power to be at all places at all times, and omniscience, the power to be fully all-knowing including knowing the future. Being a perfect human, he most certainly retained the use of 100% of his brain, unlike humans since the fall of Adam who can use only about 8%, the very opposite of human evolution.

Through verse eleven are written some of the steps in humility which Christ Jesus took to become fully human and then to return as fully God. He emptied himself of total qualities of God, was made in the image of man, became a servant and was fully obedient even to the cross. For this he was highly exalted, every knee shall bow and every tongue confess that he is Lord. Paul then tells them that they are to follow that example and serve without grumbling. Paul concludes this chapter by telling of his supreme confidence in his helper Timothy, who had been with him since just prior to his first visit to Philippi. Paul now sends Timothy back to Philippi to work with them. He also commends Epaphroditus, who had come to Rome from Philippi, and had nearly died in the work of Christ. In verse twenty-nine, no doubt sensing the rising Roman persecutions, Paul asks them to honor such men as suffer for Christ.

At the beginning of chapter three, Paul does what many speakers do. He writes, "and finally in closing," then proceeds to say or write as much as already given. Here he directly attacks those Jews who attack the Christians. The Jews call the Christians dogs, dogs who did not follow the rules and rituals of the Jews, and would eat nearly any type of food, as would dogs. In verse two, Paul turns this around and refers to those Jews as dogs who believe that simply mutilating the flesh by circumcision will save a person. He then recites his qualifications as a true Hebrew. This was done very briefly in Acts, Second Corinthians and Romans, but here he does it again to emphasize that he was a Pharisee. He now counts all of these on the loss side of his life as it was all time and effort wasted, not in the work of Christ. In verse eight he calls it *skubala*, which means refuse and waste, both food scraps for the dogs, but more explicitly bodily excrement, dung. As were the ancient Hebrews, Paul was very bluntly descriptive.

In verse nine Paul states quite simply the justification by faith of which he wrote so much to the Romans. He lost all, old friends and old fortunes, and has gained Christ, "not having my own righteousness, which is from the law, but that which is through faith in Christ, the righteousness which is from God by faith." He continues with the fact of the cross. "That I may know him and the power of his resurrection, and the fellowship of his sufferings, being conformed to his death." Here, as in chapter six of Romans, he sets forth his pure and simple witness testimony, that the purest joy is knowing and believing that you are part of the cross and resurrection of Christ into a blessed eternity with God.

He goes on to conclude chapter three by emphasizing that Christianity is a matter of the mind, which may come as a surprise to many doubters who feel that it is a matter of unthinking emotions. We are not to look back but are to run toward the goal of Christ. Paul steps beyond humility and asks that the people mark and imitate his actions, and those of similar good examples. What a bold and confident statement. They are not to walk and live as one "whose end is destruction, whose god is their belly, and whose glory is in their shame--who set their mind on earthly things."

In chapter four, beginning at verse four, Paul discusses the "peace of God," which is different from "peace with God," which is reconciliation through Christ, of which Paul wrote in chapter five of Second Corinthians and Romans. He itemizes twelve conditions or prerequisites to receiving this peace of God:

(1) rejoice in the Lord, and always;
(2) exhibit a gentle attitude of forbearance toward others;
(3) be not burdened with anxieties or worries;
(4) always pray with a thankful heart;
(5) think on praiseworthy things;
(6) be thankful to God in any condition;
(7) patience;
(8) gentleness;
(9) perseverance of God who is at hand;
(10) joy from God;
(11) value approval of God;
(12) rest in Christ.

This peace of God passes all human understanding. Again he refers to the mind. We are to do these things and the peace of God will be with us. This has caused and allowed Paul to be content, a mild form of joy, in all circumstances, whether of plenty or of hunger.

And here begin, on the following pages, the letters of Paul to Timothy and Titus.

CHAPTER 41

1 TIMOTHY, TITUS AND 2 TIMOTHY

FALSE TEACHINGS; CHURCH LEADERS; ENDURANCE

Be diligent to present yourself approved to God, a worker who does not need to be ashamed, rightly dividing the word of truth. 2 Tim. 2:15

First, let's again look at the background and settings of these three letters, and the historical stage as Paul wrote.

At the end of the book of Acts we are told that Paul lived in Rome under house arrest for two years at his own expense. During that time he preached and taught quite openly and unhindered as to Jesus the Christ. It was during this time that he wrote his long letters to the people at Colossae, at Ephesus and at Philippi. It was then about the year 63 A.D. Paul was probably fifty-three years old, and had indeed had a very rough thirty years since that experience on the road from Jerusalem northeast toward Damascus, Syria, when the risen Christ came to him. Nero had been emperor for about ten years, and was at his despotic worst. Paul may have or not have had his appeal heard before Nero, but he was released from arrest. For about five years he had been removed from his ministry to the people around the Aegean Sea and confined among the Romans. He was no doubt a physically exhausted man.

As with many dates and travels it is unsettled as to where Paul went upon his release, but there is some general consensus. He probably traveled eastward around the northern shores of the Aegean Sea to his beloved Ephesus, and to Colossae. From there many think he fulfilled his goal of visiting Spain, and a few think that trip took two years. He then returned to the area of the eastern Aegean around Colossae, Ephesus and Macedonia, where he wrote this letter called First Timothy. For about a year he continued to travel around that area, before going to Corinth, where he wrote this letter to Titus. He eventually returned to Rome where he was again arrested. This time it was quite serious with no house arrest, but being chained in the prison. During this confinement Rome burned and many blamed the Christians. Under these conditions Paul wrote this letter of Second Timothy. Within about a year he would be executed by Nero, as would Peter.

****

THE THREE PASTORAL LETTERS

Unlike his ten previous letters which were written to churches, these final three letters of Paul were written to the pastors, the clergy. For this reason they are called "pastorals". The tone of these letters are from one of authority, a senior bishop, to junior bishops. Timothy was somewhat younger than Titus and understandably the comments in the first letter to Timothy are somewhat different from those to Titus. He had previously written of the teachings of Christ, of the incarnation, the resurrection, salvation and faith. Now he writes more specifically of the administration of the church and the congregation.

Paul uses three Greek words to name the three offices of the church. The offices and the words stand tall, but many officials have fallen. From the word *diakonos*, we get our English "deacon". It means to "serve across", as the task of the deacon is to free the primary pastor from the work of actually serving tables and the people of the church, the poor and the widows, so that time may devoted to preaching and teaching the word. A deacon is under the authority of the bishop, is not necessarily waiting to become a presbyter, and is to do as instructed by the bishop, which could be to do all permitted by a presbyter, including preaching and celebrating Holy Communion. From the word *presbuteros*, we get our word "presbyter". This word is a combination of the word *pres*, which means "before", and the word *buteros*, which means "born". It means "pre-born", and refers to those who are older or elder in the faith. From that we also get our church office of "elder". The English are famous for not pronouncing all of the letters in a word, like Worcesthershire and Gloucester. Like people in the southern states of the U.S. of A., they also drop the final "r". From the word "presbyter" the English dropped three letters, the "b", the "y" and the final "r", leaving "preste" or priest. From the word *episkopos*, we get the English word "bishop". This word is a combination of the word *epi*, which means "over", and the word *skopos*, which means "see". It means "oversee" and refers to senior presbyters who oversee or superintend junior presbyters. Some churches substitute the word "pastor" for "presbyter" to avoid the word "priest". Pastor comes from the Latin word meaning to feed or take a repast, for which the sheep are put to pasture by the sheep-herder.

Although it makes no significant difference at the beginning of the twenty-first century, there must be something said in defense of Paul and against the modern challenges to the identity of the person who actually wrote these three letters to pastors. As with many challenges to scripture, there are several here, and we will mention six. Four of these are actually one, and deal with the vocabulary, the type of words, their meaning and the proper decades some words were first used. The other two have to do with subject and style. In these three letters Paul uses just under 1,000 words, of which over one-third were not used in any of his previous ten letters. Even some of the words he had previously used now had a slight shift in meaning. Some of the words had a slight shift from Greek to Latin. These challenges probably serve more to prove than to disprove that Paul dictated these three letters.

As to the first group of four reasons, those who challenge that Paul wrote these letters simply ignore the fact that the Roman empire not only had arisen but that Paul was removed from his native area of modern Turkey and locked up in Rome. During five years of arrest he no doubt was forced to develop and use the language of Rome. Some words with similar roots had very different meanings in Latin from what they had in Greek. These challengers also say the author of these three letters expressed himself in phrases not used until a century later by the early church fathers. But by this they totally ignore the shift of the leaders of the early church from those who were primarily Jews from Palestine to second and third generation leaders who followed Paul but were of the Latin language. Also, they ignore that Paul was on the cusp of this change.

The other two reasons for the challenge also ignore an obvious change of times. To Timothy and Titus Paul no longer writes of theology and doctrine, of incarnation, resurrection, faith and salvation, but of how to administer a church. When Paul began his ministry the very concept of Christ had to be explained. Now, thirty years later, Paul was at the end, congregations were planted, the new leaders had to be given guidance on the running of a church. These challengers of these three letters, also point out that the style and tone of these letters is not as aggressive, incisive and impassioned as were the previous ten. There is an understandable shift from a wandering evangelical prophet to settled pastoral minister. These challengers seem totally unaware that Paul was no longer a young man but in his mid-fifties and at the end of a physically exhausting life.

In two preceding letters from prison, Paul wrote of the Church being the body of Christ. To the Colossians he wrote of Christ himself being the head and to the Ephesians of the congregations being the rest of the body. He now continues that thought in these three Pastorals, as he writes of how this body is to function and minister to the people. In previous letters Paul had written of the grace of God, now he writes of the church as being the means by which this grace is passed to the people, of the leaders and of the ordained rites and sacraments. Most people in the world, and many in the pews, strongly challenge the content of these letters. As an administrator molds a new member into the body there is a natural resistance and rebellion. Rather than rise to the level of the word, many would bring the word down to their level. As one reads these three letters there is a sense of the passing of time, and a passing of Paul and of the Apostolic age. In his letter to Philippi Paul began to give a sense that the second coming of Christ may not be so imminent, now he is more emphatic, especially in Second Timothy. These are

Paul's dying swan song, his last Will and Testament. These three letters are as one letter in three parts. They are practical instructions as to administration.

****

FIRST TIMOTHY

We first hear of Paul meeting Timothy in the sixteenth chapter of Acts. During Paul's short first journey he met Timothy, who was a young teenager, well versed in the Jewish scriptures. Paul had originally chosen John Mark to travel with him, but Paul and his work were too intense for Mark, who left to travel with Barnabas. During Paul's second journey, Timothy accepted the invitation to travel with Paul, and he so remained for the rest of his life. After years of tutelage under Paul, Timothy was left at Ephesus to be in charge of that most loved of Paul's churches. Timothy and Titus were in a sense the first pastors of the church appointed by Paul. At the time of these letters Timothy was the senior pastor in charge of other pastors, of whom he had oversight. He was the bishop of Ephesus.

Paul begins with his normal salutation. He then gives the first of nine charges. At verse three he mentions the teachings, the doctrines of which he has spent years teaching and writing. Now he simply advises to stay with it. In his previous letters Paul had used the word "doctrine" only six times, at verse ten he uses the word and will do so fifteen times in these letters. The doctrinal teachings are now established, and the old law does not save a person. Verse fifteen is the second of four comfortable words of assurance of forgiveness as used in the Holy Communion service of the historic Anglican, Methodist and Presbyterian churches. "This is a true saying, and worthy of all men to be received, That Christ Jesus came into the world to save sinners."

Paul begins chapter two with the second charge to ministers. There is to be prayers of all types, and in the public worship service. He mentions the four primary forms of prayer, which are those for ourselves, those of praise, those for others and those of giving thanks. Keeping in mind that Paul had been and again would be imprisoned by the subordinates of Nero and then executed by Nero, he says we are to pray for kings and all who are in high positions of authority. He emphasizes that there is no mediator between humans (men and women) and God except that of Christ Jesus, no saint and no priest. In verse eight he instructs that men should pray lifting up holy hands.

Beginning at verse nine Paul sets out his third charge to ministers with some rules for public worship which speak of the women in the church. He continues to maintain that in Christ there is no difference between Jew and Gentile, slave and free, man and woman. As to physical appearance, women and men are to be attired cosmetically orderly, in an appropriately, soberly modest manner, so as not to display either physical charms nor gaudy distractions. With these verses, many ministers fail to distinguish man from husband and woman from wife. Paul continues with the concept from Ephesians chapter five. A man is not to be "a lady's man" but to be the man of his wife. Likewise, a woman is not to be "a man's woman" but to be the woman of her husband. A woman with her newly found freedom is not to usurp authority over her husband. In verse twelve it is not that a woman is to be totally silent in the church, but that she is to be peaceably tranquil. A wife is not to speak in a manner to demean her husband, nor in a manner to indicate the body of one flesh has two heads.

At chapter three Paul gives his fourth charge to ministers, as he sets out to Timothy, and other senior presbyters, the qualities of a bishop, the overseer of other presbyters. They are to be above reproach. Paul then indicates that he prefers that they be married, and only to one wife, which most likely does not mean that upon the death of his wife he should not again marry. In verse six it is specified that he should not be a recent convert.

At verse eight he gives his fifth charge to ministers, as he sets out the qualities of a deacon. These are similar to that for bishops, with the emphasis that they are first to be tested, as a postulant, an applicant for diaconate orders. The office of deacon is a separate and independent order from presbyter, and is not simply a six to twelve month holding period while one waits to be ordained or "raised" to the office of presbyter.

At chapter four Paul again emphasizes that first charge as set out in chapter one. The ministers are to guard against heresies and false teachings, which increase as time rolls on. In verse six he exhorts the minister to put the faithful instructions of the word regularly before the congregation. They are to preach the word, and avoid silly myths and tales. The minister himself is to set the example. In verse thirteen he writes that there is to be public reading of the scripture with attendant preaching and teaching. The word is to be preached, not the latest popular philosophy or political propaganda of the masses.

Chapter five begins with how the minister, the pastor, the presbyter, is to treat various groups. Older men are to be treated as should your father, older women as should your mother, younger men as should your brother and younger women as should your sister, in purity. At verse three he begins his seventh charge to pastors, and seems to set up kind of a fourth ordination group, that of widows. They are to be taken in by the congregation and work for and be provisioned by the church, just as the presbyter and deacon.

At verse seventeen Paul writes more on that fourth charge, to presbyters, to elders, to pastors. He states that ministers are not to be greedy but are to be paid a living wage, so as not to worry about personal living expenses. At verse twenty-two he cautions the people not to be in a hurry to consecrate a presbyter to be a bishop but to test him, and then to lay hands upon him.

In the next verse he plainly writes that a little wine is good for the stomach. Throughout these three letters Paul states that one is not to drink too much wine, and nowhere forbids its consumption. Paul gives this advice to the young Timothy, but not to the older Titus, who has probably long been following the advice.

At the beginning of chapter six Paul again advises those bound to work for others, slaves to a master, to bloom where they are planted, especially if their master is a believing man of God. He then returns to that first charge to ministers to preach the sound established doctrinal teachings of the scriptures. At verse ten is that often heard and frequently misquoted, "The love of money is a root of all kinds of evil, for which some have strayed from the faith in their greediness...."

First Timothy concludes at verse seventeen with the ninth charge. The ministers are told to, "Command those who are rich in this present age not to be haughty, nor to trust in uncertain riches but in the living God...." The ministers are to preach that to all who are rich, including the big donors to their church.

****

TITUS

Now let's look very briefly at this very short letter to Titus, which was written about the same time as First Timothy. We do not hear very much in the way of biography as to Titus, but may put such together from four of Paul's letters. Paul may have known Titus while at Antioch with Barnabas in his early ministry before any of his journeys. They were probably about the same age. At the time of this letter to Titus, he was serving on the island of Crete, roughly seventy-five miles off the coast of modern Lebanon. He was the senior pastor in charge of other pastors, of whom he had oversight. Titus was bishop of Crete.

Paul begins, at verse five, with what is largely a repetition of his instructions to Timothy as to the qualities of a presbyter and of a bishop. At verse ten he begins to remind Titus that he is in a particularly hostile environment, and must stand tall. He then quotes a man of the island of Crete, "Cretans are always liars, evil beasts and lazy gluttons."

In chapter two he courteously reminds his long-time friend to continue simply to teach the sound doctrinal teachings. He then, as he had with Timothy, spoke of older men, older women, younger women and younger men. At verse seven he speaks of good deeds, of good works. He will do that six more times in this short letter. We are saved by faith, but people see only our good deeds. We are to let them see our good deeds, though we are not to boast of them. Paul does not have to remind the elderly Titus, nor any other long-time faithful, of that fact. In chapter three he concludes with more words to his faithful friend.

****

SECOND TIMOTHY

Paul was again arrested and returned to close confinement in chains in Rome. From there, two years after writing to Timothy and Titus, and anticipating his coming execution, Paul writes the last letter, his second to Timothy. In reading this, one can readily sense the coming end, the end of Paul and of the Apostolic age.

Second Timothy is indeed Paul's "swan song", his last preserved letter. It is a pastoral letter, a minister's letter to both his people and to junior ministers, and is but three pages long. Recall that Timothy was bishop of Ephesus. Shortly after opening he commends Timothy on his sincere faith and then reminds him to remain bold. "God has not given us a spirit of fear, but of power and of love and of a sound mind. Therefore do not be ashamed of the testimony of our Lord...."

In chapter two he tells Timothy, and his people, that Christians are to be as a good soldier, as a disciplined athlete and as a hardworking farmer. "No one engaged in warfare entangles himself with the affairs of this life, that he may please him who enlisted him as a soldier. And also if anyone competes in athletics, he is not crowned unless he competes according to the rules. The hardworking farmer must be first to partake of the crops."

Paul further charges ministers and other teachers not to dispute over words but to tell the story and teachings of the Christ exactly. This charge is frequently used in the ordination service of new ministers. "Be diligent to present yourself approved to God, a worker who does not need to be ashamed, rightly dividing the word of truth." The phrase "rightly dividing" is a translation from Greek for plowing a straight furrow for the planting of seeds. Farmers are not to mix up seed, and ministers are not to mix up teachings and facts. There are many items teachers are to separate and not confuse as to interpretation and teaching. These include distinguishing natural from spiritual, literal from symbolic, Jew from Gentile, Church from kingdom, law from grace, this time and space from other time and space, past from future, those promises and prophecies unfulfilled from those fulfilled, and faith from works.

In chapter three Paul warns Timothy as to corrupt and heretical teachers. "In the last days perilous time will come: For men will be lovers of themselves, lovers of money, boasters, proud, blasphemers, disobedient to parent, unthankful, unholy, unloving, unforgiving, slanderers, without self-control, brutal despisers of good, traitors, headstrong, haughty, lovers of pleasure rather than lovers of God, having a form of godliness but denying its power. And from such people turn away! For of this sort are those who creep into households and make captives of gullible women loaded down with sins, led away by various lusts...."

He asks Timothy to remember Paul's own selfless devotion, conduct and teachings and reminds him of the validity of the scriptures. At the time Paul wrote this the only "scripture" was the old Hebrew scriptures as the new Christian scriptures were not yet compiled, though mostly in existence. "All scripture is given by inspiration of God, and is profitable for doctrine, for reproof, for correction, for instruction in righteousness, that the man of God may be complete, thoroughly equipped for every good work."

At chapter four Paul tells us, "I charge you...Preach the word! Be ready in season and out of season...For the time will come when (evil men and impostors) will not endure sound doctrine, but according to their own desires, because they have itching ears, they will heap up for themselves teachers....I am already being poured out as a drink offering, and the time of my departure is at hand. I have fought the good fight, I have finished the race, I have kept the faith. Finally, there is laid up for me the crown of righteousness." He then concludes with some personal greeting, in the nature of simple goodbyes.

And here begin, as on the following pages, the two letters of Peter and one of Jude.

CHAPTER 42

FIRST AND SECOND PETER AND JUDE

PERSEVERANCE AND DELAY IN RETURN; FALSE TEACHERS

You are a chosen generation, royal priesthood, a holy nation, His own special people, that you may proclaim the praises of Him who called you out of darkness into His marvelous light. 1 Ptr. 2:9

First, let's recall, remember and recognize this man Peter and his times. As told by Matthew, Mark, Luke and John, on the day after his baptism, Jesus began to call his twelve close disciples. As he walked along, Andrew joined him and spent the day with him. Andrew then ran off to get his older bother, Simon bar-Jonah, and brought him to Jesus. Simon means "to hear" and bar-Jonah means "son of fluttering dove", but Jesus then and there renamed him "the Rock", which in Greek is Peter and in Aramaic is Cephas. Peter's vocation, with Andrew, on the Sea of Galilee, was that of fisherman. They worked in a joint venture with James and John, the sons of Mr. Zebedee, owner of what may be called the "Zebedee Seafood Company". These four would continue in a three-year joint venture as followers of Jesus. Peter, James and John would be regularly at the hand of Jesus.

Like each of us, Peter grew older and changed somewhat. In the four gospels he is depicted as impulsive and impetuous. In the first twelve chapters of the book of Acts, as Luke writes, Peter is depicted as a teacher and healer with power. In his own letters he is depicted as pastoral as a result of his life experiences as he writes to Messianic Jews, Hebrew Christians.

In the four Gospels, Peter is probably the one mentioned the most. John refers to himself as "the one Jesus loved the most", but in all respects, Peter may be considered as the first disciple. He was then a strange combination of cowardice and courage, of impulsiveness and fearlessness, of loyalty and denial. Among other things, Peter is the one who--walked on the water to Jesus; was the first to confess, "You are the Christ," only to have Jesus immediately say to him, "Get thee behind me Satan"; suggested putting Jesus, Moses and Elijah in tabernacles at the time of the transfiguration of Jesus; on the walk to the garden of Gethsemane was told by Jesus that Satan had demanded to have Peter but that Jesus had prayed for him; went with James and John into the garden where the three fell asleep as Jesus prayed and then said to Peter, "Could you not watch one hour? The spirit indeed is willing, but the flesh is weak;" pulled his sword and cut off an ear of the guard in the garden; professed profound loyalty only then to deny Jesus three times; boldly passed the younger John to go into the empty tomb first; was asked three times by the risen Lord if he loved him and then told three times to tend the sheep. Peter was an unquestioned apostle of Jesus. Unlike Paul, he did not frequently have to expound upon his qualifications and reasons for being considered a full-fledged apostle.

Peter wrote so much of suffering because the persecutions of believers by the Romans was only beginning. During the early years of the work of Peter and Paul, the emperor of Rome was the unstable and vicious Claudius I. In 54 A.D. he was succeeded by Nero, who was emperor fourteen critical years, as Christianity became a religion separate from Judaism. It was during the years of Nero that Peter and Paul were actively spreading the gospel through the Roman Empire. Paul had written his epistles from 51 to 63 A.D. Peter now writes his two epistles in 63 and 67 A.D. In 64 most of Rome burned, for which many blamed Nero but most blamed the Christians, who were persecuted and dispersed. In 67 Paul was martyred in Rome, and Peter also, upside down on a cross. A year after Nero's death in 68, he was succeeded by Vespasian, who would begin the building of the Coliseum in 75, in which Domitian would feed the Christians to the lions. When Peter speaks of suffering, it is of cruel, physical torture and death for one's Christian beliefs, not just having your computer crash or having to sit through some extra long church service.

In the historical readings of most liturgical churches, Roman, Lutheran and Anglican, those assigned for Communion have six from Peter's first letter, which cover most of that letter, and one from the second letter. Three of these come around Resurrection Sunday, one at Transfiguration and one at Ascension, as Peter was an eye witness at each.

****

FIRST PETER

Let's now look at Peter's letters. The man who wrote these letters is a different man from that of the four Gospels. The three years he had traveled with Jesus, Peter was in his early thirties, physically strong and impulsive and excitable. Jesus called him "Simon" when delivering strong instruction and "Peter" when being more friendly. After experiencing the crucifixion, resurrection and ascension we find a transformed and different Peter from the one described to us by Luke in the first fifteen chapters of Acts. He was then a young man who was the first leader of the church, preached at Pentecost, healed the sick, and traveled as he steadily grew into a solid minister of the gospel. At the time of these two letters Peter is in his late sixties, had spent over thirty years as an itinerant preacher, and sensed his imminent death at the hands of Nero. He is a powerful encourager of the followers of Christ, who were by this time no longer Jew or Gentile, but mostly Messianic Jewish Christians.

Five times in his first letter and twice in his second, Peter uses the word "precious" for seven things which are valuable, respected and honored: trial of faith 1:7; the blood that redeems 1:19; Christ the cornerstone 2:4; Christ the savior 2:7; a gentle spirit 3:4; the faith 1:1; and his promises 1:4. The word "suffering" is used in some form sixteen times in this first letter, as we recall that in the Hebrew scriptures Job stayed faithful though all was taken from him in his testings. Peter describes believers as newborn babes, living stones, priest, a people of God, pilgrims, strangers, citizens, servants, stewards, wives and husbands, elders and suffering saints. Through all, Peter exhorts believers to persevere. Perseverance alone does not make one a saint, but it helps. If one hears the words of Jesus, of scripture, they become a part of him or her. These words flow continuously as Peter writes. Nine times in this first letter Peter writes words spoken by Jesus. Paul is the apostle of faith, Peter of hope and John of love: faith, hope and love.

In his opening salutation Peter addresses this first letter to the exiles in the dispersion. The Greek word used is *diaspora*, a word used to this day by the Jews for their current condition of being dispersed around the world. For Christianity it is a very descriptive word. The second part, *spora*, is connected to the root word for "sperm", which is the seed. Dispersion means to "scatter seeds," to cast seeds broadly across the fields for a good crop. The Roman Empire scattered, broadcast, the people of the gospel, and this broadcasting of the word continues to this day.

The area to which Peter wrote, Pontus, Galatia, Cappadocia, Asia and Bithynia, is north-central Turkey toward the Black Sea, east of the Dardenelles of Istanbul. This was the area of modern Turkey not covered by Paul, who journeyed in the south and northwest areas. The ministries of Peter and Paul spread westward from Palestine, not eastward into modern Iraq. Between the two they covered Turkey, Greece and into Italy.

In the first chapter Peter tells us we are God's redeemed children, and begins at verse three. Jesus had told Nicodemus he must be born again from above, and now Peter writes that God "has begotten us again to a living hope through the resurrection of Jesus Christ." Believers are the chosen, the elect, children of God and have "an inheritance incorruptible and undefiled and that does not fade away, reserved in heaven for you." Our testings will pass, as our faith is more precious than gold and will not perish, as was spoken of by the prophets of God.

Peter writes on to exhort us to a holy life. In verse thirteen he recalls the words of Jesus to "gird up your loins," as he tells us to "gird up the loins of our minds." In verse seventeen he recalls the words of Jesus to "call upon the Father." In verse nineteen is the meaning of the cross, that the "precious blood of Christ" has paid our ransom from sin. At verse twenty-two we find words again of being "born again, not of corruptible seed but of incorruptible" being fertilized within us by the living word of God. He then quotes from Isaiah as to the grass withering and the flower fading, but the word of God endures forever.

The thought of being newborn babes needing spiritual milk, not meat, is continued in chapter two, as he tells us we are to cast away all malice, deceit, hypocrisy, envy and evil talk. At verse four we are told that Jesus the Christ is the precious cornerstone of the building to the body of the church. The believers of the congregations are the living stones of the building. We are the Church, not the wood and bricks and plaster. In verse seven Peter gives a very, very critically important statement as to this cornerstone. Jesus is valuable and precious to believers, but to unbelievers Jesus is a stumbling block. In our times, everybody must deal with this stone, this Jesus. What do you, what do I, do with this stone? The Jews of that day rejected him and shortly lost their land, and the historic seed and blessing also moved to include and focus on the faithful believers in Christ.

As recorded in Exodus 19:5-6, a few verses before God gave Moses the Ten Commandments, he spoke of his chosen people, priests and a nation. In verse nine Peter quotes those verses as he writes of the followers of Christ. This is a very special message for and among the people, that believers are each one a priest and pray directly to God the Father through God the Son. This is of special importance to the churches of the Reformation.

From chapter two, verse eleven, through chapter four, verse eleven, Peter writes of the duties of Christians in this world. It is most important to bear in mind that when Peter writes of suffering, he distinguishes between suffering which is undeserved persecution, and suffering which is deserved as discipline or punishment for an offense or crime or grossly bad judgment.

First, Peter reminds us we are aliens and exiles on this earth and are to exhibit a godly conduct to others in general. Then at verse thirteen, he comments on the Social Code as he writes, "submit yourselves to every ordinance of man for the Lord's sake, whether to the king as supreme, or to governors." As Nero steps up his persecutions, which will shortly lead to the execution of Paul and Peter, they both tell us we are some how to submit to the authority of Nero and his henchmen! It is critically important that one read the entire word to have a more complete guidance as to obeying the way of Christ while obeying an earthly ruler. One is to have balance without compromise of Christ, and a sense of many verses without tangential proof-text for some position. In verse seventeen we find four standard precepts: Preciously "Honor all people. Love the brotherhood. (Reverently) Fear God. (Preciously) Honor the king." In many liturgical churches these verses are the Communion reading for the third Sunday after Pascha/Resurrection (Easter).

With those four precepts of duty pre-conditioned before all, Peter continues with these duties. As all people are to follow those precepts, then the slave of that day, and the employee of this day, is to recognize his or her position as subordinate to the superior. This is not to say anybody is to be a passive doormat. All scripture exhorts God's people to be active and to have a peace from worry, fear, anxiety and guilt. We are to imitate Christ. When Christ was reviled he did not revile in return but trusted in the judge of judges. He "bore our sins in his own body on the tree...(and) by (his) stripes you were healed." He again quotes Isaiah in writing, "You were like sheep going astray, but you now returned to the Shepherd, the Overseer (Guardian) of your souls." In many liturgical churches these verses are the Communion reading for the second Sunday after Pascha/Resurrection (Easter).

In chapter three he comments on the Domestic Code. In verses one and seven he carries these social concepts to husbands and wives, as he writes that they both are to do likewise, meaning Preciously "Honor all people. Love the brotherhood. (Reverently) Fear God. (Preciously) Honor the king." "Return to the Shepherd, the Overseer (Guardian) of your souls." As Paul told the Ephesians, a woman must be married to a man who has Christ as his head and both must be filled with the Holy Spirit. Paul and Peter both write on this matter because they are fully aware the ideal does not always exist. Should the husband not have Christ as his head and be filled with the Spirit, the wife is to endeavor to win him over by her example. She is to exhibit that very precious jewel of a gentle and quiet spirit, which is not at all to be confused with a doormat or meaningless fixture. The husband is to do likewise, being in mutual subordination to the wife, a one flesh, otherwise God may not hear his prayers.

Peter fairly recapitulates that we are to imitate Christ, and quotes part of Psalm 34 as the response to undeserved persecution. "Do not return evil for evil or reviling for reviling." In verse fifteen are words we should bear in our hearts and minds. "Sanctify the Lord God in your heart, and always be ready to give a defense to anyone who asks you a reason for the hope that is in you, with meekness and reverence." Be prepared to verbalize the belief within you.

Between the cross and the resurrection Christ was active. Two verses relate to Jesus on the "Saturday" between the crucifixion and the resurrection of pre-dawn "Sunday". Verse nineteen states that Jesus was made alive by or in the Spirit and preached "to the spirits in prison", and verse six of chapter four states that he "preached also to those who are dead." Many students understand this differently, but most consider it to mean that he went to the prison of the dead to preach encouragement and salvation to those who had died in the faith. This concept is in the Apostles' Creed as the *descensus* clause, as he "descended into hell."

The first part of chapter four is an exhortation to pure living and some nuggets for ethical living. Beginning at verse twelve Peter writes of suffering for Christ as contrasted to suffering for doing wrong, such as murder, thievery or general mischievousness. Many people maintain they are persecuted and disliked because they are Christian when in fact the problem is that the person is actually somewhat obnoxious and irritatingly rude.

Peter closes out this letter by exhorting the elders of the group to tend the flock, not by being domineering but by setting a good example. They must establish the right relationship with the congregation. The shepherds must pastor the flock. He harkens back to what God told Cain in Genesis chapter four verse seven, that sin crouches at the door like an animal, as he writes that "the devil walks about like a roaring lion, seeking whom he may devour."

****

SECOND PETER

Let's now take a brief look at the short three-page letter known as Second Peter. In his first letter Peter cautioned as to dangers from outside the congregation and now as to dangers from inside. As had Paul, Peter now also cautions the believers as to false teachers. He begins with the usual salutation and promptly writes of the precious faith and the precious promises. The first chapter is a call to adhere to the traditional faith as a guide to salvation. To the basics of the faith one is then to add virtue, then knowledge, then self-control, then perseverance, then godliness, then brotherly affection. At verse fourteen he states that he senses his death is imminent, as Roman persecutions increase. The age of the apostles and eye-witnesses is also coming to an end.

Peter concludes the first chapter with an admonition not to alter the prophetic words of scripture to one's own liking. "No prophecy of Scripture is of any private interpretation, for prophecy never came by the will of man but holy men…moved by the Holy Spirit." Then, in chapter two, he writes of the danger and destruction of false and unorthodox teachers, as had Paul fifteen years earlier in his letter to Galatia and ten years earlier in his second letter to Corinth. In ancient days, God had not spared those who did not follow his word but did save those who had obeyed, and he will continue to do so. We are to avoid false teachers who entice unsteady souls away from the accuracy of scripture. They are people of corruption who promise freedom but bring only bondage. He concludes this thought in chapter three as he warns that such scoffers and twisters of scripture will increase in the last days, but God will save those who repent and obey. In verse sixteen he tells them, and us, that Paul had written "in his epistles, speaking of these things, in which are some things hard to understand."

****

JUDE

We now make brief mention of the one-page letter accredited to Jude, who is identified as the brother of James, but who could be either the brother of Jesus or of John. Jude joins Paul and Peter as he writes to warn of both false teachers and also of apostasy, the turning away from Christ and the word of his Gospel. As had Peter, he reminds the people that in ancient days God had punished those who turned from him but saved those who obeyed. These false teachers simply cannot understand the scripture and therefore revile it. They serve "only themselves; they are clouds without water,...late autumn trees without fruit, twice dead, pulled up by the roots." He concludes with that benediction which concludes many church services. "Now to him who is able to keep you from stumbling, and to present you faultless before the presence of his glory with exceeding joy, to God our savior, who alone is wise, be glory and majesty, dominion and power, both now and forever. Amen."

And here begins, as follows on the next pages, the book of Hebrews.

CHAPTER 43

HEBREWS
FAITHFUL TO JESUS, SON OF GOD, PRIEST AND SAVIOR

Now faith is the substance of things hoped for, the evidence of things not seen. Jesus Christ is the same yesterday, today and forever. Heb. 11:1; 13:6.

The Gospel of Matthew and this book of Hebrews were written specifically to converted Jews, to Messianic Jews. This book was probably written in Hebrew then translated into Greek, in which language it has come down to us. During the early centuries of Christianity, the author of this book was deemed to have been Paul, but over the past few centuries that has been brought into serious question. There are about seven others who are in the running for author. It is not here our purpose to determine how much of which book what person may have written. The book is thought to have been written about 68 A.D., two years before the Jerusalem temple was leveled by Rome. There is no indication in the document as to whom it was written, but it is somewhat apparent that it was written to a group which was predominantly Messianic Jews. The group was probably unsteady in their beliefs and feeling the effects of the increasing persecution of Nero. On the surface this book seems very Jewish but it is written in Greek and is actually the transition from Jewish thought to Greek thought. This book is the transition, the bridge, from the Hebrew scriptures to the Christian scriptures.

Not many people are very familiar with this book. In fact, most people know very little about it. For those who do know something of the book it is usually only an awareness of chapter eleven, of what is popularly termed the "Hall of Faith", which lists the heroes of the old Hebrew scriptures who held on by faith. Due to chapter seven, which deals with that priest in Genesis, many have an awareness of that catchy name of Melchizedek. There are also a few well-known verses, such as the beginning of that chapter eleven: "Now faith is the substance of things hoped for, the evidence of things not seen. Jesus Christ is the same yesterday, today and forever."

No doubt some of the reasons for not being familiar with this book is that it is not so much a letter as a sermon and not so much a sermon as one continuous, well structured and well organized argument. The argument is interwoven and folds back over itself as it connects and re-connects. It is somewhat difficult to outline. Paul's letter to the Romans is also one long argument. It is okay to read parts of each, but both are written for one reading, and at some time should be read through in one sitting to get a good understanding. There are no stories of people living out life. This argument speaks in terms of sacrifices and priests of the old Hebrew scriptures as they relate to the New Testament. The direction of the argument is to show that Jesus the Christ is superior to all else, the prophets, the angels, the priests, temples, Moses, Joshua and Aaron.

The argument does not follow in chronological sequence. It is arranged in a multitude of contrasts. Throughout there are two levels, two worlds, two houses. The contrasts are of old and new, earth and heaven, falling away and drawing near, unbelief and belief, rebellion and loyalty, shadow and substance, disobedience and obedience. It is an encouragement, an exhortation to hold fast, to endure and persevere through the coming trials. Peter did this in ethical terms, persevering is the good life. Hebrews does it in Christological terms, persevering is for Christ. Revelation will do it in apocalyptic terms. In Ephesians Christ is the body of the Church, in Colossians Christ is the head of the Church, and in Hebrews Christ is the High Priest. Faith is comprehending and apprehending the unseen.

The writer has a pattern throughout his argument. He states his facts, then begins his effect or consequence of those facts with the word "therefore", or a similar word. Fifteen times he actually uses the word "therefore", and an additional thirteen times it is presumed. He then exhorts, calls to us, to persevere with the phrase "let us", let us do a certain action. He frequently follows that with a warning should we fail to act, with the word "lest". These warnings are grouped mostly at chapters three and twelve. Repeatedly he writes: Therefore let us do such and such lest we suffer.

Some students of the Bible think the main theme is stated at chapter four verses fourteen through sixteen. "Seeing then that we have a great High Priest who has passed through the heavens, Jesus the Son of God, let us hold fast our confession. For we do not have a High Priest who cannot sympathize with our weaknesses, but was in all points tempted as we are, yet without sin. Let us therefore come boldly to the throne of grace, that we may obtain mercy and find grace to help in time of need."

The writer himself, at chapter eight verse one, tells us what his chief point is. "Now this is the main point of the things we are saying: We have such a High Priest, who is seated at the right hand of the throne of the Majesty in the heavens, a Minister of the sanctuary and of the true tabernacle which the Lord erected, and not man." All agree that, at either point, the writer begins at the beginning with his statement of the supremacy of Christ, which is his argument, and most likely his main theme. All are excellent verses as to the overall theme which is the perfect and final revelation of God in his Son. Jesus was prophet while on earth. He is now priest in heaven. He will return as king. Prophet. Priest. King.

Most students of the Bible agree that from the very first verse through chapter ten, verse eighteen, the book argues from biblical facts that Christ is superior to all else. From there to the end the argument changes from Christ to faith. Some think at that point it also becomes more practical application to life, while others think the application to life begins at chapter twelve verse fourteen, "Pursue peace with all people."

The very first four verses probably read best in the King James. They echo the first verses of both Genesis and of the Gospel of John. None of these question the existence of God, but take it as fact. "God, who at sundry times and in divers manners spake in time past unto the fathers by the prophets, hath in these last days spoken unto us by his Son, whom he hath appointed heir of all things, by whom also he made the worlds; who being the brightness of his glory, and the express image of his person, and upholding all things by the word of his power, when he had by himself purged our sins, sat down on the right hand of the Majesty on high; Being made so much better than the angels, as he hath by inheritance obtained a more excellent name than they."

With that the writer begins his first contrast, that of Jesus to the angels. We note that without a compass that is regularly corrected a ship at sea can easily get off course one degree then two or three and totally miss its intended destination. People can get slightly off course and worship angels. Some, like a secular humanist, can get about 180 degrees off course as they discard God and put man at the center of the world. Paul wrote of that problem to the Colossians. Apparently those Hebrews to whom this letter was written had the same problem. The word "angel" means "messenger of God". In most of chapter one they and we are told of the difference between Christ and the angels. Jesus the Christ was not simply some messenger but was and is the Son who is worshipped by the angels and will sit in heaven.

Chapter two begins with one of those combination sentences, "Therefore let us pay closer attention to what we have heard, lest we drift away from it." In this book, the people are told more than this once to listen carefully and not be slow to learn. We are then told that everything is being put in subjection under his feet. This is not yet completed. Jesus is superior to and better than the angels. In verse seventeen we are told that Christ became flesh and blood so that he might be both the sacrifice for sins and the High Priest. As priest he would offer himself as a holy sacrifice.

This holy sacrifice refers to those most ancient blood sacrifices to God. The blood was applied to the mercy seat at the holy of holies. The Hebrew word for that seat is *kapporeth*, and the Greek word is *hilasterion*. Various English words are used in various translations to convey the concept for this holy sacrifice, including "propitiation", "expiation", "reconciliation", "atonement", and "perfect offering". These are very important word-concepts in Christianity as they are the cross, the resurrection and the Lord's Supper. Paul wrote of it in his third chapter to the Romans and John in chapters two and four of his first letter. The King James, New American Standard and historic Anglican Prayer Book use the word "propitiation". The Revised Standard and Catholic New American use "expiation". The New International uses "atonement". There is something of all of these English words in Christ. Propitiation and expiation are like the two sides of one coin, as the first serves to block the wrath of God and the second to remove the cause of that wrath.

At the beginning of chapter three we are told to fix our eyes on Jesus, to consider Jesus, who is both apostle and High Priest. Here Jesus is contrasted to Moses. Both were loyal and faithful servants of God, but Christ was more than a servant. He was the Son. The inspired writer cautions us to be careful lest we have an evil and unbelieving heart which will lead us to fall away. This falling away is more than a slip now and then, as with all of us. It is apostasy, a complete standing aside and away from Jesus. He tells us that this was the case with the entire generation which exited Egypt with Moses. They all rebelled and fell away and all over twenty years of age were allowed simply to die in the desert.

In chapter four we are given five of those "therefore" sentences, which are to focus our attention on the reason for what is being stated. In verse one we are again to consider, to focus our eyes upon, Jesus. At verse six we are to focus on God's rest. At verse eleven we are to labor hard lest we fall into disobedience. At verse fourteen we are to hold fast to our confession. At verse sixteen therefore we are to come boldly to the throne of grace.

The first eleven verses are a discussion on that perfect, peaceful sabbatical rest of God. "Therefore, since a promise remains of entering His rest, let us fear lest any of you seem to have come short of it." We are reminded that God rested on the seventh day, the Sabbath. The Greek word used here is *katapausis*, a compound word made of *kata*, which means "deep down" and *pausis*, which means "cease from labor," and from which we get our English word "pause". This *katapausis* sabbatical resting in God is not an idle inactivity but rather is a deep down and prolonged rest. It is a drawing near to the now accessible God, purified of sin and with no encumbering rituals. Being drawn along is not mentioned here but is an undercurrent throughout. To draw near to God is the best of good, and to draw away is the worst of bad. In verse eleven we are told to work very hard in order to enter a perfect rest. In the historic Anglican Communion service the people are bid to, "Draw near with faith" to make their confession and receive communion.

At verse fourteen begins what some think is the transition and main theme. "Seeing then that we have a great High Priest who has passed through the heavens, Jesus the Son of God, let us hold fast our confession." With that we are told to "come boldly to the throne of grace, that we may obtain mercy and find grace to help in time of need." In the historic Anglican services of Morning Prayer and Evening Prayer the minister bids the congregation to accompany him "unto the throne of heavenly grace" to make their confession.

In chapter five Christ is contrasted to the priests of old and found to be far superior. This begins with words as to human priests of old. They were very good men but weak and sinful. Being human, they understand and deal sensitively and gently with the ignorant and wayward. In verse four is a thought put forth to all those seeking ordination in our churches. The New Living Bible states, "No one can become a high priest simply because he wants such an honor. He has to be called by God for this work, just as Aaron was." Christ did not exalt himself, but was chosen by God. The writer then quotes scripture and refers to Melchizedek, who was mentioned only in three verses of the fourteenth chapter of Genesis.

At the conclusion of this short chapter five, the readers are given a slight rebuke. The writer would like to tell them much more, but they are dull of hearing and understanding. As with all who are only beginning, either life in the physical or in the faith, they must be fed milk and not yet meat. They must stretch on to more maturity before they are fed solid food.

At the first verse of chapter six, the writer quickly leads the readers on to this maturity and solid food. He begins this movement with a warning not to return to the old ways. "Therefore, let us leave the discussion of the elementary teachings of Christ and move on to maturity and completion." There will be no more discussion of repentance, baptisms, laying on of hands, the resurrection, and eternal judgment. At verse four he writes of those who completely lose faith and fall away into apostasy. This is a hard saying and not to be served with sugar or extra water to dilute it.

For those who have once fully come to Christ and then fully fall away there may be no salvation. He specifies five experiences a person cannot fully experience and then fully deny. First, is fully to have seen the light and been enlightened. Second, is fully to have had a fore-taste of the heavenly gift. Third, is fully to have partaken of the Holy Spirit. Fourth, is fully to have had a fore-taste of the word of God. Fifth, is fully to have had a fore-taste of the powers of the age to come. To have had any or all of these experiences and repented, and then to apostasize, to turn your back completely toward God, allows no more chances. Such people have effectively again crucified Christ and held him up to contempt. In verse nine the writer is quick to inform the readers that such probably does not apply to any of them. We are not to concern ourselves about others, this is the judgment we are incapable of rendering.

At verse thirteen, as the writer begins to return to his discussion of Melchizedek, we have the promise and oath of God to Abraham. God is not false. Then, in chapter seven, we are assured that these promises are realized in Christ. In verse twelve he writes that a change in the High Priest requires a change in the law, from the old to the new, and in verse nineteen that the change is required to move on to completion. In verse twenty-five is another "therefore" consequence. "Therefore, Christ is able to save to the uttermost those who draw near to God through him, since he always lives to make intercession for them."

The name Melchizedek in Hebrew means "King of Righteousness." He was at the time king of Salem, "King of Peace," the name of the city prior to the name Jerusalem. He was also a priest of the one true God, though he was not a Hebrew. Upon Abraham's return from a military victory, Melchizedek brought him bread and wine, offerings at that time and today at the Lord's Supper. He blessed Abraham, who gave him a tithe, one-tenth, of all of his prizes of victory. Melchizedek was a fore-shadow, a type, of Christ. Both are kings of righteousness and peace, both priests though neither was a Levite, both are to be offered a tithe, neither had a natural father and neither left descendants. Christ was superior to this fore-shadow, this type.

Chapter eight begins with what the writer says is the chief point of his writing. Christ is the High Priest seated at the right hand of God in the heavenly sanctuary. We are then told that the tabernacle, and temple, of Moses was but a pattern for the ministry of Christ. He quotes Jeremiah, that there is to be a new covenant, written on the hearts, and forgiveness will come through Christ. The old is not so much at fault but obsolete. This thought is continued through chapter nine.

In chapter ten at verse nineteen, is another of those fifteen "therefore" words, and a transition is made from Christ to faith. We are to have a confident faith in the blood of Christ, once and for all. We are not to neglect continuing to meet together for assurance, reinforcement and encouragement. Therefore we are exhorted to draw near with faith, hold fast our confession of hope and consider one another in love. As in chapter six, we are again warned against falling away by deliberately sinning.

Chapter eleven is that listing of the great members of the "Hall of Faith". It begins with, "Now faith is the substance of things hoped for, the evidence of things not seen." It then goes on to list thirteen heroes of faith, plus the people of the exodus and the fall of Jericho, and make mention of six others. Each of these is introduced by the words "By faith". It begins with Abel and runs through Samuel, including Rahab, the harlot of Jericho and great-grandmother of David. The point is stated in verse thirteen. "These all died in faith, not having received the promises, but having seen them afar off were assured of them." This chapter concludes, beginning at verse thirty-three, with the upside of faith, and the successes of the promises. It then goes on to state the downside which many have suffered, including torture, ill-treatment and wanderings, while persevering in the faith.

In chapter twelve these heroes are described as a great cloud of witnesses, of martyrs. We are to look to these and to that pioneer, the first leader, Christ, as we struggle against sin. We are to cast away anything that burdens us or may cause our feet to stumble. Here we have three "therefore" clauses plus six clauses with "therefore" presumed but not written, including, therefore:

strengthen your drooping hands; pursue peace; make straight paths; and serve God acceptably with reverence.

In chapter thirteen, we are exhorted to continue in brotherly love, caring for strangers and family. Hebrews concludes with that well-know benediction. "Now may the God of peace who brought up our Lord Jesus from the dead, that great Shepherd of the sheep, through the good of the everlasting covenant, make you complete in every good work to do His will, working in you what is well pleasing in His sight, through Jesus Christ, to whom be glory forever and ever. Amen."

And here begin, as follows on the next pages, the three short letters of John.

CHAPTER 44
JOHN THIRD, SECOND AND FIRST
LOVE, KNOW, ANTINOMIANS AND GNOSTICS

If anyone sins, we have an Advocate with the Father, Jesus Christ the righteous, and he is the propitiation for our sins, and not for ours only but also for the whole world. 1 Jhn. 2:1-2

****

JOHN AND HIS LETTERS

The year was probably about 26 A.D. It was in the spring of the year. Jesus was about thirty years old. He had recently been baptized by John the Baptist and was beginning to call twelve disciples, twelve apostles. He called Simon Peter and his brother Andrew. They worked as fishermen for Mr. Zebedee, along with Zebedee's two sons, James and John. That sequence is also very likely the age sequence of these four young men. The probable ages of these young men at the time of the call were Peter twenty-one, Andrew nineteen, James eighteen and John sixteen. Jesus promptly gave Simon the Greek name of Peter, Cephas in Aramaic, both meaning "Rock", and being the eldest he was put in charge. Mark tells us that Jesus named the teenage Zebedee brothers *Boanerges*, meaning "sons of thunder", as they may have had a volatile and tempestuous temperament, somewhat like Peter.

John is the only one of the twelve who did not die a violent martyr's death and is thought to have died at the age of ninety in 100 A.D. He outlived all of the others by about thirty years. He wrote five books of the new Christian scriptures. His Gospel and the Revelation are fairly long, but two of his letters are less than one page. His writings make up nineteen percent of the new Christian scriptures, Paul's thirteen epistles make up twenty-five percent, and Luke's Gospel and Acts nearly twenty-seven percent of the new Christian scriptures. John wrote all five of his documents about sixty years after the resurrection when he was in his eighties. It is thought that he began the Revelation and then wrote the Gospel and the three letters before finishing the Revelation. He completed his Gospel first, before 90 A.D., in which year he wrote the three letters, which may have been written in reverse order from the way numbered in the Bible. These writings were done while in Ephesus, before being sent into exile on the island of Patmos, where he completed the Revelation. As one becomes a little more familiar with these five writings of John, it is interesting to keep in mind that the young man called "son of thunder" by Jesus, was the same who as an elderly man wrote of love and knowledge in his Gospel and three letters.

John described himself as the disciple "whom Jesus loved,...lying close to the breast of Jesus" at the last supper. He was the one who outran the older Peter to investigate the empty tomb on that resurrection morning. However, he stopped at the entrance to look into the tomb, leaving it to Peter to go in first and find the tomb empty. This man who was a son of thunder when a teen-ager, wrote these deep and reflective documents at the end of his years. In his Gospel he emphasized the deity of Christ, Jesus as God. In all of his writings he wrote of love, light, giving, forgiving, knowing, the Way, the Truth and the Light.

At the time John wrote, the Hebrew world was increasingly merging with the Greco-Roman world. This clash between ancient philosophies and theologies caused a major problem of conflict and confusion. It had now been about 550 years since the time of Malachi, the last book of the Hebrew scriptures. It had been about 500 years since Socrates taught the young Plato in Athens, Greece. It had been about 450 years since Plato's student Aristotle had taught the young Alexander the Great. The teachings and philosophies of Socrates, Plato and Aristotle, had been spread eastward by the empire of Alexander. Now the teachings of Christ spread westward and had to be sifted, sorted and distinguished from the teachings of those great men. One of the biggest problems was what it meant to know or have special knowledge of the truth and the rules of living. John wrote on these matters, and of love. Paul was the apostle of Faith, Peter of Hope, and John of Love.

Let's look at John's letters in reverse order, first very, very briefly at the third and second very brief letters, and then at the first letter in more detail. Keep in mind that he was probably just finishing that wonderful book on the Gospel, in which he quoted Jesus as saying, "I am the way, and the truth, and the life." In a sense Third John is the Way, Second John the Truth, and First John the Life.

****

THIRD AND SECOND JOHN

These are the two shortest writings in all of the Bible. At about two-thirds of a page, Second John is the shortest, and Third John is only about twenty words longer. Paul's letter to Philemon and Jude's letter are just a little longer than these two. In both of these letters, John begins by referring to himself as "the Elder", which he no doubt is, being now in his eighties and the eldest spiritually. Both are written to an individual, the Third to Gaius and the Second to the "elect lady", the only book in the Bible addressed to a woman. We do not know the location of these two individuals or their churches, but they were most likely in the area of western modern Turkey, near the Aegean Sea.

In the second verse of Third John, we have those words of the beloved hymn, "It Is Well With My Soul." This letter has some echoes of some of Paul's letters, as John first writes of his love for Gaius and then of his dislike of the actions of Diotrephes, who puts himself first and speaks against John in disrespect of his authority. The churches always have had and always will have mumbling voices of dissent within them. Paul and John spoke openly in love and truth of these problems. He concludes by also commending Demetrius. Having gotten those few sentences off his chest, John now returns to his writings of the heights of love and truth, as in his Gospel and in his next two letters.

In Second John we hear of truth and love, as John writes of loyal obedience to Christ. He gives a taste of his coming letter, which we call his First, and of his much longer Gospel. He uses the word "truth" five times and the word "love" four times. He also uses the word "know" as he refers to those "know-it-alls" known as Gnostics, who claim to have special knowledge of the secrets of life. In verse three he emphasizes that he is not giving his readers any original or new commandment. As from the beginning, they are simply to love one another. In verse seven he cautions them not to listen to deceptive false teachers who do not preach the true gospel. That is another problem that has been within the church from the beginning to our day. He concludes with a desire that their joy be complete and calls them children.

****

FIRST JOHN

Let us now look at First John, the letter of the Life. For those people who have a Bible in which they underline, and most readers do so, the pages for this first letter are ones that will have nearly every verse underlined with some words then double or triple underlined. Many of the verses in this letter sound so very familiar to those familiar with their Bible. The verses have a majestic quality and are also repeatedly rephrased by John, so they do sound memorable. He develops his four themes of light, righteousness, love, and truth and fairly repeats them. The language is much like that of his Gospel, as he emphasizes certain teachings of that Gospel and greatly expands his second letter. Most students of the Bible outline this letter giving it the same general analysis and breakpoints. The letter was a general encyclical letter written to be circulated around the churches of what is today western Turkey.

In this letter John uses a technique similar to that which Paul used at times. To protect and recover the language, John uses the same words used by various groups of philosophers as he defines the word over and again in such a way as to sift, sort and distinguish them from the use of non-Christians. Languages change over the decades and words take on different meanings. During the latter twentieth century there was a flood of ever subtle changes in words of our primary language in the United States. This is the deconstruction of our language. It starts with soft confusion and hardens into change. Speaking of language and not of political persuasion and with the certainty of being accused by those liberated from the scripture of being illiterately stupid, here are a few changes.

Love, both a noun and a verb, meaning a sense of strong personal attachment of affection and admiration, in modern times primarily means lustful sex. Feticide and prolicide, meaning the killing of one's own child, now are to mean simply the mother's "choice" of convenience. Free will, meaning the freedom of choice of all of God's people, now is to mean rights without responsibilities. Gay, meaning joy and frivolity, now is to mean homoeroticism. Fetus, meaning the developing offspring of a father and mother within the womb, now is to mean some cancerous mass to be eliminated for the sole convenience of the mother. Fundamentals, meaning the elementary basics in education, math, athletics, and religion, now is to mean illiterate ignorance. Religion, meaning a system of devotion, faith and worship which cultivates a community, now is to mean a suppressive evil against progress and enlightenment. Church, meaning a group of Christians, now is to mean the only faith to which the government must stand in aggressive opposition.

Now here are a few words with which John had to contend in his day. These words may sound unfamiliar and difficult, but are no more so than words like hypodermic or epidemic. These contentions are present today, but we just do not know their names. Some words are Gnostic, Docetic, Antinomian, Perfectionist, Spiritualist and Propitiation. Our English word "know", as in "knowledge", comes from the Greek word *gnosis*. Gnostics were know-it-alls who thought they held a special true knowledge of life. John reclaims the word "know" and uses it thirty-five times in this letter. We are simply to "know Christ". The Greek word *dokeo* means "suppose, think or seems". From this we have the Docetics who did not believe the humanity of Christ and that he only "seemed" to suffer and die on the cross. In all languages something must be given a name to be certain it exists. Laws give specific names to various things, and the Greek word for name was modified a little into *nomos* to mean law. A person opposed to law is an "anti-nomian". Many Christians were confused and believed they did not have to obey any laws at all. Paul dealt with this problem in his letter to the Romans and John deals with it again here. As to Spiritualism, the problem was similar to that with which Paul dealt in his letters to Colossae, as the people had difficulty distinguishing angels and demons from Christ. Many believed that were they to have full knowledge and worship certain spirits they would be forever saved by God. These are each very modern problems today.

The most used word here is "love", at forty-three times. Next is "know" at thirty-five, then "sin" at twenty-seven. With those words one readily is informed as to the purpose of this letter, that we understand Love, Knowledge and Sin. John also plainly tells us, nine times, the reasons he writes to us. "We write to you...

— about the Word of life, which has existed from the beginning. 1:1
— especially in order that our joy may be complete. 1:4
— especially so that you will not sin; but if you do sin, we have someone who pleads with the Father on our behalf--Jesus the Christ. 2:1
— because your sins are forgiven for the sake of Christ. 2:12
— older parents, because you know Jesus. 2:13
— young people, because you have defeated Satan. 2:13
— not because you do not know the truth, but because you do know it and also know that no lie comes from the truth. 2:21
— about those who are trying to deceive you. 2:26
— that you might have eternal life--you that believe in the Son of God. 5:13

As John did in his Gospel book, here he contrasts light and darkness. However, in this first letter he goes on to use several more contrasts: the new or old commandment; loving the Father or the world; Christ or antichrist; truth or lies; children of God or of Satan; eternal life or death; love or hatred; true or false prophecy; love or fear; having or not having eternal life.

Now we will look most closely at the first two chapters then very briefly at the other three. As he did with his Gospel, John begins with an introduction, a prologue. He writes that he knew Jesus on this earth. "That which was from the beginning, which we have heard, which we have seen with our eyes, which we have looked upon, and our hands have touched, concerning the Word of life — the life was manifested, and we have seen, and bear witness, and declare to you that eternal life which was with the Father and was manifested to us — that which we have seen and heard we declare to you, that you also may have fellowship with us; and truly our fellowship is with the Father and with His Son Jesus Christ. And these things we write to you that your joy may be full." He says he has heard, looked upon and touched this Jesus, and now proclaims him to the people. As in his second letter, he does this that their joy may be complete.

At the fifth verse of chapter one, John begins his words on light and darkness. He also gives the first two of four conditions of being in fellowship with God, being verse seven with walking in the light, and verse eight with breaking with sin. We are to walk in the light and not in the darkness and walk in the way in which Jesus walked. At verse nine is a condition to forgiveness which is rarely emphasized from the modern liberal pulpits. "If we confess our sins, He is faithful and just to forgive us our sins and to cleanse us from all unrighteousness. If we say that we have not sinned, we make Him a liar, and His word is not in us." The unilateral act of letting go of hate is a pre-condition to the bilateral act of forgiveness, and too many counselors confuse letting go of hate with forgiving. There is no forgiveness without first repenting and confessing.

Depending upon how one counts them, in this letter John gives us about seven tests for proper conduct and deeds. Some start with, "If we say...then," and some with, "He who says...." In chapter one at verse six we are not to walk in darkness but in light. At verse eight we are not to say we do not sin but are to confess our sins. In chapter two at verse four we are not to say we know Christ but disobey his commandments. At verse six we are to walk as Jesus walked. At verse nine we are not to hate our brother in darkness but to love our brother in light. At verse fifteen we are not to love the world but to love the Father. At verse twenty-two we are not to deny Jesus as the Christ.

In chapter two he writes that obedience is knowing God. He calls us children. We are children of God. There are several Greek words which mean "child." The word John uses here is *pais*, which means a child of a true parent. John sees all of his students as his own true children.

In verse two we have one of the four places in the Bible where we hear of propitiation. We heard of this in Hebrews. This is the verse used in the Comfortable Words of the assurance of pardon in the historic communion service. "Children, these things I write to you, so that you may not sin. If anyone sins, we have an Advocate with the Father, Jesus Christ the righteous; And He Himself is the propitiation for our sins, and not for ours only but also for the whole world."

At the seventh verse we hear of love and the true light, as John also sets out the second condition to walking in the light. We are to keep the commandments, especially as to love. John makes it clear that this is "no new commandment to you, but an old commandment which you have had from the beginning." At verse twelve he gives a charge to both young and old, that we are to love the Father and not the world. "For all that is in the world -- the lust of the flesh, the lust of the eyes, and the pride of life -- is not of the Father but is of the world." This is the third condition of being in fellowship with God, being in but not of the world.

At verse eighteen, John gives us the name "antichrist." The name is used only here, in chapter four and again in his second letter. This antichrist equates to "the lawless one" of which Paul wrote in his second letter to Thessalonica. The antichrist and his followers are those who actively deny the faith of

Christ. At verse twenty-two John gives the fourth condition of walking in the Light: guard against those who are antichrists. "Who is a liar but he who denies that Jesus is the Christ? He is antichrist who denies the Father and the Son." This is the fourth condition of being in fellowship with God, being on guard against the many little followers of the antichrist.

In chapters three and four, John essentially repeats and rephrases conditions for walking in the Light as conditions for being a true child of God. In chapter three he writes of living apart from sinfulness as he uses the word "know" throughout, and couples it with "sin" in the first half and with "love" in the second half. In chapter four he writes of living in love as this apostle of love uses the word "love" twenty-five times.

In chapter five John writes of "love" in the first half and of "sin" in the second half, as he contrasts the two. We do know God exists by what may be called "heart knowledge." We just know it in our heart. We must come to Jesus in our heart, in our attitude, in our love of others. This love is not a mushy thing as we are taught by movies and television. This love, called *agape*, is simply to come to Christ, to let Jesus into your heart, and to pray and desire that others, even your enemy, come to Jesus in his or her heart. In this epistle, John uses the word "love" forty-three times and the word "know" thirty-five times. He repeats and repeats the love of God is all we must know. Even more than heart-knowledge is the evidence of witnesses. In verse seven, we are told, "There are three that bear witness in heaven: the Father, the Word, and the Holy Spirit; and these three are one. And there are three that bear witness on earth: the Spirit, the water, and the blood; and these three agree as one. If we receive the witness of men, the witness of God is greater."

Hear again seventeen wonderful verses from this short letter.

— God is light, and there is no darkness at all in him. 1:5
— If we say we have no sin, we deceive ourselves, and there is no truth in us. 1:8
— If we obey God's commands, then we are sure we know him. 2:3
— This command I am writing you is not new; it is the old command, the one you have had from the beginning. 2:7, 3
— Love your neighbor as yourself, because love comes from God. 2:10-11;4:7
— Everything that the sinful self desires, what people see and want, and everything in this world of which people are so proud, — none of it is from the Father. 2:16, 2:27
— Do not be surprised if the people of the world hate you. 3:13
— God commands that we (i) believe in his Son Jesus Christ and (ii) love one another. 3:23
— Do not believe all who claim to have the Spirit, but test them to find out if the spirit they have comes from God. 4:1

— This is how you will be able to know whether it is God's Spirit: anyone who acknowledges that Jesus Christ came as a human being has the Spirit who comes from God. 4:2

— Love is not that we have loved God, but that God loved us and the world so much that he gave his only Son to be the means by which our sins are forgiven. 4:10 (3:16)

— There is no fear in love; perfect love drives out all fear. 4:18

— Who can defeat this world? Only the person who believes that Jesus is the Son of God. 5:5

— There are three witnesses: the Spirit, the water, and the blood. 5:7

— He hears us whenever we ask him; and since we know this is true, we know also that he gives us what we ask from him. 5:15

— No child of God keeps on sinning. Keep yourself safe from false gods. 5:18, 21

And here begins, as follows on the next pages, the Revelation of Jesus the Christ to John.

CHAPTER 45

REVELATION
APOCALYPSE OF SECOND COMING

I am the Alpha and the Omega...the first and the last. Rev. 1:8,17.

****

BACKGROUND

This is not meant to be a commentary on the Bible nor to add things outside of or beyond the book itself. However, Revelation is a book very different from all of the others, as it is nearly all a book of prophecy. For that reason some background seems necessary.

Most people have an extremely limited knowledge of this book of Revelation. Many have heard, and some have read, a few verses including those of the seven churches as written in the second and third chapters; the picture of Jesus knocking on the closed door with no handle of chapter three; the four horsemen of the apocalypse of chapter six; the 144,000 martyrs of chapters seven and fourteen; the number of the beast as six-six-six of chapter thirteen; the mark of the beast of chapters thirteen and fourteen; the battle at Armageddon of chapter sixteen; the thousand year millennium of chapter twenty; the new Jerusalem of chapter twenty-one; and the Great Tribulation, which is chapters six through nineteen. They have heard but cannot put any of it together, or even find the correct verse in the book. One can sympathize with those people, of which we each are, or have been, one.

As we now discuss some of this book you will no doubt feel the depth of the confusion. It seems most churches avoid this book, especially from the pulpit. One may think this avoidance might be due to most so-called mainline churches not wanting to get into the second coming and some really powerful prophecy. It is indeed unlike any of the other books, including Daniel which has an undeserved reputation of being difficult. A person cannot even begin to get a handle on any except the first three or five chapters without first having some concept of the entire book. Even with that one needs a good outline at hand to see just where the verses being read at the time fit into the large picture.

Revelation is first and foremost a book of worship of a sovereign and almighty God. A complete analytical survey and summary of Revelation is well beyond the scope of this book, the purpose of which is to encourage the reader to read the Bible. The clear over-arching message is that God is in control, on the throne, master of all, of all nature and of all spirits. God has already defeated Satan and his evil forces and will clean away those pockets where they still operate. There is no fear or doom and gloom for those on this winning side.

Like most, or all, of the Bible, from beginning to end, Revelation also is a book of spiritual insights into the human condition and is applicable to past, present and future. It's message is that a righteous and just God is in control and that each of us is to remain steadfast when oppressed by evil and wickedness and burdens of all types, as the oppression is temporary and the victory is eternal. This message was opposed by Karl Marx, who, with his communistic material dialectic, convinced the people that some victorious god is only dreams of a non-existent future to keep the laboring class oppressed. The names of the people, nations and events are readily changeable from the past to the future. Corporations, states and nations, monarchs, republics and democracies get their power from the individual people, and it is imperative that the people choose as leaders those firmly adhering to Christian concepts.

The confusion with this book can begin with its two names. The word "revelation" is derived from two Latin words, *re-* meaning "back", or "away", and *velato* meaning "cover" or "veil". To reveal or unveil something is to take away the veil covering it. In the very first verse we are told that these things are the revelation of Jesus Christ to the writer. And it is in the singular, one continuous revelation, though of many things. The resurrected Jesus took away the veil so that John could see these matters. John may have not even fully understood all of it, but he reports what he saw as the veil was removed.

In Greek there are two somewhat similar words meaning "veiled" or "hidden". One is *kalupto* which means "veil" or "cover", in the sense that something is veiled or hidden from sight. Another is *krupto* which also means hidden but from understanding rather than from sight, as a secret sign or symbol. From this word for secret, we get the word "krypton" for the secret powers of Superman. The Greek word *apo* means "back" or "away". From the Greek word *apo-kalupto* we get our word "apo-calypse", meaning "unveiled", no longer hidden from sight. This book of the Revelation is also known as the book of the Apocalypse. This word is not to be confused with the word *apo-krupto* which we write as "apo-crypha" which are books not canonized as a part of the bible. We hear of the four horsemen of the Apocalypse (Greek), which are the four horsemen of the Revelation (Latin).

Revelation is simultaneously both extremely personal and extremely archetypal, and the two concepts cannot be separated. One's intellectual search for some absolutely objective analysis of Revelation is hopelessly impossible as one's subjective affections and religious world-view become involved as to this supremely religious book. For that reason, self-defined atheists or agnostics are self-eliminated from any understanding and readily accuse a believer of not being objective. Though difficult, strive to keep in mind that the young man, called "son of thunder" by Jesus, became the elderly man who wrote the three brief epistles on love and this apocryphal book of Revelation.

A study of this book, and of the comments of others who have studied it, reveals that nearly all outline the book in much the same manner and with much the same breakpoints. That part is revealed. The problem is how to interpret and understand, to see with the mind, things that are revealed to the eye. Several times in other scripture we are told that there are some things which we are not to know, things only the Father knows. However, we are also told to be wise as to these things. A person can spend a lifetime in a study of the Bible. A person can spend a lifetime in a study of just this one book. This book is a tool for the worship of a loving, almighty and incomprehensible God.

This book is absolutely packed with the number seven, which in the Bible is the perfect number, the number of God. The number for Satan is usually six, being less than God and the number for Christ is eight, which means on the other side of God as opposed to Satan. There are seven primary sevens in this book. At the beginning are the seven churches. In chapter six are the seven seals of judgments. In chapters eight and nine are the seven trumpets of judgments. In chapters twelve and thirteen are the seven personages. In chapters fifteen and sixteen are the seven vials or bowls of plagues. In chapter seventeen through twenty are the seven dooms as to Babylon, the Antichrist and Satan. In the last two chapters are the seven new things. All of this is mixed with some 300 symbols.

These revelations relate to heaven and to earth. Inserted at places in these stories are several interludes or parenthetical supplements to expand the stories. Here one could use a chart, and there are many available in books and bookstores. The first three chapters deal with the seven churches. Chapters four, five, the first part of nineteen, and from the second part of twenty to the end deal with heaven. All of the rest deals with earth, of which chapters six, eight, nine and sixteen are the chronological back bone of the earthly story. Chapters seven, ten through fifteen and seventeen and eighteen are parenthetical insertions to supplement the story. The book begins with five chapters of church sounding material. At chapter six, with the vision of the four horsemen of this apocalypse, the tenor and tone of the book changes abruptly and stays on that course of the second coming.

Jesus the Christ is Prophet, Priest and King and also Judge. In the four Gospels we are told of Jesus the Christ as the suffering and obedient servant, and teaching Prophet. In the epistles we are told of Jesus the Christ as the head of the Church, the Priest at the right hand of God interceding for humanity. In the apocalyptic book of the Revelation, we meet Christ the King and Judge. The Lamb is now a Lion upon the throne as King of kings, Lord of lords, and Judge of all earth. There is no more humiliation, no more apology, no more teaching. Do not look for it in this book. Here we find absolute power and sovereignty. This is the book that unbelievers forcefully try to explain away as fictitious stories of superstitious ancient mankind. This is a book to be read as worship and not to be fully understood. Genesis tells of beginnings at the starting line. Revelation tells of endings at the destination, the finish line.

A large part of the confusion as to this book is that Revelation overlaps and must be read and merged with many other parts of the Bible, especially the old Hebrew scriptures. Here are some of the primary parts. Chapter twenty-four of the Gospel of Matthew, known as the Olivet Discourse, given during the final days of Jesus on earth and discussing the signs of the end times, relates to chapter six with its seven seals, beginning with the four horsemen. In the final verses of Daniel chapter nine we have the seventy weeks of years and particularly the seventieth week, which is deemed by some to be the Great Tribulation of chapters six through nineteen of Revelation. The four beasts of Daniel chapter seven are to be distinguished from the three, or four, beasts of Revelation chapters thirteen and seventeen. A student is to keep in mind that the Antichrist is not Satan, the Devil, but is an evil and deceptive human being. There are two points of debate. One involves the sequence of the Rapture of the final verses of First Thessalonians as to the Great Tribulation. Another is the sequence of the second coming in triumph of Christ, the Second Advent, with that thousand year Millennium of a blessed, though somewhat imperfect, peace.

In general biblical interpretation all matters must be placed on the proper side at six points. (1) The matter must be placed either in the natural or in the spiritual realm. (2) The matter must be placed in the literal or in the symbolic realm. (3) The matter must be placed in the past historical or in the future realm. (4) The matter must be placed in the proper time and space, this or another. (5) The matter must be placed in its proper context. (6) Prophecy and promises must be placed in those already fulfilled and those yet to be fulfilled. The six points are applicable to nearly every verse of Revelation.

In the interpretation of Revelation, each of the foregoing six have different views of interpretation giving us essentially four groups. Each of the groups essentially agree that the first three chapters are historic, and from there the four views of interpretation spread across the charts. (1) The Preterist view is that the first three chapters were history at the time John circulated his epistle and the next seventeen were apocalyptic as to events of the late first century with the last two chapters being purely symbolic of the final victory of good over evil. (2) The Historicist view is that chapters four through nineteen are symbolic of events through modern times, including Rome, Mohammedism, the Papacy and the Reformation, with the final two chapters being symbolic of the final victory. (3) The Idealist view is that chapters four through nineteen are symbolic of the conflict between good and evil and are mostly in the past, with the final two chapters being symbolic. (4) The Futurist view, generally that of Dispensational Pre-Millennialists, is that chapters two and three, as to the seven churches, are of the church through history and that the remaining chapters are largely a literal prophecy of future events of the end times. This interpretive view is very spectacular and sells a lot of books and videos.

The second coming of Christ, the Second Advent, is not exactly one sudden event but rather a series of events. The four primary events associated with Revelation are the Rapture, the Great Tribulation, the Millennium and the Advent. Most seem to agree that the Rapture and the Tribulation come before the Millennium and the Second Coming. These four events involve two positioning problems, both of which use the prefixes pre- and post-. One involves the Rapture and the Tribulation. Does the Rapture of the saints come before, during or after the Tribulation? Most seem to agree that the Rapture will come before the Tribulation, that it is Pre-Tribulation, that the saintly believers will not suffer the great wrath of God. However, some believe that the saintly believers will suffer through the wrath, with the help of God, that is Post-Tribulation. As to the Millennium and the Second Advent, it seems most agree the Advent will come after the Millennium, that is Post-millennial. However, many believe the Advent will come before the Millennium, that is Pre-millennial, and sells a lot of books and videos.

As to the sequence of the Millennium and the Advent, which is not the Rapture and Tribulation, in addition to the pre- and post- views, there are two more views. Let's look at all four. Pre-millennialists believe that the unconverted Jews must first return to Zion, rebuild a temple and restore animal sacrifices as history proceeds downhill to a final cataclysmic denouement at Armageddon at the Advent all then followed by the Millennium, a 1000-year earthly rule of Christ. Post-millennialists believe the Millennium may already be occurring as the Holy Spirit works through democratic revolutions and the co-operation of humans world-wide and that the Advent will then come. A-millennialists believe the peaceful Millennium is not of this earth but only of a heavenly ingathering of souls. Many are Pan-millennialists, believing it will all pan out in the end.

****

REVELATION

Revelation opens with Jesus Christ the Son giving an account as given to him by God the Father of things to come. John was told to write what he was to be told and envision in a book and send it to seven churches.

The seven churches of chapters two and three were real churches at the time John the Apostle wrote this book. John was then in exile on the small Greek island of Patmos, ruled by Rome, about seventy miles off the coast of modern Turkey. These seven churches are in what is today western Turkey. They were situated in a circle, with each about fifty miles from the other. John lists them in a clock-wise direction. These seven churches are types of churches of then and of today, and, as many believe, the church through history.

Each letter to a church begins with a simple salutation. There is then usually a commendation and a complaint closing with a promise. Ephesus was a backslidden church that left its first love, but if they overcome they will eat of the tree of life. Many think this generally was also the early apostolic church of the first century. Smyrna was a persecuted church which will attain eternal life if they persevere. Many think this was also the church in general from of 100-316 A.D. Pergamos was a worldly and licentious church and called to repentance. Many think this was also the church in general of 316-500 A.D. Thyatira was a lax and paganized church, which was called to follow the commands of God and be saved. Many think this was also the church in general of 500-1517, during the Dark Ages until the Reformation. Sardis was a dead church which was warned that the coming of judgment would come as a thief in the night and only a few will be saved. Many think this was also the church in general of 1517-1750 and the Great Awakening. Philadelphia was the missionary church, the favored church of the opened door. Many think this was the church in general from 1750 until fairly modern times. Laodicea was a lukewarm church which was to be vomited out of the churches as it was not a true church but composed of those who merely profess to be Christians. Many think this is the church in general of modern times.

Chapters four and five take John to the heavenly throne room with One seated on the throne. In his right hand he holds a scroll sealed with seven seals, which no creature could open. The Lion of Judah, the Lamb, comes as the only one worthy to open the seals. The seals are apparently variously wrapped within the scroll as when they are opened a new vision appears. Chapters five through sixteen are essentially the contents of the seals. In chapter eight the seventh seal discloses seven trumpets, and in chapter eleven the seventh trumpet heralds the coming victory following seven plagues contained in seven vials or bowls. The order of the seals, trumpets and bowls is like a three-part telescope opening in reverse order. The first part contains six seals with the seventh being the opening of the second part of the telescope with the trumpets, and then the third part being the bowls. There are no time periods or sequences given. The opening of the telescope could be instantaneous and all the effects of the seals, the trumpets and the bowls simultaneous; or, as some think, the openings could take over 2,000 years and come at undetermined intervals.

At some point from here the Rapture of First Thessalonians chapter four verse sixteen could or should well occur in some fashion as to all faithful believers. In chapter six the telescopic seals begin to open. The first seal releases a white horse with a rider with a bow but no arrow. Most interpret this to be a false peace before the coming tribulations, but some think it is the Christ with some brief peace. Those who interpret all as history see this as the early apostolic church. The second seal releases a red horse and rider. Most interpret this to be war. Those who interpret all as history see this as the church going through many debates until the time of Constantine. The third seal releases a black horse and rider. Most interpret this to be famine. Those who interpret all as history see this as the church since Constantine in 311 A.D., to the firm establishment of the Papacy in 538 A.D.. The fourth seal releases a yellowish-green horse on which rides Death and Hades follows him. Some anti-Roman historicists interpret this as the period from 538 A.D. to the Reformation in 1517 A.D. These are the four horsemen of the Apocalypse. The fifth seal is a vision of those martyrs slain for the word of God, crying out as to how long it would be until the final judgment. The sixth seal releases a great earthquake as the sun becomes black and the moon becomes as blood, as the great day of wrathful judgment had begun. Historicists can find many earthquakes and red moons in the eighteenth and nineteenth centuries to support their view.

Between the sixth and seventh seal, the sixth and seventh trumpet and the sixth and seventh bowl is a parenthetical interlude, a hiatus of rest. The interlude of the seals is chapter seven, which is the sealing of 144,000 of the tribes of Israel, and a vision of the glorified martyrs in heaven. Most interpret this to be totally symbolic with the tribes meaning the entire world, and is the number twelve squared then multiplied by ten cubed and symbolically includes all of those to be sealed on the forehead by God. Some opine that the number is fixed as to 144,000 exactly of saints to be fully the bride of Christ.

Chapter eight is the opening of the seventh seal which releases the second part of the telescopic portion of the seven trumpets, which are judgments. The trumpet judgments are worse than the seven seals, and the seven bowls will be yet worse and more universal as the effect of unrepentant humans moves from fairly indirect modes to more direct individual attacks. The seals, trumpets and bowls may well be but one judgment in three or nineteen phases with increasing severity. Most interpretations may be that such is the case and all are yet in the future at final end times, and that they may all be either actual coming events or symbols of seriously terrible times.

The first trumpet blast of judgment is hail and fire mixed with blood upon a third of the earth. Most interpret this to be symbolic of the end times, but many see it as actual end times events. Those who interpret all as history see this as the invasion of a third of the Roman Empire by the Goths around

375 A.D. The second trumpet is of something like a burning mountain being thrown into the sea causing a third to become blood. In addition to being symbolic or actual at the end times, there is a view that this is the vandals' attack upon the central third of the Roman Empire from the sea around 440 A.D. The third trumpet is of a great blazing star named Wormwood falling into a third of the fresh water. In addition to being symbolic or actual at the end times, there is a view that this is the bitter attack of Attila and the Huns across the Alps, the headwaters of the western third of the Roman Empire around 450 A.D. The fourth trumpet is of a third of the sun, the moon and the stars being darkened. In addition to being symbolic or actual as to the end time, there is the view that this is the final end of the Roman Empire as the western third was overrun by the barbarian Ostrogoths around 480 A.D.

Chapter nine covers the fifth and sixth trumpets and an interlude. The fifth trumpet blows and an angel falls from heaven, and he has the keys to the shaft of the bottomless pit which he opens. From the shaft arises smoke which darkens the sun and from which come locusts like scorpions. The locusts are allowed to torture for five months those who did not have the seal of God upon their foreheads. The king of the pit is named Abaddon in Hebrew and Apollyon in Greek, meaning the Destroyer. Some interpret this as yet future symbolism and some as yet actual events, and some as the beast being Nero, while some see it as the invasion of Mohammedism from the pit of Arabia in the seventh century. The sixth trumpet sounded releasing the four angels bound in the Euphrates River to kill a third of mankind, evidently employing 200,000,000 cavalry (twice ten thousand times ten thousand). Again, some interpret this as symbolic and some as an actual event of the end times, connecting it to the Kings of the East when the Euphrates dries up in chapter sixteen, verse twelve. The problem with an actual event is the Tigris River parallels the Euphrates and this is simply an unrealistic number of cavalry if in a brief period of time. Those who see this as now a past historical event interpret it as the expanse of the Ottoman Empire from Turkey, at the headwaters of the Euphrates, with the huge cavalry being over centuries beginning in the late thirteenth century.

Chapter ten and the first part of eleven are an interlude between the sixth and seven trumpets. John sees an angel come down, who places his right foot on the sea and his left on the land and holds a little scroll open in his hand. Seven thunders sound, but John is told not to write down what they said. The angel raises his right hand and swears, "Delay no longer." He then gives John the little scroll and commands him to eat it, which he does. We do not know what the thunders said nor how the little scroll read. For those who think the seventieth week of the latter part of Daniel chapter nine is delayed until the end times, the division here between chapters ten and eleven may be the halfway point of the final week of years. Also, somewhere between the beginning of chapter eight and the end of eleven is assuredly the beginning of the great tribulation of the latter part of Matthew chapter twenty-four.

Chapter eleven may be one of the most difficult in the Bible to interpret. John is told to measure the temple, the altar and those who worship there. He is not to measure the outer temple which is given to the nations to trample for forty-two months, three-and-a-half years. Two witnesses are sent to prophesy for 1,260 days, which is probably a contemporaneous three-and-a-half years, at the end of which the beast (Satan's assistant) from the bottomless pit (from which came the locusts) will kill them. For three-and-a-half days their bodies will lie exposed in the great city, allegorically termed Sodom and Egypt. Then a breath of life enters them, and they ascend to heaven. An earthquake occurs. Those who think this refers to now past history interpret the days to be years and the witnesses to be the Old and the New Testaments which were forbidden in France around 1793. Others interpret the months and years to be a symbolic period of tribulation while still others interpret the years as actual in the end times. Some interpret the two witnesses to be Moses and Elijah and others to be Joshua and Zerubbabel.

The conclusion of chapter fifteen is the sounding of the last, the seventh, trumpet, the extending of the third and final section of the telescopic woes and plagues. Verse fifteen announces the victory. "The kingdoms of this world have become the kingdoms of our Lord and of His Christ, and He shall reign forever and ever." With this Satan and his followers are defeated and only the clean up and put away phase remains. The remaining leading characters will now all come on stage, the Dragon, the Beast of the Sea, the Beast of the Earth and the Scarlet Harlot. There will be no more time for repentance on the part of humans. Judgment has arrived.

Chapters twelve and thirteen are essentially one unit followed by fourteen, before sixteen brings the final telescopic events of the plagues of the seven bowls. Twelve and sixteen are outlined by some as seven visions and by others as seven personages or creatures. The first six verses is usually deemed one vision with three personages. A woman appears clothed with the sun, the moon under her feet and wearing a crown of twelve stars. Also appears a great red dragon with seven heads and ten horns and a crown upon each head. With his tail he sweeps down a third of the stars. The woman is pregnant and delivers a male child to rule over all nations, which child is "raptured" up to God, and the woman flees into the wilderness, where she is nourished by God for 1,260 days. Verses seven through twelve are two visions and one personage. The personage introduced is Michael the archangel who fought with the dragon, who is identified as that serpent of old, Satan the Devil. Michael and his angels defeated Satan and his angels throwing them out of heaven and down to earth. "Woe to the inhabitants of the earth and the sea! For the devil has come down to you, having great wrath, because he knows that he has a short time." In what some see as a fourth vision or a fifth personage, the Church, Satan then pursues the woman to where she is nourished for a time, and times, and half a time, evidently meaning a symbolic three-and-a-half years. Satan becomes angry and goes off to make war against those who keep the commandments and testify as to Jesus the Christ. Most interpret the woman, not as Mary, but as the Jewish people which brought forth Jesus the Christ and had other children who became the Church.

Chapter thirteen is three visions and two personages, or beasts. John sees a beast, somewhat like a leopard, rising out of the sea. As did the dragon, this leopard-like beast has seven heads and ten horns, with a crown on each horn. One of its heads appears to have a wound which should have been mortal but had healed. The beast is granted the authority of the dragon and speaks blasphemous words. John then sees this beast exercise its authority. John sees an indescribable beast with two horns like a young lamb, the seventh vision and the seventh personage of these two chapters. This beast speaks like a dragon and exercises the authority of the leopard-like beast of the sea. We are told in chapter sixteen, verse thirteen that this beast is the false prophet. It works great signs and bids the people to worship the image for the beast of the sea or die, and for all to have the mark of the beast. The mark of the sea beast is a human number, six-hundred-sixty-six, and is to be marked on the right hand or the forehead. In passing, the number of the Greek letters for Jesus Christ total 8-8-8.

Interpretations as to chapter thirteen would easily fill an average sized book. We are told the dragon of chapter twelve is Satan, the Devil, and the beast of the sea is the false prophet. But who are they? A good starting point seems to be that the dragon is indeed Satan; the beast of the sea is the Antichrist; the beast of earth is the anti-Holy Spirit; and the three compose an anti-Holy Trinity. Some interpret them to be the Pope of Rome, the Church of Rome and apostate Protestantism. Some view them as the Roman empire, its divisions and various emperors. Some view them as representing events in the future, either symbolically or as actual events with the seven heads and ten horns being some future reconstituted anti-Christian union. Some opine that the beast of the earth was indescribable as it was a U.S. bison with two small immature horns, and the false prophet of the sea is the modern paganistic United States. In chapter seven, verse three, the servants of God are sealed on the forehead. Here servants of the beast of the sea are marked with the number six hundred sixty-six (6-6-6) on the forehead, or right hand, an anti-Seal. Hebrew, Greek and Latin all use letters of the alphabet for numbers. The number total, in various languages, comes to 6-6-6 for innumerable persons, including Nero and other emperors, world leaders and the Papal office.

Chapter fourteen is an interlude of seven visions of various worshipers, some of the Lamb and some of the beast. John sees a Lamb standing on Mount Zion with 144,000 "first fruits" who have the name of the Lamb and of the Father written on their foreheads and are singing a new song. These are probably the same as in chapter seven. Then come three angels, one announcing that the hour of judgment has come, and one that Babylon the great has fallen, and one that any one who receives the mark of the beast shall suffer God's wrath. Then he sees one like the Son of Man seated on a cloud, with a crown on his head and a sickle in his hand, as it was time to harvest the earth. Then an angel swings his sickle and gathers the vintage of the earth, the wicked, and throws them into the wine press. The blood which flows from the press is as deep as the height of a horse's mouth and makes a stream the length of all of Palestine.

Chapter fifteen is another brief interlude, between the brief beginning of the final judgment and its conclusion. John sees seven angels, with the seven coming plagues, and also something like a sea of glass mingled with fire with those who had conquered the beast standing beside the sea as they sing a song of Moses. Then he sees the temple of the tent (tabernacle) of meeting (testimony) (in which God and Moses met during the exodus) and out of it come the seven angels with the plagues. Then each angel is given a bowl (vial) full of the wrath of God. No one could then enter the temple of the tent until the seven plagues of wrath were emptied in judgment.

Chapter sixteen is the judgment of the emptying of the seven bowls (vials) of plagues of the wrath of God. The end of times and the world has fully arrived. An angel pours out the first bowl on earth and ulcerative sores come upon those who had the mark of and worshiped the beast. Another angel pours the second bowl on the sea which becomes like the blood of a dead man, and all in it die. Another angel pours the third bowl on the fresh water, rivers and springs, which become blood. Another angel pours the fourth bowl on the sun which is allowed to scorch those who do not repent. Another angel pours the fifth bowl on the throne of the beast causing darkness, and because of that and their sores they blaspheme God. Another angel pours the sixth bowl on the Euphrates River causing it to dry up and prepare the way for the Kings from the East. Three foul spirits, like frogs, then come from the mouth of the dragon, and of the beast and of the false prophet. The demons work miraculous signs for all the kings of the world to gather for battle against the judgment day of God Almighty, which gathering takes place at a place called Armageddon. Another angel pours the seventh bowl into the air, and a great voice (God's) from the temple says, "It is done." Then comes lightning, a great earthquake and a storm of hail of about 100 pounds each and the great city (Babylon?, Rome?) is split into three parts. Some think these seven plagues are symbolic of the day of judgment, and some think they will occur literally as spoken apocalyptically.

The vision continues through the remaining six chapters and are separated into various groups of seven visions by various analysts, each equally accurate. In the wilderness, John sees a woman, a harlot dressed in scarlet, sitting on a scarlet beast with seven heads and ten horns. She wears gold and jewels and holds in her hand a golden cup filled with abominations and the filthiness of her fornication with the kings of the earth. On her forehead is written, "Babylon the Great, Mother of Harlots and of Earth's Abominations." John is told, "The beast that you saw was, and is not and will ascend out of the bottomless pit and go to perdition....The seven heads are seven mountains on which the woman sits. There are also seven kings. Five have fallen, one is, and the other has not yet come....The beast that was, and is not, is himself also the eighth, and is of the seven, and is going to perdition....The ten horns...are ten kings who have received no kingdom as yet, but they receive authority for one hour as kings with the beast....These will make war with the Lamb, and the Lamb will overcome them....The woman whom you saw is that great city which reigns over the kings of the earth."

Chapter eighteen begins with the proclamation by an angel of the fall of Babylon, the great commercial city. Babylon has become a dwelling place of demons and a prison for every foul spirit, and the merchants of the earth have grown rich through the abundance of her wantonness. Another voice from heaven says, "Come out of her, my people, lest you share in her sins, and lest you receive of her plagues....Her plagues will come in a single day, death and mourning and famine.... For in one hour her judgment has come." The merchants of the earth will weep for her as no one buys her luxuriant cargoes of such things as gold, jewels, silk, ivory and human souls. It's wealth will be laid waste in one hour. An angel takes up a great millstone, throws it into the sea and says, "Thus with violence the great city Babylon shall be thrown down, and shall not be found anymore."

Chapter nineteen begins with a brief hymn of praise over the fall of Babylon followed by a hymn to marriage of the Lamb (Christ) and his bride (the Church). Now come visions of the sudden and powerful Second Advent, Coming, of the Christ. The first time He came as Priest and Prophet, this time as King and Judge. The end of times has arrived! John sees the heaven open and white horse upon whom sits One called "Faithful and True," with eyes like a flame of fire and who judges and makes war in righteousness. He has a name inscribed which no one knows but is called "The Word of God," and is clothed in a robe dipped in blood. The "armies of heaven," clothed in clean white linen, follow him on white horses. A sharp sword with which to smite the nation goes out of his mouth. "King of Kings and Lord of Lord" is written on his robe and his thigh. An angel standing in the sun calls to all the birds that fly, "Come and gather together for the supper of the Great God, that you may eat the flesh of kings,...of horses and...of all people." John sees, "the beast, the kings of the earth, and their armies, gathered together to make war against Him who sat on the horse and against His army." The beast (of the sea; antichrist) and the false prophet (beast of the earth) are captured and the two are thrown alive into the lake of fire (from which there is no release). All of the rest of their armies are slain and consumed by the birds. This is the battle of Armageddon, not a battle between earthly human nations but a battle between the armies of heaven led by Christ against the kings of the earth led by the beast (antichrist).

Chapter twenty opens with the brief conclusion of Armageddon, the defeat and binding of Satan. John sees, "An angel coming down from heaven, having the key to the bottomless pit and great chain in his hand. He laid hold of the dragon (Satan), that serpent of old, who is the Devil and Satan, and bound him for a thousand years; and he cast him into the bottomless pit, and shut him up and set a seal on him, so that he should deceive the nations no more till the thousand years were finished. But after these things he must be released for a little while." As to interpretations of this section, some believe that all is literal, including the thousand years; others believe all is symbolic, the war, the key, the pit, the chain, and the thousand years, being the complete symbolic number ten cubed to the third power, another symbolic number, three. This 1,000 years is the "millennium" of which much has been heard in the late twentieth and early twenty-first centuries in the U.S., especially in such words as "pre-millennial", "post-millennial" and "amillennial".

During the "1,000 years" Satan is bound in the bottomless pit, those who had been beheaded for testimony to Jesus and to God and had not received the mark of the beast (antichrist) on them would reign with Christ. At the end of that time period, Satan will be loosed from the bottomless pit to deceive the nations. As the nations prepare for battle a fire comes down from heaven and consumes them, and the Satan is then cast into the lake of fire, the place of no release, where are the beast (of the sea; antichrist) and the false prophet. At this time John sees a great white throne and Him who sits on it. The dead stand before the throne. There are books open, one of which is the book of life, and the people are judged by what is written in the books. Death and Hades and those whose names are not in the book of life are all cast into the lake of fire.

Chapters twenty-one and twenty-two conclude the Revelation with a vision of the new heaven, the new earth and, coming down out of heaven, the new Jerusalem. God will wipe away every tear and pain and death shall be no more. The holy city has a great and high wall with twelve foundations with the names of the tribes and twelve gates of pearl (pearly gates) with the names of the twelve apostles. The street is pure gold and as transparent as glass. The foundation of the city is foursquare, and its height is equal to a side, making it either a cube or a pyramid, about half the size of the United States. The city has no temple nor any sun or moon as God and Jesus are all present. A river of the water of life flows from the throne, and on either side of it is the tree of life.

And here conclude the books of holy scripture and follows the story of your life with and in Jesus the Christ.

APPENDIX A
OLD TESTAMENT (HEBREW) BOOKS
CHRONOLOGICALLY

Years	Book	Subjects - Topics - Events
4004-1812?	GENESIS	Beginnings; Adam, Noah, Abraham, Isaac, Jacob, Joseph (Bronze / Pyramids 2900)
1900 B.C.	JOB	Will a man worship God for nothing? (Peik-Beijing) (Stonehenge) (Hammurabi 1750)
1543-1462	EXODUS	Redemption, salvation, laws, Moses, Aaron, bronze calf (191 or 347 silent years)
1463-1462	LEVITICUS	Holiness, presence, grace, sacrifices, Moses
1462+1423	NUMBERS	God salvages victory out of human rebellion, (38 year gap between chpts. 19-20)
1423 (1257)	DEUTERONOMY	Moses' three sermons God's acts, laws, covenant, to the new generation.
1406 (1240)	*JOSHUA*	God's faithfulness in a limited mission of land (1200 "Sea Peoples" from Troy?)
1380?-1050	*JUDGES*	Heroes and Zeroes of dark ages of declension and apostasy. (Iron age 1200)
-1110	*RUTH*	Love story of redemption; Naomi, Boaz, Obed. (David's great-grandmother)
1050-1000	*1 SAMUEL*	Samuel's mother gives him to God under Eli; Saul
1000- 950	*2 SAMUEL*	David restores order after Saul's chaos (and provides most for temple, 1 Chr 22)
4004- 984	*1 CHRONICLES*	Chpts 1-9 genealogies Adam to Return; 10-29 David and temple plans; similar to 2 Samuel; written at end of exile from view of God's priests. "Things Omitted."

Years	Book	Subjects - Topics - Events
995- 935	PSALMS	Five books "pentateuch" of hymns and prayers, many attributed to David-Solomon
986- 868	*1 KINGS*	**First Temple**. Solomon apostasizes from glory to disgrace; **931** Jeroboam takes ten North and son Rehoboam takes two South; 20 kings each. Elijah (then Elisha).
950- 935	PROVERBS	Collection of wise and pithy sayings for living; recommended for late teenagers.
950- 935	ECCLESIASTES	Life, wisdom, power, etc. all end in God; secular humanists should read.
950- 935	SONG OF SONGS	Explicit, erotic ideal human love poetry; young adults should read, but elderly know
984- 539	*2 CHRONICLES*	Similar to 1 & 2 Kings but covers only Southern not Northern Israel; written at end of exile from view of God's priests. "Things Omitted," out of and into Kings.
868- 586	*2 KINGS*	Israel, then Judah forsake their God and fall; Israel **721**, Judah **587**; Elijah & Elisha.
785- 775	JONAH	Israel; Divine grace is universal in its sweep. (2Kgs14; Jeroboam II) ("Phoenicia")
760- 750	AMOS	Israel; God is just and must judge sin. (2Kgs14-15) (Homer-Greece; Illiad, Odyssey)
755- 720	HOSEA	Israel; **721 Fall**; God loves Israel despite her sin. (2Kgs 14-15; Menahem-Hoshea)
737- 690	MICAH	Judah; Bethlehem-born Messiah to be Deliverer. (2Kgs 15-21; Jotham-Manasseh)
742- 681	ISAIAH*	Judah; 1-39 Judgment; 40-55 'Deutero' Salvation of captive 'Israel' (2Kgs15-21)
640- 621	ZEPHANIAH	Judah; Day of the Lord precedes kingdom blessing. (2Kgs 21-23; Josiah)
662- 608	NAHUM	Judah; Doom is to descend on wicked Nineveh. (2Kgs 21; Manasseh); (615)

Years	Book	Subjects - Topics - Events
612- 589	HABAKKUK	Judah; Justification by faith is way to salvation. (2Kgs 23-24; Jehoiakim-Zedekiah)
627- 580	JEREMIAH*	Judah; **587 fall**; Josiah; Warned of apostasy. (Obadiah?)(Zoroaster-Persia, 628-551)
586- 580	LAMENTATIONS	Jeremiah's broken-hearted acrostic 'funeral songs' re Judah
- 586	OBADIAH	Judah; Retribution must overtake merciless pride of Edom. (855-840?)
- ???	JOEL	Judah; Judgment precedes Israel's revival. (835-796??) (Possibly post-exilic, 440)
597- 571	EZEKIEL* *EXILE*	Judah captive; national apostasy("Deutero" Isaiah-Israel; Babylon, Persia; Comfort)
605- 535	DANIEL*	Judah captive; visions; Nebuchadnezzar's dream; Balshazzar's banquet; end times.
539- 458	*EZRA RETURN*	Cyrus allows release of Jews from Babylon, **538**; **Second Temple**.
- 520	HAGGAI	Exile; Lord's temple and interest are top priority; Restoration.- (Pythagoras-Greece)
519 & 480	ZECHARIAH	Exile; Lord will remember his people Israel (Buddha-India: Confucius-China)
483- 473	*ESTHER*	Jewish girl becomes queen, saves people; Ezra; Purim.(490 Marathon; 480 Salamis)
445- 432	*NEHEMIAH*	Jerusalem wall rebuilt; importance of prayer. (JOEL?) (Greece defeats Persia)
440- 430	MALACHI (470?)	The wicked are warned of judgment. (Socrates; then Plato; Aristotle; Athens)
325 B.C.	Greeks	Temple desecrated and despoiled.(430-6 BC Bible silent)(146 Romans halt Greeks)
164 B.C.	Maccabees I & II	**Temple rededicated** following desecration by Antiochus Epiphanes in 167 BC. Hannukah, "the Dedication," began as a commemoration.
63 B.C.- 400 A.D.	Romans	Pompey arrives; Herod the Great rebuilds the **Third Temple**, largest and grandest.

Years	Book	Subjects - Topics - Events
6 BC-29AD	JESUS CHRIST	A **New Covenant**; Promise of land to old nation of Israel transformed to promise of Kingdom to new Israel of individual believers.
70 A.D.	Romans	Titus sets fire to and destroys temple. (Masada) Jews restricted until 1948.

APPENDIX B
NEW TESTAMENT BOOKS
CHRONOLOGICALLY

Years	Scripture	Events
325 B.C.		Greek Empire; Maccabee-Hasmoneans and Herodians; Temple desecrated and despoiled.
167 BC.		Following desecration by Antiochus Epiphanes Temple rededicated (Hannukah).
30 BC-4 A.D. Romans.		Herod the Great rebuilds the Third temple, the largest and grandest.
6 BC		Jesus the Christ incarnate. New Covenant, from nation for land to individual believers.
0010 A.D.		Paul born in Tarsus (Turkey). Jesus 15 yrs. old.
0024		Paul, 14-yr-old, from Tarsus to Jerusalem to study under Gamaliel. Jesus 29 yr old.
0029	Acts 1:1-9:25	(Crucifixion; Jesus 34) Pentecost; Signs and wonders; Peter's two sermons; Peter and John in prison twice, Stephen, Conversion
35 AD.		Paul 25 yrs. old.
37	Gal 1:17-19	Two (this + 2) years later went to Jerusalem.
37	Acts 9:26-12:2	Peter's ministry. Cornelius, centurion, visions of him and Peter, Holy Spirit to Gentiles.
38		Paul 28 yrs. lowered from window in Damascus, Syria
44-47	Acts 13:1-14:28	Paul's First Journey. Peter escapes from prison. Death of Herod. Barnabas and Paul

Years	Scripture	Events
		to Cyprus, Pergamum, Derbe. Jerusalem Council. 34-37 (44-47?) yrs. old.
49	Gal 2;7-10	Paul, and Barnabas, to Gentiles.
49	Acts 15:13-35	Apostolic Decree -idols, fornication, strangled and blood.
49	Gal 2:11-14	Paul confronts Peter. (51) (51) (52)
50-54	Acts 15:36-18:22	Second journey. Syria, Asia, Philippi, Thessalonica, Athens, Corinth, Ephesus, Jerusalem.
51 *	1 THS 1:1-5-28	Written after leaving due to Jews' jealousy of Paul. Believers dying before parousia share.
52 ?	2 THS 1:1-3:18 S	Second coming (parousia) has not come. Persevere in spite of trouble. Paul in Corinth.
54-58	Acts18:22-19:41	Third journey. Similar to second except went across Asia Minor (Turkey) to Ephesus.
56 *	1 COR 1:1-16:24	Cosmopolitan, commercial; divisions based on sex, marriage, conscience, order, gifts.
56	1 Tim 1:3	Timothy stays in Ephesus to refute false teachings.
56	Acts 20:1	Ephesus to Macedonia.
56 *	2 COR 1:1-13:14	Some had made strong attacks on Paul. Appeal for reconciliation.
57	Acts 20:2-3	Macedonia to Corinth.
57 *	GAL 1:1-6:18	One need (should) not become a Jew to be a Christian; Judaizers.
57 *	ROM 1:1-16:27	In Corinth. Prepare people in Rome for visit, toward Spain. Justify. Sanctify.1-4, 5-8, 9-16.
57	Acts 20:4-28:16	Retracks north Aegean to Jerusalem. Arrested. Caesara. Felix. Festus. Rome. In Prison.

Years	Scripture	Events
58	Jas 1:1-5:20	Practical instructions. Actions from faith. Brother of Jesus. (Some say 44 or 80 A.D.)
60 *	PHM 1:1-25	Master Philemon to accept returning slave Onesimus. PRISON.
60 ?	COL 1:1-4:18	False teachers leading away. Only Christ is salvation. PRISON.
62 ?	EPH 1:1-4:18	To live out God's plan for unity of mankind through oneness with Jesus. PRISON.
62 *	PHP 1:1-4:23	False teachings overcome by humble attitude of Jesus, and not law. Rejoice. PRISON.
63	Acts 28:17-31	Release from Prison. (Probably arrested again) (Mark written)
63 *	1TIM 1:1-6:21	False teachings on special knowledge; foods, marriage, church admin., worship. PASTOR
63 *	TIT 1:1-3:15	Guidelines to assistant on church leaders, teaching and Christian conduct. PASTORAL
63	1 Ptr 1:1-5:14	To North Asia Minor to encourage readers to endure persecution in Christ as new Israel.
66	2 Ptr 1:1-3:18	False teachers. Apparent delay in Christ's return is to allow reconciliation.
66	Jud 1:1-25	Similar to 2 Ptr. (Brother of Jesus)
66	2TIM 1:1-4:22	Endurance. Keep on faithfully witnessing. Fine arguments do no good. PASTORAL.
68	Heb 1:1-13:25	Stay with faith. Jesus is obedient Son of God, eternal priest and savior.
66	Mark 1:1-16:20	To Roman world; Jesus as servant in action; Ox.
70	Matthew 1:1-28:20	To Jews; Davidic king; Prophetic; Lion. (Temple burned and leveled by Titus; Masada)
71	Luke 1:1-24:53	To Greeks; historical; perfect Son of Man; Man. (Jews restricted until 1948)

Years	Scripture	Events
72	Acts 1:1-28:31	Acts of the Holy Spirit in expansion of the church.
89	John 1:1-21:25	To Church; Divine Son/Word; Spiritual; Eagle.
90	1Jhn 1:1-5:18	Antinomians, grace without moral law; Perfectionists, Gnostics.
90	2Jhn 1:1-13	Personal letter on false teachings; Gnostics.
90	3Jhn 1:1-14	Private letter to thank Gaius, scolds Diotrephes.
(70-)95	Rev 1:1-22:21	New Testament prophecy; Apocalypse of John; Second coming as king.

Appendix C
Palestine-Israel-Return-Eretz (the Land)-Return/Restoration-Zionism

"If you obey then 'good,' but if not then 'out of the land.'"

Gal 3:16, 29--Paul: "To Abraham and his Seed were the promises made. He does not say, 'And to seeds,' as of many, but as of one, 'And to your Seed,' who is Christ." (A New Covenant from God.)

1850 B.C. Gen 12:1-3 If you "Go to the land, I will make of you a great nation, bless you, make your name great and will bless those who bless you and curse those who curse you." Abram left home at Harran and traveled 600 miles southwest to Shechem (north of Jerusalem) where he built an altar to the Lord. 12:7 "To your seed I will give this land." Jos 21:43,45--God did fulfill all of these promises; Put them on the land about 1850 B.C., 1422 and 539; Abraham did give rise to a great nation, under Moses, David and Solomon; he was blessed; his name became (and is) great, to Jew, Christian and Muslim; blessings and cursing went out based upon the way others treated Abraham, and even his descendants, until the end of this Old Covenant with the coming of the New Covenant, which says that each people will be blessed and cursed as they follow Christ and treat others.

Gen 13:15 "All the land which you see I will give to you and your seed forever." (About 1850 B.C.) At Bethel (just north of Jerusalem), all you can see N-S-E-W, West Bank, Medit'n Sea, into 'Jordan.'

Gen 15:6,18 v.6 Abram believed in the Lord, and the Lord reckoned him righteous. v. 18 On the same day the Lord made a covenant with Abram, saying: "To your seed I have given this land, from the river of Egypt to the great river, the Euphrates -- (19) the Kenites, the Kenezzites, the Kadmonites, (20) the Hittites, the Perizzites, the Rephaim, (21)the Amorites, the Canaanites, the Girgashites, and the Jebusites." Land from below Gaza to northern Lebanon to 'Iraq'? This is a unilateral Old Covenant from God and seems to place no conditions on Abram; however, it is obviously conditioned on that continued belief and obedience, which fact is evidenced in such conditions attached to the promise of land from this point on, as to Moses, David, Solomon and in Jeremiah; then the New Covenant.

Gen 17:1-9 God said to Abram, "I am the Almighty God! <u>Walk before me and be perfect</u>, and I will make my covenant between me and you and will multiply you exceedingly.... I have made you a father of many nations....I <u>will</u> establish my covenant between you and me and your <u>seed</u>....I will give to you and your <u>seed</u> after you the land in which you are a stranger, all the land of Canaan, as an everlasting possession; and I <u>will be their God</u>." God tells Abraham that Sarah will have a child.

Gen 18:19 "For I (God) have known (Abraham), in order that he may command his children and his household after him, that they keep the way of the Lord,...that the Lord may bring to Abraham what He has spoken to him."

1830 B.C. Gen 24:7 As the aging Abraham in Egypt tells servant to find a wife for his son but to have them live in the land promised, he is silent as to the conditions which do and will exist.

Gen 26:3 God said to <u>Isaac</u>, "Dwell in this land, and I will be with you and bless you; for to you and your <u>seed</u> I give all these lands, and I will perform the oath which I swore to Abraham your father...who <u>obeyed</u> my voice, commands statutes and laws." A new promise, as the other was personal to Abraham, and the conditions inferred to Isaac.

1740 B.C. Gen 28:4 Isaac to Jacob: "May God give to you and your <u>seed</u> the blessing of Abraham." The promises, blessing and curses are personal and related.

Gen 28:13 At Bethel, God stood at the top of <u>Jacob</u>'s ladder, "I am the Lord God of Abraham your (grand) father and the God of Isaac; the land on which you lie I <u>will</u> give to you and your <u>seed</u>." Another new promise, as those to Abraham and Isaac personal, and the conditions inferred to Jacob.

Gen 35:12 "The land which I gave to Abraham and Isaac I <u>will</u> give to you; and to your <u>seed</u> after you I <u>will</u> give this land." Jacob was at an altar he had just built to God.

Gen 46:3 God permits the Hebrews to go to Egypt, for about 400 years..

Gen 48:4 On his deathbed in Egypt, Jacob/Israel repeats to Joseph God's words, to his sons. "Behold, I will make you fruitful and multiply you, and I will make of you a multitude of people, and give this land to your descendants after you as an everlasting possession." He then continues and defines "everlasting" to refer to Jesus the Christ.

1660 B.C. **Gen 49:10** "The scepter shall not pass from Judah, nor the lawmaker from between his feet, until Shiloh (Messiah, the one to whom it belongs) come, and the obedience of the peoples to him." (Many Christians believe the Messiah has come!)

The Hebrews spend about 400 years in Egypt, which God had permitted. Gen 46:3

1500 B.C.　Exo 3:8　Boundaries of the land. God said to Moses, "I...bring them to a good land."

Exo 19:5 "If you will obey my voice and keep my covenant, then you shall be...special...and to me a kingdom."

Deu 11:13,14,16,17 "If you obey my commandments...then I will give. Take heed lest your heart be deceived...and you perish from the land."

1423 B.C.　Num 33:51-56 "If you do not drive out the inhabitants of the land..." then I will dispossess you from the land.

Deu 28:58-68　"If you do not carefully observe all of the words of this law...then the Lord will bring upon you and your descendants lagues...and you shall be plucked from off the land which you go to possess and scattered."

Deu 30:1-10 "When you and your children return to the Lord.... if you obey...."

1422 B.C.　Jos 1:3-4 The 'Land' from 'So. Gaza' to Euphrates (north of Lebanon to 'Iraq'?)

Jos 1:7-8 "Only be strong and brave, that you may observe to do according to all the law, which Moses...commanded....Then you shall prosper."

1415 B.C.　**Jos 21:43,45** "Not one good thing that the Lord had spoken of to Israel had failed to happen....**All came to pass**."

Jos. 23:14,16 "Not one thing has failed of all the good things which the Lord your God spoke concerning you. All have come to pass for you; not one word of them has failed....When you have transgressed the covenant...you shall perish quickly from the good land." Joshua states that all promises to Abraham, Jacob et als. fulfilled, including the land.

1122-622	2 Kgs 23:22 Jews would not observe the Passover for 500 years, as taken.
1014	2 Sam 7:12-16 God to David; "I will set up your <u>seed</u> after you, who will come from your body, and I will establish his kingdom...Your house, your kingdom and your throne shall be established forever."
985	1 Chr 28:7 and 1 Kgs 2:4 In David's final speech and charge to Solomon, he states the condition God had placed on him. Forever, "**<u>if</u> <u>your sons take heed to their way</u>**, to walk before me in truth <u>with all their heart and with all their soul</u>," "steadfast to <u>observe my commandments and laws</u>." (After David, apostasy.)

985 (cont.)

Psa 105:44-45 "He gave to them the lands of the nations...in order (on condition) that they <u>will</u> (habitually) <u>keep</u> his laws and (will habitually obey) his statutes."

1Kgs 3:14; 2 Chr 7:19-20 God to Solomon. "If you walk in my ways."

972	1 Kgs 8:25 As dedicates temple, Solomon repeats God's condition to "heed and walk."
962	1 Kgs 9:4-8; 2 Chr 7:17-20 God again tells Solomon of conditions, "heed and walk." These are the conditions to Solomon as given also to David.

1 Kgs 11:1-12 "Solomon did what was evil in the sight of the Lord."

Psa. 105:44-45 and 132:12 Observe the statutes, "If you keep...."

<u>1 Kgs.11:31,37,38</u> God then went outside the line of David, away from Solomon's son Rehoboam and offered all to Jeroboam, a servant. "If you will heed all that I command and walk in my ways, then I will...give Israel to you." **God actually moves the promise outside the line of David!**

1025-569	1Kgs 12-2Kgs 25 Time of prophets and apostatic Israelites. <u>Old Covenant completed</u>. Land, Seed and Blessing, LSB, moving **from Old to New** embryonic covenant.
760-750 BC	Amo 2:1-9:10 "Woe to those who are at ease in Zion...Go into exile."

Amo 9:11-15 "I will restore the fortunes of my people Israel.... never to be uprooted"

Acts 15:15-17--"In that day"? must mean Jesus the Christ and his Church.

721 B.C.   Northern kingdom **Israel** falls and **most** taken **captive** to northern 'Iraq.'

739-685   Isa 1:9 "The Lord of host left...a tiny, tiny remnant." (No nation)

Isa 11:11 "In that day the Lord will extend his hand a second time."

Isa 43:5-7 "I will bring your offspring from East, North, South." Ezr/Neh

627-580   Jer 5: 18 "Even in those days, I will not make a full end of you." Remnant.

Jer 7:5-7 "If you obey then 'good,' but if not then 'out of the land.'"

Jer 12:17 "If they refuse to listen, then I will uproot that nation and destroy it."

Jer 13:9 "I will spoil the pride of Judah and the great pride of Jerusalem."

Jer 16:14-15 "I will bring them back to their own...which I gave." Ezr/Neh

Jer 18:7-12 "If you obey then 'good,' but if not then 'out of the land.'"

Jer 19:10 "I will break the people and this city as one breaks pottery."

Jer 22:4-5 "If you obey then 'good,' but if not then 'out of the land.'"

Jer 23:3 "I will gather a remnant (not a nation) of my flock." Ezr/Neh

Jer 24:6 "I will bring back the good figs (people) of Judah." (Not a nation)

Jer 31:35-36 "I will make a **new covenant** with the house of Israel and the house of Judah, not like the old covenant." (Old covenant over)

605-530   Daniel prophesies while living in Babylon as Israel and Judah in captivity.

Dan 12:4 As to the visions of chpts. 8-11, which have valid Roman Catholic and anti-Roman interpretations, Jesus(?) told

Daniel in 12:4 to "shut up the words, and seal the book, until the time of the end." To debate them is an heretical waste.

587 B.C.   Southern kingdom **Judah** falls and **many** taken **captive** to southern 'Iraq.'

593-570   Ezk 18:31 To those in exile, "get yourselves a new heart and a new spirit"

Ezk 28:25 "I gather the house of Israel from the peoples among whom they are scattered" (Ezr/Neh did in 580 B.C.; not 1948 AD)

Ezk 36:33-35 "I will cause the cities to be inhabited, and the waste places shall be rebuilt. And the land that was desolate shall be tilled, etc..." (referring to Ezr/Neh)

Ezk 37:21-22 "I will take the people of Israel from the nations among which they have gone, and will gather them from all sides and bring them to their own land; and I will make them one nation in the land, upon the mountains of Israel; and one king shall be king over them all; and they shall be no longer two nations, and no longer divided into two kingdoms." (Ezr/Neh; when quoted for 1948 AD, they omit the underlined which clearly refers to divided kingdoms of 721 BC.)

539-450 BC Ezra and Nehemiah: Cyrus of Persia releases Jews to return, build **second temple**.

494 BC   Zech. 11:10 "I took my staff Grace (Beauty) and cut it in two, that I might break the covenant which I had made with all the peoples."

450 B.C. ??   Ezr 9-10; Neh 13; small number of Jews chose to return; they fell into apostasy.

444 B.C.   Neh. 9:8 God has "performed (his) word" by returning the exiles.

430 BC   Malachi: Apostasy continues and **Old Covenant ends**. New Covenant on horizon.

20 B.C-64 A.D. Herod begins and successors complete the **third temple**, the largest.

6B.C.-29 A.D. Jesus the Christ. Many Christians believe in a **New Covenant**.

No further mention of any return of a Jewish nation nor of any Godly temple.

The New Testament is replete with scripture as to the "New Israel" and absolutely no mention of any godly Israeli nation or temple. Act 2:38-40

Appendix D
Covenants Of The Bible

Covenant: com- with, together + -venio, to come; to come together. An agreement between two or more persons. The conditional promises made to man by God, as revealed in Scripture, as those agreements between God and the ancient Israelites, in which God promised to protect them if they kept His law and were faithful to Him.

1) Edenic:
Gen 1:28-30; 2:15-17

God gave Adam and Eve dominion over the earth and all therein and put them into the Garden of Eden, forbidden to eat of the tree of the knowledge of good and evil.

2) Adamic:
Gen 2:16-17; 3:14-24

God gave of every tree to Adam and Eve to eat except as to the knowledge of evil, and because they ate of the forbidden tree, God cursed the serpent and Adam and Eve and evicted them from the Garden.

3) Noahic:
Gen 8:20-9:17

After the flood, God told Noah the he never again would curse the ground nor cut off all flesh by the waters of a flood and as a sign of the covenant would put a rainbow in the sky.

4) Abrahamic
Gen 12:1-3; 15:18-21

In Gen 12, God told Abram (Abraham) to go from his home country to a land He would show him, and He would (i) make him a great nation, (ii) bless him, (iii) make his name great, and (iv) bless those who bless him and curse those who curse him. Abraham moved to the land and the covenant was fulfilled as the descendants were a great nation under Moses and David, he was blessed, his name became great among Jew, Christian and Moslem, and those who blessed or cursed Abraham were blessed or cursed. In Gen 15 God told Abraham that He has given to his seed (descendants, of whom there were none at the time) the land from the river of Egypt to the Euphrates, which today would cover all of Palestine/Israel, all of Lebanon, maybe most of Syria and of Jordan, a portion of Arabia and the western half of Iraq. In Gen 26:3 God told Abraham's son to dwell in the land and he will give the land to his seed and perform the covenant with Abraham, indicating conditions. In Gen 28:13 God made a similar statement to Isaac's son Jacob. God would not keep renewing the promise of the land if it were unconditional. From there on the promise as to the land is very clearly conditional on obedience. In Jos 21:43,45 and 23:14,16 Joshua says all of these promises are fulfilled. From there on the conditions were repeatedly violated and the Hebrews were several times and finally removed from the land. In Isa 43:10 et als. the Hebrews are spoken of as chosen and in vs. 19 of new things. These are the two halves of the Old Covenant, the chosen seed and the land.

5) Mosaic
Exo 20:1-20

Also known as SINAIC. Decalogue / Ten Commandments.

6) Palestinian
Deu 30:1-10

God told the Hebrews, while wandering in the desert, that when they return to Him and obey, then He will restore their fortunes.

7) Davidic
2 Sam 7:12-16

God told David his throne will be established forever, which is conditioned in 1 Chr 22:13 and 1 Kgs 2:4 upon obedience.

8) New
Jer 31:31-34; Heb 8:7-13

God begins to plant his New Covenant, as he says he will make a new covenant with Israel and Judah, writing it upon their hears. In Heb 8:7 this is further explained that the First Covenant was not faultless.

Suggested Selected Bibliography

Achtemieier, Paul J. ed. *Harper Collins' Bible Dictionary*, San Francisco: Harper & Row Publishers, 1996.

Aland, Kurt, et al, ed. *Novum Testamentum Graece*, 26th ed. Stuttgart: Deutsche Bibelgesellschaft, 1987.

Barker, Kenneth, ed. *The NIV Study Bible*. Grand Rapids: Zondervan Bible Publishers, 1985.

Bauer, Walter, ed. by Gingrich, F, and Danker, F. *A Greek-English Lexicon of the New Testament*. Chicago: The University of Chicago Press, 1979.

Beitzel, Barry J. *The Moody Atlas of Bible Lands*. Chicago: Moody Press, 1985.

Bible Works for Windows, Hermeneutika, 1996.

Bridgewater, W. and Kurtz, S. eds. *The Columbia Encyclopedia*, 3rd ed. New York: Columbia University Press, 1967.

Bright, John. *A History of Israel*, 3rd ed. Philadelphia: Westminster Press, 1981.

Brown, Francis, ed. *The New Brown-Driver-Briggs-Gesenius Hebrew and English Lexicon*. Peabody, MA: Hendrickson Publishers, 1979.

Buttrick, George A. ed. *The Interpreter's Bible*, Vols. 1-12. Nashville: Abingdon Press, 1951-1980.

Encyclopedia Britannica, 15th ed. Chicago: Encyclopedia Britannica, Inc., 1998.

Green, Jay P. Sr., ed. *The Interlinear Hebrew-Greek-English Bible, 4 Vols*. Peabody, MA: Hendrickson, 1985.

Henry, Matthew (1662-1714). *Matthew Henry's Commentary on the Whole Bible*, Vols. 1-4. Peabody, Mass.: Hendrickson Publishers, 1991.

House, H. Wayne. *Chronological and Background Charts of the New Testament*. Zondervan Publishing House, 1981

The Holy Bible, King James Version. New York: American Bible Society, (1611).

The Holy Bible, New King James Version. Atlanta: Thomas Nelson Publishers, 1992.

The Holy Bible, Revised Standard Version. New York: Oxford University Press, 1962.

Jones, Alexander, ed. *The Jerusalem Bible* . Garden City, NY: Doubleday & Company, Inc., 1966.

Keller, Werner. *The Bible As History*. New York: Wm. Morrow and Company, 1956.

Larkin, Clarence. *Dispensational Truth; God's Plan and purpose in the Ages*, Glenside, Pa.: Rev. Clarence Larkin Est., 1918.

Larkin, Clarence. *Rightly Dividing the Word*, Glenside, Pa.: Rev. Clarence Larkin Est., 1920.

Life Application Study Bible. Wheaton: Tyndale House Publishers, 1996.

Mauro, Philip. *The Hope of Israel*. Choteau, MT: Old Paths Gospel Press, (1930).

Mauro, Philip. *The Wonders of Bible Chronology*. Ashburn, Va.: Hess Publications, 1933, 2001.

Mays, James L. ed. *Harper's Bible Commentary,* San Francisco: Harper & Row Publishers, 1988.

Mears, Henrietta C. *What the Bible Is All About*, Ventura: Regal Books, 1953.

Pfeiffer, Charles F. *Baker's Bible Atlas*. Grand Rapids: Baker Book House, 1961.

Reese, Edward. *The Reese Chronological Bible, King James Version*. Minneapolis: Bethany House Publisher, 1977.

Robertson, A.T. *A Harmony of the Gospels for Students of the Life of Christ* . San Francisco: Harper Collins Publishers, 1950.

Rudolph, W. et al, ed. *Biblica Hebraica, Stuttgartensia*. 3d ed. Stuttgart: Deutsche Biblegesellschaft, 1987.

Smith, Uriah. *The Prophecies of Daniel and the Revelation*, Nashville: Southern Publishing Association, Rev. 1944.

Stein, Jess, ed. *The Random House Dictionary of the English Language*. New York: Random House, 1967.

Tenney, Merrill C. ed. *The Zondervan Pictorial Bible Dictionary*, Grand Rapids: Zondervan Publishing House, 1967.

Thomas, R.L. & Gundry, S.N. *A Harmony of the Gospels*. San Francisco: Harper Collins Publishers, 1978.

Thompson, Alfred. *A Visual Study of the Book of Revelation*. Old Tappan, NJ: Fleming H. Revell Co., 1970.

Thompson, Alfred. *The Panorama Bible Study Course*. Old Tappan, NJ: Fleming H. Revell Co., 1947.

Unger, Merrill F., *Unger's Bible Dictionary*. Chicago: Moody Press, 1966

Vine, W.E. *Expository Dictionary of New Testament Words*. Grand Rapids: Zondervan Publishing House, 1952.

Walker, Williston, et. als. *A History of the Christian Church, 4th Ed*. New York: Charles Scribner's Sons, 1985.

Walton, John W. *Chronological and Background Charts of the Old Testament*, Grand Rapids: Academie Books, Zondervan, 1978.

Wohlberg, Steve. *End Time Delusions*. Shippensburg, PA: Destiny Image Publishers, Inc., 2004.

Woodward, Dick. *New Testament Handbook*. Williamsburg, VA: International Cooperating Ministries, 1995.

Woodward, Dick. *Old Testament Handbook*. Williamsburg, VA: International Cooperating Ministries, 1995.

Zodhiates, Spiros, ed. *The Hebrew-Greek Key Study Bible* . Grand Rapids: Baker Book House, 1984.

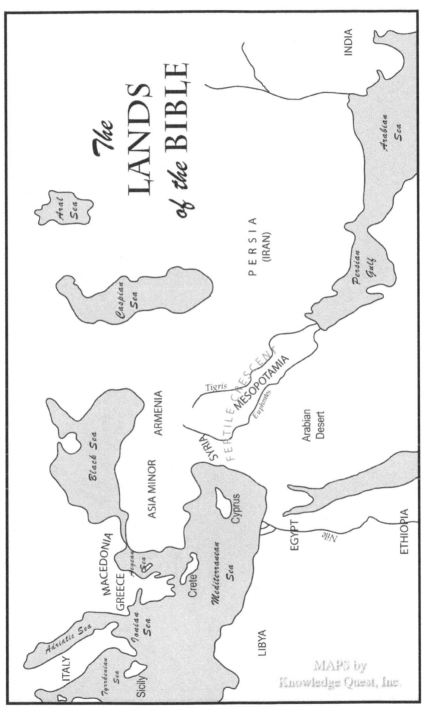

The
LANDS
of the BIBLE

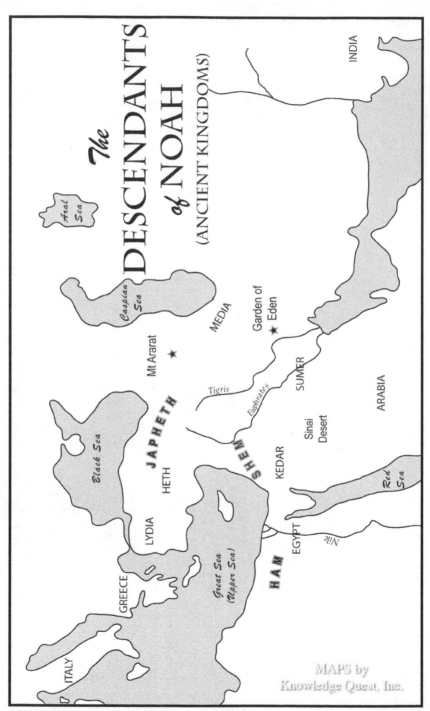

The
DESCENDANTS
of NOAH
(ANCIENT KINGDOMS)

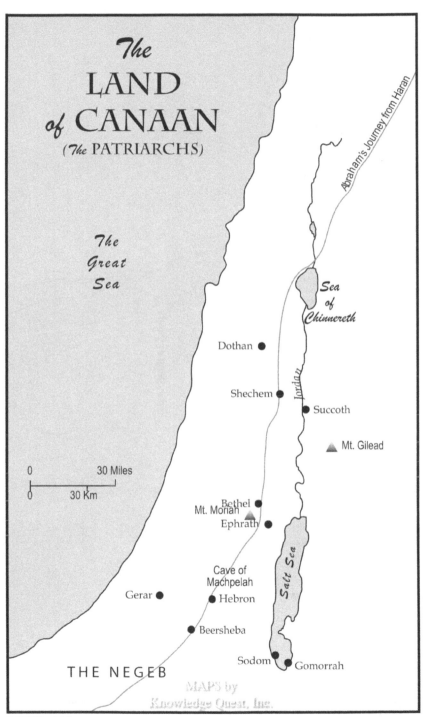

The
LAND
of CANAAN
(*The* PATRIARCHS)

The Great Sea

Abraham's Journey from Haran

Sea of Chinnereth

Dothan ●

Shechem ●

Succoth ●

Jordan

▲ Mt. Gilead

0 — 30 Miles
0 — 30 Km

Bethel ●
Mt. Moriah ▲
Ephrath ●

Salt Sea

Cave of Machpelah
Gerar ●   ● Hebron

Beersheba ●

Sodom ●   ● Gomorrah

THE NEGEB

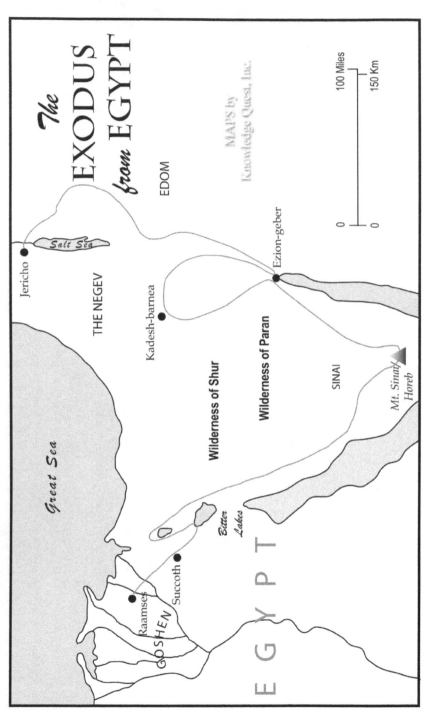

The
EXODUS
from EGYPT

MAPS by
Knowledge Quest, Inc.

EDOM

100 Miles

150 Km

Ezion-geber

Salt Sea

Jericho

THE NEGEV

Kadesh-barnea

Wilderness of Shur

Wilderness of Paran

SINAI

Mt. Sinai
Horeb

Great Sea

Bitter
Lakes

EGYPT

Raamses

GOSHEN

Succoth

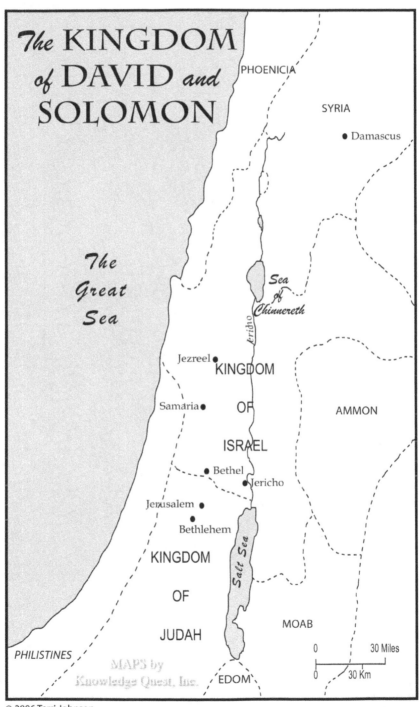

The KINGDOM of DAVID and SOLOMON

PHOENICIA

SYRIA

● Damascus

The Great Sea

Sea of Chinnereth

Jordan

Jezreel ● KINGDOM

Samaria ● OF

AMMON

ISRAEL

● Bethel
● Jericho

Jerusalem ●

● Bethlehem

Salt Sea

KINGDOM

OF

AMMON

MOAB

JUDAH

PHILISTINES

MAPS by
Knowledge Quest, Inc.

EDOM

0   30 Miles

0   30 Km

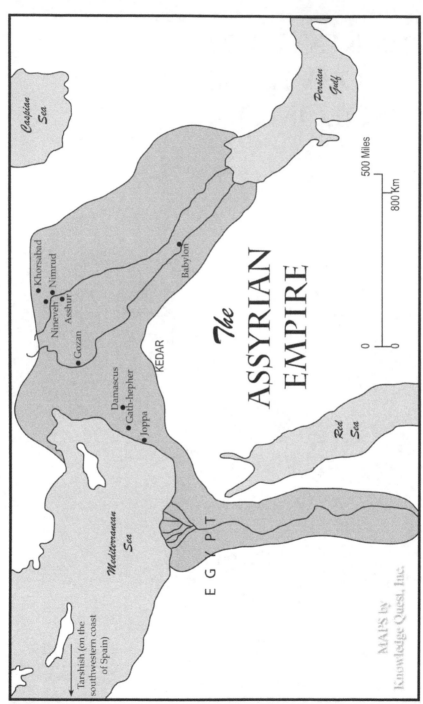

Printed in the USA
CPSIA information can be obtained
at www.ICGtesting.com
JSHW082149140824
68134JS00014B/142